1001
WAYS TO MARKET *your* BOOKS

Third Edition

Ad-Lib Publications, P.O. Box 1102, Fairfield, IA 52556-1102

Books by John Kremer

Book Marketing Made Easier

Book Publishing Resource Guide

Directory of Book Printers, 1991 Edition

How to Make the News: A Step-by-Step Guide to Getting National Publicity for Your Product, Service, Event, Group, or Idea (to be published late spring, 1991)

Mail Order Selling Made Easier

1001 Ways to Market Your Books — For Authors and Publishers

Specialty Bookseller Directory

Special Reports and Kits

How to Sell to Mail Order Catalogs (includes 550 mail order catalogs)

How to Sell to Premium and Incentive Users

Mail Order Worksheet Kit

Mail Order Spreadsheet Kit (for Lotus 1-2-3 or Quatro Pro)

Radio Phone Interview Shows: How to do an interview tour from home (includes label formats and listings for 950 radio shows)

The Top 250 National TV News, Talk, and Magazine Shows

Newsletters

Book Marketing Update (a bimonthly newsletter for publishers)

Book Promotion Hotline (a weekly marketing contacts newsletter)

PR FLASH (a weekly media contacts newsletter)

Databases

Book Marketing No-Frills Data Files
(includes 1320 wholesalers, 3100 specialty booksellers, 1450 book markets, and 1575 book services)

National Publicity No-Frills Data Files
(includes 3680 newspaper editors, 3200 magazine editors, 2450 radio shows, 960 TV shows, and 755 syndicated columnists)

1001 WAYS TO MARKET your BOOKS

FOR AUTHORS & PUBLISHERS

Includes over 100 special marketing
tips just for authors. Now you
can take a more active role in
marketing your books.

JOHN KREMER

Published by:

Ad-Lib Publications
51 N. Fifth Street
P. O. Box 1102
Fairfield, Iowa 52556-1102
(515) 472-6617; Fax: (515) 472-3186
(800) 669-0773

Printed and bound in the United States of America.

Library of Congress Cataloging in Publication Data

Kremer, John, 1949-
    1001 ways to market your books: for authors and publishers.
        Third Edition.
    Bibliography: p.
    Includes index.
    1. Books--Marketing. 2. Publishers and publishing.
3. Authorship. 4. Self-publishing. I. Title.
II. Title: One thousand and one ways to market your books.
III. Title: One thousand and one ways to market your books.
Z278.K72 1990   070.5   88-083673
ISBN 0-912411-33-3
ISBN 0-912411-32-5 (pbk.)

Table Of Contents

Brief Version

Table Of Contents

Chapter 11 — Offbeat Advertising and Promotions, *222*

Introduction

How to Get the Most Out of This Book

Let's make one thing clear right at the beginning: This book is not intended to be a textbook on how to market books. Rather, it is designed to be an organized potpourri of ideas, examples, tips, and suggestions to stimulate your creativity and to encourage you to explore new ways to market your books.

Here are a few more suggestions on how to make best use of this book:

1) Once you have reviewed the ideas in this book, make them your own. Don't just copy someone else's approach. Adapt it to your own needs, make it better, and then use it.

2) Remember the old 80/20 rule. Generally speaking, 80% of your business comes from 20% of your customers. So focus your efforts on your prime markets first. Don't scatter your attention by trying to apply all 1001 ways to market your books on each book you publish. Be selective. And maintain your focus on those markets and advertising methods which offer the best possible return for your time and money.

3) Again, I repeat, maintain your focus. Take the best ideas from this book and use them. Don't go overboard and dilute your efforts by trying to do everything at once. I've seen too many marketing efforts fail because the companies had no plan, no focus, and no clear conception of what in the world they were doing in the first place (or the second place, or the third place). That's why I devote an entire chapter to planning your marketing strategy. Planning is the first and most crucial step in marketing any book, so be sure you do it justice.

4) Study, study, study. That means, come back to this book after you've spent some time in marketing your books. Read this book more than once. Read other books on publishing and marketing, especially the companion titles to this book, *Book Marketing Made Easier* and *Book*

Publishing Resource Guide. Other superb titles are listed in the short bibliography to this book and in my extended review of books about publishing in the *Book Publishing Resource Guide*.

5) Most important, review your own marketing efforts. And do it with a critical eye. Where can you make your program better? What more can you do? Test, test, test.

Don't be afraid to mark up this book unless, of course, you've borrowed this copy from a friend or from the library—in which case, run down to your local bookseller right away and get your own personal copy. Or call toll-free **(800) 669-0773** to order direct from Ad-Lib Publications.

As you read this book, make notes to yourself. Use a marker to highlight those sections or ideas which have the greatest potential for your own marketing program. Use this book as you would a dictionary or workbook. Keep it handy. Mark it up. Scribble notes to yourself.

Above all, don't just glance through this book once and then toss it aside. If you do, you'll miss many opportunities to sell more books.

I have my own philosophy about publishing. I am dedicated to selling my books—not just for the money, or the prestige, or whatever—but because I don't believe in wasting my time. If I'm going to publish a book, then I'm going to do my best to make sure that anyone and everyone who might at all benefit from the book gets a chance to read the book. I believe that every publisher should be as committed to marketing their own books. And that's why I've written and published this book—to make it easier for you to meet that commitment. I hope it helps.

John Kremer
August 15, 1990

Authors — Scattered throughout this book are boxed notes like this one. These notes provide tips and suggestions to help writers who want to take a more active role in marketing their books. Read the rest of this book to obtain an inside look at how book publishers go about marketing books. Read these notes to learn how you can help.

Chapter 1

Some Basic Fundamentals of Marketing

The following points are basic to any marketing strategy. Read them and get to understand them before you go on to read the more practical points covered in the other chapters of this book.

1:01 Selling Is Your Responsibility

No matter how you choose to sell your books—whether through bookstores, to libraries, via mail order direct to the reader, or however else—one thing you will always have to do: You will have to sell your books. No one else can do that for you.

Even if you sell exclusively through bookstores, it is still your responsibility to see that potential readers know about your books and where to buy them. Don't expect anyone else to do your selling for you. That's your job. At best, others can only provide channels. It will always be up to you to provide the motivation for readers to buy your books.

1:02 The Two Fundamentals

There are two fundamental activities in marketing any product or service: 1) promotion and 2) distribution. In other words, you must get the word out and then you must make sure that your product is available. One does not follow the other. Both must be done simultaneously, or neither will be effective. Promotion will not be effective unless readers can readily buy your books, and distribution will be disappointing and full of headaches (and returns) unless your promotions help to move your books out of the stores.

1:03 Look Before You Leap

But even before you begin to promote and distribute your books, you must be engaged in a great number of other marketing functions. You must decide what you are going to sell (editorial). You must package your books (design and production). You must decide who your customers are and how you are going to position your book (market planning). You must set a price (financial). And much, much more.

1:04 Publishing as Marketing

If you haven't noticed by now, I consider every function of a publisher to be an integral part of book marketing. And, because I do, this book will cover more than just promotion and distribution. As far as I'm concerned, no detail is too small to consider if it will make a difference in how many readers get to know about and read a book.

So, if you happen to be with the marketing department, I encourage you to share this book with the other departments in your company. Not only will it make your job easier, but it will also, I believe, foster better cooperation among the people in your company. Indeed, if you are very wise (and very kind), you will buy a copy of this book for every employee (and every employer) in your company. I'd certainly like that.

Now, with the commercial out of the way, I want to repeat the point I've been making: Marketing is a company-wide activity. It cannot be, and should not be, restricted to one department. Too many things enter into the making of a successful book (and a successful book publishing company) to allow parochial interests to limit your possibilities.

Even the least recognized department of most publishing companies, the fulfillment division, has a crucial marketing impact. Many companies rise and fall based on their customer service (fast delivery, ease of ordering, cordial service representatives, customer confidence, and more). Any company which does not regard its fulfillment division as an integral part of its marketing will certainly fail.

1:05 Marketing Requires Commitment

It takes time to build a company (even longer to build a reputation). You must be prepared to spend years developing a list, making contacts, testing various advertising methods, establishing a network of sales representatives and/or distributors, and doing all the other jobs that go into building a company that will be around for years to come. Don't give up. If you can make it through the first few years, you'll be well on your way to success.

Of course, this same advice applies to each book you publish. Never give up your marketing efforts as long as the book is still in print.

Too many publishers have failed because they ignored this fundamental of marketing: You must be committed to what you are selling. You must believe in it. How can you sell anything if you don't believe in it — and if you're not willing to back it up with time and effort? Why publish a book if you're not going to commit your resources to marketing the book so it reaches the people who can use it and enjoy it?

1:06 Marketing as an Investment

Especially when you are just starting out, you must think of your marketing program as an investment. You cannot approach marketing as a sporadic activity. If you do, you'll just get caught up in one fad after another. That is no way to build a business.

1:07 For Most Effective Marketing, Be Consistent

Though consistency may be, as Emerson once said, "the hobgoblin of fools," it is also the basis for developing a stable business. A marketing plan is essential to any success. And that marketing plan should include a clear picture of the image you want your company to present to the public. Once you've set your goals and your means to those goals, stick to them as long as they still serve your needs.

1:08 Marketing Is the Means, Not the Goal

The last three points of this chapter have, in essence, been making the same point. Effective marketing requires commitment. It requires a stable base. It requires a long-term point of view.

I have reiterated these points because I want to ensure that as you read about the wide variety of ways to market your books, you don't lose sight of your major purpose in being a publisher. Remember: Marketing is the means, not the goal.

Chapter 2

Planning: The Basis of Successful Marketing

No company can be successful without some sort of marketing plan. Whether it be written on the back of a matchbook, carried in the mind of the company president, or formalized in a 200-page bound report, a marketing plan is a must. Without it, you might as well be gambling—the effect would be the same.

2:01 First, an Overview

Before you make any plan, you should have some idea what you are getting into. To help put the business of book publishing into perspective, here are some statistics, facts, figures, and assorted tidbits of information:

- According to a 1978 study, 45% of Americans do not read books at all. On the other hand, 95% of all Americans listen to at least one hour of radio each day. 81% read a daily newspaper. Yet when asked what they would do if they were given four extra hours of leisure, 33% of those surveyed said that reading would be one of the two or three things they would do. 26% said they'd socialize with friends, 21% said they'd play sports, and only 12% said they'd watch TV (Roper Poll).

- The average number of books read per year by those people who read regularly is 16 books.

- During any given week in 1987, 22% of American adults bought at least one book (Gallup Survey). In 1986, more than two billion books were sold for a total of $10.5 billion in retail sales. That works out to about $47.00 in retail book purchases per person per year.

- According to Tom Parker, in his book *In One Day*, Americans buy five million books every day—and over 35 million paper clips.

- In 1987, affluent Americans (earning over $50,000 per year) spent $2.3 billion on books, $34.8 billion on clothes, $7 billion on artwork, $10.3 billion on jewelry, and $3 billion on cosmetics.

- Currently there are over 700,000 books in print in the United States. U.S. book publishers produce more than 55,000 new titles per year (of which perhaps 5,000 have bookstore potential).

- According to one *Publishers Weekly* survey of five large publishers, only one in ten of their fiction books make back their advance. Even among mid-sized publishers, as many as 60% of all general trade titles may lose money. As David R. Godine admits, only 40% of the sixty titles he publishes each year are likely to be profitable.

- In 1984, over $9 billion worth of books were sold in the United States. The 15 largest U.S. publishers accounted for $5.3 billion of those sales (or 57.7%). The 5 largest accounted for 35% of all trade sales. 70% of all hardcover sales were made by the top 11 trade hardcover publishers. 95% of all mass-market paperback sales were made by the top 13 mass-market publishers. With the increasing consolidation of the larger publishers, these numbers have undoubtedly increased since 1984.

- To put these annual sales into greater perspective, U.S. pasta sales average $10 billion per year. U.S. retail liquor sales for 1984 were over $20 billion. Drug store sales were over $40 billion. In 1986, $198.8 billion was spent on gambling. Meanwhile, over 30 American companies had greater annual sales than the entire book publishing industry. Exxon, with sales 10 times greater than the entire book industry, had profits equal to 50% of all book sales.

- In 1986, school textbooks accounted for approximately 33% of all book sales. Technical and professional books accounted for another 17% of sales. Religious books, another 5%. Reference books, another 5%. Trade books accounted for the other 40% (about 20% for trade paperback and hardcover retail sales, another 15% for book club and mail order sales, and the other 5% in mass-market paperback sales).

- The average price for a hardcover book in 1985 was $26.50 (with the average for non-genre fiction being $16.95). Trade paperbacks averaged $13.95 and mass-market paperbacks $3.60.

- The average price for a hardcover book in 1987 was $29.00. Trade paperbacks averaged $14.55 and mass-market paperbacks $4.00. Ten years ago in 1977, average trade paperback prices were under $6.00.

For more statistics on the current trends in consumer book buying habits, send for the latest copy of the *Gallup Report on Book Buying*. The 1988 edition cost $95.00. Contact **The Gallup Organization, 53 Bank Street, P. O. Box 310, Princeton, NJ 08542; 609-924-9600.** Gallup, of course, also conducts many other surveys that might be of interest. Ask them for details.

2:02 Preparing Your Marketing Plan

What should a marketing plan include? At the very minimum, it should list the following items:

- the books or lines to be offered,
- the packaging, display, and pricing,
- how the books will be positioned,
- the audience or market, and
- a program for reaching that market.

In other words, you should have some idea of what you plan to sell, how you plan to package it, how you will create a desire for your books, who will buy the books, and how you intend to let those buyers know about the books (and where they can obtain them).

Other points you should consider when preparing a marketing plan include: market research, competitive titles, budgets, schedules, and how the proposed promotion fits in with major company objectives and on-going projects.

For more help with the details of organizing your marketing plan, see my book, *Book Marketing Made Easier*.

2:03 Positioning to Sell

No book manuscript or proposal should be given the go ahead until you have a firm idea how you will position the book. That means, that before you make any editorial decisions, you should always ask yourself the question: "Who will buy this book, and why?" The last part of that question is crucial. You should always be able to describe what needs and/or desires your new books fulfill.

David Ogilvy, author of *Confessions of an Advertising Man*, once listed thirty-two things he had learned during all his years as an advertising man. Of the items on that list, he said the most important was how you positioned your product. Results, he claimed, were based not so much on how the advertising was written as on how the product itself was positioned.

Positioning is vital when your book is not the first one published about the topic. For example, if you are publishing a new diet book, the first question a reader will ask is, "Why should I buy another diet book? The other four I've bought didn't work. Why will this one work any better?" If you expect readers to buy your diet book, you need to answer that question. And you will need to have answered that question long before you even begin to typeset the book. Because your answer to that question will not only affect how you market the book, it will also affect how you edit, design, and package the book.

> **Authors** — When conceiving and writing your books, you, too, should ask yourself the question, "Who will buy my book, and why?"

2:04 Scheduling the Publication of Your Books

The date of publication should not be a production decision; it must be a marketing decision. The timing of a book can be a crucial part of any marketing plan.

- For example, college textbooks must be presented to academics before March (if not a whole lot sooner) for fall adoption. Summer is too late.
- Instruction books for golf and tennis sell better in the winter when the readers are not actively playing.
- Diet books do well after the winter holidays and before the summer bathing season.
- Prima Publishing designed special Valentine's displays for their book, *How to Find the Love of Your Life*, and made sure the book was widely available early enough to encourage sales.
- To tie in with special days, you need to let retail stores know about your books at least five to six months in advance. Since the major gift industry trade shows for Christmas are held in July and August, Christmas gift books must be ready for promotion before then. Indeed, begin your promotion with the ABA Convention in June.
- Calendars need to be promoted in May and June. August is too late, since by then most stores have already bought their supply of calendars which they then put on display in September.
- Cookbooks also have seasonal trends. For example, soup and turkey cookbooks tend to sell best in the fall, as do books about entertaining at home. Books on outdoor cooking and salads sell best in the summer. Baking guides sell best in winter. Diet books sell best after the winter holidays.
- Smaller publishers can often gain more notice and reviews during January and February and in late summer before the major publishers announce their spring and fall lists. So consider setting your publication dates for those times.
- Random House required Tip O'Neill to have his memoirs ready so they could be published within three months from the time he retired as Speaker of the U.S. House of Representatives because once he was out of office his memoirs would not be as promotable.

> **Authors** — Make sure you have your finished manuscript into your publisher's hands when your contract specifies. The publisher's marketing plans could well succeed or fail based on whether you meet deadlines so they can stay on schedule.

2:05 Prepare a Marketing Budget

Set your marketing budget well in advance of publication. Be sure to have a clear plan of how you intend to spend your advertising dollars, reserving the major portion for your prime markets and media. Because word of mouth is still the most cost-effective way to advertise your books, set aside at least one-third of your marketing budget to be used for promotion and publicity. Again, there are several forms in *Book Marketing Made Easier* which should help you to organize your promotional budgets.

2:06 Repeat, Repeat, Repeat

When planning your marketing budget, be sure to include enough money to allow you to advertise to your major prospects at least several times. Repetition is a key to gaining audience recognition.

2:07 Research Your Market

If you are approaching a new market, do what you can to get to know more about that market. Ask questions, conduct surveys, read the major trade and consumer magazines for that area, attend shows and exhibits, poll retailers, and do test markets with your potential audience. For more details on researching markets, read Chapter 4.

● In preparing their new Swept Away line of young adult novels (combining elements of romance, history, and *Back to the Future*-type fantasy), Avon joined *Seventeen* magazine's spring survey of its readers. In that survey, Avon polled thousands of readers to find out what time and place teenagers would most like to visit and what famous people in history they would most like to meet. The answers to this poll will be used to plan future titles in the Swept Away line.

> **Authors** — You would do well to research your audience as thoroughly as you would if you were a publisher and your money were riding on the success of the book.

2:08 Spotting New Markets

Here are some statistics to spur you into thinking about new markets that are developing. Watch for these kinds of statistics in your daily newspaper and in trade magazines so you can spot new trends and markets before they become oversaturated with new book offerings from other publishers.

The Mature Adult Market

While many publishers are now pursuing the younger adult market (ages 24 through 39), you could be going after two new growing markets: those over 65 and those under 10.

- 10% of all Americans are now over the age of 65. 22% are over the age of 50. While senior citizens tend to be more conservative and discriminating in their buying habits, they represent a large, virtually untapped market. By the year 2000 half the people in the United States will be over the age of 50.

- In 1983 the total household income of those over 65 was $263 billion. It is estimated that people over the age of 50 control half the discretionary income and own more than 70% of all assets in the country.

- The biggest consumers of vitamins are people over 65 (from the Tufts Center for the Study of Human Nutrition).

- When given a choice on how they liked to be addressed, 78% of adults over 65 chose "senior citizens" while 64% chose "mature" and 61% chose "senior" (*USA Weekend* poll). Note: Many respondents chose more than one option.

- People over 55 average four trips per year. 23% take as many as seven trips a year (U.S. Travel Data Center).

- People over the age of 50 are the most likely buyers of gourmet foods via the mail (Gallup Survey).

If you publish books intended for this audience, use the above information and other data that you collect to target your editorial content and promotions more effectively.

Children's Books — Still a Growing Market

- Children, on the other side of the age line, now number 20% of all Americans. And we are in the midst of another baby boom, with births expected to peak in 1989 or 1990 at 3.85 million new babies each year.

- American children spend about $4.25 billion annually—$1.44 billion for snacks and sweets; $1.1 billion for toys and games; $771 million for movies and sports; $765 million on video games; and $162 million on gifts. Besides their own spending, children are estimated to influence another $50 billion in purchases each year.

- TV is the most effective medium for reaching children.
- If you want to sell books to this market, the books must have strong child appeal (play value or high interest) as well as value (since parents or grandparents make the final decision in most cases).
- Children are loyal to brands they know so, once you have sold to them, your chances of selling to them again are much improved.
- Unlike most adult books, sales of children's books tend to start slowly and, if they are good, build over time. Children's books have staying power and tend to be superb backlist sellers.
- In 1985 total sales of children's books (excluding elementary school textbooks) were $336.2 million. In 1986, they were $386.2 million. By comparison, in 1977 they were only $162.1 million.
- According to a fall 1988 *Publishers Weekly* survey of bookstores, gross revenues from children's books break down into the following categories: 27% picture books, 17% books for babies and toddlers, 20% for younger readers, 19% for middle readers, and 17% for young adult readers.
- According to recent Gallup Surveys, 82% of all children's books are bought by women. 76% are bought by middle-aged people (between 25 and 49 years old). 46% are bought as gifts.
- 70% of all children's books bought are fiction. 55% are hardcovers.

Teenagers—A Larger Market Than You Might Think

- In a spring 1988 Gallup Survey, teenagers reported spending 2 1/2 hours of each day watching television, 2 hours listening to the radio, and 1 hour 6 minutes reading books.
- In 1987, there were 24,000,000 teenagers. They spent $53.7 billion on personal items (an average of $2237 per teenager).
- 90% of all teenage girls have bought something by mail (70% have bought magazines, 25% books and records).
- According to the Rand Youth Poll, teens cited radio as the best means of reaching teens. Magazines were second, and television third.

Women—Yes, They Have Their Differences

- 55% of all Americans are women.
- Women are said to control 80% of every dollar spent on consumer goods. Indeed, according to a recent Gallup survey, 59% of all books bought each year (and 72% of all books given as gifts) are bought by women.
- What are their favorite subjects? 81% buy cookbooks, 71% children's books, and 69% buy fitness books. In fiction, they buy romances (92%), children's fiction (79%), contemporary fiction (79%), and humor (55%).

- Now that more women are working, they also value convenience. The more readily they can obtain your books, the more likely they will be to buy them.

- Women tend to be more price sensitive than men. Hence, they are much more likely to buy books at a discount.

Hispanics — Another Growing Market Segment

- Hispanics, with 10% of the American population, now represent a $55 billion annual market.

- 45% are not fluent in English. 90% do listen to a Spanish-language radio station.

- The top Hispanic markets are Los Angeles area (3.4 million), New York (2.4 million), Texas (2.3 million), Miami (744,500), Chicago (590,000), and San Diego (375,000). Note, however, that Hispanics in Texas (primarily Mexican) have a different cultural background from those in Miami (primarily Cuban) or those in New York (primarily Puerto Rican), so you cannot treat the Hispanic market as one homogeneous mass.

- Hispanics are better educated than they were even ten years ago. In 1985 48% of all Hispanics had completed high school (as compared to only 36% in 1974).

Books by Subject

- **Business books** — Business books, like children's books, tend to sell better as time passes. For example, Ingram sold 60% more copies of *Service America* in 1987 than they did in 1986, and the trend is continuing in 1988. Hence, business books have great backlist potential.

  Sales of business books rose 18.6% in 1986 (AAP estimate).

  According to Michael J. Weiss in his book, *The Clustering of America*, not all book buyers are alike. Buyers of business books, for example, have the following lifestyle characteristics in common: They drive a leased car, enjoy tennis, travel by domestic air carrier, drink imported dinner wine, own a personal computer, contribute to public TV, and own a compact disc player. Compare their lifestyle to buyers of gardening and self-help books (see below).

- **Christian books** — According to the Evangelical Christian Publishers Association, 37 million people bought at least one Christian book during 1983. 48% of those sales were through Christian bookstores.

- **Cookbooks** — The average American woman owns 15 cookbooks. Three out of ten women and one out of ten men collect cookbooks. As cookbook collecting has increased over the past ten years, so has publishers' output (from 365 new cookbooks in 1973 to 833 in 1984). $285 million were spent on cookbooks in 1984.

Bookstores sold 42% of all hardcover cookbooks bought and 31% of the softcover; supermarkets sold 9% of the hardcover and 19% of the softcover.

- **Fitness books** – Gallup Surveys in 1987 showed that 66% of buyers of diet, health, and exercise books are women. The largest percentage of buyers of fitness books (35%) are among people over 50 years old. Fitness book buyers also tend to be less educated and poorer than the average book buyer.

  Where do people go to buy fitness books? 45% go to bookstores, 13% to discount or department stores, 12% to supermarkets, 7% to book clubs, and 12% via other mail order outlets.

- **Gardening and home repair books** – Again, according to Michael Weiss, buyers of gardening and home repair books tend to have the following lifestyle activities in common: They enjoy bowling, belong to a veterans club, travel by car with camping gear, drive a sport or utility vehicle, enjoy hunting, collect records of oldies songs, and visit theme parks.

- **Self-help books** – On the other hand, buyers of self-help books share the following lifestyle activities: They buy jazz records, drive convertibles, travel by cruise ship, enjoy skiing, and belong to a health club.

2:09 Spotting Trends

Besides watching the changing statistics, you should also be watching for new trends in society. The first company to spot a trend has the best chance of capturing the largest share of the market.

- Trivial Pursuit, for example, was the first game to exploit people's fascination with trivia. As a result, it became one of the hottest selling games of the century with over a billion dollars in sales!

- Mabel Hoffman's *Crockery Cookery* was the first major book published describing how to use crockpots. It has sold over three million copies since 1975.

- Tom Clancy, with his *The Hunt for Red October*, captured a new trend in militaria and helped to put the Naval Institute Press on the map.

- Travel guides and regional titles are still selling well (though they were a hotter item in 1986). With lower gasoline prices and cut-rate airline tickets, people are traveling more.

- As more members of the baby boom generation decide to have kids of their own, childrearing books have also taken off. So have children's books in general. An indication of the growing interest in this area (and the greater opportunity for sales) is the number of new bookstores specializing in children's titles and the recent formation of the Association of Booksellers for Children.

> **Authors** — The sooner you, too, can catch a trend, the more likely you are to write books that will sell — and sell well.

2:10 The Benefits of Specialization

When planning your book list, you should carefully consider how each new title fits into your current publishing program. The more you can specialize in certain areas, the greater your chances of success in those areas. Do what you do best, and do it better than anyone else.

Here are just a few of the advantages of specialization:

1. Your company gains recognition for its expertise in your areas of specialization. For example, TAB and Que both have a good reputation for publishing practical computer books.

2. You create a readership that avidly awaits your next offerings. This creates a marketing momentum that makes each new book much easier to sell to bookstores. This becomes readily apparent in category fiction and continuing sagas such as Jean Auel's Earth Children series (whose first book in the series, *The Clan of the Cave Bear*, sold 119,000 hardcover copies its first year; while the next book, *The Valley of Horses*, sold 289,000 hardcover copies its first year out; and the third in the series, *The Mammoth Hunters*, sold 1,470,000 hardcover copies within three months of publication).

3. You can make greater use of your house list to sell new titles since your previous buyers will naturally be interested in new titles along the same lines as the books they previously bought. For example, the three titles in Ad-Lib's own book marketing series attracted the same audience as our previous *Directory of Short-Run Book Printers*, now titled the *Directory of Book Printers*.

4. As you publish more books in the same field, people in that field will become more and more familiar with your company name and reputation. Even if they don't buy your first or second or third book, they will buy eventually.

5. Specialization will strengthen your acquisitions program as well. Major writers or experts in your area of specialization will begin offering you first look at their new manuscripts. Hence, the quality of your offerings will only get better as you continue to specialize.

   Jeremy P. Tarcher publishes many new age, psychology, and self-help titles. One of their specialties within this category are books on drawing and writing. Their first book in this area, Betty Edward's *Drawing on the Right Side of the Brain*, has sold more than one million copies. As a result, they have attracted several other writers, including Mona

Brookes, author of *Drawing with Children* (with 80,000 copies in print), and Gabriele Lusser Rico, author of *Writing the Natural Way* (with more than 175,000 copies sold).

6. Finally, specialization allows you to market books together as a package, to display them together, to offer special discounts for ordering three or more different titles, to offer bouncebacks for the entire range of titles, to publish special interest catalogs, and to coordinate other cross promotions.

> **Authors** — When looking for publishers, first try those who specialize in the subject of your book. Not only will you be more likely to find them interested in publishing your book, but they are also more likely to market it more effectively than a publisher who does not specialize in the subject.

2:11 Develop Series for Continuing Sales

A variation on specialization is to develop a series of titles on the same topic. The advantages are the same as for specializing in general.

• Modern Publishing publishes 30 to 40 different series of children's books each year and then packages each series as a display unit. As Lawrence Steinberg, Modern's president, points out: One book gets lost in the midst of many other books, but six books make a display and, hence, are much more visible.

• Dover Publications publishes a collection of Ready-to-Use Alphabets and Cut & Assemble books along with many other series which they then sell by mail to regular customers.

• Globe Pequot Press offers a series of Bed & Breakfast guide books for different parts of the country. Each book helps to sell the others, just as Fodor, Fielding, Frommer, Baedeker, and other travel guides continue to sell year after year.

• Bantam has sold almost forty million copies of their two series aimed at teenage girls, Sweet Dreams and Sweet Valley High. New titles in these series regularly hit the bestseller lists for young adult titles. As a result of the success of these series, Bantam has gone on to create several other series for young adults, including On Our Own, Varsity Coach, The Carlisle Chronicles, Time Machine, Dark Forces, Kelly Blake, and Sweet Valley Twins.

• Since 1973, Random House has sold over 50 million copies of its Pictureback line of children's books. In two years, its follow-up Step-into-Reading series of 37 titles has sold over one million copies. And, now,

Random House has started a new series, SteppingStones, for ages 7 through 9.

- Writers often develop series when one of their books hits big. It's a natural follow-up. Once you've written one book on the subject, the second is that much easier to write (and to sell).

Spencer Johnson and Kenneth Blanchard have written a good number of One Minute books since their first (originally self-published) *One Minute Manager* became a bestseller. Now there's *The One Minute Father, The One Minute Mother, The One Minute Salesperson, Putting the One Minute Manager to Work, Leadership and the One Minute Manager, The One Minute Manager Gets Fit*, and *One Minute for Myself*. Similarly, Laurence Peters has come out with *The Peter Plan* and the *The Peter Pyramid* since hitting it big with *The Peter Principle*.

- When *What to Expect When You're Expecting* by Arlene Eisenberg, Heidi Eisenberg Murkoff, and Sandee Eisenberg Hathaway became a bestseller (it now has sold over 500,000 copies), the authors wrote a second book taking off where the other left off. Their *What to Eat When You're Expecting* has already sold more than 85,000 copies.

> **Authors** — Whenever you conceive a new book, consider the possibilities for related titles. Does the subject you are writing about lend itself to one book or a series of books? When you send a book proposal to publishers, let them know if you have any plans for additional related titles. Publishers love series because the first book in the series helps to sell the following books (and the following books, in turn, help to sell more copies of the original titles in the series).

2:12 Category Books: Sales after Sales after Sales

Category or genre books can be viewed as a combination of a book series and a magazine. They tend to develop a regular following just as any magazine does. Hence, if you publish a line of romances or science fiction or westerns (such as Silhouette romances or DAW science fiction), you begin to establish an expectation in your readers. They begin to look for your new releases. This repeat readership allows you to forecast sales much more readily than for non-category fiction (which is always a gamble at best). This consistency of sales also makes it easier to convince booksellers to carry your books.

Category books, of course, need not just be fiction. Non-fiction categories such as cartoon books, automobile repair books, and computer books have also developed a regular and predictable customer base.

2:13 Annuals and Perennials — Directories

Another form of series that can ensure consistent sales and income for your company is to develop an annual directory or guide. These directories can form the foundation for an entire line of related books.

● As mentioned before, Ad-Lib's own *Directory of Book Printers* has generated the customer base for our other books and newsletters on publishing and marketing.

● R. R. Bowker, Gale Research, and a good number of other companies have established a strong sales base from their annual directories and guides. Many of their customers are repeat customers, year after year.

● And, of course, annuals can become perennial bestsellers such as the J. K. Lasser and H & R Block tax books.

Directories, of course, come in at least 57 varieties, among which are yellow page listings, telephone directories, apartment guides, tourist guides, menu listings, bibliographies, field guides, consumer guides, Who's Who, buying guides, surveys, catalog collections, and more.

Authors — Note that writing a directory has one major advantage and one major disadvantage. The advantage? If the directory sells well, you may have a regular source of income for years to come. The disadvantage? A directory always needs updating. Are you ready to commit to that?

2:14 Develop Standing Orders

Another benefit of developing a specialty, a series, or an annual directory is that you can solicit standing orders from libraries and customers who require the latest information.

● Third Sector Press has established a standing order policy whereby their customers are sent each new title for a free 60-day examination. Only customers who have prepaid or paid previous invoices within five weeks are offered this review privilege. The customers benefit from this standing review policy because they get to see each new title at least three to four months before publication date (at the same time that reviewers are sent copies). And Third Sector benefits because they thereby establish a strong continuing customer base.

2:15 Develop Continuity Series

Continuity series are a variation on the standing order idea mixed with the negative option of the book club. In a continuity series, customers sign up for the first title in a series and are sent all further titles until they either cancel their participation or the series is completed. In such series it is not unusual to have as many as 50% of the initial customers drop out by the fourth book in the series. Nevertheless, the series can still be a success if you start with a large enough customer base.

- Time-Life Books has run such continuity series for years with remarkable success. Their revenues for 1985 were over $550 million. Of course, not all that revenue came from their continuity series.

- Knapp Press has developed a 24-book continuity series titled *Cooking with Bon Appetit*. Several of the books in this series have sold more than 100,000 copies.

2:16 The Value of Bestsellers

When planning your lists, always be on the lookout for any title that has the possibility of becoming a bestseller. Then do everything you can to make it a bestseller. Why? Because a bestseller can put your company on the map.

- The Naval Institute Press had that happen to them when they published *The Hunt for Red October*. Not only did booksellers and librarians look more carefully at the Institute's new titles, but they also began buying more of their backlist titles as well. Book reviewers also gave more serious consideration to new titles published by the Press.

- North Point Press reported similar results after Evan Connell's *Son of The Morning Star* hit the bestseller lists.

- It's not even necessary for a title to hit the bestseller lists to have an impact on a company's growth. Ginny NiCarthy's *Getting Free: A Handbook for Women in Abusive Relationships* has sold over 70,000 copies, which has enabled Seal Press to afford other projects.

  Note that a book can make a major bestseller list with as few as 59,000 copies shipped. That's how Patrick Suskind's *Perfume* made *PW*'s list.

- Another side effect of publishing a bestseller is that you begin receiving many more submissions from established writers who can provide you with more bestselling titles.

  Acropolis Books has developed a line of books from their bestseller by Carole Jackson, *Color Me Beautiful*. They now offer *Your Colors at Home* by Lauren Smith and Rose Bennett Gilbert, *Always in Style with Color Me Beautiful* by Doris Pooser, *Alive with Color* by Leatrice Eiseman, and *The Winner's Style* by Kenneth Karpinski.

One word of caution: If you are serious about promoting a book so it becomes a bestseller, be sure you are prepared to deal with all the accompanying headaches: reprintings, distribution, fulfillment, returns, collections, and the cash flow crunch. More than one small company has found itself in bankruptcy because its owners and managers were not prepared to handle the demand, either materially or psychologically.

Authors — Can you add something new to a bestselling topic, just as Doris Pooser and others did for *Color Me Beautiful*? If you can, you have a chance to tailgate on their success—and have a bestselling book of your own.

2:17 Develop a Perennial Bestseller

Developing a perennial bestseller is often more a function of luck and happenstance rather than careful planning, but when it does happen it sure can put a small company on solid ground.

- Ten Speed Press has become a well-recognized press because of Richard Bollen's *What Color Is Your Parachute?*, which has been a perennial bestseller for years.
- Because it is used in so many classes, William Golding's *Lord of the Flies* continues to sell 300,000 copies a year in paperback.
- Similarly, every year the University of Chicago Press sells 150,000 copies of its *Manual for Writers of Term Papers, Theses, and Disertations*. Over 4.6 million copies have been sold.
- Other perennial bestsellers include *The Joy of Cooking*, *The Elements of Style*, *The One Minute Manager*, *Color Me Beautiful*, and *Think and Grow Rich*.
- Of course, many annual guides have also become perennial bestsellers, such as the *World Almanac*, the various tax and travel guides, the *Rand McNally Road Atlas*, the *Guinness Book of World Records*, and *Kovel's Antiques & Collectibles Price List*.

2:18 Develop Brand Names

Even book publishers can develop brand names that help to promote their titles. Brand names can be developed not only from company names (to be discussed in greater detail in the next chapter), but also from series titles, authors, and individual books. Brand names, if they represent quality or consistency, can help to build a loyal customer base.

- It wouldn't be an exaggeration to say that the One Minute series has become a brand name. Personally, I'm still waiting to read the *One Minute Lover*. It's only a matter of time before it comes out.

- Publishers' imprints such as Laurel, Dolphin, Plume, Torchbooks, Vintage Contemporaries, and Linden Press have also established strong reputations for quality. As a book reviewer in the *Philadelphia Inquirer* noted, "If I had to pick a line of paperbacks I would buy sight unseen, title unknown, it would be the Laurel series."

- Annual directories can often develop brand name qualities as well. How many of you would not recognize the LMP and the PTLA? Almost anyone who has been in the book industry for a few years would recognize those two books as Bowker's *Literary Market Place* and *Publishers' Trade List Annual*.
  We at Ad-Lib Publications are looking forward to the time when our BPRG (*Book Publishing Resource Guide*) achieves the same level of recognition.

- Simon and Schuster's series, Harold Robbins Presents, sells more because of the headline name than because of the contents of the books themselves. International rights guarantees for the series exceeded $225,000. Here's an example where one author's reputation is carrying an entire line of books, none of which are written by him.

- Other brand name authors (whose new books are almost sure bestsellers) include: James Michener, Danielle Steel, John Jakes, Kathleen Woodiwiss, Barbara Taylor Bradford, John le Carre, Stephen King, Robert Ludlum, John D. MacDonald, Dick Francis, Robert Heinlein, Judy Blume, Toni Morrison, James Clavell, Elmore Leonard, Robin Cook, Judith Krantz, Ken Follett, Dr. Seuss, Shirley MacLaine, Erma Bombeck, Joseph Wambaugh, Jeff Smith (the Frugal Gourmet), Tom Clancy, Gary Larson (the Far Side), Jim Davis (Garfield), and Isaac Asimov (who even has a magazine named after him).
  These names are in no particular order, just off the top of my head. The list is obviously incomplete.

- *Timescape*, a Nebula award winning book by Gregory Benford, became the brand name for a superb series of science fiction books from Pocket Books.

- Price/Stern/Sloan's Wee Sing series of books and cassettes have consistently been in the top ten of B. Dalton's juvenile bestseller list.

- The *World Almanac* has given rise to a number of subsidiary titles like the *Kids' World Almanac of Records and Facts*, *World Almanac Book of Inventions*, *World Almanac Book of the Strange*, *World Almanac Book of World War II*, *World Almanac Consumer Information Kit*, *World Almanac Dictionary of Dates*, and the *World Almanac Guide to Natural Foods*.

2:19 The Importance of a Lead Title

Even if you do not develop any bestsellers or brand names, you should set priorities for your new titles. Usually this means that you will feature one or more lead titles each season. And, although these lead titles will take most of your time and money in promoting them, they do not need to detract from your other titles. Indeed, if chosen carefully and promoted well, lead titles can actually help to attract attention to your other titles.

• One way lead titles can help is by opening doors to reviewers and booksellers who would not otherwise look at any of your titles. One of the lead titles for New Society Publishers in 1985 was a wall calendar featuring *Cat Lovers Against the Bomb*. The calendar appealed to many general readers, especially cat lovers, who would not otherwise have been immediately attracted to New Society's line of social justice books. Once readers bought and enjoyed the calendar, they were more likely to look into the other books published by New Society (many of which were listed on the back page of the calendar).

• Para Publishing's lead title for the fall of 1985, *Is There a Book Inside You?*, was a natural lead-in to Para's other books on self-publishing.

Authors — Don't be jealous if your book isn't the lead title. Be happy your publisher is promoting its lead titles because these lead titles, if successful, often pull along the entire line, resulting in more sales for your book as well.

2:20 Whatever You Do, Build a List

Good list building is the only way to ensure steady income over a number of years. If you rely solely on your new titles, your company will always be on a boom or bust cycle. So when selecting new titles, be sure to look for titles that will have a lasting value — books on health rather than fad diets, books with real content rather than instant non-books, books written with style and depth rather than by formula.

2:21 Build a Superb and Deep Backlist

As a corollary of the above dictum, when you prepare your marketing plans you should be thinking ahead to how new titles will fit into and contribute to your current backlist. Think backlist. It truly forms the solid backbone of any successful book publisher.

- Bantam's backlist now includes well over 2,000 titles, of which 250 sell more than 10,000 copies per month.
- Harper & Row's backlist titles account for 70% of all their paperback sales.
- According to a recent Huenefeld survey, 65% of all sales for mid-sized book publishers comes from titles more than a year old. College textbook publishers obtained over 80% of their sales from backlist.
- Cookbooks are perennial backlist sellers. At one time, six of the ten top backlist sellers for HarperCollins were cookbooks. 80% of Waldenbook's sales of cookbooks are backlist titles.
- A strong backlist title rarely gets returned—one good reason for developing a quality backlist.
- Backlist titles will sometimes come back to the forefront due to new promotions. *Out of Africa and Shadows on the Grass* by Isak Dinesen became a new bestseller as a result of the release of the movie, *Out of Africa*, starring Robert Redford and Meryl Streep.
- Farrar, Straus & Giroux has an active backlist of 300 titles. When Flannery O'Connor's letters were published in 1979, her *Collected Stories*, which had been published 8 years before, also picked up in sales. Her stories have now sold 200,000 copies and continue to sell 15,000 each year.
- Independent booksellers welcome any publisher with a strong backlist. Backlist titles allow independent booksellers to compete with the discounters, chains, and supermarkets which primarily feature frontlist titles.

2:22 Plan for the Long Term

The main point of much of the above chapter has been to encourage you to develop a long-term marketing plan rather than focus only on short-term seasonal marketing plans. Your publishing company will become much stronger if you do so. Ideally, your long-term and short-term plans should mesh in such a way that each contributes to the other. If done well, your frontlist will then merge into your backlist, making it even better and better as the years go on.

Chapter 3

Establishing and Marketing Your Company

An integral part of marketing your books is marketing your company name and image. If booksellers, librarians, and readers do not have a strong awareness of your company, you will have a difficult time selling your books. So you must, as Humpty-Dumpty pointed out to Alice, begin at the beginning.

3:01 Do the Obvious

Although it may not be necessary to point out the obvious, in the interest of being complete, I will mention that you should start your company out on the right foot. That means you should register your company, acquire all the proper permits, rent or arrange a separate workspace, get a phone, print up official stationery and business cards, and get down to business.

3:02 Use Your Business Cards to Network

To maximize your networking among aquaintances and business associates, learn how to use your business cards. And be sure your employees, sales people, and authors also know how to make best use of them. Here are some hints:

- Carry your cards with you wherever you go. Hand them out to everyone you talk to (on the street, in an airplane, at the market, wherever). More often than not, these people will be interested in your books and what you do — and will contact you again later. This technique is especially effective for authors.

- When visiting key contacts, give out two cards—one for them and one for their secretary (for the Rolodex).

- Exchange cards. Don't just give your card away. Be sure to get the other person's card as well. In fact, an easy way to make sure the other person gets your card is to ask for theirs. Once you have their card, write a note on the back reminding you of the conversation and any follow-up you want to do.

- When giving out your card, write your home phone number on the card before you give it to the other person. Do this only for people you really want to mark as being special.

- Have your office hours printed on the card, or note when you are commonly available. This will make it easier for the other person to contact you.

- Business cards are an absolute must at conventions, exhibits, meetings, and conferences. Don't leave home without yours.

In Issue #12 of the *Book Marketing Update* newsletter, I list about 20 companies which can produce business cards for you—in whatever shape, size, style, and price range you want. [Back issues of the *Book Marketing Update* newsletter are available for $5.00 each as long as supplies last. Call toll-free (800) 669-0773 to order, or write to Ad-Lib Publications at the address listed on the title page.]

Authors — You should have business cards printed up with your name and the title of the book or books you are currently promoting. You might even want to have the cover of your main book reproduced on the back (or front) side of the card. Once you have the cards, give them to everyone you meet who might have any interest (however remote) in your book.

3:03 Choose a Company Name

Give careful thought to what you call your company. Here are a few hints:

- Avoid names that are hard to pronounce or whose spelling is not immediately obvious. I often have cause to regret my own decision to name the company, Ad-Lib Publications. It's not an easy name to catch over the phone. Plus, people have come up with innumerable ways of spelling it (not quite as many ways as with my own last name— but I didn't have a choice in that matter).

- Peggy Glenn, in her book on *Publicity for Books and Authors*, describes how she came to change her company name from Pigi Publishing (P.G. from her initials, but often pronounced "piggy") to Aames-Allen. First, borrowing an old trick from the telephone book, she began her company name with two a's. That way her company would always be first in the various trade listings. It's a small quibble, and I certainly wouldn't recommend that anyone else follow suit because then the LMP would begin to look like the yellow pages of any major city. As publishers, we must remember that there are twenty-six letters in the English alphabet.

  Peggy's second reason for naming her company Aames-Allen is well-conceived. It sounds very English. Plus it has the hyphenated name associated with many established publishers, such as Addison-Wesley, McGraw-Hill, Prentice-Hall and others. Hence, it not only sounds like proper English, but it also sounds familiar, as if it had been around for a long time.

- Don't use the word *enterprises* at the end of your company name. It usually marks the amateur in the business world. Don't ask me why that is the case, but when I was working in the gift and toy industry, any such company name was always suspect. The situation may have improved in the past nine years, but I wouldn't bet on it.

- Many smaller presses have wonderful names like The Lunchroom Press, The Green Hut Press, Bear Tribe Publishing, The Spirit That Moves Us, Devil Mountain Books, and Peanut Butter Publishing. The disadvantage with such names is that they sound like small presses, and some booksellers still hesitate to order from small presses because of past problems getting orders or receiving credit for returns. On the other hand, these names project an alternative image that many presses want to promote – and which many readers find appealing.

- In the final analysis, you must pick a name that appeals to you and projects the image you want to project. Whatever you do, choose a company name that helps you to reach your ultimate audience. Your company name should be – and is – part of your company image. Make sure it fits.

3:04 Create a Brand Name

One of your first goals as a publisher should be to establish your company name as a brand name – one that will be immediately recognized and respected by readers. A brand name can be worth thousands, even millions of dollars, in advertising every year.

- One scholarly publisher with an established imprint tested a new imprint name in a direct mailing to its regular audience. The mailing under its established imprint outpulled the new mailing by over 200%.

- The Bantam sales and marketing directors both asserted in a *Publishers Weekly* article that they sell the Bantam name as much as any individual titles when they sell to bookstores.

- Kiplinger Books has established a brand name as a result of its newsletters and magazines. Now, all their books carry the Kiplinger name displayed prominently on their front covers. Kiplinger's *Make Your Money Grow* has sold over 300,000 copies.

- Because both the Penguin name and logo are familiar to most English-speaking readers, Penguin promoted Penguin boutiques (separate sections devoted solely to Penguin titles) in various bookstores. And many bookstores bought the idea.

- Repetition is the key to creating a brand name. If you decide to try to establish your company name as a brand name, be sure to repeat it in all your ads and to feature it on the covers of all your books.

- Harlequin has done such a thorough job of establishing its company name as a brand name that it comes close to being a generic term for romances.

3:05 Become a Joiner

To help establish your company name, you should join the standard trade associations for the book industry. Besides giving you more visibility in the industry, membership in a trade association can help to foster working relationships with other publishers, provide you with the latest news and resources, enable members of your company to attend informative seminars, and provide a number of other educational and marketing opportunities.

- The Association of American Publishers is the oldest trade association for book publishers in the United States. It functions mainly as a networking and lobbying association for the major publishers. **AAP, 220 East 23rd Street, New York, NY 10010-4686; (212) 689-8920; Fax: 212-696-0131.**

- Smaller companies might find it more useful to join COSMEP or PMA. COSMEP (the International Association of Independent Publishers) publishes an informative newsletter, sponsors an annual conference, and offers co-op book exhibits at the ABA and ALA shows. **COSMEP, P. O. Box 703, San Francisco, CA 94101; (415) 922-9490.**

- Publishers Marketing Association (PMA) publishes a great newsletter, sponsors regular seminars, and exhibits member books at the ABA, ALA, and many other conventions. It also offers an array of co-op promotional mailings, including Books for Review, Library Mailings, and Target Mailings (to buyers and reviewers of cookbooks, self-help, new age, and other topics). PMA also sponsors the annual Benjamin Franklin Awards for the best books of the year published by independent publishers. **Publishers Marketing Association, 2401 Pacific Coast Highway #102, Hermosa Beach, CA 90254; (213) 372-2732; Fax: (213) 374-3342.**

- If you publish new age books, you should join the New Age Publishing & Retailing Alliance. Besides sponsoring a new age bestseller list, the group also offers co-op marketing opportunities, exhibit services, mailing lists, awards, and more. Write to **New Age Publishing & Retailing Alliance, P. O. Box 9, Eastsound, WA 98245; (206) 376-2702.**

- Join your regional book publishers association. For instance, the Mid-America Publishers Association covers the upper midwest. For more information, write to **Mid-America Publishers Association, 51 N. Fifth Street, Fairfield, IA 52556-3226; (515) 472-6130; Fax: (515) 472-3186.**

- The Rocky Mountain Book Publishers Association even sponsors a joint catalog of books published by their members. They are currently looking into arranging a joint distribution agreement with a major regional wholesaler. For more information, write to **Rocky Mountain Book Publishers Association, 755 Brook Road, Boulder, CO 80302; 303-277-1623.** Other regional associations have also arranged joint catalogs and distribution arrangements.

- Many other regions (and subject areas) have active publishing associations which publish newsletters, sponsor seminars, and organize various co-op marketing promotions. For the names, addresses, and phone numbers of over 65 publishers associations in the U.S. and Canada, see the listings in my *Book Publishing Resource Guide*.

- While you are at it, don't overlook the booksellers associations. Membership in the American Booksellers Association can benefit your company in a number of ways: You receive the monthly *American Bookseller* magazine and the weekly *Newswire*, which keep you informed of other publisher's activities as well as the major concerns of booksellers. Meanwhile, you are helping to support an association that can only strengthen independent booksellers—which, in turn, means that you are helping to strengthen one of the main outlets for your books. **American Booksellers Association, 137 West 25th Street, New York, NY 10001; (212) 463-8450; (800) 637-0037; Fax: 212-463-9353.**

  Among the services that ABA offers to its member stores is the instant availability of any publisher's address, phone number, and terms just by calling ABA's toll-free phone number.

- There are many worthwhile regional booksellers associations as well, such as the Upper Midwest Booksellers Association, to which Ad-Lib belongs. UMBA holds an annual trade show in the fall, publishes a bimonthly newsletter which publicizes regional authors, and sponsors a holiday books catalog that is mailed to over 300,000 people. For more information, write to **UMBA, P. O. Box 40034, St. Paul, MN 55104; (612) 934-7422.** Many of the other regional bookseller associations also hold trade shows and sponsor holiday book catalogs.

For a complete list of bookseller associations, again see the *Book Publishing Resource Guide*.

• If you are a specialty publisher, you might also want to join a specialty booksellers association such as the Christian Booksellers Association or the Association of Booksellers for Children (ABC).

Christian Booksellers Association, P. O. Box 200, 2620 Venetucci Boulevard, Colorado Springs, CO 80901; (719) 576-7880.

Association of Booksellers for Children, Caron Chapman, Learn Me Books, 175 Ash Street, St. Paul, MN 55126; 612-490-1805.

• Finally, if you publish books of interest to specific trade and professional associations, you should also join those associations. Since you are publishing in that area, you probably already know which associations are most active. Join those.

Authors — You should join authors associations where you can network with others writing similar material. If you write books in specific subject areas, you should also join the trade and professional associations representing that subject.

3:06 Become a Reader

If you are serious about marketing your books, you should read everything you can to keep you up to date on current events in the industry. Plus, you should never stop learning. Continue to read new books on book marketing, publicity, advertising, publishing, printing, graphics, and anything else that applies to the fields in which you publish.

• Above all, you should subscribe to at least one trade magazine such as *Publishers Weekly* or *Small Press* (see addresses in Chapter 9).

• If possible, read some issues of the other book trade magazines, such as *American Bookseller, Library Journal, School Library Journal, Quill and Quire, Magazine and Bookseller*, and others.

• Look into subscribing to various newsletters such as the *Huenefeld Report, Book Marketing Update, Book Promotion Hotline, BP Report, International Publishing Newsletter*, the newsletters published by the publishing associations, and others.

• Read the books listed in the Bibliography of this book.

Again, refer to the *Book Publishing Resource Guide* for addresses of the major publishing trade magazines and newsletters. This resource guide also includes annotated listings and publishers' addresses for more than 250 books on publishing, printing, publicity, and marketing.

> **Authors** — You should also read these trade magazines. Not only will you get a better idea how the industry works, but you will also be able to keep up on what other authors and publishers are doing.

3:07 Get the Notice Out

Once you've established your company, don't hide under a bucket. Get the word out. Let the key people in the industry know that you are in business.

- Send notices to all the trade journals. *Publishers Weekly*, *Small Press*, and *Small Press Review* all list new ventures as a regular feature. Don't forget the library and bookseller journals as well. And the appropriate specialized trade magazines.

  The addresses for the book trade journals are listed in Chapter 9. The addresses for many specialized trade magazines are listed in *Book Publishing Resource Guide*, *Standard Periodical Directory*, or *Gale's Directory of Publications*.

- Also send notices to key contacts in the industry: wholesalers and distributors such as Baker & Taylor and Ingram, book store chains such as B. Dalton and Waldenbooks, book clubs, catalogs, and any other businesses who you think might be interested in what you are doing (and can help you to do it).

  The addresses for these major contacts are also listed in *Book Publishing Resource Guide*. Since I could not possibly list all the major book marketing resources in an Appendix to this book, I've listed them in *Book Publishing Resource Guide*, the 320-page companion volume to this book.

3:08 Get Listed Wherever Possible

As part of your publicity, be sure to have your company listed in all the appropriate industry reference books. Not only will such listings help get you orders from booksellers and librarians, but they will also add legitimacy to your company.

Certainly the most important listings for your company and its books are the Library of Congress Cataloging in Publication office, the ISBN office, and the Bowker Books In Print series. For details on how to get listed in these places as well as dozens of other places, see the companion book in this Ad-Lib book marketing series, *Book Marketing Made Easier*.

3:09 Continuing Publicity

Don't be shy about announcing other achievements as your company continues to grow. Anniversaries, new book publications, author signings, new discount and return policies, changes in employees—these are all news and should be announced to any key contacts and trade magazines which would be interested. See Chapter 9 for more ideas.

3:10 Get Involved, Become a Sponsor

When you join associations, don't just fade away into the woodwork; become an active member. Get to know fellow publishers, booksellers, librarians, and others involved in the industry. Get to know their concerns, their needs, their desires—and let them know yours.

- As part of your active participation in the industry, sponsor awards or contests or scholarships to give others recognition and to help them grow in their profession. Or, work with your associations when they sponsor such awards and scholarships. Any such activity may not immediately show on your balance sheet, but they do help your company to gain recognition in the industry and further the image you want for your company (as long as the activities you sponsor are compatible with the image you want to project).

- You could also sponsor marathons, bake-offs, and other such events. For instance, several book publishers helped to sponsor the 1984 LA Olympics. Such sponsorships have certainly helped gain recognition for Budweiser, Miller Light, Pepsi, and Pillsbury. If your company's line of books would lend itself to such sponsorship, you should give it serious consideration. For example, why couldn't a publisher of auto books help sponsor the Indy 500 or the Daytona 500? Or a publisher of cookbooks sponsor its own bake-off? Such sponsorships take time and commitment, but they can pay off in the long run.

- Since the first edition of this book was published, Bridge Publications has become the first book publisher to sponsor an Indy 500 racing team, the Dianetics/Penske team. They've done so as part of their promotional campaign for *Dianetics*, their perennial self-help best-seller, which has already sold over 10,000,000 copies.

3:11 Create a Unique Selling Proposition

When you are considering how to build up your company image, try to create a unique selling proposition that can set your company apart from others. To be honest, I'm not aware of any publishing companies that have a widely recognized unique selling proposition, such as those of

Seven-Up's Uncola or Avis's "We Try Harder." Wouldn't it be nice to position your company the way Perrier positioned itself? After all, it is just water, isn't it?

Can you name the companies or products associated with the following slogans?

Let your fingers do the walking.
A _____ is forever.
When _____ talks, people listen.
Reach out and touch someone.
Look, mom, no cavities!
Snap, crackle, pop!
We build excitement — _____!
Ring around the collar.
Don't leave home without it.

Of course, gaining such name recognition usually requires quite a bit of mass-market advertising. But your company name need not be recognized by everyone; it only needs to be recognized by your prime prospects. So even a publisher with a limited audience can promote its unique selling proposition to that audience — and make them remember it.

● Dan Poynter of Para Publishing has done that with the slogan for his *Self-Publishing Manual* — "The Book That's Launched a 1000 Books!"

● Dustbooks calls itself, with justification, "the information source for the small press world."

● Kiplinger has recently been using the following slogan in the trade ads for its consumer finance books: "Kiplinger: Brand name help for generic problems." A great slogan!

3:12 Persistence Pays

Follow the rules. Ignore the rules. But whatever you do, stick it out. Persist. And you will win out. One of the basic secrets of marketing is persistence. Marketing takes time. If you can persist long enough, your company will eventually get the recognition it deserves. You must give the prime book marketing tool, word of mouth, a chance to operate.

● For example, it took us four years and three editions of our *Directory of Book Printers* to gain the recognition it deserved. Libraries have finally discovered the directory, with the third edition selling ten times faster than the second. Moreover, B. Dalton finally started carrying the book. Even then, we still get people calling us to ask, "Where have you been all these years?" Right here, folks.

- May-Murdock, a self-publisher in Marin County, quietly published books about railroading for a number of years. Finally the word got around. As a result, a leading San Francisco television personality asked them to publish his collection of commentaries.

  Not only, then, will your books sell better as you gain experience and exposure over the years, but you will also begin to receive more proposals and ideas that have greater commercial potential as writers and other contacts discover your existence.

- Penguin Books celebrated their 50th anniversary on July 30, 1985, and gained an incredible amount of publicity as a result. So another advantage of persistence is that someday you, too, will be able to celebrate your golden anniversary. Please invite me when you do. I love parties.

Chapter 4

The Customer Is Always Right

To build a loyal customer base, you must begin by offering basic customer services such as the acceptance of major credit cards, toll-free phone service, and fast response. Even more important, however, you must treat your customers with respect.

Remember: Your customers are almost always right. Make it a point to develop a loyal customer base. Treat your customers with respect. Listen to them. Serve them well, and they will continue to buy from you.

4:01 Accept Credit Cards

One way to develop a steady customer base is to accept credit cards. Why? Here are a number of good reasons:

- Credit card holders have better credit histories, greater household income, and more disposable income than others.
- Credit card customers tend to spend more on each order.
- Credit card holders are more likely to buy by mail.
- Accepting credit cards makes it easier for your customer to order from you — and to pay you.

How do you go about accepting credit cards? For VISA and Master-Card, check with your local bank. You may have to check more than one bank before you find one that will allow you to process credit card orders through their system.

If you are selling to businesses, you should also accept American Express since many businesses provide employees with this card for travel and miscellaneous expenses. To contact American Express, call (800) 528-5200. In Alaska and Hawaii, call (800) 528-4800.

For Sear's Discover card, call (800) 322-4566. For Carte Blanche and Diners Club, call (800) 525-7376.

4:02 Install an 800 Number

If you are serious about providing customer support and service, you should install an 800 number to make it easier for your customers to call and order from you. Such 800 numbers are so inexpensive nowadays that you really cannot afford to offer anything less.

If you do install an 800 number, be sure to let your key customers and contacts know that you have such a number. Have it printed on all your sales literature, catalogs, news releases, and other out-going mail. Above all, be sure it's on your order forms.

To be sure its customers have the number handy, Peachtree Publishers sends a label with its toll-free number highlighted, as follows:

TOLL-FREE

800-241-0113

404-876-8761 Atlanta

Peachtree Publishers, Ltd.
494 Armour Circle, NE—Atlanta, Georgia 30324

Here's just a small list of the advantages of having an 800 number:

1. An 800 number makes it more convenient for your customers to order from you.
2. It speeds response to your direct mail offers. You can begin to receive orders as much as a week or two faster than by mail.
3. It has been known to triple the response to such offers.
4. It produces larger orders because it allows you to interact with your customer. If your telephone order takers are alert, they can increase sales by letting customers know about other books you publish that are similar to the ones the caller ordered.

5. People buying by telephone have a better payment record and tend to be better credit risks.

6. Toll-free phone numbers encourage impulse buying.

7. Toll-free service builds good will. It demonstrates that you are responsive to the needs of your customers and open to their feedback.

8. A toll-free number allows you to offer better customer service. It makes you more accessible to your customers so they can clear up any questions they might have about your books or service. The sooner you clear up questions, the quicker you diffuse any possible dissatisfaction — thus ensuring that the word of mouth about your company and your books remains positive.

9. Reviewers and other publicity outlets are more likely to mention a toll-free order number where they might not mention a mailing address or ordinary phone number. They view toll-free numbers as a service to their readers while they view mailing addresses as a service (free advertisement) for the publisher.

10. You can save money on sending out review copies. Since a review copy is only a toll-free phone call away, reviewers are more likely to respond to your news releases by calling for a review copy.

After all this promotional talk about toll-free numbers, you're probably wondering what Ad-Lib's toll-free phone number is. It's 800-669-0773. We're sold on having a toll-free number. Here are a few notes on our experience with offering a this service:

• In a three month study we conducted during the months of December 1986 through February 1987, we found that 28% of our orders were coming in over the phone. Since that time the percentage has increased considerably.

• During that three month period, 45% of our sales revenue came from phone orders.

• The average order size from phone calls was $57.19 as compared to an average order size of $27.04 from incoming mail.

• It costs us about $1.00 in phone charges and 50¢ in labor to take an order via our toll-free number. These added costs are more than covered by the $30.00 difference in average order size between phone orders and mail orders.

To set up your own in-house toll-free phone number, call one of the following telephone companies:

• **AT&T — (800) 222-0400.** Besides a dedicated toll-free phone number, AT&T also offers ReadyLine 800 service which uses your regular telephone lines. If you want to offer a toll-free number on a trial basis, ReadyLine is probably the way to go. It costs a lot less to install than the dedicated 800 number (and can be installed within five days). If, however, you expect lots of calls, you might want to install a dedicated

800 phone line right away since ReadyLine costs about 25-30% more per minute. ReadyLine costs $20.00 per month with a 22¢ to 27¢ per minute charge; basic installation costs $43.50.

- **MCI Telecommunications** — **(800) 777-1099.** Calls come in over your regular line. Installation is now free with a $20.00 monthly charge plus per minute rates ranging from 20¢ to 29¢. When your monthly usage tops $50.00, you get an additional 5% discount.

- **TeleConnect** — **(800) 728-8888.** Calls come in over your regular phone line. They charge a one-time set-up fee of $25.00 plus $2.75 per month plus 22¢ to 29¢ a minute for incoming calls. Unlike AT&T's, their billing statement is itemized so you will know where your toll-free calls are coming from. Allow one week to 10 days for installation.

- **US Sprint** — **(800) 347-3300.** Calls come in over your regular line. Installation is now free with a $10.00 monthly charge plus per minute charges of 21¢. Allow 4 to 8 working days for installation.

  In the summer of 1988, Ad-Lib switched from AT&T dedicated service to a Sprint 800 service. As a result, we've been saving at least $100.00 per month in charges.

- **Worldwide 800** — **(800) 950-3800.** They offer international 800 services for those seeking to offer a toll-free number to overseas customers.

To use a toll-free number effectively, you must accept credit cards. You must also have someone to answer the phone during regular business hours and, if your are marketing to consumers, 24 hours a day. And, if you are doing a major consumer promotion, you may well need more than one toll-free line.

For those of you who are not ready to establish an in-house 800 line, you might want to sign up with a toll-free answering service. A list of about 25 such services are listed in the *Book Publishing Resource Guide* and/or my new book, *Mail Order Selling Made Easier*.

4:03 Fax for Fast Service

A major new development in business to business communications is fax service (where a copy of a document can be sent over your phone lines from your fax machine to any other company with a fax machine). Within ten years, I predict, as much as 75% of all business-to-business correspondence will occur via fax. Faxes, for the most part, have already replaced telexes.

What are the advantages of fax machines?

1. They are faster than letters sent by mail.
2. You can send complete documents as is, even with illustrations — something you cannot do with telexes.

3. Fax machines are easy to use.

4. A fax costs only a few cents more than a first class letter to send.

5. If your fax machine is connected to a dedicated phone line, you can keep it hooked up and available for orders 24 hours a day—and with minimum labor costs.

6. Faxes, like telexes and unlike letters, carry a sense of urgency; hence, they tend to get delivered as soon as they are received.

7. Unlike phone orders, fax orders are less susceptible to errors since all information is written or typed by the sending party.

More and more companies are now offering to receive (and send) purchase orders via fax. If you decide to buy a fax machine, it will cost you anywhere from $400 to $3,000, depending on what features you want (most fax machines even do double duty as primitive copiers). You can lease a fax machine for about $50.00 a month.

Many copy centers also offer fax services where they allow you to print their fax number on your sales material and then charge you for each fax they receive and deliver to you.

• The *Official Facsimile Users' Directory* lists 27,000 fax numbers. The 1988 *FAX Phone Book* lists 130,000 fax numbers in the U.S. and Canada. According to *Newsweek*, there were some 785,000 fax machines in use in 1988. That number was expected to double by mid-1989.

• Houghton Mifflin now offers a toll-free number for fax orders (800-458-9501) and prints it on its invoices and in its catalogs.

• The current edition of the *ABA Book Buyers Handbook* lists the fax numbers of about 500 book publishers.

At Ad-Lib Publications, we have not actively solicited orders by fax, but one or two orders still come in each week. We use our fax machine primarily to communicate with media. While we started with a fax card in our computer, we soon switched to a stand-alone fax machine. Why? Because it was impossible to send many of our most important documents via a fax card. By the way, Ad-Lib's fax number is **(515) 472-3186**.

4:04 Create a Customer

The first three sections of this chapter have dealt with setting up a few specific mechanisms that will enhance your service to your customers. The rest of this chapter will focus on how to create and keep customers.

Don't just make a sale; create a customer. Satisfied customers are repeat buyers. So do whatever you have to do to keep your customers happy. Make customer service part and parcel of your daily operating philosophy and way of doing business.

4:05 Fast, Friendly Service (with a Smile)

Never delay any response to your customers. Always respond to any orders, inquiries, or complaints with fast, friendly service.

• Process orders as fast as possible. One reason so many independent booksellers shop with Ingram (or other wholesalers) is because Ingram fulfills orders the same day and ships right away. If you process your orders the same day you receive them, you'll begin to pick up orders that would otherwise go to wholesalers (at a higher discount). Plus, since booksellers will be able to obtain books while the books are still hot, faster order processing will mean increased sales and less returns.

• Respond to inquiries the same day you receive them. The faster you respond (whether by phone, mail, or a sales representative), the greater your chances will be that the inquirer will order from you.

• Acknowledge immediately any back orders, out of print titles, or other books that cannot be shipped right away. Be as specific as possible about the date you will ship the order.

• Answer complaints right away. In fact, don't just answer the complaints, resolve them. Remember, no matter how petty or ill-conceived the complaint, the customer is always right. Don't take that statement as just another platitude; make it a working philosophy that all your personnel adhere to without question.

• Send refunds as soon as they are requested. Stand by your guarantee, and your customers will stand by you.

• Ship by UPS rather than book rate when the order needs to be shipped quickly or when you need to make sure it gets there at all.

The value your company puts on customer service must permeate the entire company, from top management down to the mailroom. Alan Mirken, President of Crown Publishers, used to spend one day a week at their warehouse—not only to check on their fulfillment services, but also to emphasize the value the top management placed on customer service.

4:06 Answer Your Phone

Keep your phone lines open for customer service and orders. If you are a small company and have no one available to answer the phone, then install an answering machine (and then make sure you get back to callers right away). If you are a larger company with a telephone operator and three tiers of secretaries, make sure they know when a call should come through to you rather than be terminated somewhere along the chain of command. As Tom Peters has noted in *The Excellence Challenge*, "The only magic of the $40 billion giant IBM is that in a $500 billion industry they happen to be the only company that answers the phone."

When you do answer, never let a caller hang up until you have completely answered their questions—and have gotten their name and address so you can send them further information.

4:07 Don't Run Out of Stock

Always try to keep your titles in stock, readily available for any orders that might come in. Plan ahead so you don't run out right before a big promotion. Work with your various printers so that you always have good turnaround times on reprintings. And, finally, keep track of your inventory so you don't have any costly surprises.

4:08 Everyone Wins

One of the key rules of marketing is to structure your product, prices, and services so that everyone wins. Give your customers good product (contents, style, design, and promotion). Offer it at a fair price. And give them fast service. Then they win by getting what they want, when they want it, at a price they can afford. You win because you've gotten your books into the hands of the people who can use them—and you got paid for doing it.

4:09 Go for the Additional Sale

Never fulfill an order without going for the additional sale. Include bounceback offers in your shipping package. Or put order/inquiry cards describing related titles in the books you ship out. Don't feel shy about letting your customers know about other books that might interest them. Such notices should be an integral part of your service to them.

4:10 Do What You Do Best

Again, do what you do best. Create the best books you can, offer the friendliest and fastest service in the West, and always let your customers know that they are important to you. Then you need not fear competition from any other source.

4:11 Offer Satisfaction Guaranteed

Offer a firm guarantee of satisfaction, and then stand by it. Sears, the largest retailer in the world, built its business on its unconditional guarantee of satisfaction. Why should you offer less?

- In 1986, Stein & Day advertised a full refund to anyone who did not find Oliver Lange's novel *The Devil at Home* "one of the most moving experiences you've had in fiction in a long time." Their print ads announced the book as "the only guaranteed fiction in America." Any dissatisfied reader was invited to return the book to the publisher with comments (and the sales slip) if they wanted a refund.

- In 1984, Warner Books offered an even more daring guarantee. They put a belly band around their newly published diet book, *The Pasta Diet*, announcing a money-back guarantee if the book buyer did not lose 10 pounds in 14 days. According to their reports, very few refunds were requested.

- In January 1988, Villard Books placed a full-page advertisement in *USA Today* announcing A Great Diehl! on William Diehl's novel, *Thai Horse*:

  We guarantee it! Villard Books is so sure you will love Thai Horse *that we'll prove it with a MONEY-BACK GUARANTEE! Not only that, we'll let you read the entire first chapter—excerpted below—for free! Because we think that once you begin this novel, you'll have to finish it. So start reading. Experience the adventure of a lifetime*—guaranteed!

- Enterprise Publishing offered a four-point "Risk-Free, Postage-Free, 100% Money-Back Guarantee" for its *Basic Book of Business Agreements*:

  (1) *The* Basic Book of Business Agreements *must save you at least $695 (10 times what you paid for it) within 6 months of purchase!*

  (2) *You will recover the full cost of the book in saved legal fees the first one or two times you use it.*

  (3) *Regardless of how much money it saves you, you must be completely satisfied. Look it over at our risk for 30 days. If you don't think it lives up to our claims, we'll refund your money.*

  (4) *You may return the book using the postage-free return label on the reverse* [of their guarantee].

- Boardroom Books offers a $100,000 guarantee good for a whole year:

  If the Book of Inside Information *doesn't give you at least $100,000 worth of money-making/money-saving ideas, return it at any time up to a full year from the date you receive the book. We'll promptly refund the money you paid, no questions asked.*

- Margaret Kent's self-published book, *How to Marry the Man of Your Choice* (which originally sold for $95.00 per copy) later appeared on the bestseller lists as a $14.95 hardcover from Warner Books. Their unique guarantee still stands: If the reader isn't married to Mr. Right within four years, she can get her money refunded. This guarantee brought the book oodles of publicity via major TV shows, radio shows, and newspapers.

Note how these publishers used dramatic guarantees to gain wide publicity for their books. Whatever money they had to pay out in refunds was certainly minimal compared to the value of the publicity and customer goodwill they received in return.

Guarantees, of course, can also be used to state your company's philosophy of doing business. Note the philosophy of these companies:

- Sierra Club offers the following guarantee on all items in its catalog: **"Lifetime Guarantee**—At Sierra Club, our work spans lifetimes. So in the spirit of the Club, we offer you a lifetime guarantee on any merchandise you purchase from our catalog. If you are not unconditionally satisfied with your selection, you may return it for a prompt refund, repair or replacement."

- The following guarantee is printed on the front inside cover of *Marketing Without Advertising* by Michael Phillips and Salli Rasberry:

  Nolo Press, the publisher of Marketing Without Advertising, *is confident that you will find this unique small business book to be worth far more than your purchase price. If for any reason you do not agree, we will refund your full purchase price, no questions asked, no reasons requested. (We thought about asking for a copy of your financial statements before and after reading this book to make sure your business didn't in fact improve, but decided what the heck, if you trust us, we trust you.)*

  The reason we make this unusual offer is that we firmly believe Marketing Without Advertising *authors Phillips and Rasberry when they write that for any small business to successfully market goods and services over the long term, they not only need a quality product, but must also go out of their way to provide excellent customer service. This is done by assuring customers in advance that if they are dissatisfied with the product they have easy to understand rights to effective recourse. One of these is to be able to ask for and promptly receive a full refund.*

  So, while we look forward to not hearing from you, we will promptly and cheerfully refund your money if we do.

- Jerome K. Miller of Copyright Information Services offers a personal guarantee at the end of his sales letters: "I am very enthusiastic about this book. If you buy it and don't like it, I will immediately refund your money."

4:12 Give a Little Extra

Always give your customers more than they expect. Make your books the best available. Add bonus reports or little gifts (bookmarks, cards, whatever) when you ship their orders. And, especially with your key customers, send them something special around the winter holidays, or for Valentine's, or some other appropriate occasion.

4:13 Keep in Touch

Keep in touch with your key customers and contacts. Let them know you appreciate their business. Send them advance announcements and pre-publication specials for your most important titles. Send them complimentary advance review copies of attractive titles. Whatever you do, don't give them a chance to forget you.

4:14 Always Say Thank You

Whether you overtly say thank you with every order, or you choose to say thank you by demonstrating to your customers their importance to you (by responding to them quickly and courteously), you should always let your customers know that you appreciate their business.

4:15 Satisfied Customers Spread the Word

Not only are satisfied customers repeat buyers, but they are also your best advertisements. When you create satisfied customers, you are also creating walking/talking billboards for your books. So when planning your fulfillment and customer service systems, remember that word of mouth is the most productive advertising available to book publishers—and that the best word-of-mouth advertising comes from satisfied customers.

Chapter 5

How to Open New Markets

There are a few basic steps you should take whenever you are opening a new market for your books or other products. These basic steps apply whether you are attempting to sell to libraries, wholesalers, bookstores, other retail outlets, catalogs, corporations, individuals, or special sales.

The following points should be considered as general guidelines. As you read the rest of this book, keep these guidelines in mind.

5:01 Ask Questions

The best way to scout a new market is to ask questions of everyone you can locate—store owners, wholesalers, sales representatives, consumers, magazine editors, and so on. Don't be afraid to ask stupid questions. In this first stage of researching your market, you should not be shy or reserved. Be open. Let them know that you are new to the market and would like to learn more. My experience is that most people are quite willing to share their knowledge and experience, whether in person or over the phone.

Start by questioning people you know. Use your local resources. Talk to your local bookseller, retail outlet, library, or anyone else who might be qualified to answer all or some of your questions.

5:02 Ask the Right Questions

Of course, it's not enough to ask questions. You have to ask the right questions. And the right people. Here are just a few of the questions you might ask:

- **Retail Store Owners**

  Where do they buy their goods? From whom? At what discount?
  What trade magazines do they read?
  Which ones do they use to make their buying decisions?
  How do they find out about new products?
  Do they respond to direct mail or telemarketing?
  Or do they require visits from sales representatives?
  Which wholesalers do they use most often? Why?
  Which sales representatives give them the best service?
  Which wholesalers or representatives do they trust most?
  Have they noticed any new trends? Any new consumer demands?
  What marketing help would they like to have from their suppliers?
  Also get their feedback on your books' titles, covers, and contents.

- **Consumers**

  Where do they go to buy books (or other products) similar to yours?
  What factors affect their decision to buy?
  How do they find out about new products?
  What magazines do they read?
  Do they respond to advertisements in magazines? To direct mail?
  Are there any books they'd like to see published?

- **Wholesalers**

  What discount do they require? What terms?
  What is the average size of their opening order?
  How do they find out about new products?
  What magazines do they read? What trade shows do they attend?
  What markets do they serve? How do they reach their markets?
  Do they publish a catalog?

- **Sales Representatives**

  What territory do they reach? What markets do they serve?
  What percentage do they require for their commission?
  What kind of discounts do the wholesalers and retailers require?
  How do they find out about new products?
  What magazines do they read? What trade shows do they attend?
  What new trends have they noticed?
  Is there anything retailers want that other suppliers are not providing?

- **Trade Magazine Editors**

  What is the size of the market?
  How do products get distributed in this market?
  What are the standard terms and discounts?
  Who are the most reputable wholesalers and sales representatives?
  Have the editors noticed any new trends in the market?
  What are the critical marketing months for this market? Lead times?
  What trade shows are most effective?

In all of the above cases, you should also ask for suggestions on where to go to find out more information. Get names, addresses, and phone numbers where you can. Also get feedback on the design and usefulness of your book or other product (and any displays, advertisements, or promotional material you have available).

Authors — You, too, should be asking questions. Indeed, if you have done your homework in writing your book, you will have talked to many of these people anyway. While you are gathering material for your book, also keep on the lookout for any information that could be useful in marketing the book.

5:03 Read the Trade Magazines

Read the trade magazines to find out how distribution works in a particular market, what retailers are looking for, what the new trends are, how to approach advertising to this market, and other insider information. And, if the magazine is not providing the knowledge you want, write to the editor. These magazines are usually very responsive to the needs and desires of their readers.

* In the gift market, you should read *Gift and Decorative Accessories, Giftware News,* and *Giftware Business.*
* In the toy market, read *Toy and Hobby World* and *Playthings.*
* In the premium and incentive markets, read *Incentive Marketing, Potentials in Marketing,* and *Premium/Incentive Business.*
* For sporting goods, read *Sporting Goods Dealer, Sporting Goods Review,* and *Sports Merchandiser.*
* For direct marketing and catalogs, read *Catalog Age, Catalog Business, DM News, Direct, Direct Marketing,* and *Target Marketing.*
* For gardening, read *Garden Supply Retailer, Lawn and Garden Marketing, Nursery Manager,* and *Yard & Garden.*
* For hardware and home improvement, read *Hardware Age, Hardware Merchandiser,* and *National Home Center News.*
* For special gift shops, read *College Store Journal, Hospital Giftshop Management, Jewelry & Gem Business, Museum Store Magazine,* and *Souvenir & Novelties,* among others.
* For health foods, read *Health Foods Business, Health Foods Retailing, Natural Foods Merchandiser,* and *Whole Foods.*

- For pets, read *Pet Age, Pet/Supplies/Marketing,* and *The Pet Dealer.*
- For crafts, read *Creative Product News.*
- For office supplies, read *American Office Dealer* and *Geyer's Office Dealer.*

Most of these trade magazines will send you a sample copy or even a free subscription if you request it on your letterhead. For the addresses of these magazines and many others, check the *Standard Periodical Directory, Gale Directory of Publications, Book Publishing Resource Guide,* or the *PR Flash No-Frills Data Files* (computer data files updated by Ad-Lib Publications). You should be able to find the directories in your local library.

5:04 Read Appropriate Consumer Magazines

Besides reading the trade magazines, you should also read the consumer magazines that cover the subjects you publish. When you read these magazines, read the ads as well as the articles. Which ads appear issue after issue? (Those appearing more than once are probably successful.) What angles are the advertisers using to reach this market? What benefits do they stress? What are the buzz words for this market?

When reading the articles, what topics get the most coverage? What subjects are covered in their regular columns? What are the concerns of the readers, as reflected in their letters to the editor? Remember, magazines are sold month by month. If the editors do not deliver what the readers want, the magazines will not continue to sell. Hence, editors are very sensitive to their readers needs and tend to pick up on new trends long before book publishers do.

- For example, if you want to sell to camera shops and photographers, read *American Photographer, Aperture, Darkroom Photography, Lens Magazine, Modern Photography, PHOTOgraphic,* and *Popular Photography* as well as the photography department in *Popular Mechanics.*
- If you publish business books, read *Business Week, Forbes, Fortune, In Business, Inc., Money, Savvy Woman, Success, Venture,* and *Working Woman* as well as your regional business magazine and the business sections of *USA Today, Wall Street Journal,* and your local newspaper.
- If you publish books for children or on child care, read *Child Magazine, Family, Family Circle, Fathers Magazine, McCall's, Mothers Today, Parenting, Parents, Redbook, Rodale's Children, Woman's Day, Working Mother,* and *Working Parents,* among others.
- If you publish new age titles, read *Body, Mind & Spirit, Brain/Mind Bulletin, Longevity, Mediation, Monk, New Age Journal, New Frontier,* and *Yoga Journal,* among others.
- For gardens, read *Fine Gardening, Flower & Garden, HG, Horticulture, National Gardening,* and *Organic Gardening,* among others.

Both the *Gale Directory of Publications* and the *Standard Directory of Publications* list magazines by primary subject interest. You'll find that most subject interests are covered by at least 20-25 magazines. Use these directories to find the magazines' addresses and editors. To get a sample copy of any magazine, write to its advertising department. Ask for their ad rates at the same time.

Authors — Again, you should also be reading the trade and consumer magazines that cover the subject of your book. Read them to make sure you are covering your subject as completely as possible. Read them to get a better understanding of the audience for your book. Read them to get ideas for new books. And, finally, read them to help you figure out the best ways to market your book.

5:05 Join Trade or Professional Associations

As part of your continuing research, join the trade and/or professional associations in your subject areas. Most such associations publish a trade magazine or newsletter to help you keep track of the news, people, trends, and upcoming events. Many also sponsor conventions, trade shows, seminars, or other networking meetings; publish books or reports (and market other publishers' books); keep a job bank or referral service; and offer other services that could be invaluable in researching and marketing your new books.

Here are just a few of the associations you might want to join:

● For crafts and hobbies, join the Hobby Industry Association, American Home Sewing Association, Association of Crafts & Creative Industries, Southwestern Craft & Hobby Association, and National Needlework Association, among others.

● For psychology, join the American Psychological Association, Transpersonal Psychologist Association, American Family Therapy Association, and others.

● To research the premium/incentive market, contact the following associations: Incentive Federation, Incentive Manufacturers Representatives Association, National Premium Sales Executives, and Promotion Marketing Association of America.

● To learn more about direct marketing and mail order, join the Direct Marketing Association (or one of its local chapters) or the National Mail Order Association.

To locate these associations, look in the *National Associations of the U.S.* (Gale) or *National Trade & Professional Associations of the U.S.* (Columbia Books), which are available in most libraries. Note that many national associations also have local chapters where you can network person to person.

Authors — If you don't already belong, you should join the appropriate trade and professional associations. They provide the best opportunity to meet other people interested in the same things that fascinate you. Network with these people. It's a great way to discover background information, uncover new trends, meet opinion leaders, find out new marketing possibilities, and more.

5:06 Attend Trade Shows and Conventions

Each market has its own trade shows (and usually more than one). Attend at least one trade show as soon as possible. There is no better place to get completely immersed in a new market. All the major players attend (media, manufacturers, other suppliers, services, distributors, and buyers). You can make more contacts during a two- or three-day show than you could in a year of correspondence. When you return home from the show, of course, be sure to follow up on those contacts.

Also, if you have time, attend any appropriate seminars that might run concurrently with the trade show. These seminars can often provide a goldmine of information and/or contacts.

- If you sell to the gift market, you'll want to attend the National Stationery Show (mid-May in New York), the New York International Gift Fair (late January and mid-August), the Chicago Gift Show (early February and late July), the Washington Gift Show (mid-July), the Wisconsin Gift Show (late August), the Boston Gift Show (mid-September), the Missouri Gift Show (mid-September), or other regional gift shows. Attend the show nearest you.

- For other general merchandise markets, you might want to attend the National Back-To-School Variety Merchandise Show (mid-February in New York), the Mid-Year Variety Merchandise Show (mid-June in New York), and the National Merchandise Show (late September in New York).

- For the toy market, attend the American International Toy Fair (mid-February in New York) and the Atlanta Spring & Summer Toy Fair (late September).

- For the craft and hobby markets, attend the National Craft and Hobby Expo (late October), the Craft, Model and Hobby Convention (mid-January), and the National Craft Supply Market (mid-March) as well as the regional craft and hobby shows.

- If you want to sell your books as premiums, you should attend the Premium Incentive Show (early May in New York) or the National Premium Incentive Show (also known as Motivation '92; late September in Chicago).

- If you want to know more about direct marketing, attend the DMA Annual Conference (late October), the National Mail Order Merchandise Show (late March in New York), and Mail Expo (mid-September in Washington, DC).

- For health food markets, attend the Natural Foods Expo (East) in mid-October or other regional shows.

- For sporting goods, attend the World Sports Expo in mid-October, the National Sporting Goods Association Fall Market in mid-September, and the Mid America Sports Market in late February, among others.

- For housewares, attend the Houseworld Expo (mid-April in Chicago), the International Housewares Exposition (mid-January in Chicago), and the Mid America Hardware Show (late February).

There are many other professional meetings and seminars. For a complete list, read the appropriate trade and professional magazines. Or look into these directories, some of which should be available at your local library:

- *Association Meeting Directory* — Lists 9,000 meetings. Available from Association Meeting Directory, 1000 Connecticut Avenue NW #1035, Washington, DC 20036. $245.00.

- *EventLine* — Lists 17,000 trade shows and other events worldwide. Available on-line or as software for $1,100 to $1,900 a year. From EventLine, P. O. Box 57101, Philadelphia, PA 19111; 215-572-7424.

- *Exhibits Directory* — Lists 250 book shows worldwide. $90.00 to non-members. From the Association of American Publishers, 220 East 23rd Street, New York, NY 10016-5825; 212-689-8920.

- *Trade Shows Worldwide* — Lists 5,000 trade shows, conventions, and exhibits. Available from Gale Research Company, 835 Penobscot Building, Detroit, MI 48226-4094; (800) 877-GALE. $169.95. Gale also publishes and/or distributes many other valuable directories and provides mailing lists. Write or call for their catalog.

- *Tradeshow Week Data Book* — Lists U.S. trade shows. Available from Trade Show Week, 12233 W. Olympic Boulevard, Los Angeles, CA 90064; 212-826-5696.

- Or contact the **Trade Show Bureau**, 1660 Lincoln Street, Suite 2080, Denver, CO 80264; (303) 860-7626.

> **Authors** – If you ever get a chance, you should also attend any appropriate trade shows, conferences, or seminars that might cover the subjects you write about. Again, they are the best way to immerse yourself totally in a new field. And a great place to make new contacts

5:07 Check Out the Directories That Cover the Field

You can discover a lot about a new market by exploring the various listings in the directories that cover a particular field. Most markets are covered by at least one if not two or more directories that list sources, buyers, consultants, suppliers, magazines, and more.

- For new age topics, read these directories, among others: *Alternative America, Holistic Resources, National New Age Yellow Pages, New Age Directory, New Age Marketing Resource Directory, New Consciousness Source Book,* and *Whole Again Resource Guide.*

- To sell to catalogs, read the *National Directory of Catalogs, The Catalog of Catalogs, Directory of Mail Order Catalogs, Great Book of Catalogs,* and *The Wholesale by Mail Catalog.*

- To market to libraries, check out the *American Library Directory, Directory of Special Libraries and Information Centers,* and *Directory of Federal Libraries.*

- To market to gift shops, try the *Gift Shop Directory* or the *Gift and Housewares Buyers* directory.

- For hardware buyers, try *Hardware Distributors, Hardware Wholesalers,* or *National Hardware Wholesalers.*

To locate more of these directories for specific fields, refer to Gale's *Directory of Directories,* Ad-Lib's *Book Publishing Resource Guide,* or the Book Services section of Ad-Lib's *Book Marketing No-Frills Data Files.*

You can also ask the directors of the related associations as well as the editors of the applicable trade journals. Both of these groups should be able to tell you which directories cover the field most thoroughly.

> **Authors** – To research your books and the potential markets for your books, these directories can be invaluable. Go through them with a fine-tooth comb. You'll find it worth the time.

5:08 Contact the Distribution Network

Each market operates differently, with varying terms and discount structures. To begin feeling out the territory, contact at least one or two distributors or sales representatives right away and ask them how to approach the market.

Some markets rely primarily on distributors, while others rely primarily on sales representatives, while still others (like the book market) use a combination of the two. Adapt your sales program to fit within the established structure of that particular market. Don't try to force some new terms or "creative" programs on that market until you have first become established. If your books don't fit, no one will carry them. Design your displays and programs to match the available resources within that market.

5:09 Network with Other Publishers

When approaching a new market, first talk to a few other publishers to find out what they know about the market. Somewhere along the line you will meet a publisher who has experience selling to the market or knows another publisher who does. Invite them out to lunch. Then pick their brains (while sharing your own experiences with them).

One of the great things about the publishing world, especially among independent publishers, is that people are willing to share information. I have never found any independent publisher who was not willing to share his or her experiences, resources, and knowledge—and I talk to about 2,000 publishers every year!

Of course, when you talk to other publishers, remember the golden rule. If you expect them to share ideas and resources with you, you should also share your ideas and resources with them. That's only fair.

> **Authors** — You should network with authors and publishers you know. You can learn a lot from others, especially if you share what you know with them.

5:10 Use Your Local Library

One of the best resources you have for finding out anything—and everything—is your local library. And, especially, your reference librarian. Here are just a few of the things your local librarian can do for you:

- Help you find the directories of periodicals, associations, and other marketing possibilities.
- Let you know what topics and authors are hot with their patrons.
- Help you keep track of new books (especially competitive titles) from other publishers.
- Provide you with books, magazines, and other resources to research new books or verify facts in manuscripts submitted by your authors.
- Give you feedback on your titles, covers, contents, bibliographies, and indexes of your forthcoming books.
- Help you locate authors, experts, and celebrities who can write new books for you.

> **Authors** — You should also get to know your local librarians. They can help you research your books, find out what books compete with yours, let you know which publishers are publishing books similar to the ones you are working on, and help you locate experts and opinion leaders who can help you promote your books.

5:11 Use Your Government Resources

Most government departments maintain statistics and other research that can aid you in finding out more about new markets. Your librarian can help you locate those local, state, and national government departments which might be able to assist you.

Most of the information available from government departments is free or low cost. Not only do these government departments publish research, but they can also provide consultants or experts who can answer other questions for you (whether by mail, by phone, or in person). Or if they cannot provide an answer, they can direct you to someone who can.

5:12 Target Mailings

In testing a new market, start by doing targeted mailings to a few prime buyers in that market. Test your offer (titles and contents of your books). Test your copy. Test your lists. Follow up with phone calls to verify your results — and your assumptions.

Once you've tested your offer, you can roll out with more mailings or with advertisements and distribution via the normal channels for that market (whether via sales representatives, distributors, or wholesalers).

5:13 Test, Test, Test

Again, I repeat: Start small. And always test your marketing programs before spending a lot of money. Make sure your advertisements and products are designed well—and work. Then, and only then, roll out to the larger market.

5:14 Plan and Prepare

Make sure you have a good marketing plan. Then stick with it.

Remember: First impressions last. Make sure the first impression you create in a new market is the one you want to live with. Then go ahead.

5:15 Be Persistent

Once you commit yourself to a new market, stick with it. Be patient. It can take time to open a new market, sometimes as long as a year or two. While you are waiting for orders, keep in touch with the major players in that market. Let them know that you are still actively interested in their market—and that you intend to be in that market for the long run.

5:16 Go Slow

Don't enter a new market until you have exploited your prime markets thoroughly. Remember the 80/20 rule. Spend most of your marketing time and money promoting to the 20% of your potential market which is most likely to produce the most buyers of your books. Only then should you explore other markets.

As a corollary to this principle, don't try to open too many new markets at the same time. You'll just spread yourself too thin and won't have the time or money to do justice to any of the new markets.

Chapter 6

Editorial: The First Step

The first step in marketing any product is to produce something worthwhile, something people want or need, something people will buy. As products, books involve a combination of content, author, title, design, packaging, and price. All these elements must work together to create a bestselling book.

6:01 Strive for Excellence

Regardless of what kind of books you publish, the books must have some sort of content. Yes, it is possible to sell books with no content at all (witness the Anything Books and diaries), but that is a limited market. Most publishers must give priority to content. And rightly so. Indeed, the reason most of us are in publishing is because of the content. We want to create books with lasting value, with significance, with substance.

Excellence of content does not come out of thin air. You must seek it out. And the first step in finding what you want is to define as clearly as possible what it is that you are seeking. Set a firm objective, make it clear to your editorial staff, and then let them go to work.

Here are a few guidelines your editors should have:

- Seek the best available—the best authors, the best subjects, the best content.
- Make sure the book fits into the company's current and projected lines of books.
- Always be aware of the marketing implications. As an extension of this responsibility, your editors should participate in your major marketing meetings and decisions.

• When reviewing a proposal, consider not only its potential for direct sales but also for subsidiary rights, international sales, and special sales.

• Think big — not that all books have to be bestsellers, but rather that all books should have grand possibilities, either for sales or for the enlightenment of the world, or for both.

6:02 Edit for Clarity and Simplicity

Don't let a book out your door which has not been edited carefully by an experienced editor. Edit for clarity. Edit for a readable style. Edit for ease of use. The more accessible you make the contents of a book, the more likely readers will be to finish the book ... and recommend it to their friends and associates.

• *Mail Order Know-How* by Cecil Hoge, Sr. could sell many more copies if only it had been edited more thoroughly. It could have been cut by thirty per cent without detracting from its content. It would have made an outstanding 300-page book. As it is, the superb content is lost in the rambling, unedited nature of the book.

Authors — Work with your editors to create the best book you can write. Don't be offended if they suggest changes to make the book better. Let them do their job. Don't be so married to your words that you let the words get in the way of the message. A good editor can make your book clearer and simpler so more readers will be able to read and use it.

6:03 Edit for Promotional Clout

When editing a manuscript, consider ways to insert material into the book to make it more promotable.

• For example, if you are editing a book on gardening, why not list specific seed and tool companies as resources in the appendix? Not only will such lists benefit the reader, but they will also provide you with potential premium sales. Any company with marketing savvy would jump at the chance to use your book as a premium to give away or sell to its customers — especially if that company is mentioned in the book as a prime resource.

• Another way to increase the promotional value of a book is to expand a special chapter or section so the book attracts a wider audience.

While editing the fourth edition of my *Directory of Short-Run Book Printers*, I renamed it the *Directory of Book, Catalog, and Magazine Printers* and featured not only book printers but also those capable of printing catalogs, magazines, and other bound publications. I thus expanded the potential audience from just book publishers and self-publishers to businesses and organizations as well. This slight change in editorial matter has increased the bookstore sales of the directory.

Authors — Look for ways to include extra chapters or additional information that might be useful to potential readers — and to people who might not otherwise buy the book. Is there any material you can add that will increase the audience for your book?

6:04 Look for Tie-In Possibilities

Your editors should be on the lookout for any manuscripts which could tie in with current television programs, movies, or other products already being promoted. The resulting book can then hitch a ride on an already rolling promotional wagon. As Ralph Waldo Emerson once recommended, "Hitch your wagon to a star."

- **Television** — Avon sold over ten million copies of *The Thorn Birds*, many after the TV miniseries. *Shogun* also sold well after its release as a TV miniseries.

- **Television** — Already two Sniglets books have hit the bestsellers lists. Certainly it hasn't hurt their sales to be indirectly promoted on HBO's *Not Necessarily the News* every week.

- **Television** — The Muppets shows and movies have given rise to a great variety of licensed products including books by Holt, Rinehart & Winston, Random House, and Fenmore Associates and software by Simon & Schuster. Many gift stores have included these books in the Muppet Boutiques organized and promoted by Henson & Associates.

- **Radio** — *Lake Wobegon Days* would not be the bestseller it is now without the prior exposure of Garrison Keillor and Lake Wobegon on the weekly National Public Radio series, *Prairie Home Companion*.

- **Movies and Television** — Pocket Books sold over two million copies of the book tie-in to the movie, *Star Trek: The Motion Picture* and over a million for the tie-in to the third Star Trek movie, *The Search for Spock*. Their Star Trek series of original novels regularly sell over 300,000 copies each. It's a continuing gold mine for them.

- **Movies** – Avon sold over 2,800,000 copies of their *Gremlins* movie tie-in book. Ballantine sold over 1,500,000 copies of their movie tie-in, *Indiana Jones and the Temple of Doom*.

- **Movies** – A number of companies brought out books to tie-in with the movie biography of Isak Dinesen, *Out of Africa*. Two of these titles became bestsellers, Vintage's combined edition of Dinesen's *Out of Africa and Shadows on the Grass* and St. Martin's biography of *Isak Dinesen: The Life of a Storyteller* by Judith Thurman.

- **Movies** – Alice Walker's *The Color Purple* stayed on the top of the mass-market bestseller lists for months after the release of the movie.

- **Magazines** – Consumer Guide, Rodale Press, and many other magazine publishers regularly publish books that draw upon their editorial expertise.

- **Magazines** – When Collier published the *People Magazine Guide to Movies on Video* (taken from reviews in its Picks and Pans section, HBO bought a five-figure quantity to use as premium giveaways to its cable accounts.

- **Catalogs** – Addison-Wesley has published an entire series of Eddie Bauer sporting guides. *Items from Our Catalog*, a take-off on the L. L. Bean catalog, became a bestseller.

- **Sports** – Too many to mention (from biographies and team histories, to baseball card price guides and hall of fame pictorials), but most are steady sellers.

- **Food Products** – *Campbell's Creative Cooking with Soup* cookbook is the only one that comes readily to my mind, but many other product tie-ins including at least one for Hershey's chocolate have been published.

- **Toys** – Random House has published four books featuring Wrinkles (the 1985 Canadian toy of the year) as well as other books featuring the Berenstain Bears, Sesame Street, and the Muppets. In 1988, for the first time, Random House exhibited at the Toy Fair as a toy manufacturer. Indeed, besides books, Random House now produces crayons, electronic games, board games, and puzzles.

- **Other Products** – Computers (in all makes and models), computer software (for all makes and models), automobiles (including the classic, *How to Keep Your Volkswagon Alive*), and many other products have been featured successfully in books.

- **Cities and Regions** – Everybody loves their own hometown, so regional and city-specific titles almost always sell well. Not only the usual tourist coffee-table books with plenty of pictures, but also other titles such as *How to Live (Fairly) Elegantly on (Virtually) Nothing in Los Angeles*, *The Boston Ice Cream Lover's Guide*, and *The Washington Driver's Handbook: A Guide to Capital Cruising* have all found strong audiences, both local and tourist.

6:05 Get the Best Authors You Can Afford

When selecting possible books for publication, look to the author's qualifications, experience, and promotability. In one survey of children's booksellers, they rated the author's reputation as the third most important criteria (after contents and illustrations) when selecting books for resale.

Here are a few pointers on how to select authors:

- Select authors on the basis of past performance. Authors who have previously written books tend to be more reliable, are less likely to cause problems, and are generally more promotable. If they are also a "big name," so much the better. As mentioned previously, there are a number of authors whose new books are almost guaranteed best-sellers.

- If you have a choice between a celebrity author and an unknown, choose the celebrity (as long as the books are fairly equal in content and quality). Someone who is better known is more promotable — even if they have never authored a book before. Movie stars, sports heroes, political figures, company presidents, and other celebrities are all promotable authors (provided that they have help from ghost writers if they need it).

  Not only was Lee Iacocca a well-recognized television spokesman for Chrysler, but his biography had a pre-sold market. Hundreds of local car dealers gave away thousands of copies of the book to people who took a test ride in a Chrysler.

- When selecting celebrity authors, it is best if you can publish the book while the celebrities are at the peak of their fame. As mentioned before, Random House required Speaker of the House Tip O'Neill to have his memoirs ready in time for the book to be published within three months of his retirement — before he disappeared from the limelight.

  In another case, Pergamon Press began to re-advertise their collection of Deng Xiaoping's speeches and writings within weeks after *Time* magazine named the Chinese leader Man of the Year for 1985.

- If the author is an authority on the subject, again so much the better. And if the author is an authority, don't keep it a secret. Play up his or her expertise in your promotions.

  For example, a diet book by a doctor, a book on early childhood learning by a teacher or a psychologist, or a book on the science of hitting by Mickey Mantle or Rod Carew — all are more promotable because of the acknowledged expertise of their authors.

- If you have the choice between an author with adequate style, such as myself, and someone with superb style, choose the author with superb style. Well-written books will tend to sell better, provided the style fits the subject.

- While focusing on celebrities and established authors, don't forget the unknowns. Do what you can to develop new writers as well. Remember: All established writers had to begin somewhere — and that was as unknowns.

  If that is not enough to convince you to develop new writers, note that first time novelists are often more promotable than second or third time novelists whose first books were only mid-list sellers. Finally, there is nothing really as exciting in the book world as discovering a new talent and sharing that talent with others.

Authors — Don't give up just because you are an unknown. Instead, do everything you can to get better known. Write for magazines. Write for local newspapers. Write for small press journals. To get better known, you have to get your name out there in the marketplace. If you cannot do it through writing, then emphasize your areas of expertise. Become an expert — one worth publishing.

6:06 Editors as Stars

When publishing an anthology, textbook, or other compilation, choose an established author to head the editorial effort. The name quality of the author will help to sell the compilation.

- Houghton Mifflin's anthology series, *The Best American Short Stories*, sold only 6,000 to 7,000 copies a year until they began using a different celebrity author as guest editor each year. Sales now total close to 35,000 copies per year, a five-fold increase.

- A great number of science fiction anthologies have been produced by the team of Isaac Asimov, Charles G. Waugh, and Martin Harry Greenburg. The sales of these anthologies, of course, were not hurt by the fact that Isaac Asimov was associated with them, though by now both Waugh and Greenburg are probably as well known by the readers of these anthologies.

6:07 Other Sources of Editorial Material

In your continuing search for new authors and new material for your line of books, you might want to research some of the following sources. You might be surprised by what you find in these sources. Seek and ye shall find.

- **Self-Publishers** — Self-publishers are an excellent source of new book material. Here are just a few of the major bestsellers which were originally self-published:

  The Elements of Style by William Strunk, Jr.
  The Encyclopedia of Associations by Frederick G. Ruffner
  Feed Me, I'm Yours by Vicki Lansky
  The Handbook of Higher Consciousness by Ken Keyes, Jr.
  How to Avoid Probate by Norman F. Dacey
  How to Keep Your Volkswagen Alive by John Muir
  Mary Ellen's Best of Helpful Hints by Mary Ellen Pinkham
  The One Minute Manager by Spencer Johnson and Kenneth Blanchard
  What Color Is Your Parachute by Richard N. Bolles
  Winning Through Intimidation by Robert Ringer

  Collier published a paperback edition of *Joshua*, a parable originally self-published by its author, Joseph F. Girzone, a retire priest. The book had sold 45,000 hardcover copies in its self-published edition; it sold over 100,000 copies in Collier's trade paperback edition — and is still selling well.

- **Local Celebrities** — Jennifer James, a Seattle talk radio personality and local columnist, sold 50,000 copies of her self-published book, *Success Is the Quality of Your Journey*, in the Pacific Northwest alone. Later, Newmarket Press brought out the book in an expanded paperback edition for national distribution.

- **Syndicated Columnists** — Almost every syndicated columnist can generate one or two books a year just by editing their collected columns. And many of these can become bestsellers. Witness the books by Ann Landers, Lewis Grizzard, and Erma Bombeck.

  Syndicated columnists can also create new books about their field of expertise. Edith Lank, whose "House Calls" real estate column is syndicated to more than 100 newspapers across the country, has written *The Complete Homeseller's Kit*, which is more than just a collection of her columns.

- **Sponsor Contests** — Avon/Flare sponsors a biannual Young Adult Novel Competition for authors between the ages of 13 and 18. Winners receive a publishing contract and an advance of $2,500. Avon has already published Lee J. Hindle's *Dragon Fall* in 1983 and Tamela Larimer's *Buck* in 1985.

- **Do Research** — To research its new line of Swept Away romances, Avon participated in *Seventeen* magazine's market research questionnaire. They also sponsored a contest in which students were asked to finish the following sentence: "If I could travel through time, I would most like to see, experience, and meet . . . ." (in 150 words or less). The winner received $200 plus recognition in the book inspired by his or her essay.

- **Specialty Booksellers** — More than anyone else in publishing, booksellers know what is selling and what is in demand by readers. Why not make use of their expertise to generate new titles? Ask for their feedback on proposed titles. Ask for their recommendations on up and coming authors.

   You might even create an entire line of books with the store's imprint. That's what Farrar, Straus & Giroux did with Kitchen Arts & Letters, a specialty cookbook store in New York. Their first title, *Christmas Memories with Recipes*, came out in the fall of 1988.

   Similarly, Warner Books has begun publishing a joint imprint with the Traveller's Bookshelf, another New York specialty bookstore. Already they have published eleven titles in Karen Brown's Travel Guides series. Directors of the bookstore suggest authors, ideas, and titles as well as approve book covers. They also do a lot of promotion.

   Peter Glassman and James Carey, owners of the Books of Wonder children's bookstore in New York, have their own Books of Wonder Classics imprint with Morrow Junior Books. Besides suggesting titles, authors, and illustrators, they also work with the art director to ensure top quality production. Peter Glassman also writes an afterword for each edition. Thus far Books of Wonder has published seven titles.

   Otto Penzler, owner of the Mysterious Book Shop (another specialty bookseller in New York), established his own publishing imprint, The Mysterious Press, in 1976. Recently, he has joined in a partnership with Warner Books where he retains full editorial control and ownership, while Warner provides financing, subsidiary rights sales, marketing, and publicity. Ballantine distributes the books to the book trade, while Warner Publishing Services distributes to the mass market. The Mysterious Press and Warner Books share the profits.

- **General Booksellers** — While all of the above examples involve New York specialty booksellers, it should be possible to make similar arrangements with some of the top-rated booksellers in your region — whether they are general booksellers or specialty booksellers.

   For example, if I were a publisher in Colorado, I would certainly try to arrange a co-publishing agreement with the Tattered Cover Bookstore, one of the largest independent booksellers in the country. Or how about an imprint featuring Powell's in the Pacific Northwest?

- **Other Publishers** — The major publishers often let a book go out of print long before its natural sales cycle has been exhausted. Why not take advantage of their short-sightedness?

   When Harper & Row let *The Martha's Vineyard Cookbook* go out of print (because there are only two bookstores on Martha's Vineyard), Globe Pequot Press was able to pick up the rights free. Since then, they've sold more than 20,000 copies of the book to gift shops, gourmet shops, and other retail outlets (even bookstores!) throughout the New England area.

6:08 Using Celebrity Forewords and Blurbs

If you can't sign celebrities or established authors, the next best thing is to obtain a foreword or blurb from such people. Anyone with visibility or name recognition is a good candidate for writing forewords for books by unknown authors.

- Robert Miller's *Most of My Patients Are Animals* was given a big sales boost by James Herriot's rave introduction to the book. The book, published by Paul S. Eriksson, was also chosen as a featured alternate by both the Literary Guild and Doubleday Book Club.

- Don Dible's *Up Your Own Organization* received such favorable advance comments that he decided to make use of them to help promote his book. In the end, three known business leaders, Robert Townsend of Avis, William Lear of Lear Motors Corporation, and John Komives of the Center for Venture Management, wrote an introduction and foreword to his book. Of course, he made sure their well-known names were featured on the front cover of his book.

> **Authors** — Do you know any well-known authors or other celebrities who could write a foreward, introduction, or other blurb for your book? If so, ask them to write a foreword. It will make your book more saleable. If you don't know anyone personally, write to a few well-known experts or celebrities who would be appropriate for your book. Your librarian will help you locate their addresses (in *Who's Who* or *Contemporary Authors* or some other biographical resource).

6:09 Titles: The First Impression

A good title alone can make the difference between a mediocre seller and a bestseller. The title of a book, like the headline of an advertisement or news story, often makes the difference between a reader passing the book by or picking it up and giving it more careful consideration. More often than not, the reader gives less than a moment's attention to any book title; if you don't capture the reader's imagination or curiosity or desire in that short moment, you will have lost the sale.

More important, however, is that many distributors, bookstore buyers, reviewers, and subsidiary rights buyers also judge a book by its title (and its cover). They know from experience that a good title sells more books. As Gloria Norris of the Book-of-the-Month Club once noted, "We can break out good writers—especially if their books have good titles."

Here are a few suggestions on how you can create titles that will sell more books:

• Test your titles beforehand, either by using focus groups, your key contacts, or small test markets. Classified ads are a cheap and workable way to test the effectiveness of titles, since the title alone either sells the book or it doesn't. In one such case, a publisher tested two different titles for two books by advertising the books in full page ads in leading newspapers across the country. Which of the following titles do you think did best?

1. The Art of Courtship vs. The Art of Kissing
2. Care of Skin and Hair vs. Eating for Health

Here are the actual results: *The Art of Kissing* sold over 60,000 copies in one year while *The Art of Courtship* sold only a little over 17,000 copies. *Care of Skin and Health* outsold *Eating for Health* by 52,000 copies to 36,000. In each case, both titles had the same number of exposures to the same number of readers.

• The above examples point out one other factor in titling your books: Be specific. Let the readers know what they can expect to get from the book. Specific benefits are usually more effective than general benefits in appealing to book buyers.

• Use subtitles to provide further explanation or description of the book's contents or benefits. Here are two examples of superb benefit subtitles: Herb Cohen's *You Can Negotiate Anything: How to Get What You Want* and Callan Pinckney's *Callanetics: 10 Years Younger in 10 Hours*.

Here's the rather long subtitle of *A.P. & Me*, an upcoming publicity book from Ad-Lib (spring, 1991): *How to Use Comedy Story Development to Transform Your Benefits-Oriented Press Release into a Worldwide Publicity Event*. It's rather long, but it does describe the contents of the book more thoroughly than the title alone. And it offers a prime benefit that the main title does not convey.

• Choose titles that play off the titles of other well-known books. Melvin Powers of Wilshire Book Company wrote a parody of Jim Everood's bestselling book, *How to Flatten Your Stomach*, which he titled, *How to Flatten Your Tush*. His parody made several bestseller lists.

Charlotte Peche titled her book on gynecology, *The One-Minute Gynecologist*, thus drawing on reader's familiarity with the other One-Minute books. The subtitle for her book helped to clarify what it was all about: *One Woman's Search for the Quick and Painless Visit*.

• Choose familiar leads to your titles. For example, *The Joy of Sex, The Joy of Lex, The Joy of Cooking, The Joy of Photography*, and so on. Or, *Mail Order Selling Made Easier, Astrology Made Easy, Tennis Made Easy, Book Marketing Made Easier*, and other such titles.

Or, that classic book title lead-in: *How to* ... do just about anything. Or, finally, how about *101 Ways to* ... do just about anything?

- Use the subject of your book as the lead-in to the title. In that way your book will be listed in the title index of any reference work just where inexperienced readers would look for a book on that subject. That is one reason we changed the title of one of our books from *The Directory of Book Marketing Opportunities* to *Book Publishing Resource Guide*. It's also a good argument for such titles such as *Book Marketing Made Easier* and *Iacocca: An Autobiography*.

- If you expect your authors to tour or do interviews, make sure the title is one they can pronounce. I wrote one book about kinetic optical illusions (illusions created when you spin a pattern on a record turntable) with a working title of *Dizzy Discs and Other Kinetic Illusions*. However, I would never use that title for the book, because I have an impossible time pronouncing the word "discs"—that "c" between the two "s's" is incredibly awkward.

6:10 Choose Uniquely Wonderful Titles

This suggestion for titling your books is the most important of all: Choose new titles, wonderful titles, titles that speak of romance, glory, wonder, or delight. This advice is absolutely important when titling novels. Nonfiction books can get away with being prosaic, but novels must be enticing, or startling, or daring, or warm.

- As I was writing an earlier chapter of this book, I reviewed the catalog offerings of New Society Publishers. One of their book titles immediately attracted me: *Heart Politics*. What a wonderful title, full of contradiction, conflict, warmth and promise. I was so attracted to the title that I stopped writing this book long enough to write a check and send for the book.

Here are a few of my other favorite book titles (not in any particular order and certainly not complete):

Cold Sassy Tree
The Unbearable Lightness of Being
Parachutes and Kisses
Stolen Ecstasy
Ancient Evenings
The Lonely Silver Rain
Bus 9 to Paradise
Zen and the Art of Motorcycle Maintenance
The Hunt for Red October
The Little Drummer Girl
A Confederacy of Dunces

Outrageous Acts and Everyday Rebellions
The Winds of War
The Lonesome Gods
Silk Lady
Angels of September

And here are a few titles that work well, that do a good job of selling the nonfiction book (again, in no particular order):

Color Me Beautiful
In Search of Excellence
How to Be Your Own Best Friend
Think and Grow Rich
Dress for Success
Everything You Always Wanted to Know about Sex
    But Were Afraid to Ask
Thin Thighs in 30 Days
Complete Book of Mask Making
Chocolate: The Consuming Passion
The Dieter's Guide to Weight Loss During Sex
Eat to Win
The One Minute Manager
The Beverly Hills Diet

6:11 A Rose by Any Other Name

Don't be afraid to change a title if you can make it better. Never stop playing with the title. Even after the book has been published, it is still possible to change a title. It's been done more than once. And done successfully.

- One paperback publisher changed the title of a book from *Five Days* to *Five Nights*. The second title sold much, much better than the first.

- One of the first books I published was titled *FormAides for Direct Response Marketing*. What a horrible title! The book was well-reviewed, but its sales were anything but spectacular. It was a superb book, with a poor title and poor cover design. Fortunately, we finally did sell out of that edition and have recently brought out a revised and much-expanded edition of the book under the title, *Mail Order Selling Made Easier*. Book club rights for this new edition were sold to The Executive Program, and preliminary sales have been fantastic.

- Garden Way sold 1,500 copies of *The Squash Book*. After changing the title of the book to *The Zucchini Cookbook*, they sold over 300,000 copies.

Here are some other title changes, all of which I feel were made for the better:

- *The Pineapple Diet Book* to *The Beverly Hills Diet Book* — The second is much more glamorous and enticing. Pineapples pucker my mind.

- *Tomorrow Is Another Day* to *Gone with the Wind* — and the heroine's name was changed from Pansy to Scarlett O'Hara. Which title do you think has sold millions of copies and gone on to become a major motion picture? Do you think the original title would have done as well?

- *Catch 18* to *Catch 22* — The second has better rhythm and assonance.

- *Your Guide to Coping with Pain* to *Conquering Back Pain* — The Canadian title was changed when Prentice-Hall came out with a U.S. edition so that the title would better reflect the book's contents. And better reflect the American way of viewing problems.

- *Notes from a Teacher's Wastebasket* to *Up the Down Staircase* — The first has the flavor of an old maid teacher; the second catches the chaos and joy of teaching.

- *Chapters in the Life of a Young Man* to *The Portrait of the Artist as a Young Man* — There is more romance in being an artist. Plus the vibrant "portrait" enlivens the title much more than does the rather stale "chapters."

- *John Thomas and Lady Jane* to *Lady Chatterley's Lover* — The first could be a simple tale of married life between a commoner and a noble; the second clearly suggests an illicit romance which makes for a far more exciting tale.

- *Cain Mark* to *East of Eden* — The first title is ambiguous; the second hints of oriental romance.

- *The PRE-Reading Experience* to *Developing the Early Learner* to *The IQ Booster Kit* — Note how the title becomes more specific while at the same time offering greater benefits. Which would you buy? Which do you think sold best?

- *Trimalchio in West Egg* to *The Great Gatsby* — Which would you rather recommend to a friend? I can't even pronounce the first title, but, oh, the second title! Look out, Tony the Tiger, here I come!

- *Hunting Caleb* to *Searching for Caleb* — The first suggests morbid violence, while the second suggests longing and desire.

Authors — Be open to suggestions for changing the title of your book. Don't insist on your title. Allow your publisher an opportunity to give the book a title that will sell more copies. Indeed, you should always be developing and testing new titles yourself. Keep trying out new titles till you find one that clicks — not only with your inner sense, but also with friends, booksellers, librarians, and strangers on the street.

6:12 Titles as Point of Purchase Advertising

Whatever you title your book, remember that the title of your book must serve at least three purposes:

1. It must attract the attention of the book buyer.
2. It must indicate what the book is about. For nonfiction, the title should be as clearly descriptive as possible; for fiction, the title should be appropriate for the specific genre.
3. It must, if possible, create the desire to buy.

The best titles, like all good advertising headlines, serve all three functions at the same time. Remember that the title (and cover) of your book is often the only advertising message any buyer ever sees. Make sure the message is clear and effective.

Chapter 7

Designing Your Books as Sales Aids

As mentioned in the previous chapter, the marketability of a book is determined not only by its editorial content and the qualifications and fame of the author but also by the design, packaging, and price of the book. In this chapter, we'll discuss the last three elements in greater detail.

7:01 You Can Sell a Book by Its Cover

It's an old maxim that you can't judge a book by its cover, but this maxim does not hold true in the real world of commercial bookselling. People do judge a book by its cover — not only readers but also bookstore buyers, reviewers, and distributors.

Here are just a few reasons why you should place major attention on the cover design of your books:

- The cover or jacket is used by your sales representatives and distributors to sell your book to bookstore buyers. Often the cover is the only thing the buyers ever see — the only thing that can either make the sale or lose the sale.

  At Falker-Verlag, a German trade publisher, cover designs originate with the marketing and sales department. No book is sent out whose cover has not been approved by the sales representatives.

- The cover is featured in your advertisements, catalogs, and reviews. If it is well-done, it will increase your sales. If it is boring or unconvincing, it will detract from your sales.

- In marginal buying situations, the first impression that the book creates is the only impression it creates.

- For bookstores, the cover is important for a number of reasons:
  1) it must fit into the atmosphere the bookstore is trying to create,
  2) it must fit into (and yet stand out from) other titles in the same category, and
  3) it must attract the casual browser.

- The cover is often the only advertising a book buyer sees. It is the ultimate in point-of-purchase advertisements. It either works, or it does not. And it has only about 8 seconds to do so, since the average bookstore browser, according to the *Wall Street Journal*, spends only 8 seconds on the front cover of a book—and then only if the reader is attracted enough to the book to pick it up in the first place.

  As Judith Clinton of Tor Books has observed, "We believe that the cover is a point-of-purchase advertisement of major importance in the marketing of the book."

- Book covers are also important for advance sales at exhibits or with key wholesale, chain store, and book club buyers. Again, it is often the only part of the book that they see first hand before the book is produced. And many of these buyers must make their purchase commitments months in advance of any book's publication date.

  At the 1983 ABA Convention, Alan Gadney of Festival Publications took many large orders for three computer books based solely on the sample covers he had produced. The sales could not have come from the contents of the books, because Alan hadn't written the books yet.

- To many buyers and reviewers, the cover design reflects the attention the publisher has put into the book (and will continue to put into the book by way of continued promotions). Hence, your books will get far more reviewer attention if you yourself put more attention into designing an effective cover. As the former book editor of *Newsday*, Leslie Hanscom, has commented, "I know when I see a really attractive jacket that the publisher is behind the book and, of course, I pay attention to it."

- For some kinds of books, a well-illustrated cover increases the value of the book. For example, in the science fiction and fantasy fields, the cover illustration is often the number one criteria by which book collectors in that genre judge a book. Indeed, the annual Hugo awards granted by the fans has separate categories for both fan artist and professional artist. And the art shows at the various SF conventions are often better attended than the seminars and speeches.

- Design is crucial, of course, with non-books such as diaries, the Anything book series from Crown, and personalized recipe books like Nancy Edwards's *With Love From My Kitchen*, published by Paint Box Studio. In such cases, the design is the book.

- Cover design, when standardized for a series, can help readers to identify other books in the series.

SAMS has standardized the cover type, logo, and graphic window design for all its computer books. It has helped them gain valuable customer recognition for the entire line; indeed, it has helped to establish SAMS as a brand name for high quality computer books.

Vintage Contemporaries, Penquin, and NAL Plume all have uniform cover formats for their series of literary novels. The books in these series tend to be displayed together in the bookstores, often face out. This grouping (and the uniform design) helps readers to recognize the books as a series. When they buy one and like it, they come back for more. Booksellers seem to love it.

7:02 Elements of Good Cover Design

The basic rule of cover design is that the cover should match the contents of the book. That means that the style, format, and message of the cover should be compatible with the style, format, and message of the book itself. An effective cover design should have at least some of the following elements:

- Use a standard format. The book should look like a book, and especially like other books with similar contents. If you want to attract the attention of buyers of a specific genre, your books must look like other books within the genre. Just as all oatmeal boxes look alike, so must all romance novels that hope to sell to repeat buyers. In the case of romance novels, this means a cover with a feminine typeface combined with an illustration of a man and woman caught in a wild embrace (the woman with long wind-blown hair and at least one naked shoulder).

- At the same time, the book must look different. It must be able to stand out in the crowd. That is one reason Zebra Books printed holograms on the covers of its romance novels. It hoped to distinguish its line of books so the books stood out on the paperback racks and thereby attracted more attention from potential buyers.

  Bantam put an embossed silver foil dustjacket on Leona Blair's novel, *Privilege*, so it would stand out from all the other hardcovers on the shelves.

- The front cover of a book should be bold and simple, more like a billboard (which it is) than a full-page display ad. The cover should be uncluttered, easy to read (with highly readable type), and simple enough that the casual browser can catch the title and author without searching for either.

- Generally speaking, the title of the book should be featured at the top of the cover. It's the first thing the reader should see. If, however, the author is well-known and more important than the title, then feature the author's name in bold type at the top of the cover.

- Besides the author and title of the book, feature any other information that could be useful in selling the book. Touchstone, for instance, took advantage of the controversy surrounding the movie, *The Last Temptation of Christ*, to bring out a new edition of the book by Nikos Kazantzakis featuring the artwork from the film's lobby card.

- The typography of the front cover should match the style of the book. For example, a simple typeface is more appropriate for a serious book while a fancy script typeface might be more appropriate for a romance novel. Novelty books, on the other hand, might use a casual typeface such as Hobo (one of my favorites).

  Typefaces come in all sorts of characters from simple to complex, from feminine to masculine, from strong and bold to light and airy, from romantic to businesslike. Be sure that your graphic designer selects a typeface that matches the style and subject of the book.

- Fiction should almost always have some illustrative element on the cover while nonfiction can easily do without any illustration or graphic elements at all. Indeed, serious nonfiction books may be better served by a simple bold headline and little else. Again, the design of the cover depends on the style and subject of the book as well as the intended audience.

- Full-color covers are almost a requirement for coffee-table books, high-priced cookbooks, pictorial travel guides, and most fiction. Full-color covers also encourage impulse sales for almost any book.

  Indeed, while walking the floor of the ABA Convention this year, I noticed that covers of all books are becoming more and more attractive, even dramatic—most with full-color covers. Many publishers reported that switching from one- or two-color covers to full-color covers has had a significant impact on their sales.

- Not that all covers need to be full-color. Javan has successfully self-published a series of poetry gift titles with a simple cover design: just the title and the author's name printed in italics, brown ink on a light brown antique cover. Booksellers reportedly like the cover just as it is.

- If you are publishing a series, there should be some continuity in the cover design so that bookstore browsers can readily see the connection. For example, Wei-chuan's Cooking uses the same format for all four covers of their line of Chinese cookbooks.

  The two complimentary titles from Advocacy Press, *Choices* and *Challenges*, both had similar cover designs though one was feminine in style and the other masculine—matching the audience for each book.

- Try different sizes of books. 101 Productions was the first publisher to use an 8" x 8" format for trade cookbooks, a format that allows for more flexibility in the layout of pages while enabling the book to lie open more easily without breaking the spine. In the past fifteen years, 101 has sold more than four million copies of their cookbooks.

Comstock's line of popular western history, biography, folklore, and fiction is published in mass-market format rather than the trade paperback format standard for this type. Why? Because it sets the books apart from all the rest.

- Here's a little quirky hint: If one of your books happens to have a publication date of mid-March, you might want to give it a green cover. More than one bookseller has been known to display a window full of green books for St. Patrick's Day. Customers reportedly love it.

- Besides being your major point-of-purchase advertising for the book, the cover must also protect the book. If it is a paperback book, have the cover varnished, film laminated, or coated with a UV plastic. If it is hardcover, use a jacket (which also allows for more promotional copy than a cover by itself).

Authors — Don't insist on your own cover design for your books. Rely on the judgment of your publishers. They are far more likely to be in tune with the trends of the marketplace — and certainly know better than you do what they can sell. This doesn't mean that you can't give them suggestions; just don't be married to your own ideas.

7:03 Don't Forget the Spine

More than once in my own publishing career I have forgotten to add copy for the spine before sending the materials to the printer. Thus I had to rely on the printer to set the type and place it appropriately—a procedure that I do not recommended if you like to sleep at night. Anyway, the spine of your books should always have at least the following elements:

- the full title of the book,
- the name of the author, and
- your company name and logo (if there is room).

Since most books in libraries and bookstores are displayed spine out, make sure the title is large enough to read.

Also, leave some space on the lower portion of the spine for libraries to place their shelf stickers. Either leave this space blank or use it for some information that you don't mind having obliterated by the sticker.

One other note: Make sure the spine reads from top to bottom when the book is shelved with the front cover facing the right side of a shelf. This is the standard way to place the copy on the spine. If you place it the other way, browsers will have a harder time reading the title of your book.

7:04 What to Put on the Back Cover

While the front cover should act as a billboard to attract potential buyers, the back cover should serve as a display advertisement to encourage the buyer to get the book. Hence, the back cover can be more complex, more wordy, more detailed. How much more complex? The average book now has about 10 to 15 words on its front cover and from 70 to 100 on its back.

What should the back cover contain?

- First and foremost, it should have more details about the book, anything about the book that will encourage the reader to buy the book. List an abbreviated form of the table of contents, or use a section from the author's introduction, or, in the case of a novel, write a short synopsis of the crisis/setting/characters of the story.

  Above all, emphasize the benefits not the contents of the book. The back cover should resell the book after the front cover has done the initial job of attracting the browser.

- Second, it may contain blurbs from reviewers and experts — blurbs, of course, that praise the book. Testimonials or endorsements help to instill confidence in the book.

- Third, include some details about the author, anything that will establish his or her credentials to write the book. If the author is a celebrity, be sure to include a recent photo of the author, either at work or at play depending on the nature of the book.

- Fourth, list the price of the book. For the convenience of the bookseller, the price must appear somewhere on the cover. For most mass-market paperbacks the price is listed on the front cover, most trade paperbacks on the back cover, and most hardcovers on the inside front flap.

- Fifth, print the ISBN number and Bookland EAN symbol on the back cover. Why is this information so important?

  1. Most library and bookstore orders are now placed using the ISBN number as the sole designator of a title.

  2. With many libraries and booksellers using computers, the ISBN number is the most convenient short-hand code for the book's title and author.

  3. The ISBN number and Bookland EAN allow for complete inventory control through all the channels of distribution, from the publisher to the wholesaler to the bookstore.

  4. Waldenbooks has sent a letter to its major vendors requesting that all publishers print the Bookland EAN symbol on all new titles by the end of 1988. As price scanners become more common, other chains and booksellers will clearly follow suit.

The Bookland EAN symbol should be printed on the back cover with high contrast ink (either black on white, or dark blue on white) with at least an 1/8" of white space around the edges. The ISBN number should be printed in OCR-A font above the Bookland EAN symbol:

To get camera-ready copy for the Bookland EAN, you should contact one of the following bar code suppliers who will know how to prepare the code once you have assigned an ISBN number to the book:

- **Accession Inc.,** Richard Oaksford, P. O. Box 2299, Lynnwood, WA 98036-2299; (800) 531-6029; Fax: (206) 672-9063.
- **Book Industry Bar Codes,** Landy & Associates, 5311 N. Highland, Tacoma WA 98407; (206) 752-5099.
- **GGX Associates,** 11 Middle Neck Road, Great Neck, NY 98407; (516) 487-6370; Fax: (516) 487-6449.
- **Precision Photography,** 1150 N. Tustin Avenue, Anaheim, CA 92807; (800) 872-9988; CA: (800) 872-9977; Fax: (714)-630-6581.
- **Symbology Inc.,** P. O. Box 13262, St. Paul, MN 55113-0162; (612) 631-0520; (800) 328-2612; Fax: (612) 631-8155.

If your books are sold in groceries, drugstores, or other mass-market outlets, the Universal Product Code (rather than the Bookland EAN) should be printed on the back cover. You can sign up to participate in this program by writing to: **Uniform Code Council, 8163 Old Yankee Road, Suite J, Dayton, OH 45458; (513) 435-3870; Fax: (513) 435-3870.**

- Sixth, leave space on the top right corner of the back cover for those libraries which use bar-code scanners for checking the books out. How much space should you leave? One inch down by three inches wide. Again, leave this space blank or use it for information you don't mind having obliterated by the bar-code sticker.

One of the things you could print on the top right corner of the back cover is the subject of the book. Make the subject clear so the bookstores do not shelf the book in the wrong area. Prentice-Hall's *National Rifleman's Bible* ended up in the religious section of many bookstores because it lacked this vital information.

Remember that whatever you put on the back cover should serve one purpose: to inspire the reader to buy the book. Few browsers look beyond the front and back covers; hence, the covers have to be so designed that they encourage the browser to buy the book right away or else open the book to learn more about it contents.

7:05 Jacket Flaps

The jackets of hardcover books usually include a short synopsis of the book on the front flap and a short biography of the author on the back flap. This arrangement allows the back cover to be used for testimonials and blurbs from advance reviews. Since a hardcover book is usually higher priced, use this extra space to include more copy that will overcome the casual browser's price resistance.

7:06 Selecting the Right Binding

There are five basic binding options currently available: hardcover (whether perfectbound or smyth-sewn), perfectbound paperback, saddle-stitched paperback, comb or spiral bound, and loose-leaf binders. How do you choose how to bind your new titles? Here are a few guidelines:

Hardcovers

Use hardcovers for gift books, library editions, permanent collections, major works of fiction and non-fiction, and professional reference titles.

- Since hardcovers are still taken more seriously by booksellers, reviewers, and subsidiary rights buyers, publish hardcover editions of your books if you want to reach a wide general market through book reviews and author tours.

- Libraries still prefer hardcover editions because they wear better under heavy use. For the same reason, professionals prefer hardcovers for their expensive reference manuals.

- Most higher priced books are published in hardcover because such covers are viewed as being more expensive. An exception to this rule, however, are high priced annual directories, such as *Literary Market-Place*, because they are expected to wear out quickly and be replaced with a new edition each year.

- Cookbooks often sell better in trade paperback editions except around Christmas time when many people are buying cookbooks as gifts for others; then the hardcover edition has a much higher perceived value.

- Hardcover editions are also indispensable for books which are destined to be collector's items — anything from a cookbook to a limited edition.

Perfectbound paperbacks

Use for most mass-market titles, inexpensive editions, novelty books, travel guides, poetry, literary novels, and any book with an ephemeral topic. According to one study, 58% of all small press titles are now published in trade paperback.

- As mentioned above, many annual directories are published in perfectbound paperback format because they are expected to last only a year until the next edition comes out.

- Most genre novels are published in mass-market format because, again, they tend to reflect changing tastes and aren't likely to be read again and again.

- The main reason to use this format is to keep the retail price down so more readers can afford to buy the book. It also cuts your upfront costs in publishing a book, leaving you more money to put into advertising and promoting the book.

- Of course, you could publish both a hardcover and a paperback edition (either simultaneously or, as is more common, the hardcover first, followed by the paperback). Publishing two editions expands the potential audience of the book.

- Publishing two editions also allows you to sell each edition to a different book club without endangering the exclusivity of either club. Festival Publications did this with one of their titles, selling the $15.95 paperback to one book club and the $23.95 hardcover to another.

Saddle-stitched paperbacks

Use mainly for workbooks, manuals, reports, newsletters, and other expendable publications.

- Because saddle-stitched books have no spine and thus cannot be shelved with the spine out, they are hard to sell to libraries and booksellers. Don't use such binding if these are your major markets.

- The main value of saddle-stitched books is that they are less expensive to produce. Hence, they make superb workbooks and lab manuals.

- They also lie flat more easily than perfectbound books — another reason they make good workbooks and atlases.

Comb-bound and spiral-bound books

Use primarily for cookbooks, computer manuals, and other books where there is a great need for the book to lie flat while allowing the reader's hands to remain free.

- A survey by the Benjamin Company showed that 54% of cookbook buyers consider it essential that a cookbook lie flat. An additional 32% considered it nice but not essential.

Loose-leaf binders

Use primarily for subscription services and any other books which require periodic updating or removal of the pages.

- A collection of forms may either be published as a perfectbound book with perforated pages (which does not allow the pages to remain together in a neat way) or as a loose-leaf binder (which allows for the pages to be removed, copied, and then returned for safe keeping).

- Loose-leaf binders are usually sold only by mail to end users because librarians and booksellers do not like stocking books whose pages can be removed easily. In addition, binders do not sit neatly on most bookstore and library shelves.

- Loose-leaf subscription services are among the highest priced publications, generally priced between $99.00 and $500.00. Some of the major loose-leaf publishers are Prentice-Hall, Research Institute of America, the Bureau of National Affairs, Commerce Clearing House, Warren, Gorham & Lamont, Law Publications, Matthew Bender, Aspen, J. B. Lippincott, and Longman Trade.

7:07 Pricing Your Books

Generally speaking, your books should be priced from five to eight times your production costs. Within this projected range, you should set the retail price of your books to be competitive with other books covering the same subject and in the same format. Here are a few guidelines:

- **Mass-market paperbacks** — Prices range from $2.50 to $5.95. The average price for a mass-market paperback in 1987 was $4.00. The highest average prices for mass-market paperbacks were $12.38 for art books and $11.52 for technology books. The lowest average price was $2.80 for juvenile paperbacks.

  The *Twin Cities Gold Book*, a directory of advertising and creative services published by Prime Publications, was one of the highest-priced mass-market format paperbacks. It sold for $16.00.

- **Trade paperbacks** — Prices range from $3.95 for a thin book up to $30.00 for a larger trade paperback. The average price for a trade paperback in 1987 was $14.55. The lowest average prices were around $9.25 for fiction, poetry, and books on religion.

  One of the highest priced paperbacks in 1988 was the 1000+ page *Literary MarketPlace*, which sold for $95.00.

- **Hardcovers** — Prices range from $6.95 for some juveniles and novelty books to $99.95 on up for professional reference books. The average hardcover price in 1987 was $36.28. The lowest average prices were $11.48 for juveniles and $18.19 for fiction. The highest average prices (around $60.00) were for books on medicine, science, and technology.

Perhaps the highest-priced hardcover is the $22,000 facsimile edition of Audubon's Birds of America, a combined publication of Abbeville Press and the National Audubon Society. In three years they sold 335 copies of this edition—that's over $7,000,000 in sales.

- **Saddle-stitched books**—Prices range from 99¢ to $10.95 on up. Play books for children range from 99¢ to $4.95. Professional reports range from $9.95 all the way on up to $6,750.00 for a report on *European Drinking Habits* from Business Trends Analysis.

- **Comb-bound or spiral-bound books**—Prices range from $3.95 to $19.95. Cookbooks average between $6.95 and $12.95 for comb-bound books. Comb-bound software manuals are generally higher prices. The highest priced comb-bound book is probably *Electronic Publishing Markets* published by Market Intelligence Research Company for $995.00.

7:08 Good Books Come in Unusual Packages

While in most cases your books should look like books, there are arguments for packaging your book in unusual ways to reach a new market. In many such cases, it's a good policy to publish two editions, one for the standard book market, the other for the special market.

- Unusual packaging can allow you to reach other markets, just as the unique packaging of L'eggs allowed it to reach into grocery stores to sell nylons. Para Publishing die-cut its *Frisbee Player's Handbook* into a circular shape and then packaged it inside a frisbee, thus encouraging sales to toy and sports shops that might not otherwise have carried the standard edition of the book (which sold better to bookstores and libraries).

- Unusual packaging can set your book apart from other books. The Pet Rock, for instance, was really just a short book, *The Care and Feeding of Your Pet Rock*, packaged with a plain rock in a fancy box. It wasn't the rock or the fancy box that really caught the imagination of the public; it was the book with its humorous approach to something as commonplace as a little rock.

- Even small format changes can make a difference in sales. Dial added a fancy ribbon marker to Paula Wolfert's *The Cooking of Southwest France*, thereby setting the book apart from other cookbooks. So, even though the book had few illustrations and a high price, it still sold well because of that little touch of class.

- Richard Scary's *Biggest Word Book Ever!* from Random House is two feet high—almost taller than many of its intended users (ages 3 to 5). But its size sets it apart from other books, and it fits the title. Of course, the size also allows Random House to justify the high price tag of $29.95.

- You can use unusual packaging to adapt your books to particular seasons, celebrations, or events. Little Simon, the juvenile publishing division of Simon & Schuster, repackaged its Hatchling line of small board books into see-through Easter eggs which were then nestled on top of green paper grass inside a large counter-top display. These books sold well during the Easter season.

- Unusual book packages such as pop-ups, die-cuts, sticker books, and board books are often used in creating books for children. Such books combine play-value with content to help attract and keep the attention of children. Hence, they sell almost as well as toys.

- Metro Files, a subsidiary of Rolodex, published a directory of toll-free numbers, *1-800-Toll-Free*, not as a book but as a set of Rolodex cards. Not only did this make it easier for readers to use, but it also sold more Rolodex filing systems.

- Redpath Press published a series of twelve short stories as "Perfect Presents" — individually bound short stories designed as gift items. These Perfect Presents were a little smaller than standard greeting cards, include a story and illustrations, and sell for $4.95 or $5.95.

- Jeff Cook self-published 18 varieties of *Cook's Canned Speeches*, one-page speeches that were packed inside a can with an applause sign and a plastic carnation. With most of his orders coming from such gift store chains as Spencer Gifts, he sold more than 35,000 copies at $6.95 within a very short time.

- More than two million wands and seven million workbooks in the Questron line of electronic workbooks have been sold by Random House.

- When Little, Brown and Company was faced with 25,000 leftover copies of *Blue Highways* after a year on the bestsellers lists, they decided to package the book as a gift so they could extend its selling life for one more season. They clipped the price off the jacket flap (so the book could be given as a gift), gift wrapped the book, and bound the package with a band that was printed with the name of the author, the title of the book, the price, the ISBN number, and the Bookland EAN bar code. As a result, they sold another 15,000 copies of the book during the holidays. In 1988, they did a similar gift promotion for Cleveland Amory's *The Cat Who Came for Christmas*.

- For fancy coffee-table books, booksellers prefer to have copies either shrinkwrapped or boxed. Not only does this make it easier to gift wrap the books, but it also ensures that these expensive books will remain in pristine condition. To help the bookseller display these higher-priced books without damaging the copies for sale, offer the bookseller a 60% discount on a browser's copy (with an order of five to ten additional copies at your normal discount). Or provide extra covers. Or provide sample pages from the inside of the book.

7:09 Combine Books with Other Items

One way to expand the market for your books is to repackage them with other media, from audio tapes to frisbees, and then sell the package as a kit. This repackaging will make it easier for you to sell your book in other retail markets, especially gift stores.

- As noted above, Para Publishing packaged its *Frisbee Player's Handbook* with a frisbee. This combined package actually sold better than the book alone and helped to get the book into several catalogs.

- Many children's books are now packaged with an audio tape so the children can listen to the audio tape as they read the story or look at the pictures.

- Harper & Row published a novel by Ursula LeGuin, *Always Coming Home*, which was accompanied by an audio tape. The book told the story of a future Amerindian society while the audio tape contained songs and poems from this fictional future.

- When Jim Humberd published a book on travel to a European country, he contacted that country's tourist office. They supplied him with thousands of road maps of the country which he then packaged with the book. Other items you could package with a travel book: some small gift item from the country or region featured in the book, travel accessories, translation cards, currency exchange rates.

- Computer software is almost always packaged with a manual or set of manuals explaining how to use the software. Certainly the software sells better because it has printed documentation. Of course, the documentation is often inadequate; otherwise, there wouldn't be the large market that now exists for computer books explaining how to use the software.

- W. W. Norton packaged a software program to accompany the paperback edition of Richard Dawkins's *The Blind Watchmaker*, a defense of Darwinism. The software allows readers to simulate the evolution of biomorphs.

- Rodale packaged a free radon testing kit with its books, *Radon: The Invisible Threat* by Michael Lafavore.

- Klutz packaged a set of measuring spoons with its cookbook for kids, *Kids Cooking: A Slightly Messy Manual*.

- Workman packages Hugh Danks's *The Bug Book* inside a plastic bug-catching bottle.

- Midwest Financial Publications packaged courses that contained two or three books, a collection of cassette tapes, and other information which they then sold via hour-long television shows. The packages were priced at almost $300 — well over the total price that could have been charged if each item were sold separately.

> **Authors** — When writing your book, brainstorm various ways that your book could be combined with some other item to create a more saleable package in special retail outlets. While your publisher might not go for the idea, it won't hurt to come up with some suggestions. And, if your publisher cannot do it, perhaps you could test the idea yourself.

7:10 Designing the Inside

When designing a book, take some time designing the inside as well as the outside of the book. Here are a few inside design elements that can affect the marketability of books:

- Use acid-free paper for books that must last a long time: library editions, limited editions, professional texts, and any other books worth preserving. If one of the main markets for the book will be libraries, acid-free paper could double the sales of the book.

  The following symbol should be printed in all books that are printed on acid-free paper:

- Be sure that the typeface you use for the text of the book is readable. And, if the book is to be used by many older people, make sure the type size is large enough. New England Press once published a superb cookbook (practical content, great reviews, attractive design, and reasonable price), but the book did not sell well. Only by chance did they discover the problem. When watching bookstore browsers pick up the book and page through it, they discovered that the typeface was too small for use in a kitchen.

- Use color inside high-priced books, pictorial books, and children's books. Few coffee-table books, pictorial travel guides, or expensive cookbooks will sell without full-color photos. Even fewer children's books will sell if they are not colorful and attractive. In the cookbook buyers survey conducted by the Benjamin Company, 48% of the respondents said that color photographs accompanying the text were essential for cookbooks.

- Illustrations help to sell books. Photographs, line drawings, tables, graphs, charts, sidebars, and other illustrations all make a book more attractive and useful. Especially in this visual age where many readers have grown up watching TV, graphic elements help to sell books.

- Give a sense of spaciousness to your books. Now, here again I have not always practiced my own advice (certainly my *Book Marketing Made Easier* and *Directory of Book Printers* are both crowded to the gills). Nevertheless, if your major distribution outlet is bookstores, your books should be as attractive and as inviting as possi-ble, both inside and out. Remember: As many as two-thirds of all bookstore sales are impulse purchases. The more attractive you make your books, the more likely they are to sell.

- Since many readers still equate size with quality, you might want to use high-bulk paper to make your books look bigger and to add a feel of substance. Nat Bodian gives a case in point:

  In 1982, two titles were published on the same subject by two different publishers. The first, printed on machine-coated stock, measured one inch thick and sold for $17.95; the other, printed on antique finish paper, measured one and a half inches thick and sold for $24.95. The thicker book, which actually had 19 fewer pages, sold much better in bookstores.

> **Authors** — Above all, don't forget the content. That is the most important thing you can put into your book. Pack your book with information that is practical, complete, and indispensable to the reader. It's the content that will generate satisfied readers, and it is satisfied readers that will tell their friends to buy the book as well.

7:11 Front and Back Matter

The front and back matter of your books can be used to help market the books. Front matter such as forewords and dedications can help to promote the purpose of your books, while back matter such as appendices and bibliographies can increase the resource value of the books and, hence, their marketability. Here's a list of front and back matter which can be used to increase the promotability of a book:

- **Inside front cover (or end papers)** — These may be used for maps, family trees, or other illustrations which add to the reader's understanding of a book. Illustrations printed on the inside covers or end papers are easier to refer to while reading.

  In my book *Tinseltowns, U.S.A.*, a trivia/quiz book, I printed sample questions from the book. Then I gave the page numbers where the answers could be found. If the bookstore browser wanted the answers, he or she would have to open the book!

- **Half-title page** – If included at all, this page is most often used to list only the title of the book. It may, however, also be used to print additional testimonials and endorsements or an enticing lead-in paragraph to the story itself.

  For example, Warner Books printed a series of questions on the half-title page of the mass-market edition of Jerry Gillies's *Moneylove*. If you answered "no" to any of the questions, "you are on the way to discovering the enriching truth about the road to prosperity . . . and you can get it with *Moneylove*."

- **Verso of half-title page** – If you include a half-title page in your books, use the opposite side to list other books by the author (especially those published by you). It's an inexpensive and unobtrusive way to let readers know about other books by the author.

- **Title page** – List the title of the book, including any subtitle or explanation; the author, authors, or editor; and the name and logo of your company. Also, list your company's address and phone number on this page; it will make it easier for readers to order more books from you.

- **Copyright page** – List the copyright notice, ISBN number, CIP information, and company name and address (if not listed on the previous page). The copyright notice, of course, is required to secure the fullest protection of the copyright law. The ISBN number allows booksellers and librarians to reorder copies more easily. The CIP information makes it easier for librarians to catalog your books; hence, librarians are more likely to order your books if this information is included.

  If the book is available in two editions (both hardcover and paperback), print that information on this page as well.

- **Dedication** – Encourage your writers to include some human interest in their dedications, anything that will speak to the readers and make the dedication more memorable. Robert Holt included the following dedication in his self-published book, *Hemorrhoids: A Cure and Preventative*: "To the silent sufferers." His dedication was picked up by several reviewers who used it as the lead to their reviews.

> **Authors** – If you decide to include a dedication in your book, spend a little time to make it the best dedication you can write. Include some human interest.

- **Foreword** – Forewords to your books should be written by celebrities or by experts in the subject of the book – someone, in short, who will add legitimacy or interest to the book. As mentioned in the previous chapter, that's why Don Dible got Robert Townsend, president of Avis Rent-a-Car, to write the foreword to his book, *Up the Organization*.

- **Preface**—The preface should not only establish the author's authority or expertise but also reveal why the author chose to write the book. Many bookstore browsers read the preface before anything else, because the preface often reveals the author's motivation for writing the book, gives them insight into the author's style and approach to the subject, and provides background on the author and the research behind the book.

> **Authors** — Use the preface to establish a rapport with the readers of your book. Give them some insight into yourself, your reasons for writing the book, and some reason to want to find out more about the subject of the book. Make it personal, and make it interesting.

- **Acknowledgements**—Acknowledgements are a great place to thank those who helped you research and write the book, especially the experts and other resource people who provided the necessary background facts and examples. Such acknowledgements help to establish the reliability of your information.

> **Authors** — Use the acknowledgement to recognize the help and love you've received from your friends, family, and resources. Of course, it doesn't hurt to know that everyone listed in the acknowledgement will probably want to buy at least one copy of the book (or receive one as a gift).

- **Table of contents**—After the front and back covers, the first thing most bookstore browsers look at is the table of contents. In preparing a table of contents, be as specific as possible. Let the reader see at a glance what your book offers. Include not only the chapter titles, but also major subheads. (Here's one reason why your chapter titles and subheads should be lively, interesting, and informative.)

  Nat Bodian, in his two volumes of the *Book Marketing Handbook*, included not one but two tables of contents. The first was a short two-page table of contents listing only the major chapter titles; the second was a fifteen-page listing of the major chapter titles and all the subheads. The first provided the reader with a brief summary of the book's contents, while the second provided a complete and detailed overview. *1001 Ways* provides both tables of contents as well.

When preparing the table of contents, consider the possibility of using the table as part of the advertising brochure for the book. Many professional and how-to books use this approach very successfully, since readers of such books are most interested in what the books cover. Well-prepared tables of contents provide the best overall summary of what the books have to offer.

> **Authors** — You can make your table of contents much more interesting by creating intriguing, challenging, benefit-laden, humorous, or just plain interesting chapter titles. Remember: One of the first parts of the book any bookstore browser looks at is the table of contents. So make it meaty, enticing.

- **Lists of illustrations/tables/charts** — If the book includes many illustrations, charts or maps, you should include a list of illustrations. Such a list makes it easier for the reader to locate a specific illustration. (Such a list, of course, also makes the book more attractive and useful to librarians, because it makes the book easier to use as a reference resource.)

- **Introduction** — Use the introduction to lead the reader into the rest of the book. After the table of contents, most bookstore buyers will look at the introduction. The introduction must be so well-written that the reader is enticed to read on. Chances are that once a bookstore browser reads a well-written introduction, he or she will buy the book.

With fiction, the first chapter often serves the same function as an introduction in a nonfiction book. The first chapter, indeed the first sentence, must entice the reader into the book.

Earlier today I picked up one of the Fletch mystery novels by Gregory Mcdonald. Well, say no more. Honest, I was just going to glance at it, but the first chapter was so delightful that I had to keep reading. I just finished the book a few minutes ago. Sorry for the interruption (Did you notice it?).

> **Authors** — Because the introduction can be so important in convincing a bookstore browser to buy your book, don't just tack on an introduction. Make it an integral part of your book. And make it as good or even better than any other part of the book.

Back Matter

Most of the traditional back matter (appendix, glossary, bibliographies, footnotes, and index) serve one major purpose: They provide readers with access to more information, to additional resources. For that reason, they are considered essential by many librarians. At the very minimum, a nonfiction book should contain a complete index and bibliography.

- **Bibliography**—Librarians love to see bibliographies in books because bibliographies let readers know where they can go for more information on the subject, thus making the librarian's job easier. Also, of course, bibliographies indicate that a book has been well-researched and, therefore, is probably more accurate and complete.

  The real bibliography for this book was so long I had to publish it as an extended section of a separate book, *Book Publishing Resource Guide*. The new edition of this bibliography lists and reviews over 250 books on publishing, printing, graphics, publicity, and marketing.

> Authors — If you have done the research for your book, you should have no trouble preparing a complete and useful list of books that will show your readers where they can go for more information. Librarians will love you for it.

- **Index**—Librarians also love indexes—and for good reason. Indexes make any book more accessible to readers. All nonfiction books (and many convoluted novels) should have indexes.

  The index for the first volume of Nat Bodian's *Book Marketing Handbook* was 50 pages. The second volume not only reprinted the index from the first volume but also included its own index of 58 pages. That's 108 pages of indexes—about 1/5 of the book. Yet those indexes are worth every extra page, because they make all the detailed tidbits of Bodian's books far more accessible.

> Authors — You are responsible for preparing the index for your book. In many cases, the publisher will hire a professional indexer to do the job, but I feel that authors should do their own indexes because they know their books better than anyone else. At least, they should. And because they do, they should have a better feel for what is most important in the book—the topics people will want to come back to again and again. I always prepare my own indexes.

- **Appendix**—A good appendix should list all the resources readers will need so they can follow through on the recommendations you make in your book. In more than one case I've recommended books solely because of their appendices which provide access to so many resources.

  A complete and detailed appendix makes your book more attractive as a reference work. As such, your book might qualify to be listed in such resource bibliographies as the *Directory of Directories* which can lead to extra sales. Tom and Marilyn Ross's *Encyclopedia of Self-Publishing* was listed in the *Directory of Directories* because of its extensive resource list.

  It's also possible to so expand an appendix that you actually begin the writing of another book. My *Book Publishing Resource Guide* grew out of the appendix I had planned for this book. The list of resources got to be so large that it would have made this book cumbersome to use. So I broke the book down into two parts. Now the latest edition of this directory is 320 pages long—and has grown into a significant computer database of well over 18,000 records.

  > **Authors** — An appendix is a great place to add material that could increase the marketability of your book with special audiences. For example, in a travel guide you could add a resource section for handicapped travelers. Or you could add a calorie chart in a dessert cookbook. Or you could list prime resources (who might later buy multiple copies of your book for giveaways to their major customers).

- **Glossary**—If your book is highly technical and/or introduces many new terms, you might want to add a glossary. Again, librarians love glossaries. So do reviewers.

  One of the elements that distinguishes Marilyn and Tom Ross's *Complete Guide to Self-Publishing* from Dan Poynter's *The Self-Publishing Manual* is that the Ross book includes a glossary of 400 publishing terms. Since both books are superb, and it is not easy to recommend one over the other (they both have their partisans), the glossary could make all the difference in marginal buying situations where a buyer could only afford one of the two books.

  > **Authors** — If you have used a lot of new terms in a book, you would be wise to add a glossary. It will make your book more understandable and, therefore, more saleable.

7:12 Bonus Inserts and Features

To add value to your books, look into the possibility of offering certificates, coupons, or other bonuses for the buyers of your books. Are there any bonus items you can give the reader? Are there any companies that would be interested in offering free samples to readers of your books? Here are a few examples of what other publishers are offering as added incentives for buying their books:

- In his self-published book, *How to Solve Your Small Business Advertising Problems*, William Witcher included coupons worth $75.00 in free offers (a free trial issue of the Clipper Creative Art Service, a free audiocassette *In Praise of the Self-Employed*, and a free book, *Tax Strategies for Preserving the Business Owner's Estate*, from Arthur Andersen & Company). The cover of his $14.95 book proclaimed: "FREE Bonus Offer—$75 value. See Inside!" Who could pass up such a bargain?

- Bantam printed a back-of-book coupon offering a free copy of *The Sweet Dreams Model Handbook* in every copy of the "Kelly Blake, Teen Model" series of young adult novels. They also promoted this offer in the floor displays and consumer advertising for the series.

- In 1989, Berlitz launched a new series called "Berlitz More for the Dollar." The books in this series of travel guides were each filled with over $4,000 in valuable coupons.

  Do you have any travel guides which could benefit from such added value? How many travelers do you know who would be willing to pay $9.95 or $14.95 for $4,000 in money-saving coupons?

- Many directory publishers include coupons for services provided by companies listed in the directory. Since many directories already accept advertising, offering coupons is just another way of bringing in more advertising income *and* providing another valuable service to their readers.

Authors — While doing the research for your book, don't overlook any possibilites for enhancing the value of your book by offering bonus coupons for services or products supplied by key companies serving the field. You might explore possibilities with companies before you submit the book to a publisher, but don't sign any contracts without first getting approval from your publisher. Indeed, you should never make any outside commitments without first getting approval from your publisher. You could easily void your contract if you go ahead without such approval.

7:13 Ask for the Order

Placing an order form in every book you produce is an inexpensive way to increase the sales of all your titles, especially those related to the book. This order form can be designed in a number of formats, from a gift certificate for friends . . . to a listing of your related titles . . . to a coupon requesting your catalog . . . to an order blank headed by the question, "Did you borrow this copy?"

Order blanks encourage orders from customers who first saw the book in a library or at a friend's house or on an associate's desk. Other orders will come from repeat buyers who are buying extra copies as gifts for friends. Still more orders will come for other titles in your line that are related to the book from which the order form was taken.

- Such order forms are now quite common in most mass-market paperbacks, especially in the genre titles such as science fiction, western, and mystery novels. For example, in the mystery novel by Gregory Mcdonald that I read today, Warner Books had two pages of advertisements for other books, one page listing four other Fletch titles by Mcdonald, the other page listing ten titles by P. D. James.

- Dover Publications routinely includes listings of other related titles in their various lines of books. I've bought a good number of books from them in this way.

- Janet Martin of Redbird Productions reports that most of the orders for their *Cream and Bread* book are placed via the order blanks in the back of the book.

- To build interest in forthcoming titles, Bantam prints 16-page previews of upcoming titles in related books. For example, they printed a 16-page preview of a new Nero Wolfe adventure written by Robert Goldsborough in the reprint editions of Rex Stout's original Nero Wolfe series.

One problem with printing actual order forms in the back of your books is that bookstores do not look kindly on such blatant advertising for direct orders by publishers. Obviously, they would prefer that the reader come to them for any additional books. If your book is sold primarily through bookstores, you might want to replace the blatant order form with a simple listing of your titles and prices plus your company name, address, and phone number. That's what we've done with this book. See the half-title verso page (page 2 of this book).

One further comment: Never offer quantity discounts in your books, especially not to consumers—not if you want to sell your books in bookstores. Booksellers rightfully resent publishers who offer consumers better discounts than the booksellers can possibly offer. It's okay to say that quantity discounts are available to volume buyers (25 or more copies); just don't list the actual discounts. Have readers write for the information.

7:14 And Ask Again

Rather than print the order form in the book itself, many publishers slip an order card in each book they send out. A separate order card makes it easier for the reader to send in an order.

- Barron's includes comment cards in most of their new cookbook titles. These comment cards serve at least four functions:

  1) They get feedback from the users of the book.

  2) They find out where the readers bought the book.

  3) They elicit opinions from readers on what other titles they'd like to see produced.

  4) They allow readers to request Barron's complete catalog of cookbook titles. Barron's has added 15,000 names to their mailing list in this way.

- Fulcrum inserts the following card into every book they publish. Not only does the card help them to build their mailing list, but it also gives them and their authors feedback on the titles they produce. Their authors love the feedback.

FULCRUM *The Reader's Publisher*   COMMENT CARD

At FULCRUM we believe that the two most important people in the publishing process are the author and the reader. If you have a comment for the author of this book, please use this card. If you would like to see our other titles, please ask for our catalog. Our books are available through your local bookstore or library.

Send Catalog ☐

Book Title (please print) _____

Comments _____

_____

_____

Name _____

Address _____

City, State, Zip _____

- Knopf inserts attractive full-color postcards featuring the book into some of their books. Their hope, of course, is that the reader will send the card to a friend, along with a favorable note about the book.

- Bantam inserted a Tell-A-Friend postcard into 75,000 copies of the first printing of Leona Blair's novel, *Privilege*. Like Knopf, they hoped that this would help to generate favorable word of mouth.

- Falcon Press inserts the following card into every book that they publish. They also offer toll-free numbers to make it easy for readers to request the catalog.

  One note: They also advertise the availability of special discounts. This might get them into trouble with booksellers. Thus far, though, they have reported no such difficulties.

A few good reasons why you should have our free catalog

In it you'll find:

☆ *One of the best selections of guide books available—for Arizona, California, Colorado, Idaho, Montana, Utah and Washington.*

☆ *Beautiful geographic books in full color for most western states.*

☆ *Gorgeous wildlife and scenic calendars—at modest prices.*

☆ *A great selection of western classics.*

☆ *And advance notice of new titles, along with special introductory discounts.*

All absolutely free! No purchase necessary—ever

Simply fill out the information below and we'll send you our current catalog right away. Why wait—send us this card today.

YES! *Please send me your FREE catalog which may entitle me to special discounts— no obligation. (please print)*

NAME _____

ADDRESS _____

CITY/STATE/ZIP _____

Or call **Toll-free:** **1-800-582-BOOK** *(outside Montana)*
1-800-592-BOOK *(in Montana)*
and ask for a FREE catalog

• Writer's Digest Books includes comment cards in all their new titles. They encourage readers to use the cards as bookmarks while reading the book and then to write down their reactions to the book after they have completed reading it.

When the readers send in the card, they may also request information regarding five of Writer's Digest services: other books published by Writer's Digest Books, the Writer's Digest School, the Writer's Digest Book Club, the *Writer's Digest* magazine, and the *Photographer's Market Newsletter*.

Chapter 8

How Authors Can Help to Promote Their Books

Many publishers are quite hesitant about having authors get involved in the marketing of their own books. Publishers often have good reasons for such reluctance: Many authors get a little too enthusiastic and demanding. Nevertheless, an author's help is indispensable to the active promotion of any book. If you make it clear to your authors right from the beginning where you need and expect their help (and where you don't), you will gain invaluable marketing assistance. Use it. It can make the difference between a poor seller and a bestseller.

8:01 Publishers: A Few Basic Guidelines

The best single advertisement for a book, other than giving away lots of review copies, is the author. An author is a walking/talking advertisement for his or her own book. So, don't ignore your authors. Here are a few basic guidelines on how you can make best use of your authors:

- The first and foremost rule is this: Listen to your authors. Let them know that you are interested in using their knowledge and experience. Don't brush off their suggestions. Use their good ideas, and tell them why their other ideas are not workable for you.

- Before you sign a new author to a contract, find out what he or she will do to promote the book. Get it down in writing. Then follow up.

- Have all your authors fill out an Author's Questionnaire (for a very complete sample that you can use, see pages 62 to 67 of my *Book Marketing Made Easier*). Make sure they understand the importance of completing this questionnaire as soon as possible. Let them know that you will be using the information they provide to plan a marketing campaign in which they will play a central role.

- Offer your authors sizeable discounts (at least 40%) if they want to buy books to sell on their own. Remember: They can be their own best salespeople.

- Keep your authors informed of new marketing developments—book club sales, major reviews, special sales, and so on.

- Work with them on special promotions. For more details, read the rest of this chapter—even the sections, such as the next one, which are directed towards authors.

8:02 Authors, Please Note!

Although you have a right and duty to help market your books, don't get in the way of your publishers. Remember, above all, that your publishers will generally have had more experience in editing, designing, producing, promoting, and marketing books than you. Let your publishers do their job; you do yours. Here are some suggestions on how you can help your publishers do their job more effectively:

- Work with your editor. Your editor should be your main contact with your publishers. If you have any suggestions for different ways to market your book, channel those suggestions through your editor. Your editor, in turn, should pass those suggestions on to the appropriate departments within the publishing company.

- Listen to your editor when he or she makes suggestions on ways to improve the style, content, or approach of your book. That doesn't mean you shouldn't give your editor feedback based on your own knowledge and experience, but it does mean that you should listen carefully to his or her suggestions and, in most cases, follow those suggestions.

- Consider ways to change your book's contents so the book becomes more marketable. For details on how you can improve the contents of your book, re-read the two preceding chapters.

- Answer all questionnaires and other requests for information from the publisher promptly and completely. Use these requests as an opportunity to suggest other ways to market your books—especially those ways which draw on your own experience, associations, and expertise.

- Provide your publisher with a detailed biography of your life, including your activities and interests. The publisher may have contacts or knowledge that can turn some of your activities or interests into promotions for your book.

- Never stop thinking of ways to market your books. Pass on those suggestions which would be most appropriate for the publisher to carry out. Also consider ways you yourself can market your books. More suggestions along this line are listed below.

> **Authors** — Read the above notes one more time. They are
> the most important pointers you can pick up from this book.
> Above all, establish a good working relationship with your
> editor and, secondly, fill out (in detail) the author's question-
> naire your publisher sends you. If they don't send you one,
> create your own. Or use the Author's Questionnaire on pages
> 62 to 67 of my *Book Marketing Made Easier*.

8:03 Use Your Authors' Connections

Although some authors are famous for their love of seclusion, most
authors do have associations, connections, contacts, and friends who can
be of assistance in promoting their books. Use those connections. They
are a prime audience for the book.

● Ask your authors to compile four lists of individuals they know:

1) those who might be interested in buying the book for personal use,
2) those who might purchase the book in quantity (for businesses,
    associations, clubs, and other organizations),
3) those who can provide their expertise in reviewing, commenting on,
    or perhaps writing a promotional blurb or foreword for the book,
4) those in the media who might review the book or provide other
    exposure for the author and/or the book.

● Other lists your authors might be able to provide include:

1) the names of individuals involved in the subject area of the book,
    especially opinion leaders.
2) buyers of products or services described in the book,
3) companies or other organizations that might be interested in the
    book (either for resale to their members or for use as premiums),
4) membership directories of clubs and associations in which the
    author is an active member,
5) a list of media for the city in which the author lives (or has lived
    previously),
6) names of individuals who have expressed an interest in the author's
    previous books, articles, or other activities.

● Ask your authors to arrange announcements about the publication of
their books in the newsletters of any associations to which they belong,
in their companies' in-house magazines or newsletters, in appropriate
alumni publications, and other club bulletins.

- If your authors work for a company or other institution, encourage them to ask the company's public relations department to issue its own news release.

- If the author is a regular contributor to a magazine or newspaper, that periodical might be interested in doing a review or special advertising promotion for the author's current book, especially if the book fits its editorial profile.

  Because Robert Miller was a regular contributor to their magazines and because his book, *Most of My Patients Are Animals*, fit into their editorial focus, *Veterinary Medicine* and *Western Horseman* took 8,000 copies of the book to sell to their subscribers.

- Explore any sales opportunities with your author's college. Stetson University College of Law ordered a special alumni edition of Steve Rushing's book, *A Funny Thing Happened on the Way to Court*. 1,000 copies of the book (with the Stetson logo imprinted on the cover) were given to donors to the college.

Authors — Help your publishers ferret out these special sales and promotional opportunities. You are the one with these special connections. Make a list of them and then help your publisher follow up on these prime sales leads.

8:04 Provide Authors with Sales Material

Since your authors' family, friends, colleagues, and other connections are prime prospects for their books, provide your authors with any promotional material which might help stimulate sales to these special audiences.

- For instance, you could print your regular news release on legal-size paper with a tear-off order coupon at the bottom of the page. These announcements can then be sent by your authors to all their friends and acquaintances. This procedure not only allows your authors to announce the publication of their books, but also relieves them of having to let each individual acquaintance know where to obtain their books.

- Let your authors know that you will also supply similar announcements, advertising copy, or more formal brochures to any organization or individual acquaintance wanting to promote the author's book in their newsletter, membership mailings, or other promotions. You could have the orders come direct to you, go to the organization or individual sponsoring the mailing, or have the recipients order through their local bookstore.

> **Authors** — If your publisher offers you the opportunity to mail out some promotional materials, take it—even if you have to share expenses (as long as you also share profits).

8:05 Keep Your Sales Force Informed

Your authors are your best sales force for their own books. Encourage them to carry a copy of the book with them wherever they go, to talk up the book with any individuals or organizations they encounter, and to always let you know what they are doing in the way of personal promotions.

The last point in the above paragraph is perhaps the most important of all: Make sure your authors keep you informed of any of their activities, speeches, or other events that might have an impact on the sales of their books. In turn, you should let your sales representatives and distributors know of all such activities so they, in turn, can take advantage of any such promotions.

> **Authors** — Be sure to keep your publisher informed of anything you are doing to promote your books. That way, your publisher can coordinate your activities with their own activities—and those of their distributors.

8:06 Authors as Self-Promoters

Your authors can do many things on their own to increase the sales of their books. Give them room to act. Indeed, encourage them to do their own promotions. But, of course, make sure they also keep you informed so you can tie their promotions into your own.

The following comments will be address directly to authors; see that your authors know about these ways to promote their books during their day to day activity.

> **Authors** — Read the following pages very carefully. They list about ten ways that you can promote yourself and your books more effectively. Try those you feel you can do well.

Become a Speaker

There are a good number of ways to use speaking engagements to sell books. Here are just a few of them:

1) Simply mention your books in any talks you give, whether to the Lady's Auxiliary, Rotary Club, or an association meeting. Integrate the subject of your book into the subject of your talk so you can mention your books as a natural part of the talk. Then let the audience know they can buy copies of your book in the back of the room after the talk (these sales are known in the speaking trade as back-of-the-room sales) or from their local bookstore.

   • I know of at least one speaker who earns over $1000 per talk from sales of his books.

   • Sir Edmond Hillary used to sell at least two books for every person who attended his lectures.

   • At one of his Super Seminars in Los Angeles, A. L. Williams sold 7,600 copies of his book, *All You Can Do Is All You Can Do, But All You Can Do Is Enough*, in just two hours and fifteen minutes.

2) Here are a few other places you might want to give a talk: libraries (especially meetings of the Friends of the Library), bookstores, clubs, churches, civic groups, chambers of commerce, schools, colleges, PTA's, writer's clubs, garden parties, businessmen luncheons, workshops, seminars, professional meetings, cruise ships, museum shows, conferences, ski lodges, and anywhere else that welcomes speakers and entertainers.

   • The Indiana Chamber of Commerce has set up its own speakers bureau. Check to see if your own local or state Chamber has a similar program.

   • Your local Rotary group (and other service groups such as the Lions, Kiwanis, etc.) needs a new speaker every week. They are hungry for speakers.

   • The program chairs of your local Toastmasters Speakers Bureau meet monthly to pass on names of good speakers and to hear presentations from new speakers. Why not track down your local Toastmasters group to see if you can speak to them?

3) Give something free to everyone who attends your lectures. Art Fettig of Growth Unlimited offers everyone a free copy of one of his verses, illustrated and ready for framing. Each verse has his name, address, and phone number. He gets many bookings and book sales through this means alone.

4) Give everyone a brochure and order blank. Hand them out free during the lecture, or just afterwards. If you include some points from your talk or a list of resources that the audience can follow up on after the talk, they are more likely to take your brochure home with them.

5) Offer to accept MasterCard and VISA orders (if you are set up to do so). Again, when Art Fettig offers one of his higher priced book/tape combos, he tells members of the audience to just write their charge card number on the back of their business card. In this way, he often gets over $1,000 in orders each lecture.

6) If you are giving a seminar to a corporation or a talk to a professional association, you might try preselling your books to the program planner so that each attendee receives a free copy of your book as part of the program. If your books will make the meeting that much more effective, the corporation will probably jump at the chance.

One speaker raised his fee from $325.00 per person for each seminar he gave to $495.00 and then included his book as part of the materials for the seminar. He met no price resistence when he raised the price of his seminar.

7) Have the toastmaster announce that you will be available after your talk to autograph books and to speak to anyone with any additional questions. Of course, those people who do not already have a copy of your book will want to buy one from you so they can get your autograph at the same time.

8) If you are speaking at a newsworthy event, let the media know about your speech. Also, send them an advance copy of your talk so they can quote accurately from your talk if they do decide to cover the event.

9) Remember, as a professional you should also charge for speaking to any major seminars, conferences, clubs, and so on. These fees will help to pay your way to other speaking engagements and help to keep your promotional show on the road.

On the other hand, Bruce Sievers does not charge for his poetry readings, but he does insist on his right to sell his books after the readings. And does he sell!. In one year alone he sold over 25,000 books just as a result of his poetry readings.

10) If the topic of your book is of interest to a specific national association with local chapters, why not set up a speaking tour with these local chapters?

Linda Salzer, author of *Infertility: How Couples Can Cope*, funded her lecture tour by visiting local chapters of Resolve, the national support group for infertile couples.

11) As you travel, plan ahead. Try to arrange speaking engagements wherever you travel.

Beverly Nye, self-publisher of *A Family Raised on Sunshine*, bought a 30-day bus pass to tour five cities where she had previously lived. In each city she arranged with Mormon church groups and homemaking classes to give lectures, where she talked about her own methods of homemaking. Not only did she make money on the admission fees charged for the lectures, but she also sold over 1,500 copies in 30 days.

12) Finally, remember that it was through such speaking engagements that Wayne Dyer, Leo Buscaglia, and Robert Allen all became bestselling authors. Robert Allen traveled to different cities, offered "A Free Evening with Robert Allen" seminars, got people excited about his ideas for creating wealth, and sold loads of books.

Become a Teacher

A good number of self-publishers and writers have found that lecturing at colleges and adult education classes is a superb way to market books.

- Melvin Powers, publisher of Wilshire Books and author of *How to Get Rich in Mail Order*, has been teaching for many years in the California college system. Not only does a description of his course get mailed to over a million potential students, but in the course description he recommends that his own book be bought and read ahead of time. He suggests that students buy the book at a local bookstore or check it out of their library. As he notes, "The result was phenomenal from a standpoint of sales."

Write Articles

Besides selling first or second serial rights to your books, you might also consider adapting chapters of your book or writing related articles for magazines.

- Tom and Marilyn Ross did this for their *Encyclopedia of Self-Publishing*, selling short articles about self-publishing to such diverse magazines as *Southwest Airlines Magazine, Toastmaster Magazine, Pro-Comm Newsletter*, and others. In each case, they insisted that the magazine include an endnote telling readers where they could order the book.

If you can sell these articles, all the better; but even if you don't, you should try to place articles in any magazine where readers might be interested in the topic of your book. Be sure to coordinate any such freelance writing with your publisher (who may already have approached the magazine about second serial rights).

Write a Column

To gain greater visibility, write a regular column for an appropriate trade journal or newsletter.

- Luther Brock, a direct mail copywriter, wrote regular columns for *Direct Marketing Magazine, Mail Order Connection*, and *Information Marketing Newsletter*. He did no advertising because these columns brought him all the business he could handle.

- While I was writing the first edition of this book, I also wrote a regular column for the COSMEP newsletter. Not only did the column help members of the association, but it also provided additional visibility for my publishing activities. Moreover, many of the columns were taken straight from books I was about to publish. Of course, I mentioned the books at the end of each article.

Become a Joiner

Do anything you can to become visible. This means joining appropriate trade and social associations related to your topic (if you don't already belong). But don't just join; become active in the association's activities. If you were interested enough to write a book about the subject, you should be interested enough to become active in working with a related association.

- That's why I'm a member of COSMEP and also why I was a member of its board of directors for four years – not just because it's good for business, but because I really am concerned about the problems and possibilities of smaller book publishers.

Become an Expert

As a published author, you automatically become an expert in the subject area of your book. To become recognized, however, as an expert, you must also establish yourself as a reliable source of news or information. Hence, do not respond to a reporter's question if you do not know the answer. Admit the limits of your expertise if you want to become quoted as "a reliable source."

- As an author of a number of books about publishing, I am often called upon to consult with smaller publishers and non-profit associations about book production and marketing. I help where I can, and when I don't know the answer I send them to people who can help them. In the same way, many editors and publishers have sent people my way because they knew I could answer the questions from their readers. I've received many book orders from these referrals.

Become a Talker

The subhead above means just what it says. Talk to anyone and everyone you meet. As a self-promoting author, you should not hesitate to talk about your book and your writing. Let people know you are an author. Naturally, they will then ask what you've written. Don't just tell them; show them the book (especially when your book is first published, be sure to carry a copy around with you at all times so you can show people the actual book). Be sure to let them know where they can order the book.

- One author of a guidebook for handicapped travellers happened to sit next to Abigail van Buren on an airplane flight. Of course, during their conversation the author happened to mention her book. Some time later, Abigail found an opportunity to mention the book in her syndicated column, *Dear Abby*. Over two sackfuls of mail — all orders — resulted from that one little mention.

Leave Parts of Yourself Behind

Besides carrying around a copy of your book, you should also carry extra copies of any promotional brochures, bookmarks, and news releases about your book. Give these away to people you meet. Leave some lying around the doctor's office, in the laundromat, on the bulletin board at your local grocery store, at the airport, and wherever else you go — especially places where other people have to wait and are, therefore, likely to be looking for some reading material to pass the time.

Nice looking bookmarks (printed with the title of your book, the publication date, the name of the publisher, the retail price, your name and address, and an illustration from the book cover) have proven to be an effective way to keep an author's name before potential readers. Give these to people you meet during your day-to-day activity. Bookmarks work especially well in casual social occasions where giving out a business card would be inappropriate.

Here are a few other parts of yourself which you can leave behind:

- If your books are stocked by your local retailers (and they should be!), print up some stickers or cards that point out that you are a local author. Ask the stores if they would mind if you placed these stickers on the copies of your books in stock. 90% of the stores will appreciate this bit of help.

- Offer to autograph the books as well. That makes the books more valuable — and more likely to be bought. Again, provide a sticker or card that points out that these copies have been autographed. Note that bookstores cannot return books that have been autographed.

  Whenever I am in a different city, I always visit at least one bookstore. When I do, of course, I check to see if they have any copies of my books. If they do, I always offer to autograph them. When I did this at the main Kroch's and Brentano's store in Chicago, they placed a band around the autographed copies that announced that the books were autographed — and then placed the books on a special table up front.

- Give bookmarks, copies of the book's cover, or autographed copies of the book itself to the people at the cash register — or the person in the store most likely to have contact with potential buyers.

- Above all, leave a good impression. Wherever you go, dress well, speak well, and act with good manners.

Work with Bookstores and Distributors

Bookstores and distributors are generally happy to work with local authors. As mentioned above, most will appreciate any copies you have time to autograph. But they also respond to visits from authors. Indeed, some actively pursue continued contact with authors.

- Not only was Jacqueline Susann a superb interview subject for TV shows, but she was also a tireless self-promoter, going so far as to get up at six in the morning just to meet the drivers for mass-market paperback jobbers and encourage them to place her books in the prime spots. And they responded to her personal attention. Wouldn't you?

- Ron Hickman, book buyer for Florida East Coast News, actively seeks contact with authors. Not only does he attend the Florida Writers Conference, but he also regularly invites authors to speak to his monthly sales meetings with the drivers. He even supplies copies of the book for the author to autograph. When Maggie Davis, author of the novel *Satin Doll*, spoke at one of these monthly meetings, sales of her book in that region were much greater than in areas where she had not spoken to the drivers.

- When you send promotional material to bookstores and wholesalers, send them a personal note as well. Such personal touches help to get your material to the top of the stack—and read! Indeed, Dan Berger, book buyer for the Raleigh News Company, has said as much. He definitely pays more attention to writer's own promotional material, especially if it's newsy and interesting.

- As an author, you might want to publish your own small promotional newsletter (two or four pages), which could be send to major chain buyers, wholesalers, jobbers, and other buyers and opinion leaders. Keep them up to date on any new promotions, publicity, and sales that might encourage them to take a second look at your book. If you have a fan club, send your club newsletter to these buyers. That will save you from having to write two newsletters.

Sell Your Books Door-to-Door

Don't laugh. Door-to-door selling can be one of the most effective ways to sell your books. People love to meet and talk with authors—and they love reading books by people they've met personally. Who wouldn't buy and cherish a personally autographed copy?

- Gary Provost, author/publisher of *The Dorchester Gas Tank*, began his career this way. He'd take a suitcase of books to downtown Boston every day, settle down at some busy corner (around City Hall, the public library, a subway entrance, or plaza), and begin peddling his books to anyone who'd listen. He'd sell 20 to 25 books a day. That's more sales than most books make per day.

- Another author sold his novel, *A War Ends*, door to door. While knocking on doors one day, he met a reporter for a Los Angeles newspaper. The reporter was so taken by the author's approach to selling books that he featured him in a story. That story not only brought the author many local sales, but it also inspired a number of other feature stories nationwide, thus bringing more attention to the novel ... and more sales.

- Peter Gault sold 5,000 copies of his self-published novel, *Goldenrod*, by traveling across Canada setting up tables and selling books to anyone he met. At one point, he even sold books on the street in front of the offices of Canada's major newspapers. Not only did he get lots of attention there, but he also received many reviews for his book from the major book critics.

  Later, while selling his books in front of Lincoln Center in New York, he met another writer, Richard Kalish, who bought his book, liked it, and introduced Gault to Martin Shepard of The Permanent Press. In the spring of 1988, The Permanent Press published a hardcover edition of Gault's book for the U.S. market.

Form Alliances with Other Authors

Besides joining organizations for writers, you should also try to work out arrangements with writers in other parts of the country to promote each other's work in your home areas.

- When visiting bookstores and distributors, you can check to see if they stock not only your own books but also the books of the other authors with whom you are working.

- You can leave promotional material for each other wherever you go.

- You might even co-publish a newsletter that carries news and features about you and the other authors.

- And, if you go on tour, you can stay with your friends across the country (and they with you). That alone would make an author tour more cost-effective for your publisher.

Set a Record

One way to get publicity for your book is to set a world record (a record that can somehow be related to your book). Note that you don't have to set a world record to gain publicity, you only have to attempt it. Actually, if you're not into setting world records, you could sponsor an attempt or announce a contest and prize for such an attempt — anything at all that associates you and your book with the world record.

For more details on how to go about getting in the record books, read Clint Kelly's self-published book, *The Fame Game*, available from Performance Press, P. O. Box 7307, Everett, WA 98201.

Do It for Charity

While you are attempting the world record or, for that matter, while you are doing other promotions for your book, do them for a charitable cause. Not only will this help you in getting publicity for your book, but at the same time you will be doing a good turn for the charitable cause by bringing publicity (and money) to it as well.

- Kathryn Leigh Scott has sold her book, *My Scrapbook Memories of Dark Shadows*, to several PBS stations to use as a premium in their annual pledge drives. As part of the deal, she spent several days shooting generic spots for pledge drives across the country.

Do Everything

If you have the time, you can be your own best salesperson. Sharon Scott is responsible for selling thousands of copies of her two books, *Peer Pressure Reversal* and *How to Say No and Keep Your Friends*. Here are just a few of her activities that have helped to sell her books:

- She conducts in-service training programs for teachers, counselors, and parents.
- Through seminars and workshops, she has trained 25,000 students.
- She speaks at many conferences, both regional and national, for professionals working with youth.
- She writes a *Positive Parenting* column which appears in many school newsletters.
- She is a frequent guest on local and national TV and radio shows.
- She is now producing several videos based on her work.

Authors — Be careful not to overcommit yourself to the promotion of your books. Do what you can, but be sure to save time to write new books. That's what you do best.

8:07 Publishers — How to Help Your Authors

Not only can your authors help you with the promotion of their books, but you can also help them. It's a two-way street where both of you can benefit if you are willing to work together. Don't be afraid to ask for your authors' cooperation in your marketing plans.

On the following pages I've listed a few suggestions on how authors can help you and how you can help them. Use these suggestions. You might be surprised on how much help your authors can give you.

- Have your authors autograph several hundred copies of their books. When sending review copies to major reviewers and other key contacts, send these autographed copies. Indeed, if your authors are willing, have them personalize the autographs for each key contact. These personalized copies will get more attention than ordinary copies.

- Support your authors with material for doing bookstore appearances and media interviews. For major titles and other books that lend themselves to a national tour, help to organize such a tour and pay the author's expenses. National tours are one of the best ways to establish a nationwide demand for a book—and such widespread demand can often propel a book onto the bestsellers list.

  In January 1989, sixteen Florida writers boarded a Romance Writers Caravan bus for a three-day, four-city promotional tour of the state. As part of the tour, they autographed books, talked to aspiring writers, and met with booksellers and distributors in Miami, Fort Lauderdale, Orlando, and Tampa - St. Petersburg. If your authors ever have a chance to participate in such a tour, sponsor them.

  In the fall of 1988, the Minnesota Independent Publishers Association organized autograph parties featuring regional authors. The autograph parties were held over four weekends in different Twin Cities shopping centers. Why not work with your regional publishers or booksellers association to organize a similar program in your area?

- Send your authors to appropriate trade conventions and other conferences. One publisher sent the author of a book on child-raising to a baby products fair. While there, the author not only sold books but also made contacts that got her TV appearances as well as invitations to speak before people who bought still more books.

  Even if you cannot afford to display at a convention or trade show, you should still attend. Even without a display, you and/or your authors can still make many good contacts. The opportunities for networking at a convention are wide open.

- Encourage the formation of fan clubs for your regular authors by providing special membership cards, posters, and other promotional material for any fans who request help in forming such a club. Also exploit existing fan clubs.

  Janet Dailey, author of *The Great Alone* and *The Glory Game*, has such a fan club, and Pocket Books sends regular mailings to club members announcing new titles. It's a great way to establish a stronger bond between authors and their most ardent fans (who are also their strongest word-of-mouth supporters).

  When Kathryn Leigh Scott sent out a flyer announcing her book, *My Scrapbook Memories of Dark Shadows*, to the membership of the Dark Shadows fan club, she got a 28% response to the mailing. Fans do respond—and respond well.

- If your author is agreeable, print your author's home address in the back of the book so readers can write direct to them. Either that, or else encourage readers to write to you with the assurance that you will forward all mail to the author the same day you receive it.

- Promote tie-ins with other authors, books, or events wherever possible. For example, be on the lookout for promotions such as the one run by the Village Green bookstore in Rochester, New York. One of their staff members happened to read in one of Alice Walker's books that Zorah Neil Hurston was her favorite author. So the Village Green, building on the publicity from Walker's bestselling book *The Color Purple* and the movie of the same name, ran a promotion for Hurston's book, *Their Eyes Were Watching God*. The store sold 365 copies of Hurston's book during the Christmas season alone.

- Be sure your authors are listed in Gale's *Contemporary Authors*, other directories of writers, and any appropriate *Who's Who* listings. These listings not only help to bring greater immediate recognition to the writers, but they also make it easier for media, librarians, and other researchers to find out more about the authors.

- When you sign a contract with your authors, give them a copy of *1001 Ways to Market Your Books*. It is the most important thing you can do for your authors — and for me. Thanks. Actually, self-interest aside, it really is the most practical way to introduce your authors to the world of book marketing. Give a copy of this book to every author you sign. [Quantity discounts are available from Ad-Lib Publications.]

8:08 The Value of Awards and Honors

When one of your authors or books wins an award, make sure everyone knows about it. Send out press releases. Prepare new brochures announcing the award. When reprinting the book, add the announcement to the cover of the book. Also, when publishing new books by the author, let people know that the author is an award-winning author.

Also, don't forget to submit your best designed books for consideration in many of the annual graphics or design competitions, such as the Boston Bookbuilder's and AIGA awards. These give added prestige to your company and will also result in many orders from libraries.

Some literary awards which have a major impact on sales include the following (obviously, not an all-inclusive list):

American Book Awards (fiction, first fiction, nonfiction)
Caldecott Medal (illustrators of children's books)
Golden Medallion (romance)
Golden Spur (westerns)
Heartland Prizes (for a novel and a nonfiction book written from or
    about the midwest; sponsored by the Chicago *Tribune*)

Hugo and Nebula awards (science fiction and fantasy)
National Book Critics Circle Book Awards (biography, criticism,
     fiction, nonfiction, and poetry)
Newbery Medal (authors of children's books)
Nobel Prize (literature)
Poe Award (mysteries)
Pulitzer Prize (biography, fiction, nonfiction, poetry)
R. T. French Tastemaker Awards (cookbooks)

• It has been estimated that the annual Hugo awards in science fiction
  are worth over $50,000 to the winners in increased sales of their books,
  higher advances and royalties, and greater subsidiary rights sales. Although the winners do not receive a cash award with the Hugo, they
  become instant celebrities within the genre and each subsequent book
  is heralded with the banner, "by the Hugo award-winning author."
  That banner alone sells thousands of extra books each year. Plus, the
  fact is that almost every Hugo award winning novel is still in print (the
  first Hugo was awarded in 1953).

• In 1985, the trade paperback edition of Harriet Doerr's *Stones for
  Ibarra* sold over 100,000 copies. Sales were undoubtedly helped by the
  fact that the book had won the 1984 American Book Award for First
  Work of Fiction.

• Again, in 1985 William Kennedy's 1984 Pulitzer-winning book, *Iron-
  weed*, sold over 180,000 copies in trade paperback. If you'd like your
  books to be considered for the Pulitzer Prize, send four copies of each
  book, a photo of the author, a short biography of the author, and a
  $20.00 entry fee to the **Pulitzer Committee**, Graduate School of Jour-
  nalism, 706 Journalism Hall, Columbia University, 116th Street and
  Broadway, New York, NY 10027.

  Even if your books don't win the Pulitzer, a nomination will still boost
  sales by a wide margin. Of course, only a few books are actually
  nominated for the award, and only one is selected. This weeding out
  process is one reason awards boost sales, because readers are then
  alerted to a book which has passed inspection more than once.

• Awards can also help sell subsidiary rights. Dick Lochte's *Sleeping
  Dog*, winner of the 1985 Nero Wolfe Award for Best Mystery Novel,
  was optioned for a movie and also obtained $41,250 for paperback
  reprint rights.

  Similarly, the winner of the Jonathan Cape Young Writer's Award,
  Joseph Olshan, had his book *Clara's Heart* optioned by Warner
  Brothers for a movie, plus sold paperback rights for $14,300.

• Winners of the Ernest Hemingway Award for first fiction receive
  $7,500. Winners of the Martha Albrand Award for first nonfiction
  receive $1,000. To submit books for consideration, write to the **PEN
  American Center**, 568 Broadway, New York, NY 10012.

- Winners of the 1986 Western States Book Awards for poetry, fiction, and creative nonfiction got more than just a fancy certificate and some prize money ($2,500 to the author, $5,000 to the publisher), they also got distribution by Kampmann & Co., were carried by Ingram and Baker & Taylor, and were stocked by many B. Dalton stores across the country.

- When the Czechoslovakian author Jaroslav Seifert won the 1983 Nobel Prize for Literature, the only English translation of any of his books published in the United States was a poetry book, *The Casting of Bells*, published by The Spirit That Moves Us Press. As a result, the small publisher was swamped with orders for the book and had to return to press for another printing.

- Similarly, when Bishop Desmond Tutu won the 1984 Nobel Peace Prize, Eerdman's Publishing became swamped with orders for his book, *Hope and Suffering*. Here's one example where a non-literary award had a great impact on the sales of a book.

- Macmillan had one of its book covers (for *Unknown California*) win an Award of Distinction in the 1985 Andy Awards competition sponsored by the Advertising Club of New York.

- Be on the lookout for other awards that your authors might be eligible to win. Here are just a few awards they might qualify for:

National Jewish Book Awards in these categories: Autobiography/ Memoir, Children's Literature, Children's Picture Book, Contemporary Jewish Life, Fiction, Holocaust, Israel, Jewish History, Jewish Thought, Scholarship, Visual Arts, Yiddish Literature. For more information, write to JWB Jewish Book Council, 15 East 26th Street, New York, NY 10010; (212) 532-4949.

The **Golden Rib Award** for the best barbecue book is awarded each year by the Diddy-Wa-Diddy National Barbecue Sauce Contest. The 1988 award was won by Greg Johnson and Vince Staten for their book *Real Barbecue*.

Best Cookbook of the Year is awarded each year by the International Association of Cooking Professionals and Joseph E. Seagram & Sons. The 1987 award was won by Yamuna Devi for *Lord Krishna's Cuisine: The Art of Indian Vegetarian Cooking*.

- Don't overlook other awards and honors. If they do come your way, make sure to publicize the awards.

The Mathematics Calendar by Theoni Pappas was selected as one of the "Top 100 Products of the Year" by *Curriculum Product News*.

The Hawaii Visitors Bureau selected M. J. Harden's *Magic Maui* as the best new guidebook in Hawaii.

Joe Tanenbaum's *A Man in the Mood: Poems for Laughing, Loving and Living* won the Champion Imagination Award for its cover design.

8:09 Sponsor an Award Yourself

One way to draw attention to your books is to sponsor award competitions which are in some way connected with the book. For example, if you were publishing a book on cooking with woks, you might sponsor a wok recipe contest.

● Addison-Wesley sponsored a national Best Teacher Award competition in connection with their book by Marty and Barbara Nemko, *How to Get Your Child a Private School Education in a Public School*, which emphasized the value of committed teachers.

Another way to draw attention to new books while you are also soliciting new material from unpublished authors is to sponsor an award for an unpublished work of fiction or nonfiction.

● Viking Penguin recently instituted the Malcolm Cowley Prize for an unpublished work of fiction or nonfiction by an emerging American writer. The winner not only gets published by Viking Penguin, but they also receive $2,500 over and above whatever their contract specifies. Of course, when their book is published, Viking Penguin promotes the book as the winner of the Malcolm Cowley Prize.

> **Authors** — Help your publishers. Be on the lookout yourself. While many book publishers are aware of the major literary awards, they are not as likely to be aware of other awards that you or your book might be eligible to win. If you discover any such possible awards, let your publisher know.

8:10 Encourage Interaction

Your authors can do much more than just a few media interviews and bookstore signings if you work with them and allow them to work with you. To get the most help from your authors, you should have a procedure in place by which your authors can interact not only with their editors but also with your marketing and public relations people.

This procedure should have some safeguards so your marketing people are not continuously bombarded with suggestions or wild phone calls from your authors. If you can set up such a procedure, I believe you will find that your authors are quite willing to work more closely with you in the promotion of their books—and that this closer cooperation will lead to greater sales.

8:10 A Dramatic Example of Persistence

Here's one example of how an author, through persistence and a little bit of luck, promoted her book onto the bestseller lists—a year after the book was given up as dead by her publishers! The book: *Callanetics*. The author: Callan Pinckney.

The book was first launched by Morrow in September 1984 and, after a first round of publicity and 10,000 copies sold, went into a second printing of 5,000 copies. But there the book died. Because Callan Pinckney was not a celebrity and because the book was competing against another exercise book by Victoria Principal, Morrow was not able to get any more media interviews for Pinckney.

On her own, Pinckney continued to promote the book but with little effect until a fan in Chicago called her to ask if she would be coming to Chicago any time soon. Pinckney, of course, said she would be able to come if she could do a TV show in the area. Well, the fan was determined to have Pinckney come so she arranged for the producers of *A. M. Chicago* to contact Pinckney. And the rest is history.

Within hours of Pinckney's appearance on the show, Kroch's & Brentano's had taken over 400 orders. That was in August, 1985. From there Pinckney went on to do other shows in many other smaller cities, and each time she created another spurt of sales for her book. During this time she also personally called the major book chains to let them know that Morrow still had books in print, stored in their New York warehouse. Finally, after about three more months of such promotion, her book reached the bestseller lists and remained on those lists for almost a year.

Furthermore, Morrow arranged for a new author tour of the major cities, and Pinckney finally got on a major TV show, the Phil Donahue show. The book sold well over 250,000 copies, and paperback reprint rights sold for almost $200,000.

Chapter 9

Tips on Publicizing Your Books

There is an old definition of publicity that still applies today as it did years ago: Publicity is doing good, and then telling the world about it. Here, then, is the essence of getting good publicity: 1) Produce a good book, and 2) let people know about it. It really is that simple. But both steps do require patience, and persistence, and attention to detail.

Never think that publicity is free. It is not. You must pay your dues. If you're going to invest your time and money in promotions, make sure much of it is committed to your publicity efforts. Remember: Publicity does sell books, more books that any other means of promotion.

9:01 The Three Basics of Gaining Publicity

The three basics of gaining publicity are: 1) You must create real news about your book, something worth publicizing. 2) You must locate and cultivate the appropriate media contacts. 3) You must be persistent; you must follow through.

1. A book with solid content and style will help immensely in fulfilling the first basic requirement for gaining publicity. Of course, a highly promotable author also helps.
2. For help in locating appropriate media contacts, refer to the *PR Flash No-Frills Data Files* or one of the national media directories.
3. Ron Gold, author of *The Personal Computer Publicity Book*, asserts that the three most important PR jobs are: 1) followup calls, 2) followup letters, and 3) followup calls. In other words, you must be persistent. Any PR professional will say the same thing: Persistence pays. If you knock on enough doors enough times, you are bound to get through.

9:02 Dealing with the Major Book Reviewers

Of all the book review media, there are about ten to twenty that are most important for establishing your books as critical and commercial successes right from the beginning. These include the trade magazines for booksellers (*Publishers Weekly* and *Kirkus Reviews*), the major library review media (*Library Journal, School Library Journal, Booklist, Choice,* and *Horn Book Magazine*), and the book review sections of the large city newspapers (*New York Times Book Review, Los Angeles Times Book Review, San Francisco Chronicle, Washington Post Book World,* and *New York Review of Books*)

Of course, not all would be appropriate for every book you publish since *Choice* only reviews books appropriate for college and high school libraries, *Horn Book* only reviews children's books, and *School Library Journal* only reviews books that might be acquired by school libraries.

Here are some guidelines for getting your books reviewed by some of the major review media (note that the following names and addresses are subject to change):

- **Publishers Weekly**—Published weekly as a trade magazine for book-sellers, librarians, and publishers, this magazine reviews about 5,000 books per year. They review almost any sort of book except reference books. Send galley copies at least three to four months before publication date to the appropriate editor, as follows: Sybil Steinberg, fiction; Genevieve Stuttaford, nonfiction; Penny Kaganoff, paperbacks; Diane Roback, children's books; and Molly McQuade, how-to books. Send to PW Forecasts, *Publishers Weekly*, 249 West 17th Street, New York, NY 10011; (212) 463-6758; Fax: (212) 463-6631.

- **Kirkus Reviews**—Published biweekly as a prepublication review for booksellers, libraries, agents and publishers, this newsletter reviews 80 to 100 books per issue, about 2,500 per year. They review almost any fiction or non-fiction book, except poetry, mass-market paperbacks, and picture books for toddlers. Because they are a prepublication review service and try to run reviews at least two months prior to publication date, they like to see galley copies at least three to four months in advance, the sooner the better. Ann Larsen is fiction editor; Jeffrey Zaleski is nonfiction editor; Joanna King is children's book editor. Send review copies to *Kirkus Reviews*, 200 Park Avenue South #1118, New York, NY 10003-1543; (212) 777-4554.

- **Booklist**—Published biweekly by the American Library Association, this magazine reviews about 7,000 books per year. They review almost any book that would be of interest to a general public library, including fiction, nonfiction, children's and young adult books, and reference. Send books or galley copies as soon as they are available. Martin Brady is the editor of adult books, Sally Estes of young adult books, Barbara Elleman of children's books, and Sandy Whiteley of reference books. Write to *Booklist*, American Library Association, 50 E. Huron Street, Chicago, IL 60611; (312) 944-6780; Fax: 312-440-0901.

- **Library Journal**—Published monthly for public librarians, this magazine reviews about 5,000 books per year. They will review almost any book that is appropriate for a general public library. Send the finished book or galley copy three to four months before publication date to Nora Rawlinson, Book Review Editor, *Library Journal*, 249 West 17th Street, New York, NY 10011; (212) 463-6819; Fax: (212) 242-6987.

- **School Library Journal**—Published ten times a year, this magazine reviews about 2,500 books per year. They will review any book appropriate for school library use. Send galley copies or finished books to Trevelyn Jones, Book Review Editor, *School Library Journal*, 249 West 17th Street, New York, NY 10011; (212) 463-6757; Fax: 212-463-6631.

- **Horn Book Magazine**—Published bimonthly for anyone interested in children's literature, this magazine reviews about 400 children's and young adult books per year. Send two review copies (finished books or galley copies) to Anita Silvey, Editor, *Horn Book Magazine*, 14 Beacon Street, Boston, MA 02108; (617) 227-1555; Fax: (617) 523-0299.

- **Choice**—Published eleven times a year by the Association of College and Research Libraries, this magazine reviews over 6,000 books per year. They will review any books appropriate for college and high school libraries. They have many subject editors. Send finished books to Book Review Editor, *Choice*, 100 Riverview Center, Middletown, CT 06457; (203) 347-6933.

- **New York Times Book Review**—Published every week as part of the *New York Times* Sunday edition, this review does about 3,000 book reviews each year. They do not review how-to books (cookbooks, diet books, etc.) except at Christmas time. They prefer that you send galleys as soon as available and then send books when printed. The best times to send them books for review are in time for January, February, July, or August reviews. Rebecca Sinkler is editor of the *Book Review*; Eden Ross Lipson is children's book editor. Christopher Lehmann-Haupt is the main book reviewer for the daily *New York Times*. Send review copies to the *New York Times Book Review*, 229 West 43rd Street, New York, NY 10036; (212) 556-1234.

- **Washington Post Book World**—Published weekly as part of the Sunday *Post*, this supplement reviews about 2,000 books per year. They review general fiction and nonfiction books. Send review copies to Nina King, Editor, *Washington Post Book World*, 1150 15th Street N.W., Washington, DC 20071; (202) 334-6000; Fax: (202) 334-4480.

- **San Francisco Chronicle Book Review**—Published weekly as part of the Sunday *Chronicle*, this review does about 1,000 book reviews per year. They are open to almost any books and are especially interested in books produced by California publishers and authors. Send review copies to Patricia Holt, Book Review Editor, *San Francisco Chronicle*, 275 Fifth Street, San Francisco, CA 94103; (415) 777-7042.

• **Los Angeles Times Book Review**—Published weekly as part of the Sunday *Times*, this supplement reviews about 2,000 books per year. Like most other newspapers, they review general fiction and nonfiction books. They do not welcome visits to the newspaper offices and also prefer that you do not follow up with phone calls. Jack Miles is book review editor. Send review copies to Jack Miles, Book Review Editor, *Los Angeles Times Book Review*, Times Mirror Square, Los Angeles, CA 90053; (213) 237-7000; Fax: (213) 237-4712.

• **New York Newsday**—This daily newspaper reviews primarily general interest books—fiction, history, politics, biographies, literary criticism, poetry, and others. They do not review how-to books. Jack Schwartz is the book editor. He suggests that if you have a book that doesn't fit their book review guidelines, send the book or a news release to the appropriate departmental editor at the paper. Send review copies to Jack Schwartz, Book Review Editor, *New York Newsday*, 2 Park Avenue, New York, NY 10016; (212) 303-2930; Fax: (212) 696-0298.

• **Chicago Tribune Books**—The Sunday section reviews general fiction and nonfiction. Send review copies to Diane Donovan, Book Review Editor, *Chicago Tribune Books*, 435 N. Michigan Avenue, Room 400, Chicago, IL 66011-4022; (312) 222-3232; Fax: (312) 222-3143.

• **USA Today**—Published five times a week, this national newspaper reviews fiction and nonfiction every Friday. They also review books in their three special sections: sports, money, and life at least once a week. Books are also featured in news stories and other regular features. Send all review copies to Robert Wilson, Book Editor, *USA Today*, P. O. Box 500, Washington, DC 20044; (703) 276-3400; (800) 368-3024. UPS address: 1000 Wilson Boulevard, Arlington, VA 22209.

• **New York Review of Books**—Published biweekly for the general public, this tabloid reviews about 1,000 nonfiction books per year. They not only review books but also use excerpts and buy serial rights. Send review copies to Robert B. Silvers or Barbara Epstein, Editors, *New York Review of Books*, 250 West 57th Street #1321, New York, NY 10107-0169; (212) 757-8070; Fax: (212) 333-5374.

• **San Francisco Review of Books**—This quarterly magazine reviews academic, scholarly, and literary books with a special emphasis on books published in the West (no self-help or how-to books). Ms. Elgy Gillespie is the editor. Send review copies to *San Francisco Review of Books*, 1117 Geary Street, San Francisco, CA 94109; 415-771-1252.

• **Voice Literary Supplement**—This monthly supplement of the *Village Voice* newspaper reviews all types of books but with a special focus on literary fiction. Send review copies to Ms. M. Mark, *Voice Literary Supplement*, 842 Broadway, New York, NY 10003; (212) 460-1477.

To give you an idea what sort of books their readers are interested in buying, here are some statistics drawn from a 1984 reader survey: While the average American buys 7.6 books a year, the typical *Village Voice* reader buys an average of 18.7 books (6.3 hardcovers and 12.4 paperbacks). What kind of books do they read? Their top picks are fiction (78.3%), biography (51.5%), art/photography (49.9%), history (41.7%), current affairs (36.9%), psychology and self-help (35.1%), mysteries (33.3%), science (32.6%), science fiction & fantasy (30.9%), cookbooks (30.5%), drama (28.8%), poetry (28.0%), travel (26.9%), literary criticism (22.8%), and other subjects (15.6%).

- **The Bloomsbury Review** — This bimonthly literary review features more book reviews of small press titles, both fiction and nonfiction, than any other publication. Send review copies to Tom Auer, Editor, *The Bloomsbury Review*, 1028 Bannock Street [zip: 80204], P. O. Box 8928, Denver, CO 80201; (303) 892-0620; Fax: (303) 892-5620.

  The Bloomsbury Review seems to have an effect: 75% of their readers have bought books reviewed therein, while 70% have bought books advertised in the *Review*. 45% of their readers buy four or more books per month.

  Here are some of the subjects that their readers bought during one six-month period: literary fiction (74%), popular fiction (57%), history (57%), biographies (52%), poetry (49%), and art (41%).

- **Small Press** — This bimonthly magazine reviews about 100 to 150 small press titles every issue. Any and all subjects are reviewed. Brenda Mitchell-Powell is the editor. John Kremer writes the Books for the Trade column (which features books on publishing, printing, graphics, publicity, marketing, and other business topics). Send review copies to *Small Press Magazine*, Meckler Publishing, 11 Ferry Lane West, Westport, CT 06880; (203) 226-6967. Send review copies for the Books for the Trade column to John Kremer, c/o Ad-Lib Publications.

- **Small Press Book Review** — This bimonthly newsletter reviews 80 small press titles per issue. The *Review* is targeted primarily for libraries. Send review copies to Henry Berry, Editor, *The Small Press Book Review*, P. O. Box 176, Southport, CT 06490; (203) 268-4878.

- **Small Press Review** — The original small press book review periodical, this monthly reviews primarily poetry and literary fiction. Write to Len Fulton, Editor, *Small Press Review*, Dustbooks, P. O. Box 100, Paradise, CA 95969.

- **Rave Reviews** — This bimonthly book review magazine for consumers focuses on nonfiction bestsellers and all genres of fiction (except westerns). Reviews primarily mass-market paperbacks. An up-and-coming magazine with 100 reviews each issue. Send review copies to Marc A. Cerasini, Editor, *Rave Reviews*, 55 Bergen Street, Brooklyn Heights, NY 11201; (718) 237-1097.

As you may have noticed, one of the most important things to do if you want reviews from these major review media is to send books as early as possible — preferably four months in advance of the book's publication date. Send galley copies if finished books are not yet available at that time; then send the finished books when they do become available.

If you have any questions about their review policies, don't hesitate to call the magazines and ask. All the book review editors I've ever talked with have been very willing to answer questions and make suggestions.

> **Authors** — Make it a habit to read a few of these major review media every week. Not only will this reading help you to keep up on new trends in publishing and book marketing, but it will also help you to target publishers who are most likely to be interested in publishing your new titles.

9:03 Don't Overlook the Special Interest Review Media

Besides the major book review media listed on the previous pages, you should also mail review copies to the book review sections of other major newspapers and magazines. Finally, you should also send review copies to any special interest review media. Here are just a few of them (for a more complete list, see my *Book Publishing Resource Guide*):

- **Feminist Bookstore News,** Carol Seajay, Editor, 456 - 14th Street #6, P. O. Box 882554, San Francisco, CA 94188; (415) 626-1556. This bimonthly newsletter is sent to 350 feminist bookstores. The book reviewers, all owners of bookstores, review books on all topics of interest to feminists, from art and children's books to mysteries and poetry.

- **New Age Retailer,** Duane Sweeney, Editor, P. O. Box 224, Greenbank, WA 98253-0489; (206) 678-7772. They are the major review newsletter for new age booksellers. They ask that you send two review copies of every book — one for their library and one for the reviewer.

- **Romantic Times,** Suzanne Perry, Managing Editor, 55 Bergen Street, Brooklyn Heights, NY 11201; (718) 237-1097. This bimonthly magazine reviews all genres of romances (historicals, gothics, contemporaries, etc.). Besides newsstand distribution, it is also sent to all major mass-market jobbers. If you are a writer of romances, you should defintely read this magazine.

- **Science Fiction Chronicle,** Andrew Porter, Editor, P. O. Box 2730, Brooklyn, NY 11202-0056. One of two major review magazines for science fiction and fantasy books.

• **Sci/Tech Book News**, Jane Erskine, Managing Editor, 5600 N.E. Hassalo Street, Portland, OR 97213; (503) 281-9230. This newsletter, published 11 times per year, reviews high-level scientific, technical, and medical books. Jane also edits two bimonthly newsletters, *Reference & Research Book News* and *University Press Book News*.

Authors — Many of these special interest review media may not be known by your publisher, especially if your publisher does not normally publish books in that subject area. Hence, you can help your publisher by scouting out these specific review media as well as other special interest magazines that might be open to reviewing your books.

9:04 Major Media Directories

Besides sending review copies to the book review sections of major newspapers and magazines, you should also be sending review copies or news releases to other general interest and special interest magazines. To help you locate those media, here are a few of the major media directories, some of which you should be able to locate in your local library:

• **Advertising and Publicity Resources for Scholarly Books**, American University Presses, 584 Broadway #410, New York NY 10012; (212) 941-6610. Features 3,200 scholarly periodicals.

• **All-in-One Directory**, Gebbie Press, P. O. Box 1000, New Paltz, NY, 12561-0017; (914) 255-7560. Features general media.

• **Bacon's Publicity Checker**, R. H. Bacon Company, 332 S. Michigan Avenue, Chicago, IL 60604; (800) 621-0561; (312) 922-2400. Features newspapers and magazines. Bacons also publishes a radio and TV directory covering 9000 radio shows and 1300 TV shows.

• **Black Media Directory**, Burrelle's, 75 E. Northfield Avenue, Livingston, NJ 07039; (800) 631-1160. Features all black media. Burrelle's also publishes other minority media directories.

• **Book Publishing Resource Guide**, Ad-Lib Publications, 51 N. Fifth Street, P. O. Box 1102, Fairfield, IA 52556-1102; (800) 669-0773; (515) 472-6617; Fax: (515) 472-3186. Ad-Lib also produces the *PR Flash No-Frills Data Files*, which include more than 11,000 media records (3,650 newspaper editors, 3,200 magazine editors, 3,685 newspaper editors, 2,465 radio shows, 970 television shows, and 755 syndicated columns).

• **Catholic Press Directory**, Catholic Press Association, 119 North Park Avenue, Rockville Centre, NY 11570;4182; (516) 766-3400. Features Catholic newspapers, magazines, and book publishers.

- **CBIC Media List**, David Hunt, Director, Canadian Book Information Centre, 260 King Street E., Toronto, Ontario, M5A 1K3 Canada; (416) 362-6555; Fax: (416) 361-0643. Features all Canadian media interested in books.

- **College Alumni & Military Publications**, BPI Media, P. O. Box 2015, Lakewood, NJ 08701-9896; (201) 363-5633; (800) 336-3533. A division of Billboard Publications, BPI Media also publishes the following directories: *News Bureaus of the U.S.*, *Radio Contacts*, *Syndicated Columnists*, *Cable Contacts Yearbook*, *TV News*, and *TV Contacts*.

- **Directory of Literary Magazines**, Council of Literary Magazines and Presses, 666 Broadway, New York, NY 10012-2317; 212-614-6551. 450 literary publications.

- **Directory of Woman's Media**, National Council for Research on Women, 47-49 East 65th Street, New York, NY 10021-7021. Lists 750 periodicals, 120 women's publishers, 150 feminist bookstores, 79 special library collections, 20 woman's radio/TV groups, and more. A new edition will be available at the end of 1990.

- **Gale Directory of Publications and Broadcast Media**, Gale Research Company, 835 Penobscot Building, Detroit, MI 48226-4094; (313) 961-2242; (800) 877-GALE. Features 25,000 magazine and newspaper editors as well as 10,000 radio, television, and cable contacts. Gale also publishes *Newsletters in Print* as well as many other directories.

- **Hispanic Media USA**, The Media Institute, 3017 M Street N.W., Washington, DC 20007; (202) 298-7512. Features 300 Hispanic print and broadcast media (last updated in 1987, but planning new update).

- **Hudson's Subscription Newsletter Directory**, The Newsletter Clearinghouse, P. O. Box 311, 44 W. Market Street, Rhinebeck, NY 12572-1403; (914) 876-2081. Features 4,380 newsletters. Also publishes *Hudson's Washington News Media*, which features DC media contacts.

- **National Radio Publicity Outlets**, Morgan Rand Publishing Company, 2200 Sansom Street, Philadelphia, PA 19103; (515) 557-8200; (800) 354-8673; Fax: 215-557-8414.. Features 5,000 radio stations. Also publishes *TV & Cable Publicity Outlets* and *Feature News Publicity Outlets*.

- **Standard Periodical Directory**, Oxbridge Communications, 150 Fifth Avenue #636, New York, NY 10011-4311; (212) 741-0231. Features 78,000 magazines and newsletters. Oxbridge publishes several other directories of magazines, newsletters, catalogs, and mailing lists.

- **Ulrich's International Periodicals**, R. R. Bowker Company, 245 West 17th Street, New York, NY 10011; (212) 645-9700. International magazines and other periodicals.

- **Working Press of the Nation**, National Research Bureau, 225 W. Wacker Drive #2275, Chicago, IL 60604; (800) 456-4555. 5 volumes covering 28,000 publicity outlets: newspapers, magazines, radio, TV, feature writers, and internal publications.

9:05 The Importance of Book Reviews

Book reviews are critically important to any hardcover book that is targeted at a general audience. No publisher can afford to advertise in all the general newspapers and magazines which reach a wide audience, so the only major way to reach the most people with the least money is to obtain reviews or other mentions in newspapers and magazines. Almost any general trade publisher who relies on bookstore sales will tell you that reviews are a key factor in generating word-of-mouth and, hence, sales.

- For example, the Mexican writer Carlos Fuentes has written many books in the past twenty years, all of which received critical acclaim. However, in almost every case the reviews came too late to have a great impact on the sales of his books. A few years ago, though, his new novel, *The Old Gringo*, received top billing in almost every major book review supplement (including front cover stories in the review sections of the *New York Times, Los Angeles Times, San Francisco Chronicle*, and *Chicago Tribune*). All these reviews appeared within three weeks of the book's publication date. As a result, the book hit the *New York Times* bestseller list within six weeks of publication.

- Melvin Power's book, *How to Get Rich in Mail Order*, was reviewed by Og Mangino in *Success* magazine. That one review brought in over 1,600 orders for the book.

- When the *New York Times Book Review* reviewed Michael Rogan's *Ronald Reagan, the Movie*, the University of California Press received calls from wholesalers the very next day. They took orders for 500 copies that day.

- Karen Friedman and Evonne Weinhaus sold 20,000 copies of their self-published book, *Stop Struggling with Your Teen*, after positive reviews in *Family Circle* and *Woman's Day*, plus author appearances on the *Today* show, *Hour Magazine*, and *Sally Jesse Raphael*. Three years later they sold the reprint rights to Penguin.

- Barbara Harris has sold 750,000 copies of her self-published book, *Let's Cook Microwave*, without paying one cent for advertising. The sales are all the result of publicity and word of mouth.

- Leila Albala has sold over 50,000 copies of her four books by receiving notices in *Family Circle, Vogue, Redbook*, and UPI.

- When *Parade* magazine featured Vic Spadaccini's *The Home Owner's Journal*, Vic received 1,710 orders in the first week, another 1,210 orders the second week, and a total of more than 5,400 orders over the next six months.

- Allan Bloom's *The Closing of the American Mind*, quickly rose to the top of the bestseller lists on the strength of reviews, beginning with a favorable review by the *New York Times Book Review* and followed by other favorable reviews in major newspapers across the country.

- Reviews may not always carry a book to the top of the bestseller lists, but sometimes they can make all the difference in keeping a book in print. For example, Noam Chomsky's first book for South End Press, *After the Cataclysm*, sold very few copies until an impassioned review appeared in the *Village Voice*. Only then did bookstores begin to feature the book or, for that matter, begin to carry it at all.

- Even one review can sometimes make a difference. Hugh Nissenson's book about Johnny Appleseed, *The Tree of Life*, stayed alive only because of a favorable review in *Time* magazine.

- Besides sales, there is one other major benefit of publicity: You can attract better authors. The reason Tama Janowitz, author of *Slaves of New York*, signed with Crown was because they offered her a real commitment to building up her public image.

9:06 How to Get Reviews: Rule #1

Send out review copies. Send out lots of them. Send out more than you think you should. Hit every major newspaper and magazine which you think might be at all interested in the subject of your book. In most cases this means sending out somewhere between 300 and 500 review copies.

Don't be stingy about sending out review copies. For every hundred copies you send out, you'll get perhaps ten reviews. And those ten reviews will bring you anywhere from twenty to one hundred direct sales and many more indirect sales. Even at a conservative estimate, you'll receive 200 orders for every 100 copies you send out. That's cheap advertising. And if your list of media is selective and your book appeals to a wide potential audience, that rate of return will be even higher. (Note that the above estimate is based on sending your review copies to media which regularly review books similar to the book you send them.)

For other possibilities on your media list (that is, those media which are not prime prospects for reviewing your book), send a news release, brochure, and reply card offering a review copy upon request. Then send them a review copy if they request one.

Here's one example of the impact of giving away sufficient (even abundant) review copies:

- When Epson came out with their first dot matrix printer, they sent 500 printers to the major opinion makers in the computer industry. They did not say, "Use this printer for 90 days and then send it back." No, instead they said, "It's yours. Keep it. Use it any way you want. Enjoy." As a result, by the time other dot matrix printers got their promotional campaigns underway, Epson had already established itself as the standard among the movers and shakers in the industry. So, of course, when these people wrote about computer printers, they naturally talked about Epson — simply because that was the printer they used.

Note, however, that this giveaway policy would not have worked if Epson had not produced a solid, reliable printer. Similarly, sending out review copies will not help you unless your book is actually worthy of review.

A major literary agent for some of the best-known cookbook authors says that one of the most effective ways to promote cookbooks is to send out plenty of review copies to anyone involved with food—from newspaper and magazine food editors to teachers at cooking schools and owners of gourmet cooking shops. The word-of-mouth these people create is worth any amount of regular advertising.

Budget 5% to 10% of your first printing as giveaways—for reviewers, booksellers, and key opinion makers. The majority of these review copies should be given away in the first four months.

9:07 How to Get Reviews: More Tips

Here are some general tips on how to go about getting reviews for your books. Use those tips which make the most sense to you within your own procedures for sending out review copies.

- Don't just send review copies to book review editors. In many cases, especially with cookbooks and how-to books, you'd be better off sending your books to the food or lifestyle editors. Indeed, many book review supplements at major newspapers do not review how-to books or cookbooks except around Christmas time or other special occasions. So, watch for other opportunities for reviews: newsletter editors, specialty shop owners, in-house magazines, trade magazines, freelance writers, and other authors writing books in the same subject area.

- Some magazines and newspapers have special sections or theme issues where they review certain types of books. Have your advertising manager let you know about any such special themes or issues (note: more often than not, your advertising manager is the one who will be sent notices of these special issues). For example, *Scientific American* does an annual review of science books for children in their December issue. Also, as noted above, the *New York Times Book Review* only reviews cookbooks and how-to books at Christmas time.

To find out the editorial schedules of many general magazines, you can also refer to one of the following two services:

Bacon's Media Alerts, Bacon's PR and Media Information Systems, 332 S. Michigan Avenue, Chicago, IL 60604; (312) 922-2400; (800) 621-0561. Lists the editorial calendars, profiles, and lead times of 1,900 magazines and 200 major daily newspapers. Also includes an extensive listing and cross-index of appropriate trade shows and conventions. Cost: $195.00 (1991 edition).

Special Issues, Standard Rate & Data Service, 3004 Glenview Road, Wilmette, IL 60091; (800) 323-4588. Includes regular departments, detailed 12-month editorial calendars, and personnel listings for 3,800 business publications, 1,150 newspapers, 1,500 consumer magazines, and 400 farm publications. Published 5 times per year. Cost: $199.00.

• Have several hundred copies of your book's cover overprinted with the heading, "Advance Reading Copy — Not for Sale." Also include the publication date and retail price. Send these copies to potential reviewers. Such advance review copies offer several advantages:

1. The heading clearly indicates to the reviewers that they are receiving advance copies.

2. Such exclusive review copies tend to receive greater attention than ordinary copies.

3. The other printed information (publication date and price) provide the essential data that any reviewer requires.

• Alternatively, you could print labels that provide the same information and attach them to the outside of the cover or the inside front cover.

• The basic information every reviewer needs to have at hand when reviewing a book includes the following:

1) title of book (including the subtitle),
2) author or authors of book,
3) publication date,
4) ISBN number,
5) whether the book is available in both hardcover and softcover,
6) the price(s) of available editions,
7) the name and address of the publisher,
8) the address where individuals orders should be sent, and
9) any handling charges for individual orders.

• Send a cover letter or press release with the book. These may never be read (and may well be thrown out when the receiving clerk unwraps the book), but they are indispensable for media which do have a policy of saving such enclosures. The press release or cover letter should contain the following information:

1) the basic facts about the book (what does the book do?),
2) the significance of the book (what benefits does it offer?),
3) the intended audience (who will the book help?),
4) a biography of the author (how is the author qualified?), and
5) a list of the author's previous books.

The first three points of the press release should provide a quick summary of why readers would be interested in the book. The last two points clarify the author's credentials and background, the final point indicating any previous publishing history.

For more details on writing news releases, see section 9:10.

- Note the final point in the above suggestion: If the author has been published before, be sure to indicate that. Reviewers are more likely to review a book by an author who has already had several other books published. Why? Because an author who has been published more than once has demonstrated that he or she can write books that readers will be interested in reading. The reasoning here is that publishers would not continue to publish an author whose books have not performed well or at least broken even.

- For special reviewers, you might write a personal letter to accompany the review copy. You might also have the author autograph the review copy. Some book reviewers will notice these little touches, and some will even appreciate the extra attention.

- At least one reviewer has pointed out, "You get my attention by sending letters addressed by hand. I don't open letters addressed by machine."

- Hand deliver review copies where practical.

- Clean up your list of reviewers so you are not sending multiple copies to the same reviewer. In an article in *Publishers Weekly*, Rita Coughlin, book editor of the *Detroit News*, castigated publishers for wasting her time by sending out duplicate copies of books. One publisher actually sent her six copies of a novel!.

- Do something special to draw attention to your book—to put your book at the top of the pile of review copies.

  When Crown published Elizabeth Alston's *Muffins* cookbook, they accompanied review copies with a basket of homemade muffins.

  When Morrow published Paul Prudhomme's *Louisiana Kitchen*, they invited a group of key wholesalers and booksellers to New York to sample a dinner cooked by Prudhomme.

  Bantam packaged the review copy of Jonathan Kellerman's novel, *The Butcher's Theater*, with a letter opener piercing the cover of the book.

- Finally, and above all, follow up. Every review copy you send out should be followed up by a phone call or a handwritten note. When you phone, simply ask if they received the review copy and whether they need any further information or would like to talk to the author?

  The more I talk to those publishers who have been successful getting reviews and features, the more I'm convinced of the value of follow-up calls. According to the publishers I've talked with (and my own experience), it is not uncommon to discover that either the media did not receive the review copy, or they received it but can't find it, or any of a hundred different variations on these themes.

  Most media do appreciate the follow-up call, and most do respond either by asking for a review copy, by putting the review copy they received higher up on their pile of things to do, or by passing the book on to an editor who will be able to use it in a news or feature story.

Authors — Cooperate with your publishers. Volunteer to help by autographing copies of the book, writing personalized letters to major reviewers, hand addressing envelopes, and doing anything else that you can do to increase your chances for reviews. Above all, be sure to provide them with enough information about you as a person so they can write a great author biography that will attract the attention of reviewers.

9:08 Any Review Is a Good Review

Don't worry about the kind of reviews your books receive. Any review is a good review, whether the reviewer liked the book or not. Even a bad review helps to bring attention to the book and to fix the book's title in the minds of readers. Many readers will buy a book despite a bad review—if for no other reason than to prove the reviewer wrong. Others buy out of curiosity. Still others buy because they remember reading about the book but do not remember whether the review was good, bad, or indifferent.

- *The One Minute Manager* by Spencer Johnson and Keith Blanchard did not receive good reviews from most of the critics. Nonetheless, readers loved it. So, although good reviews can help put a book on the bestseller lists, they are not absolutely necessary.

9:09 What to Do After the Reviews

To make your book review program really effective, you must follow up your efforts. Here are a few suggestions on how to make the most of your book's reviews:

- Write a thank you note to the reviewer. Moreover, if you have gotten a good response from the review, let the reviewer know what the response was. All review media are interested in what their readers respond to, and if your book received a good response and you let them know about that response, they will be more likely to review similar books in the future (and if your list is specialized, those books will be yours).

- If your books are hardcover, print a limited number of book jackets in the beginning. Then, when the reviews start coming in, print additional dust jackets featuring the best reviews. This procedure is more costly than printing all the jackets at once, but if the reviews are good, the extra expense could well be worth it.

- Make copies of the best reviews and include them with news releases and review copies you send out after the first big wave of publicity. These reviews will help to convince later reviewers that the book is important, worthy of review, and of interest to their readers. When making copies of reviews, underline the most favorable and important comments. Also, be sure to include a tag line identifying the name of the periodical and the date the review appeared.

- Also send copies of major reviews to your key bookselling contacts (your sales reps, distributors, chain stores, wholesalers, book clubs, foreign rights buyers, periodicals that buy second serial rights, etc.). Keep these key contacts informed of your book's publicity.

- Send copies of any reviews to the author as well. Not only does this notify the author that you are promoting the book, but it also provides important feedback which the author can use in revising the book (or writing a new book which covers material left out of the current book). Some of the reviews might also cause the author to think of other possible review media or promotions.

- You might also feature copies of reviews in the bounceback offers you send to direct mail customers.

- Quote the best reviews in all your continuing advertisements, brochures, catalogs, and other promotional materials.

- When you get a large response from a review, consider advertising in that magazine or newspaper. Obviously, if readers were interested in the book as a result of a review, other readers will probably order the book if they see another notice of the book. And since you are not likely to get two reviews in the same periodical, the only way you can get additional notices of your book in the periodical is to advertise.

After receiving a favorable review and response to that review in *Entrepreneur's Magazine*, Wilshire Book continued to advertise their book, *How to Get Rich in Mail Order*, every month for the next year. Their ads continued to produce superb results for the whole year.

- Advertise in a periodical after a review rather than in the same issue as the review. That way, if the review is favorable, you can quote from the review in your ad. Plus the repeated exposure of the book in the periodical will produce better results than two exposures (one ad and one review) in the same issue.

- Subscribe to a press clipping service so you can keep tabs on all features that appear in any print media. Note that few media will automatically send you copies of reviews that they publish; hence, the only way you will know about these reviews is to subscribe to a clipping service. You cannot count on reader inquiries and orders to alert you to all reviews and features that appear, and you certainly cannot expect them to send you copies of the reviews when they order.

Here are several clipping services you might want to use:

Bacon's Clipping Bureau, 332 S. Michigan Avenue, Chicago, IL 60604; (800) 621-0561.

Burrelle's Press Clipping Service, 75 E. Northfield Road, Livingston, NJ 07039; (800) 631-1160.

Luce Press Clippings, 420 Lexington Avenue, New York, NY 10170; (212) 889-6711.

Pressclips, Inc., 1 Hillside Boulevard, New Hyde Park, NY 11040; (516) 437-1047.

- Keep copies of all reviews in your files, along with copies of any other promotions. Each book should have its own file.

- Also place a copy of the review in your media file for that particular newspaper or magazine. If you don't already have a media file, you should begin one. The file should include a record of that publication's name, address, phone number, book reviewer, other important contacts (editors, producers, etc.), subjects they review, and other notes. File a copy of every review, notice, feature, or other publicity which that publication prints about your company or your books.

9:10 How to Write a News Release

When sending out review copies or when soliciting requests for review copies, you should always send a news release. Often a news release is all you need to send to generate effective publicity. Here are a few guidelines I use in writing news releases. They work for me.

- Hold the news release to one page. Double-spaced. If you require two pages, edit more vigorously.

- If you simply cannot cut any information, try to excerpt part of the news release and put it into a separate background release or author bio. Too many news releases contain details which detract from the main news story rather than add to it.

- Focus on the news and/or benefit value of the book, not its contents.

- Focus on one main benefit or idea. When writing a news release, keep it as simple as possible.

- Avoid making judgments about your own book, unless you are quoting someone. Such statements as, "a must reference resource," or "the new standard in the field," or "the most complete directory," are completely out of line.

- Use quotes. Quotations from the author or another expert not only help to jazz up a news release and make it more personal, but they also make a release appear more like a regular news story. People like to read about people. That's why reporters look for people to interview as part of a story.

- Quotations also allow you to make stronger points that would be out of place in a straight news story. Here's a quote I've used in my news releases for the *Directory of Book, Catalog, and Magazine Printers*: "It doesn't matter where you are located. With this new edition you can find a quality book printer who specializes in the quantities, sizes, and bindings you want to use—at a price you can afford."

- Top the news release off with a great headline. You want to write a headline that will attract the attention of the editor as well as the readers. Keep it short and keep it punchy.

- The news release should read like a standard news story. It should answer the questions: Who? What? Where? When? Why?

- Use the inverted pyramid style of news stories. Start with the most important news or feature, then the supporting news, and end with the least important information. Note: Most newspapers, when they edit, start by cutting from the bottom of the news release.

- Speak the language of the intended audience. If you have a book that appeals to a number of different audiences, you might print up special press releases focusing on the benefits of the book for each particular audience. For example, with our own *Directory Book, Catalog, and Magazine Printers*, we sent one news release to magazines for writers and publishers, another release to business magazines, and still another to association and club magazines. For media which seem to fit no particular category but whose readers would still be interested in our *Directory*, we sent a personal letter to the editor outlining the benefits of the *Directory* for his or her readers. We've done this for school journalism newsletters and genealogy magazines.

- For important editors, attach a personal note to the news release.

- According to one newspaper editor, the glitzy press kits are the first to hit the trash. The news releases with a handwritten note tend to get read. A trade magazine editor has also noted, "I'd rather see a well-written release any day than all the fancy packaging on Madison Avenue."

- With newspapers, emphasize the local angle (if one exists).

- Here's an option: Instead of a standard news release, have someone write a feature article about the book or author. Send that out to your key contacts. If it's good, some publications might well print it as is.

- Here are a couple of other ways to spice up your news release:

    Glamorize your subject—For instance, for a book on country inns, what famous people stayed at the inns featured in the book?

    Stand out from the pack—Is your book the most complete? Then point it out in an usual way: "Weighs over three pounds!"

    Take the road less traveled—Take a different angle on the subject. Don't copycat other publishers' promotions.

Write an anecdote—In 25 words or less, what can you tell others about the book? Is there a story behind the book, something interesting about the author, a story in the book that can be excerpted? Tell a story. People love stories.

Localize the story—Slant the news story to a local angle. People like to read about themselves and their home towns. For my book, *Tinseltowns, U.S.A.*, we added a line at the end of each news release: "Your city, Minneapolis, is featured on page 73!" or whatever city name and page numbers were appropriate. That line got the book many local features.

Tie-in to other events or stories—See section 9:22 for 20 ways to tie your book into other events or stories.

9:11 Added Touches

To improve the reception of your news release, supply the media with added material that will help them create a story their audience will heed. Here are a few examples of things that you could add to make your news release more acceptable.

- **Press kits**—Press kits package a news release with many of the other items listed below. To publicize her *Easy Halloween Costumes for Children*, Leila Albala put together a dramatic press kit: press release, catchy cover letter, bio, photographs, copies of previous articles featuring her books, and the book itself—all inside an orange folder with a color snapshot of Halloween costumers glued to the front. That press kit worked. Her book was featured in all major Canadian newspapers as well as many American newspapers.

- **Photos**—As the publisher of *Time* magazine noted in one of his letters to readers, "As is often the case, eye-catching photography was crucial to the choice of subject. The strength of a picture will often make or break an item. ... We want the usual subjects doing unusual things."
  Romantic Times includes a note in many issues asking authors to send their own photos: "New authors—be up-to-date and send professional publicity photos and introduce yourself."

Authors — Arrange to have a professional publicity photograph taken of you. Make sure your publisher has a print, and keep several on hand for sending out with your personal press releases. Photos can add that personal touch that makes the difference on whether a press release is noticed or tossed out.

In some cases, you might want to send a photograph alone in place of the news release. Remember: A picture can be worth a 1000 words. Just send a captioned photo. If you try this, make sure that: 1) The photo tells a story. 2) The caption is catchy. 3) The media uses photos.

- **Clip sheets**—In place of or in addition to a photo, you could send a clip sheet of reproducible artwork of different sizes to fit various column widths and lengths. The artwork could consist of logos, book covers, illustrations from the book, or other camera-ready art related to the subject of the book.

Clip sheets, like photos, have two distinct advantages: 1) Visuals add to the attractiveness of a news release and make it more likely that people will notice it—and editors will feature it. 2) Features that use artwork or photos tend to take up more space in the publication.

Here is some camera-ready artwork used to promote Duane Shinn's recent book, *How to Dress Up Naked Music on the Piano!*

● **Brochures or other promotional material**—Richard J. Oddo sends
bookmarks that feature illustrations and quoted excerpts from his
book, *Within a Miraculous Realm*. I probably would not have opened
the review copy except I was so taken with the bookmark illustrated
below that I ended up reading the entire book.

Art Plate #4 ~ What difference would it
make if my stomach was full, but my
heart was empty—I might as well be dead.
My body may starve, but as long as I am
graced to roam this bountiful land of
beauty and wonder, let my soul smell the
flowers, and breathe in the fragrance of
life's miraculous existence . . .

From~ *Within A Miraculous Realm*
A book by~ Richard J. Oddo ©1988
P.O. Box 7012, Halcyon, Ca. 93420

- **Pitch letter**—A pitch letter should be personalized for the target media. It should plant a potential story idea in the editor's mind. Or a special angle on the news for that publication. Sign the letter. Make it as personal as possible.

- **Author biographies**—Always include a biography of your author. Spice it up with interesting tidbits about the author. Humanize the author. What incidents or experiences led the author to write the book? Again, people like to read about people.

- **Background releases**—If the book is technical or about a relatively new subject, you might want to add a background sheet that describes the history of the subject or how the book is tied into current events. Background releases can be used effectively to flesh out a one-page news release and fill in background information that a reporter would need to write a feature article. The background release might even include information that is not in the book.

- **Fact sheet**—A fact sheet states the basic facts about the book (title, author, publisher, number of pages, size, ISBN number, publication date, binding, and price). To convince an editor to open the book, it might also offer some enticing tidbits from the book.

  For Leonard Mogul's *Making It in the Media Professions*, Kate Bandos of Globe Pequot Press prepared the fact sheet that appears on the following two pages. Note how this fact sheet really makes the book sound fascinating. What editor could resist the questions? This fact sheet makes superb use of details from the book. To find the answers, you have to read the book!

- **Excerpts from the book**—If you do not send a copy of the book, then add a page or set of pages excerpted from the book. To enhance her news releases, Jane Hoffman sends out sample experiments from her book, *The Original Backyard Scientist*. She gives permission to reprint the experiments with their review or feature article about her book.

- **Copies of previous articles**—If the book or author has been featured in previous reviews or articles, enclose copies of a few of the most important ones—those from major media, those that feature the book in an effective way, or those that are visually attractive.

- **Other supporting material**—Enclose any other items that might support the news release. For example, if your book is about making home videos, prepare a videotape of great bits from home videos and enclose the tape with the news release.

Authors — Provide your publishers with any material that will help enhance their press kit: photos, copies of previous features about you, a good bio, and whatever else is suitable.

Making It in the Media Professions

Well-known or esoteric, handsomely paid or simply exciting, jobs in the media fields--newspapers, magazines, book publishing, television, movies, radio, and advertising--offer something for everyone.

A bit of history . . .

* In France, magazines emerged in the 18th century and were edited by such giants of letters and philosophy as Rousseau, Diderot, and Voltaire. (p. 42).
* The phenomenal expansion of radio in the early 1920s caused overextension by many businesses in this field. Radio-company stocks worth $160 million in 1924 fell to $65 million in 1926. (p.168).
* Cable television grew extraordinarily quickly. It's birth was only in the 1940s. HBO was the first to distribute the "pay TV" service and became the "king of the hill in Hollywood" when it bought rights to so many movies that it seemed to control the film industry. (p.152)
* Original radio commercials were called "a dollar a holler." (p.168).

Did you realize . . .

* New York City, the nation's number-one media market, produces only about five newspapers today--the venerable New York Times plus a few others. In the 1930's, there were many more--from the Brooklyn Eagle to the Daily Telegram. (p.1).
* People who sell advertising space for magazines eat fancy lunches with clients and agency people almost every day. They also earn a great deal of money . . . but the glamour and excitement still lies in the editorial department. Maybe it's seeing their byline or feeling the adrenalin rush when the sentences start to pour out upon the page. (p.49).
* "Time, Inc., is a giant in consumer-magazine publishing. Its flagship, Time magazine, had a recent weekly circulation of 4.6 million, and its Sports Illustrated boasts a weekly circulation of 2.8 million. Also in its stable are the monthlies Life and Money, the biweekly Fortune, and the weekly People, all highly successful publications. Time, Inc. seldom makes mistakes." (p.43).
* Despite people's desire to kick the television habit or to make it become a more educational force, the immediacy of television coverage cannot be equalled by any other form of mass media. After all, no newspaper or magazine could get moment-by-moment coverage of the attempted assassination of Lee Harvey Oswald by Jack Ruby. (p.121).
* Commercial prices for television are outrageously high, especially for special events. Popular sitcoms bring in high charges--a 30-second commercial during "Family Ties" costs $300,000. The 1987 Super Bowl tipped the scales with a whopping $600,000 per 30-second advertisement. (p.122).

--more--

The Globe Pequot Press, Inc.   Old Chester Road, Chester, Connecticut 06412. Tel. 203-526-9571   *Book Publishers*

* Although lower than that at a more established paper like The Wall Street Journal, the salary at a smaller newspaper for a copy editor with five years' experience is about $18,000; for an editorial writer/columnist with 13 years' experience, $44,000. (p.11).
* Television is certainly no fading business. Television households view an average of more than 52 hours a week. (p. 123).
* Times are changing in the movie business--today, almost 60% of all U.S. households have a VCR, and more films are watched on VCRs than in cinemas. (p.196).
* A television producer makes $40,000 - $60,000, while a television director makes about $25,000 - $35,000. (p.128).
* Each October, thousands of book publishers gather at the Frankfurt Book Fair to sell books and book rights. Buildings are full of people, books, and chatter--the effect is mind-boggling. There is never a dull moment--at the Israeli booths, armed guards patrol the area. Publishing overcomes political differences--if only for a few days. (p.80).
* In the publishing field, a regional sales manager makes about $21,000 -$35,000, an international sales manager $27,000 - $41,000, and a sales representative just starting out about $12,500. (p.96).
* Television reporters must be aware of all legalities when reporting a story. "Quoting cancer statistics (during a news report), for example, would have to include a disclaimer stating the uncertainty of whether the cancers were a direct result of the toxic dumping." (p.128).
* The power of the radio is still going strong. In 1987, radio had advertising revenues of more than $7 billion annually--about a third of television's revenues. (p.170).
* Television is not the only media to offer pay service. There is also "pay radio"--for 24 hours a day of rock, jazz, classical, or country-and-western music without commercial interruption. (p.171).
* Deejays and radio announcers just starting out get paid very little, but the supply still exceeds the demand. Perhaps it is the job they love--the sheer excitement of talking over the air--or perhaps it is the aspiration of becoming the general manager--the boss--who has absolute authority over the station. (p.173).
* Most radio stations look for personalities with strong personal styles to fill their deejay and announcer positions. But at some hard-rock radio stations, a frantic personality seems to be one of the foremost requirements for the job. (p.174).

Making It in the Media Professions
by Leonard Mogul
8½" x 11"   300 pages
$15.95 paperbound
Publication date: February 1988
For additional information, contact: Kate Siegel Bandos, Promotion Director
                                1-800-243-0495 (in CT, 1-800-962-0973)

The Globe Pequot Press. Inc.   Old Chester Road. Chester. Connecticut 06412. Tel. 203-526-9571   Book Publishers

9:12 23 Ways to Break into the Media

My experience, and that of many other independent publishers, is that it is far easier and, in most cases, more effective to get news and feature write-ups than it is to get reviews in most media.

How effective can features be? Here are a few examples:

• Last year *USA Today* featured Gregory Stock's *The Book of Questions* in a week-long series on the front page of the Life Section. That same week, Workman had to go back to press for another printing of 25,000 copies. The last time I looked, the book had sold over 550,000 copies and had been on the *Publishers Weekly* trade paperback bestseller list for months. Plus, it sold to Book-of-the-Month Club and negotiations were in the works for spinoffs of the book as a game and as a TV series.

• Peter Workman, publisher of *The Book of Questions* and *The Silver Palate Cookbook* (which has sold over 800,000 copies), believes that newspapers features are the best way to promote a cookbook. People try the recipes, then buy the book and, if the book is good, then word of mouth does the rest.

• When Abigail van Buren mentioned Jim Trelease's *The Read-Aloud Handbook* in her Dear Abby column, sales of that book were boosted to over 200,000 copies.

So, how do you get your books featured in newspapers and magazines? Here are 23 ways you can break into print. These are not listed in any particular order of priority.

1. **Work with local columnists**. Many newspaper columnists will feature books by local authors or publishers. For example, I've seen books mentioned in Herb Caen's column for the *San Francisco Chronicle* and in David Cataneo's Hot Stove sports column for the *Boston Herald*.

> **Authors** — Help your publishers. You know your local newspaper and its columnists better than your publisher or, at least, you should. Write a personal, localized note to the columnist you think would be most interested in your book. Hand deliver it if you have time. Or, better yet, if you have the gumption, invite your local columnist to lunch.

2. **Work with specialized columnists**. Again, many local newspapers have specialized columnists such as Lee Svitak Dean's Tidbits column for the Taste Section of the *Minneapolis Star Tribune*, or Pat Gardner's Tender Years column for the same paper.

Dean featured *Uncle Gene's Bread Book for Kids* in his Tidbits column
and even printed the address of the press—Happiness Press of
Montgomery, New York.

3. **Work with syndicated columnists.** There are some 1,500 nationally syndicated columnists who write about everything from home decorating
   and repairs to advice about relationships, from real estate to entertainment, from business to child care. Almost all of them mention books
   at one time or another.

   To locate columnists, look in the Syndicated Columnist section of the
   PR Flash No-Frills Data Files (available for IBM-PCs. Macintoshes, or
   compatibles) or in BPI Media's *Syndicated Columnists* directory.

   - *Dr. Gott*, a syndicated medical column by Peter Gott, M.D., recom-
     mended Jack Yetiv's self-published book, *Popular Nutritional Prac-
     tices: A Scientific Appraisal* in answer to the following question from
     a reader: "I am confused about diet, weight loss, vitamin supple-
     ments, and the relation of diet to disease. Is there any up-to-date
     book on these subjects." Yetiv's book would not have received this
     superb commendation if he had not sent a copy to Dr. Gott.

   - Since Jane Brody featured *Kicking Your Stress Habits* in her column
     on personal health, Whole Person Press has sold over 100,000
     copies of the book by mail order.

   - In one of her recent columns, Ann Landers recommended Anna
     and Robert Leider's *Don't Miss Out*, as a solution to the college
     financing blues. According to Longman Trade, the publisher of the
     book, over 50,000 of her readers responded to the notice.

4. **Set up an information bureau.** Reebok, manufacturers of athletic
   shoes, sends out many of their background information releases under
   the auspices of their Reebok Aerobic Information Bureau. The Associated Press recently featured one of their releases about a study conducted by USC researchers that showed that exercising improves
   problem-solving abilities, concentration, and short-term memory.
   What a way to sell shoes! Why not books as well?

5. **Sponsor a poll.** Conduct a survey related to one of your books. Then
   announce the results. Indeed, many books are nothing more than a
   summary and comment upon a survey (such as *The Hite Report*).

   Gallup did a poll for *Talk to Win*, a book by speech therapist Lillian
   Glass. The results of that poll were featured in many news stories.

6. **Solicit information or entries for an upcoming book.** *USA Today* often
   features such solicitations in the Lifeline Section. Here are just a few
   such requests that have appeared recently:

   - Mifflin Lowe, author of *The Cheapskate's Handbook*, sought the
     USA's biggest cheapskate. The winner received economy air fare to
     New York or Los Angeles. The runner-up won a $50 K-Mart gift
     certificate.

- CCC Publications requested contest entries for the most humorous answering machine messages for their forthcoming book, *No Hang-ups III*. They offered prices of $1000, $100, $50, and 50 fourth place prizes of $5. I would not be surprised if all entries received some sort of promotion about the first two books in the series.
- Sandy Soule asked readers to name their favorite country inns for her book, *America's Wonderful Little Hotels & Inns*.

7. **Get listed in community news.** When your authors go on tour (or even just to visit another city), arrange for an autograph session at local bookstores or libraries. Then make sure your local contact gets the event listed in the Calendar or Events section of the local newspaper.

   Note that some newspapers publish more than one calendar. For instance, the *Minneapolis Star Tribune* has a separate calendar for events of interest to senior citizens and families and another for art events.

8. **Don't forget the wire services.** The wire services can spread the word about your books to hundreds of newspapers across the country. What is the best way to reach these services? Talk to the local bureau. If you don't know the address of your local bureau, then call or write to the national headquarters as follows:
   - **Associated Press** (AP), 50 Rockefeller Plaza, New York, NY 10020; (212) 621-1500. Phil Thomas is the books editor.
   - **United Press International** (UPI), 1400 I Street N.W., Washington, DC 20005; (202) 898-8000. Jill Lai is the book review editor.
   - **Reuters**, 1700 Broadway, New York, NY 10019; (212) 603-3300.

   When you contact your local news service bureau, you will have a better chance of interesting them in an article if your book or author has already been featured in the local paper. Then, all they have to do is send that article out over the wires.

9. **Submit your story to your local news bureau.** Major media often have bureaus in other cities. According to Allan Hall, technology editor at *Business Week*, when submitting news stories to the major magazines, submit the story twice — one copy to the main editorial office and the other to the nearest bureau of the magazine. The chances are far greater that your local bureau will respond to your news release. Why? Because it is their job to find local newsworthy events, people, and products.

10. **Track down the right reporters.** Sometimes you might have to contact four or five different editors at a newspaper before you find the one who would be most appropriate for your book. I know one publisher who had to send three review copies and make five calls to five different editors at *USA Today* before he located a writer who was interested in reviewing his book/tape combos. But his persistence paid off — with a front page feature in the Life Section of *USA Today*.

When I sent a review copy of my *Tinseltowns, U.S.A.* to *USA Today*, I sent it to Tom Gliatto, then compiler of the Lifeline section, rather than the book editor. As a result, the book was featured in Today's Tip-Off at the top of the front page of the Life Section.

11. **Track down freelance writers.** To get into some newspapers, it often pays to track down a freelance writer who does a lot of work for those newspapers *and* who specializes in writing about subjects related to your book. Here's how one publisher located a freelance writer:

"I called and asked who the family editor was. I wrote her but I received no response. So I called again and this time asked for the assistant family editor. I wrote her as well. As a result of these two letters, one of them contacted a freelance writer living nearby. She wrote a superb article featuring our book."

Be on the lookout for any freelance writers who are working on books or articles dealing with subjects covered by any of your books. Send them review copies of appropriate books. For example, in the March 14, 1986 issue of *Publishers Weekly*, Marilyn Stasia requested review copies of mystery paperbacks for a feature article she was doing for the *New York Times*.

Authors — You can help your publisher by tracking down freelance writers, reporters, local news bureaus, and other media contacts that your publisher's publicity department has not yet discovered. You can be their minor league scout.

---

12. **Submit to a different department.** Again, sometimes one section of a newspaper or magazine will reject your news release where another will eagerly embrace it. It isn't always easy to tell which will like it. So, even though your news release was rejected by one department, it doesn't mean you cannot resubmit the news to another department.

For instance, if the What's Up This Week department of *Parade* magazine (which features forecasts of movies, records, and books) does not pay attention to your book, submit it to the Bright Ideas to Make Life Better department (which features new ideas on gardening, nutrition, health, parenting, and other how-to subjects).

13. **Write a letter to the editor.** Or, better yet, submit a guest editorial to the newspaper. Write something you care about. Write about the subject of your book.

Don't think that op-ed pages are worthless for publicity. They can be very effective. When Anthony Lewis praised *Under a Cruel Star: A Life in Prague 1941-1968* in the op-ed pages of the *New York Times*, the publisher had to go back to press for a second printing of 3000 copies.

> **Authors** — This tip is primarily for you. Who better to write an editorial about your subject than you? As the author of a book, you have the credentials. Use them.

14. **Offer something free.** Many magazines have special departments that feature notices about new products, free reports, free samples, informational brochures, and other things that people can write away for.

    • *USA Today* regularly features free offers in its Today's Tip Off on the front page of the Life Section. In October 1988, they featured a free booklet, *Acupressure for Your Beauty and Health*, from Kim's Publishing. When readers sent for the booklet, they also received promotional material on Kim's other books. The free offer was a perfect way for Kim's to develop a list of interested readers.

    • *Lady's Circle* magazine has a Things for Free department.

    • *Family Circle* magazine has a column, Circle This, which consists of three pages of short items about new and unusual products. Some publishers have sold as many as 20,000 books as a result of one mention in *Family Circle*.

    • *The Mother Earth News* features short items about craft, garden, and outdoor products in its Access Department. In one issue, they featured our *Directory of Book Printers*.

    • *Freebies*, a bimonthly newsletter that publishes all sorts of free offers, is especially interested in items for kids, crafts, home and garden, and teachers. Send your items or news releases to *Freebies*, 407 State Street, Santa Barbara, CA 93101; (805) 962-9135.

    When you make a free offer, make it something useful. And be sure it is related to one of your books (or an entire line of books). Then, when readers write in for your free offer, send them your report or brochure plus your catalog or advertisement for a related book. To cut your costs, ask them to send a self-addressed stamped envelope with their request.

15. **Join a press association.** Freelance writers and journalists often join press associations to mingle and network with other journalists. There are press associations for many interest groups, including a Catholic Press Association and a Computer Press Association.

    If you write or publish computer books, you should belong to the Computer Press Association. Why? Here are a few reasons:

    • Find professional writers for new titles.

    • Make connections with magazine and newspaper editors, radio and TV journalists, and freelance writers.

    • Be the first to learn about editorial changes (most press associations notify members of such changes before others know).

Authors – If you write regularly in one subject area, you should look into joining the press association that covers that subject. It will give you an opportunity to meet and network with other writers and editors. Then, when you submit articles to these editors, you should get a better reception.

---

16. **Send info to News Ahead-Lines.** News Ahead-Lines is a bimonthly news futures service that provides story leads to newspapers and other media (they charge the media $50.00 per month for this service, so you know the media value it). Among the upcoming events, they list birth dates, anniversaries, special weeks and days, awards, deadlines, association meetings and conventions, and historical tie-ins.

While no book publication dates were listed in the sample I've seen, they might list one if it was particularly newsworthy. The primary focus of these listings is political, with some business, education, sports, science, medical, and other listings.

To have your upcoming events (especially anniversaries and awards) listed in this publication, write to News Ahead-Lines, Congressional Quarterly, 1414 22nd Street N.W., Washington, DC 20037-9665; (303) 887-8528.

17. **Use PMA's Books for Review newsletter.** Publishers Marketing Association does a co-op mailing to 3,700 book reviewers four times a year. The mailing consists of a 4-page brochure listing about 40 books (with cover photo, short description, subject, and pricing. Those who receive the mailing are provided a postcard which they can return to request review copies of any titles in the mailing. For more information, write to PMA, 2401 Pacific Coast Highway #206, Hermosa Beach, CA 90254; (213) 372-2732.

Those publishers who have used this service average about 20 or more requests for review, with about half that number resulting in reviews. Their cost for participating in this program? $135.00.

18. **Distribute news releases via a PR service.** If you want to get the news out fast nationally, you might try the following service (or one like it):

PR Newswire, 150 East 58th Street, New York, NY 10155; (212) 832-9410; (800) 832-5522; Fax: (212) 832-9406.

They distribute news releases electronically to 1,000 newsrooms across the country (both newspapers and broadcast).

19. **Fax it.** Most media now have fax machines and are equipped to receive new releases via fax. If you have a machine and access to the media fax numbers, you might try sending some releases via fax. If you don't have a fax machine, you might want to try one of the new fax services that have started up.

The PR Flash No-Frills Data Files have recently been updated to include fax numbers for all media which are open to receiving news releases via fax. The data files contain over 500 media fax numbers. Available for $149.95 from Ad-Lib Publications, P. O. Box 1102, Fairfield, IA 52556-3226; (800) 669-0773; Fax: (515) 472-3186.

20. **Teleconference.** If you are holding a press conference or major media event, you might want to arrange a teleconference hook up with distant media.

Several years ago, Dow Jones-Irwin conducted a workshop based on its new book, *Service America*, that was beamed via satellite to 150 universities and corporate sites across the country. As a result of that initial push in publicity, the book sold 55,000 copies in the first year.

21. **Put your notices on computer bulletin boards.** If you publish books that would be of interest to computer users, you might want to leave an electronic copy of your news release or other promotional material on some of the computer bulletin boards run by CompuServe, the Source, Dialog, or various user groups.

You might offer specials to those who order because they read the notice on their bulletin board. You might even excerpt part of the book just to entice users to want more—and, therefore, buy the book. Note that many members of the computer media often read these bulletin boards as well.

22. **Volunteer to be an expert.** Let the media know that your authors are available as experts. Send them an author bio and a background news release about the author's latest book. Later, follow up with copies of other articles that feature the author (attach a For Your Information note to any follow-up copies). The key point is to keep your author's name continually in front of the media contact.

Don't expect an immediate response. You won't always get one. Sooner or later, though, if you have matched your author's expertise to the media's needs, some will contact you to speak to your author.

- Every week *USA Today* features a special department, Ask Money, where they invite readers to ask questions which are, in turn, answered by leading experts around the country. Do you have any authors who are qualified to answer such questions? If so, let *USA Today* know.

- *USA Today* uses experts often. In a recent article describing a survey they conducted on sex, they interviewed about ten authors, including Judith Sills, Maggie Scarf, Maxine Rock, Paul Pearsall, and David Viscott.

- The *Minneapolis Star Tribune* has a regular column called Fixit, which answers readers' questions about consumer problems, from insurance to real estate. Sometimes they turn to authors to answer their readers' questions.

- *Playboy* magazine mailed out packs of Rolodex file cards to important media contacts. Each card in the pack was categorized by subject of expertise at the top and included the name of a *Playboy* editor who could serve as an expert. Addresses and phone numbers were also listed. Experts were provided in the areas of art, sports, music, movies, photography, books, fashion, travel, and sex. Perhaps, you could send out a pack of Rolodex file cards featuring your authors as experts. The program has worked for *Playboy*.

Authors — You don't have to wait for your publisher to volunteer you as an expert. You can do it yourself. Just keep your name before the editors of those newspapers or magazines where you would like to be featured as an authority.

---

23. **Establish yourself as a prime source.** Here's an idea from State Farm Insurance. They prepared a short report, *A Reference Notebook of Insurance Sources*, which listed over 200 organizations that could provide further information on insurance topics (the top insurance companies, trade associations, arson associations, and research groups). They then placed ads in the major journalism publications (*Editor & Publisher, Quill, Columbia Journalism Review,* and *Washington Journalism Review*) inviting the media to send for a free copy of the report. Of course, State Farm was listed prominently as a source in the report. But, more important, the fact that they were able to compile such a report clearly suggests that they are the best source for information on insurance issues.

If you publish a series of books on the same subject, you can have a member of your staff prepare a similar directory for that subject area. Or you can ask your authors to do it for their subject areas. And then send the report out to important media contacts.

9:13 The Importance of Author Interviews

Author interviews are useful in propelling a book to bestseller status. Few radio and television shows actually review books, but many of them do interview authors. And despite what you might think, radio and television shows are not incompatible with either selling or reading books. Research shows that book sales are helped by television exposure (via talk shows and interviews), and that people who watch a lot of TV also read a lot of books. Indeed, it might be fair to say that key television shows sell more books than reviews in such major print media as the *New York Times Book Review*.

Interviews, of course, can appear in print as well. Both print and audio/video interviews have certain advantages over book reviews. Here are a few:

1. They tend to be more personal and intimate. They give the reader a better feeling for the author's intent in writing the book as well as the author's qualifications.
2. More people watch radio and TV talk shows than read book review sections of newspapers.
3. The author has greater control over what will be covered in the interview; hence, the author can be sure to include more promotional comments about the book.
4. Most interviews are longer than reviews and, in general, the greater the length, the greater the impact.

9:14 Tips on Obtaining Interviews

The basic guideline for obtaining interviews is the same as obtaining any publicity. You must be persistent, and you must follow through. Of course, you'll have an easier time arranging interviews if your authors are interesting and entertaining speakers and if your books appeal to the personal interests of a wide audience.

Here are a few tips on how to arrange interviews in the various media:

• Know your media. Don't try to get interviews on a show or in a newspaper section where your book doesn't fit.
• Demonstrate to editors or producers that your author will be a good interview subject and that the book will interest and benefit their audience.
• Prepare a professional press kit which includes a copy of the book, a biography of the author, a news release or brochure describing the book, a list of questions that will produce a good interview, and a list of previous author interviews (where and when), including copies of any print interviews.
• The list of questions is crucial. Make sure the questions are interesting, concise, entertaining and, above all, cover the important points you want to make during an interview. Many interviewers will not have time to read the book, so the only thing they have to go by is the information you provide. One question almost all interviewers ask: "How did you come to write this book?"
• Telephone the stations or newspapers and make contact with someone who can make decisions on interview subjects. Then mail your press kit to them. A week or two later, follow up with another phone call to your contact. At this time, ask if he or she is interested in setting up an interview or requires any further information about the author.

- Don't give up. If the first person you contact is not interested in an interview, try someone else at the same media. While arranging interviews for Peter McWilliams, author of the *Personal Computer in Business Book*, Ron Gold was rudely turned down by the business editor of a major Southern newspaper. But he didn't give up. His next call was to the computer editor at the same paper. As it happened, that editor had been wondering how to get in touch with McWilliams; hence, he was only too glad to set up an interview.

- When you send out review copies, indicate those parts of the book which would be most appropriate for the interviewer to read. You might want to attach Post-It™ notes to the relevant sections of the book and highlight the liveliest passages.

- For some easy-to-use forms to help you research the media, set up interviews, and book author tours, see *Book Marketing Made Easier* or my new book, *How to Make the News* (coming in Spring, 1991).

> **Authors** — Prepare a list of interview questions and give these to your editor (who should hand them on to the PR department). Also, you should highlight those sections of your book which would be of most interest to interviewers. Work with your publisher to refine the questions and the sections of the book to be highlighted.

9:15 The Value of Print Interviews

Don't neglect press interviews when you are arranging author tours and interviews. Press interviews have several advantages over radio and TV interviews:

1. They are more concrete.
2. They tend to linger longer in the minds of readers.
3. Readers can read them at their leisure.
4. You can collect and copy press clippings more easily and send them to key contacts.
5. Print interviews are more likely to be syndicated, which can result in features being published in as many as 200 other newspapers.
6. Print interviews are more likely to inspire other feature stories.

William Zimmerman, self-publisher of *How to Tape Instant Biographies*, is also a firm believer in the power of the press. He's had feature spreads in *Business Week*, the *Washington Post*, and the *New York Times*. The *Times* feature story brought in over 2,000 inquiries for his book.

9:16 Radio Interviews Via Telephone

Radio interviews are an easy and effective way to promote your authors and books. In many cases, radio stations will handle interviews with the author over the phone. It is possible to organize a "national author tour" without your author ever leaving his or her home. Such telephone interviews are becoming more and more commonplace.

Radio stations like the idea because it means that any author, no matter how famous or how busy, can be accessible to them even if they broadcast from Missoula, Montana. Besides, authors usually make superb guests; they are articulate, intelligent, know a lot about their special areas of interest, and are usually better prepared than many celebrities to answer impromptu questions.

Authors, of course, love the idea because they do not have to bear the long hours of travel (though it may be difficult sometimes to have a real conversation with a disembodied voice). Publishers love the idea even more because such interviews are far less expensive than full author tours. Plus they are easier to arrange. There need not be any time conflicts or tight schedules to fit.

For those publishers with limited funds, here are a few ways to get the name of your books and authors in front of the people who schedule such interviews:

- You can pay for a listing or display ad in the *Yearbook of Experts, Authorities, & Spokespersons*, which lists individuals and organizations willing to speak on just about any topic. This yearbook is distributed free to more than 5,000 media, including 1,526 radio producers Write for their 16-page information kit. **Broadcast Interview Source,** Mitchell Davis, Editor, 2233 Wisconsin Avenue N.W., Suite 540, Washington, DC 20007-4104; (202) 333-4904; Fax: (202) 342-5411.

- You can pay to be listed in one of the following interview services:

  Newsmaker Interviews, 8217 Beverly Boulevard, Los Angeles, CA 90048; (213) 655-2793; Fax: (213) 275-2602. This subscription-based newsletter features free bios on select authors and experts.

  Radio Interviews Mailing, Para Publishing, P. O. Box 4232, Santa Barbara, CA 93140-4232; (805) 968-7277. This twice-yearly co-op mailing is sent to 800 of the top radio and TV stations.

  Radio-TV Interview Report, Bradley Communications, 135 E. Plumstead Avenue, P. O. Box 1206, Lansdowne, PA 19050; (215) 259-1070; Fax: (215) 284-3704. This bimonthly newsletter is sent to 4,700 radio and TV producers. A 175-word listing costs $85.00.

  Spotlight, P. O. Box 51103, Seattle, WA 98113; (206) 363-2145. This quarterly co-op brochure advertises authors available for interviews. Three issues are sent to 400 TV and radio shows; a fall issue is sent to 5,000 radio stations.

- Buy the special report, *Radio Phone Interview Shows: How to Do an Author Interview Tour from Home*, and control the mailing yourself. This report features full information about 890 radio shows that do phone interviews (name of show, station, address, phone number, host, subject interests, and more). The report also includes 22 pages of addresses formated to copy onto labels with any photocopy machine. This report is only $30.00. To order, call toll-free (800) 669-0773 or write to Ad-Lib Publications, P. O. Box 1102, Fairfield, IA 52556-1102.

- Pay to have a news service send your story out by satellite feed. Here are a few such services that feed radio stations:

  News/Radio Network, 9431 W. Beloit Road, Milwaukee, WI 53227; (414) 321-6210.

  Audio/TV Features, 149 Madison Avenue #804, New York, NY 10016; (212) 889-1327.

- Send a review copy and author information to a radio news service, such as the following:

  Copley Radio Network, 350 Camino de la Reina, P. O. Box 190, San Diego, CA 92112; (619) 293-1818; (800) 445-4555. They send a twice-weekly show prep service called *Wireless Flash* to many radio stations. This service offers lifestyle news, trivia, and entertainment features.

  Jericho News Service, 924 Broadway, New York, NY 10010; 212-260-3744. 50% of their stories feature books and authors. Their stories go to 1,100 subscribing radio stations.

- Send an audiotape interview of the author or someone reading the book to radio stations. When William Morrow published John Irving's novel, *A Prayer for Owen Meany*, they sent a boxed cassette reading by the author to the book trade and major media.

9:17 How to Do TV Talk Shows

One appearance on a major network or syndicated TV talk show such as *Good Morning America* or the *Phil Donahue Show* can sell thousands of books. As a Waldenbooks manager once noted, "Give me a *Phil Donahue Show*, and I'll sell you a million books."

Even local TV talk shows can produce dramatic sales. Again, don't ignore TV shows just because you think TV viewers do not read. As noted above, that is not the case. TV viewers do read, and they do respond to reviews and interviews they see on TV.

- Bill Sand's book about his life in prison, *My Shadow Ran Fast*, did not sell well when first published. However, during an appearance on the *Tonight Show*, he so captivated the audience that he was invited back for a second show. Those two appearances alone were enough to put the book on the *New York Times* bestseller list.

- Louise Hay's appearances on *Oprah Winfrey* and *Donahue* catapulted her book, *You Can Heal Your Life*, onto the bestseller lists. Even before the book hit the bestseller lists, it had sold over half a million copies.
- Within two weeks of his appearance on *The Tonight Show*, James Randi's *Flim-Flam* sold 7,000 copies.
- After Paula Begoun appeared on *The Oprah Winfrey Show*, her self-published book, *Blue Eyeshadow Should Be Illegal*, sold 40,000 copies.

9:18 How to Arrange TV Talk Shows

Here are a few more tips on how to arrange TV appearances for your authors (these tips supplement the general suggestions for obtaining interviews outlined in previous sections):

- Allow four to eight weeks lead time for TV talk shows. That means you must begin contacting the show producers at least four weeks ahead of the date your author will be available.
- When you call, first talk to the receptionist at the station to confirm the name of your contact. In this business people change jobs often so even if you use the most up-to-date directory, chances are that some of your major contacts will have moved on.
- Once you've confirmed the name of the booking agent (producer, talent coordinator, or whatever their title might be), have the receptionist transfer your call to that person. At this time you simply want to introduce the subject of your book and/or the credentials of your author and to encourage the person to watch for more information in the mail.

  This pre-call can save you time and money because often the person will either tell you that the show does not do such interviews or will refer you to someone else at the station who would be more likely to be interested in your particular author or subject.
- Once you've alerted the person that you will be sending him or her something in the mail, mail your press kit that same day by first class mail or UPS. You should not send it by express mail unless you're under a tight deadline. Express mail is expensive and a bit ostentatious. Other gimmicky deliveries are also rarely appropriate.
- Within five days of the day you expect the person to receive your press kit, follow up with a phone call. Don't wait for anyone to call you. They're not about to. In this follow-up call, you must make your best pitch. The pitch should be well-rehearsed and short (no more than 30 seconds). If you cannot get your pitch down to three or four sentences, then you are not likely to get anyone's attention. Remember that the attention span of a person while watching TV is very short, so your

description of why anyone would be interested in what your author has to say must be equally short. Don't become pushy; such tactics rarely work. If someone says no, go on to call the next person on your list. If the person indicates they will think about it, suggest that you'll call them back again in a few days. Then do so.

- When you do receive a booking, send a letter out to the person right away thanking him or her for the booking and confirming the exact time and place. This confirmation letter will prevent any later misunderstandings or mishaps.

- The real secret, of course, in obtaining interviews is to keep on calling. If the first person rejects your pitch, call the second; if the second also rejects your pitch, call the third. Continue calling until you get a booking. If your author or the subject of the book is at all interesting, you should not have trouble obtaining a good number of interviews.

- It's best to start your new authors out with appearances on local shows so they can get more experience dealing with the hectic environment of a TV studio during the taping of a show.

- You might find it easier to book the national network shows by working through your local network affiliate. If your author makes a good impression on their talk show, then the local affiliate might be willing to help you book the author on a national show.

- When sending out your press kit to major local and national shows, you might want to include a videotape of your author in action. This videotape could be taken from a previous interview where the author performed well, or it could be a demo tape of the author during a simulated interview taped especially for the press kit. In either case, the tape should give program directors a great opportunity to see how well your author comes over on TV.

- Here are two things you should bring to a TV interview:
  1) any visual aids or props that will help to make the interview more interesting (for example, fire extinguishers or alarms for a book on fire safety), and
  2) an index card with the author's name typed on one line and the title of the book on another (just in case the show's production crew needs this information so they can flash the information on the screen while the author is talking).

- When booking shows, don't overlook the local cable TV stations and cable networks. Also, when sending out review copies, send them to anyone who might be interested in the book (not just the show hosts).

  When Warner Books published Stephen Davis's story of the rock group Led Zeppelin, *Hammer of the Gods*, not only did *Rolling Stone* magazine serialize the book, but MTV got wind of the book and began plugging the book free of charge. As a result, this hardcover book sold over 70,000 copies.

9:19 More Ways to Obtain TV Coverage

Author interviews are not the only way to get coverage on television. Here are a few more options:

• Send information on your books to various television syndicates, such as the Parenting Network, which used to produce three weekly news features which they sent to 25 top stations around the country.

• Search out the new satellite networks that are available to dish owners. Jane Hoffman's *The Original Backyard Scientist* was featured on a brand new series, *Report Card for Home Schoolers*, which aired on Station Three of the Angel Broadcasting Network.

• Send out video news releases. If you choose this option, have it produced by professionals. Make sure it is identified as a PR release, is one to four minutes in length, and features more than a stand-up news reporter or two talking heads.

To support a national tour by Dr. Bernard Lown for the book *Peace: A Dream Unfolding*, Simon & Schuster sent out four-minute *Peace* videos to stations across the country.

• Set up an author tour via satellite. By producing an interview locally and feeding it to stations across the country via satellite, your author can do a 20-city television tour in less than four hours. One company that specializes in producing such author tours is **On the Scene Productions**, 5900 Wilshire Boulevard, Los Angeles, CA 90036; (213) 930-1030.

• Send out video news releases (VNR) via satellite. There are many new companies which can provide this service. Here are a few of them:

J-Nex Satellite News Services, 5455 Wilshire Boulevard #2004, Los Angeles, CA 90036; (213) 934-4356.

Medialink, 708 Third Avenue, 23 Floor, New York, NY 10017; (212) 682-8300. This company distributes but does not produce VNRs.

Orbis Productions, 3322 N. Lakewood Avenue, Chicago, IL 60657; (312) 883-9584.

Pro Video News Service, 8075 W. Third #504, Los Angeles, CA 90048; (213) 857-0777; Fax: (213) 939-9475.

Visnews International, 630 Fifth Avenue, New York, NY 10111; (212) 698-4500.

Worldwide Television News Corporation, 1995 Broadway, 9th Floor, New York, NY 10023; (212) 362-4440.

The cost of having one of the above companies produce, distribute, and monitor a video news release ranges from $8,000 to $20,000. Distribution only costs from $2,500 to $8,000, depending on coverage.

> **Authors** — Visit your local TV stations yourself. Since you are a celebrity, they should be happy to interview you, if even for a short two-minute interview. Get experience doing local shows before attempting to hit the national shows.

9:20 Organizing Effective Author Tours

Author tours can be expensive, a hassle to put together, and very wearing on the author, but for some books they can make a great difference for sales. In general, author tours are not productive unless the author is a celebrity or the subject of the book has a wide appeal or is somehow connected to a current issue of interest to many people.

Author tours are not easy to arrange. Not only do you have the additional expense of long-distance phone calls, but you must also fit interviews into a tighter schedule since you cannot afford to pay for the author to stay more than a day or two in any one city. Nevertheless, for certain authors and books you will want to arrange such tours.

My books, *Book Marketing Made Easier* and *How to Make the News*, both include a number of forms and procedures to help you organize such author tours with a minimum amount of effort. Here are a few additional suggestions to make the tour more effective:

* Consider doing several short tours rather than one long one. Not only would this be easier on your author, but it could also save you money (especially if you can organize the mini-tours around your author's normal business or vacation travel).

* Arrange for a local contact in each city, someone who can pick the author up at the airport and take care of any other driving during the author's stay in the city. This local contact could be one of your sales representatives, a friend or relative (yours or the author's), or a professional escort service.

* When booking interviews, don't forget other possible appearances that could boost sales for the author's book. Check to see if any bookstores would be willing to host an autograph session. Try to schedule a speaking engagement for the author with a local club, association, or business. Have the author visit any key wholesalers, distributors, or other sales outlets. How about any local celebrations or other events?

* Give a copy of Peggy Glenn's book, *Publicity for Books and Authors*, to each of your authors you send on tour. In this book, Peggy describes how to prepare for interviews, how to dress for travel, what to pack and, in general, how to survive the wear and tear of an author tour. The list of what to pack is by itself worth the price of the entire book.

- Call the regional bureaus of Associated Press and United Press International and ask that your author's appearances be listed in their Day Book. The Day Book is a calendar of events which is checked every day by media sources which subscribe to the AP or UPI services. This could, again, result in additional interviews or other coverage.

9:21 Distribution Is Everything

Make sure you have distribution before arranging an extensive author tour or major media interviews. If there are not enough books in the stores to cover the anticipated demand, the entire effort can be wasted. This means, at the very minimum, that you should give advance notice to the booksellers in each city the author will be touring. Even better, you should have your sales representatives or distributors make sales calls just prior to your author's appearances.

Here are a few other things you can do:

- Pay for a short listing of your author's tour in the weekly *ABA Newswire* newsletter published by the American Booksellers Association. For more information and advertising rates, write or call the **American Booksellers Association**, 137 West 25th Street, New York, NY 10001; (212) 463-8450; (800) 637-0037; Fax: (212) 463-9353.

- Arrange for distribution yourself. When Beverly Nye organized her own author tour, as she arrived in each city she checked the yellow pages for retail bookstores. She called each store to let them know that she would be doing interviews and to confirm how many of her book they had in stock. She then drove around to each store peddling her books and confirming that each store would have sufficient stock to cover the demand.

- Work with one of the major book chains to ensure that your books are carried in each city your authors will be visiting. Then have your authors mention that the books are definitely available at that chain if the viewer cannot find them elsewhere.

Waldenbooks worked with Fairfield Press to ensure that the Press's reissue of *The TM Book* was in stock when TV shows promoting the Transcendental Meditation program were aired in different cities.

- If all else fails (and you don't have your own toll-free order line), have your author give out the phone number for one of the following toll-free book sources. Before doing so, however, notify the company far enough in advance so they can have copies of the book in stock when the show airs. Most of these companies will be happy to work with you to ensure that your books are available.

Book Call, 59 Elm Street, New Canaan, CT 06850; (203) 966-5470; (800) 255-2665.

Discount Booksource, 1933 Whitfield Loop, Sarasota FL 34243; (813) 758-8094; (800) 833-0720; Fax: (813) 753-9396.

9:22 How to Make Waves by Making News

Besides being featured in reviews and interviews, your authors and books can also be publicized via regular news or feature stories. Indeed, some of the best publicity for books and authors comes outside the normal review/interview channels. Don't overlook any chance for publicity. Make news. Find a news hook. Connect your books or authors with news that's already happening or about to happen.

Here's just a short list of ways you can hitchhike publicity for your books with other news (in no particular order):

• **Anniversaries**—Schedule the publication of your book to coincide with an appropriate anniversary. Here are just a few anniversaries that have been used as tie-ins by publishers:

College—Globe Pequot Press published *The Illustrated Harvard* to coincide with that university's 350th anniversary.

Current events—Congdon & Weed's published the book *One American Must Die* to commemorate the anniversary of the terrorist hijacking of a TWA jetliner.

Deaths—Grove Press published Warren Beath's *The Death of James Dean* on the anniversary of Dean's death.

Sports—Donald I. Fine set the publication date of Maury Allen's *Roger Maris: A Man for All Seasons* to coincide with Maris's 25th anniversary of breaking Babe Ruth's homer record.

State—Putnam's *Make Way for Sam Houston* tied in with the Texas Sesquicentennial celebration.

TV show—the CBS/Library of Congress "Read More About It" book promotion project featured a number of books about soap operas on the 30th anniversary broadcast of *As the World Turns*.

• **Book anniversaries**—Celebrate the anniversaries of book classics by republishing the classics or by publishing new related titles.

To celebrate the 50th anniversary of the publication of Margaret Mitchell's *Gone with the Wind*, Macmillan published a golden anniversary facsimile of the original edition. Meanwhile, Outlet Books excerpted part of Ronald Haver's *David O. Selznick's Hollywood* for release as *David O. Selznick's Gone with the Wind*. Several other book publishers also brought related titles.

Dutton celebrated the 60th anniversary of the publication of A. A. Milne's *Winnie-the-Pooh* by publishing *The Winnie-the-Pooh Journal*.

- **Authors' Birthdays** – You can also celebrate authors' birthdays by publishing (or re-releasing) their books. For example, July offers the following birthdays: George Sand (1st), Hermann Hesse (2nd), Franz Kafka (3rd), Nathaniel Hawthorne (4th), Beatrix Potter (6th), Robert Heinlein (7th), Jean Kerr and Marcel Proust (10th), E. B. White (11th), Henry David Thoreau and Pablo Neruda (12th), Isaac Bashevis Singer and Irving Stone (14th), Erle Stanley Gardner (17th), William Thackeray and Yevgeny Yevtushenko (18th), Ernest Hemingway and John Gardner (21st), Stephen Vincent Benet and Amy Vanderbilt (22nd), Raymond Chandler (23rd), Alexandre Dumas, pere and John D. MacDonald (24th), Paul Gallico and Carl Jung (26th), Alexandre Dumas, fils (27th), Gerard Manley Hopkins (28th), Alexis de Tocqueville (29th), and Emily Bronte (30th), among many others.

- **TV series** – Publicize books that are tied in to continuing TV series such as the various soap operas or to miniseries such as *Roots* or *Shogun*. Genealogy books, for example, have always sold better after showings of *Roots*.

  The miniseries, *Dreams West*, was part of the CBS/Library of Congress "Read More About It" book promotion project. The project, in connection with this miniseries, promoted books about America's westward expansion.

  After the six-part PBS series, *Joseph Campbell and the Power of Myth*, appeared, the Princeton University Press saw its 39-year-old Campbell title, *Hero with a Thousand Faces*, hit the bestseller lists. Doubleday sold over 250,000 copies of the companion book to the series.

  As a result of the airing of Shirley MacLaine's miniseries, *Out on a Limb*, the book by the same title once again hit the bestseller lists. Indeed, all four of MacLaine's previous books went right back onto the bestseller lists. One of the books featured in this miniseries (the book fell on MacLaine's head, thereby starting her on her quest) was *A Dweller on Two Planets*; within a week Harper & Row received 2,000 orders for the book. Meanwhile, sales of all new age and metaphysical books jumped 95% at B. Dalton stores.

  After the airing of *World without Walls* (a documentary about aviatrix Beryl Markham) on the local PBS station, North Point Press sold 20,000 copies of Markham's book, *West with the Night*, within two weeks – in the Bay area alone! Once the show aired nationally, the book hit all the major bestseller lists and sold over 375,000 copies.

- **Broadway shows** – While broadway shows don't have the national impact of television series, they can still be used as promotional tie-ins.

  Marion Boyars set the publication date of Charles Marowitz's *Potboilers: Three Black Comedies* to coincide with the October opening of of the Broadway show, *Sherlock's Last Case*, starring Frank Langella.

- **Local interests** – Make special note of any local angles when sending out press releases or review copies. For example, if the author has lived or still lives in the region, note that fact (perhaps by placing a label on the cover of the book announcing that the author is a local resident).

- **Retailing promotional tie-ins** – Whenever you can associate your book with a retail promotion, whether local or national, do so. Fredrick Warne published several Beatrix Potter books to tie in with "The World of Beatrix Potter" department store display which toured eleven major cities.

- **Holidays** – Many books are already published to coincide with the major holidays, such as Christmas, Hanukkah, Easter, Thanksgiving, Valentines, and others.

  Dolphin scheduled the publication date of Bill Cosby's book *Fatherhood* for Father's Day, 1986.

  The publication date for the book, *How to Make Love All the Time*, by sex therapist Barbara De Angelis was set for Valentine's Day.

  Sierra Club Books launched *Peace: A Dream Unfolding* by Patrick Crean and Penney Kome on November 11th, Veterans Day.

- **Special months** – Time your book's publication date with a month that suits your book's subject. September is back to school month; June is dairy month; May is Barbecue Month; April is school media month.

  Learning Publications found out the hard way. They sent out press releases in June for their book called *Joyful Learning – Learning Games for Children Ages 4 to 12*, but they did not receive any reviews for the book until September because that is the time when people's interest again returns to educational issues.

- **Special weeks** – Try to arrange your book's publication date or big promotions to fall within weeks that tie in with the subject of the book. April has Library Week and Secretary's Week; October has Children's Book Week and Fire Safety Week; June has Gay Pride Week; July has Special Recreation Week for the Disabled; and August has Psychic Week, National Smile Week, and National Scuba Diving Week. For any subject, there's a week that fits.

  Peggy Glenn arranged for major publicity during Secretary's Week for her book on *How to Start and Run a Successful Home Typing Business*. As a result, the book received feature stories in a number of major newspapers and magazines.

  You can sponsor your own week. Every year, for instance, Liberty Publishing Company sponsors Muffin Mania Week during the first week of February. In 1988, *USA Today*, among other media, published a notice about the week. As a result of this annual publicity, Liberty has received many inquiries from individuals and libraries which, in turn, has resulted in many sales for their book, *Muffin Mania*.

- **Special days or celebrations** – As there are weeks and months for almost everything, there are also special days and/or celebrations as well. For example, besides Mother's Day, May also has Biographers Day, Native American Day, and Armed Forces Day.

  Look in *Chase's Annual Events* (available at your local library) to discover other special days, weeks, and months that might fit in well with your books.

  For its new book *Tall Ships of the World*, Globe Pequot Press planned a promotional tie-in with the Fourth of July Tall Ships Parade in New York City.

  Grove Press scheduled the beginning of a nationwide author's tour to coincide with World Hunger Day, October 16th, for *World Hunger: Twelve Myths*, by Frances Moore Lappe and Joseph Collins.

- **Current events** – Scan the daily newspapers for any current news that you might use to further publicize your books. Be on the lookout for the offbeat as well as the headline news.

  For example, the author of a book on how to stop snoring noticed a short item about a wife filing for a divorce because she could no longer stand her husband's loud snoring. The author quickly sent off a copy of his book to the judge hearing the case. The judge, in turn, announced in court that he felt the book could save the couple's marriage. Of course, that statement made the local news and was later picked up by the wire services. Soon there were feature articles all over the country, every one of the stories spreading the word about the book. As a result, the book went into four printings.

Authors – Here is a good reason for you to read your daily newspaper or weekly news magazine. Your publisher cannot possibly notice or follow up on all the potential tie-ins to current events. You are in a far better position to do so. Hence, when you notice a potential tie-in, either let your publisher know or follow up on the item yourself.

- **Natural events** – Associate your book with a natural event, anything from eruptions like Mt. St. Helens to regular events such as the coming of Halley's Comet. The predictable events obviously work best because you can plan your publishing calendar around the events.

  For example, a number of publishers brought out books to coincide with the return of Halley's Comet, including Hunter House's *Tales of the Comet* and Polestar-Nexus's *Mr. Halley and His Comet* (which was also the premier book in a new series of children's books about men and women of science).

- **Conferences and conventions** – Set your publication date to coincide with an important conference or convention.

  Ad-Lib Publications scheduled the publication date of *Book Marketing Made Easier* for the Saturday of the 1986 American Booksellers Convention in New Orleans.

  Similarly, Princeton University Press scheduled their main publicity campaign for the book, *Makers of Modern Strategy from Machiavelli to the Nuclear Age*, to coincide with a major conference on "War in History and War Today."

  The University of North Carolina Press publicized the book, *North Carolina Quilts*, to tie in with a quilt exhibit at the North Carolina Museum of History.

- **Charity events** – Contribute your books as prizes for a charity event, anything from the semiannual public television fundraisers to special campaigns such as the recent Statue of Liberty renovation.

  For an auction to benefit the Mercantile Library in New York City, Isaac Asimov offered to include the name and occupation of the highest bidder in his next short story.

  B. Dalton gave $3,000,000 to fund a four-year program to improve literacy. This program has involved over 16,000 volunteers in over one hundred cities.

  Barron's donated a portion of its profits from the children's book, *Pickles*, to North American Riding for the Handicapped Association.

- **Local book fairs and other festivals** – Tie-in the publication of your book with a local book fair or ethnic festival.

  For example, if your book is aimed at an Hispanic audience, one of your best promotions would be to give away sample chapters of your book to people attending a festival celebrating one of their holidays such as the Cinco de Mayo.

  Redbird Productions promoted their book on growing up in a Scandinavian community, *Cream and Bread*, at any festival or event where people of Scandinavian descent might attend. As a result, in less than two years they sold over 27,000 copies of their self-published book.

Authors — Be on the lookout for any of the above promotional tie-ins for your book. Indeed, if you know of any such promotional tie-ins when you are submitting your manuscript or book proposal to publishers, tell them about the tie-in right away. Such tie-ins make the book more attractive. As a result, you are far more likely to interest publishers in your book.

9:23 37 Other Publicity Ideas

Here is a checklist of 37 additional ways to obtain more promotional exposure for your books and authors:

• Send out announcements of any major author appearances (at local bookstores, national conferences, or other events).

• Announce any major author signings, subsidiary rights sales, premium sales, reprintings, new editions, or other newsworthy sales news. Send this information to the major book trade publications.

• Send out unusual news releases. Ballantine, as part of its promotion for Robert Shea's *All Things Are Lights*, sent out postcard releases featuring the cover of the book. They also sent out custom-made candles tied into the book's title.

• Janet Martin and Allen Todnem of Redbird Productions developed a funny skit to help promote their book, *Cream and Bread*, on local radio shows.

• They also developed a slide show based on the book to present at meetings of Scandinavian-related organizations.

• Simon & Schuster produced a 90-minute cassette of one-minute tax tips to help promote its perennial bestseller *J. K. Lasser's Your Income Tax 1986*. They sent this tape to radio stations in thirty major cities with a request that one tip be featured each day for three months. As an added incentive, they also sent each station 90 copies of the book to be given away as prizes over the three-month period.

• To promote their *The Book of Inventions*, World Almanac produced a one-minute videotape, *History of Inventions in 60 Seconds*, which they sent to television stations nationwide.

• World Almanac also sponsored a contest for the best invention by a reader of the book. As a prize, the winner of the contest was featured in a later edition of the book.

• Don't forget your own local newspapers. They are sure to be interested in any local company which is expanding or offering new products. Let them know of your company's new books, big sales, any expansion plans, new personnel, and other items that might interest local readers.

Ad-Lib Publications has had a number of such stories in our local press—and we've always gotten orders for our books as a result. In a town of 10,000 people you'd think everyone would already know about us, but that isn't the case. Think of the possibilities if you're located in a city of 100,000 or more.

• Send releases to appropriate college newspapers, in-house publications, association newsletters, alumni newsletters, and other off-the-beaten-track publications.

- Try alternate news hooks. Learning Publications originally publicized their book *Joyful Learning* as a fun way to learn. Nothing new there. But when they began publicizing the book as a way to help underachievers, the media jumped on the story. Now the book filled a definite need.

- Create a splash with your publication parties. Try something unusual. Hold the press party at a unique place—on a ferryboat, in a penthouse, at a haunted house, in the middle of Yankee Stadium, at an art gallery.

  When Crown published George Lang's *Cafe des Artistes Cookbook*, they invited the press to a black-tie dinner at a major restaurant. Of course, the press came (they rarely turn down a free lunch, much less an extravagant dinner).

  For *Eating Rich: Recipes from America's Wealthiest Families*, Peter Pauper Press held a publication party at Lyndhurst, the palatial home of Jay Gould.

  For the book, *The Best Companies for Women*, Simon & Schuster held a party at Time, Inc. headquarters (Time was one of 52 companies named in the book). They then invited representatives from all 52 companies to attend the party.

- Hold your author signings at unusual locations. Yankee Books featured a special author signing at the Mondavi winery in California when they published *Italian Provincial Cookery* by Bea Lazzaro and Lotte Mendelsohn.

- Write a letter to the editor responding to something having to do with one of your books. I've seen such letters in local and national newspapers, trade magazines, and other consumer magazines.

- Reply to television commentaries and editorials. When you hear the announcement that "this station welcomes opposing views from responsible spokespersons," why not respond—especially if the subject is related to your book and you can contribute a new insight or way of looking at the situation.

- Write to Mary Ellen with a helpful hint. Write to Sylvia Porter about some money matter. Write to Ann Landers with a comment or question. Write to any major columnist if you can somehow tie your question or comment in with your book.

- Have your say in the pages of *Publishers Weekly*. More than one author (and publisher) have written columns for the "My Say" section—a perfect way to gain exposure before the most important people in the book trade, all of whom read *Publishers Weekly* every week. Send your 850-word essay to Daisy Maryles, "My Say," Publishers Weekly, 249 West 17th Street, New York, NY 10011.

- Send an interesting anecdote regarding one of your books or authors to Leonore Fleischer, *PW* columnist for the "Talk of the Trade."

- Also send subsidiary rights sales information to Paul Nathan at *PW*.

- When writing or editing a book, look for ways to mention the name of the major trade journal or consumer magazine covering the subject of the book. Mention the periodical either as a resource or in some other complimentary way.

  Notice how many times I've mentioned *Publishers Weekly* in this book. It was not all by accident. I doubt, though, that *PW* would review this book just because I've mentioned them fifty times in this book, but when they do review the book they might look more favorably on it. Who knows? Look what happened to the group who recorded the song, "On the Cover of *Rolling Stone*." They made it, didn't they?

- Give something away free. When promoting our *Directory of Book Printers*, we offered a free report on how to save money in the production of your books. Many periodicals published this free offer where they might not have published the news release about the *Directory* itself.

- Give a copy of your book to a major news figure. Jeffrey Lant sent a copy of his *Unabashed Self-Promoter's Guide* to Rosalyn Carter when her first book came off the press. As a result, he received mention in several news articles.

  Proctor Jones, who self-published his own collection of photographs as *Classic Russian Idylls*, sent a copy to President Reagan. A few weeks later he received a phone call from Reagan thanking him for the book. Of course, he let the news media know about the President's reaction to his book.

- Run for president or some other high office. That always makes news. Back in the late 60's Pat Paulsen ran an off-the-wall campaign for the presidency. Meanwhile, he received lots of press coverage which helped boost his career as a comedian. Later he wrote a book about the campaign.

  Of course, if you win the election, all the better. By this time I think almost every major political figure has published at least one book — and many of their books are novels (which sold not so much for their literary value but because of the people who wrote them).

- Make a prediction. Forecast a trend. Predict anything related to your book that is likely to happen. Predictions can make news, especially if an expert makes the prediction (and authors are considered experts).

- Write a song. Carol Bayer Sager wrote a song to celebrate the publication of her first novel, *Extravagant Gestures*. Johnny Cash also wrote a song to accompany his book *Man in White*, the story of the apostle Paul's conversion.

- Use celebrity spokespeople. Michael York and Dudley Moore talked about the Capra Press book, *Voices of Survival in the Nuclear Age*, during their appearances on major TV talk shows.

- Promote your mistakes. When Cliffhanger Press found out that they made 15 typographical errors in the first edition of Arlene Shovald's mystery, *Kill the Competition*, they promoted a Find-the-Typo Contest. Anyone who could locate 15 or more errors in the book were given their choice of an error-free second edition or copies of three other titles from the company's list. This contest got a lot of ink—indeed, probably more than if the book had been error-free.

- Give an award. South-Western Publishing Company gives a Gold Book Award to any of their authors who have sold more than one million copies of a book. Thus far, they've given out 64 such awards. Each time, of course, they've received press coverage for both the company and for the book and author receiving the award.

- Set up a hotline number. To promote his copywriting services, Robert Bly set up the Advertising Hotline. When you dial (201) 599-2276, you will be treated to one of a number of 3-minute taped marketing seminars, such as *10 Ways to Stretch Your Advertising Budget* or *12 Questions to Ask before You Create Your Next Ad Campaign*. The messages are changed about once a week.

  You might want to set up your own hotline number to help promote your books or services. How about tax help? Or gardening tips? Or recipes? Or travel tips?

  The cost to you is minimal. You will need a dedicated phone line, an answering machine with a long continuous-loop tape, and someone to write and record the tips.

  To promote his piano books, Duane Shinn offers a 3-minute Dial-a-Piano lesson by calling (503) 664-6751. This lesson provides a free sample of the teaching style he uses in his books.

- While few media that publish bestseller lists will tell you what stores are polled for the list, you might still use the polling to promote your book. For instance, Bill Chleboun, compiler of the local bestseller list for the *San Francisco Chronicle*, has made the following offer to local publishers:

  After he polls bookstores every Tuesday, he will tell you which books are on the list. Also, if you call Bill and tell him that you are interested in finding out how one of your books is doing in the local stores, he will be happy to check on this for you as he makes his round of calls. What a great way to create awareness of an important title with major booksellers!

- Send out news releases on floppy disks. Dialogic Corporation sent out a floppy disk with the news release provided in 19 different IBM word processing formats. For editors accustomed to using a computer (such as those working for computer magazines), such a news release makes great sense. Not only do you make the editor's job easier, but you also attract their attention. If you do decide to try this, however, make sure you include a printed hard copy of the news release as well.

- Make your news release visual. For instance, for a Campbell geneal-ogy, you could include a photo of the author in kilts, or print a plaid border around the news release.

- Mount a campaign. Josh McDowell, author of *Why Wait? What You Need to Know about the Teen Sexuality Crisis*, has worked closely with the national Why Wait? campaign. In the first five months the book has sold over 90,000 copies.

- Name a street after one of your authors. City Lights celebrated its 35 years in publishing by encouraging the city of San Francisco to rename twelve streets after local authors and artists. Now when you visit San Francisco, you can walk down streets named after Ambrose Bierce, Richard Henry Dana, Dashiell Hammett, Jack Kerouac, Jack London, Frank Norris, William Saroyan, and Mark Twain.

- Send copies to opinion makers. When Warner Books published John Naisbitt's *Megatrends*, they sent copies of the book to the chief execu-tives at the 500 largest corporations in the country. As a result, they generated very effective word of mouth for the book.

- Encourage your authors to read their books for the blind. Blind people are not likely to buy a book anyway, but they will talk to their friends about books they've heard.

- Five promotions a day. That's all it takes. It need not require much time or money to gain public exposure for your books. Just make five promotional contacts every day, and your book will get noticed.

Authors — If you really want to help your publisher promote your book, take the last point to heart. Just make five con-tacts each day. Mail a letter. Send out a news release. Phone someone. Take an editor to lunch. It need not require much time — 15 to 20 minutes is enough — but it can make a world of difference on how well your book sells.

9:24 Publicity Generates More Publicity

When you are pursuing media exposure, remember these four essen-tial points:

1. 75 to 80% of all news is planted. That means, that most of the news you read in newspapers and magazines has come out of news releases sent to the media by businesses, associations, government offices, and other organizations or individuals with something interesting to say.

2. If you can provide real news for the media, they will be glad to feature your authors and books. That's why you should keep refining your news hooks until you find one that really meets a need. Don't send out a press release announcing any of your books until you can show that the book provides at least one benefit for potential readers—whether that benefit be entertainment, information, instruction, or enlightenment.

3. Publicity begets more publicity. Once you get the ball rolling, it will often go on by itself. Local news features are often picked up the wire services and spread across the country. Local radio and TV shows can lead to bookings on network shows. One or two features in the major review media, and soon every newspaper in the country is calling to ask for a review copy (or simply reprinting the review from one of the major sources).

4. If at first you don't succeed, try, try again. Persistence, above all, is the key to success in generating favorable publicity for your books and authors. Believe in your books and authors, keep on plugging away, and the reviews will come.

Chapter 10

Tips on Advertising Your Books

The most effective way to promote your books is to combine advertising with publicity efforts. Although publicity and word of mouth may be sufficient by themselves to put some books on the bestseller lists, most books will benefit from some well-planned and well-placed advertising.

As one librarian noted in *Publishers Weekly*, "I confess I tend to buy books that are advertised. I have learned that, in most cases, books that are advertised have a real commitment from publishers."

When advertising to consumers, you have five basic options: direct mail, telemarketing, magazine advertising, newspaper advertising, and radio/TV commercials. Of course, you can apply these five basic options in a variety of ways. Moreover, there are many other lesser known advertising approaches which have been used successfully by book publishers.

When planning your advertising campaign for each book (or for your entire line of books), you must decide which approach or method will produce the best results for that particular book (or series of books). In making your decision, you must consider the subject of the book, its audience, its price, its format, your advertising budget for the book, its method of distribution, and its competition. In addition, you must consider how the advertising will fit into the promotions for your other books and with the company image you want to project.

10:01 Some General Guidelines

No matter what approach you decide to take with your advertising, there are certain basic principles that apply to almost any kind of advertising. On the following pages I've listed a short list of such principles:

- **Test, test, test.** Whenever you place any ad or do any direct mailing, be sure to test before committing your entire budget to that specific approach. Test everything that is important. Test the advertising copy. Test the lists or media. Test the price. Test the offer. Don't, however, waste your time testing little details such as the color of the envelope, or small changes in copy.

- **Select your audience carefully.** Choose magazines or other media with a reader profile similar to your book buyer profile. Select lists made up of recent book buyers rather than a compiled list.

- **Track the results of your advertising** so you know which media are producing the best return on your investment. Use these results to guide you in placing further advertising, not only for the current book but also for future related titles. The basic principle here is to continue using the advertising media and approaches which are producing results before trying other media or approaches.

- **Focus your advertising efforts on a few select approaches.** Don't scatter your attention by trying to advertise everywhere in every way. It won't work. Only when your prime approaches no longer produce a good return should you test other approaches.

- **Make sure you have distribution.** For example, if you are going to advertise on national television, make sure you have mass distribution—that your book is available in all the local bookstores. Of course, if you are going for a direct sale on television, then you don't need mass distribution. In that case, however, you will need to make it easy for people to order by offering a toll-free number, charge card or C.O.D. privileges, and a clear and firm guarantee of satisfaction.

- **Have enough books in stock** to handle the anticipated demand created by your advertising. Don't roll out a big advertising campaign if you don't have enough stock on hand and a smoothly functioning fulfillment department.

- **A toll-free 800 line and acceptance of credit cards** will generally increase response to any advertising regardless of the media.

- **Focus your advertising on a prime objective**: more sales for a particular book, more sales for your entire line of books, creating an image for your company, creating a brand name, or whatever. The clearer you are in your own mind about what your objective is, the more effective you will be in creating and carrying out an advertising campaign.

- **Set a marketing budget,** and stick to it. Most general trade book publishers spend about one dollar per book for advertising, or about 6% of the retail price of the book. About half that amount is spent on push advertising (ads directed to bookstores, wholesalers, libraries and other institutional buyers) and half on pull advertising (ads directed to the consumer). Decide for your own company how much you will spend for each book and where you will spend it.

10:02 The Advantages of Direct Mail

I must admit that of all advertising methods I prefer direct mail. Here are just a few of the advantages of direct mail:

- It is quick. You can prepare and mail a small promotion within days rather than weeks or months. Hence, it is perfect for testing prices, titles, and potential audiences. Of course, more elaborate and carefully targeted promotions do take longer to prepare, but even then they usually require a shorter lead time than most magazines.

- Not only is a direct mailing quicker to prepare, but response time to direct mail is usually quicker as well. Thus you can project the final results of a mailing more quickly and accurately than you can with most other advertising.

- It can be cheaper, especially for smaller tests. Using a computer to generate the sales letters, Ad-Lib has done personalized mailings to lists as large as 500 for only the cost of paper, envelopes, and postage (about 30¢ per piece).

- It does not require as much design time. A standardized direct mail format (letter, response card, folder or brochure, and return envelope) is much easier to design and produce than a magazine advertisement or a television commercial.

- It can be highly targeted. If you choose your lists carefully, you can target your mailings much more selectively than you can with most other media. You can reach almost any market segment, buyer profile, or area of the country you feel is most appropriate for each book.

- Direct mail allows you to reach audiences you might not be able to reach through any other method. Rodale Press has sold over a million copies of their book *Stocking Up* since its 1977 publication. Only 10% of those sales were made through bookstores.

- It is more flexible. After testing a promotion, you can change almost anything right away without waiting. You have complete control over the media, the audience, and your offer.

- Mailing packages can offer more details than can any other form of advertising. You can pack a lot of information into one envelope, far more than you can on a full-page magazine or newspaper ad, or in two minutes on radio or TV.

- Your advertising message does not have to compete with other advertising messages or editorial matter. At least, it doesn't have to compete once the envelope is opened.

- Direct mail can be more personal than any other advertising media. Not only can letters be personalized via mail-merging techniques, but you can use more informal language in writing your letter and can direct your letter to the specific interests of the reader.

- The inclusion of an order card and return envelope makes it easier for the consumer to respond to direct mail as compared to magazine ads (unless, of course, you include a bind-in card opposite the advertisement or include a toll-free order number).

- A direct mail piece is more likely to be retained for future reference than a magazine ad since many readers will either find it inconvenient to tear an advertisement out of a magazine or will be reluctant to do so. Other forms of advertising (radio, TV, and telemarketing) offer nothing to retain.

- You can build an advertising campaign with more confidence by testing small lists, then building to larger lists, and then rolling out to a full list or lists.

  Strawberry Hill Press turned to direct mail after selling only 3,000 copies of Stephen Chang's *The Book of Internal Exercises*. They started small with a four-page direct mail letter to a list of 10,000 proven buyers of health books. When that mailing pulled a 9% response for a net profit of over $9,000, they tested a variety of other lists which, in turn, produced a net profit of $40,000. When they finally rolled out to larger lists, they sold almost 100,000 copies of the book within a year (for a net profit of $150,000).

- Direct mail allows you to build and maintain an in-house list of prime prospects for your future books (and backlist books). Furthermore, you can make money renting the list. Strawberry Hill Press, in the example noted above, also had over $20,000 worth of list rental income in that same year.

Disadvantages

Just to be fair, there is one major disadvantage of direct mail if you market your books primarily through bookstores. Bookstores do not appreciate it when publishers advertise books for direct sale to consumers; they would much prefer that you send those consumers to them.

Several years ago one bookseller in Manhattan returned 20 copies of *The Great Getty* to Crown Publishing after he noticed a coupon soliciting direct orders in a *New York Times Book Review* ad. Indeed, there have been other cases when several booksellers boycotted publishers who were soliciting direct mail orders for titles normally sold through the trade.

10:03 15 Ways to Use Direct Mail

Direct mail advertising can be used for other reasons besides making a direct sale. Here are just a few other ways you can use direct mail to increase the sales of all your books:

- **Obtain inquiries** – You can use an inexpensive direct mail package to obtain inquiries about your books which you then follow up with a more expensive and elaborate informational package to obtain a sale.

- **Obtain leads** – Use direct mail to obtain leads for direct sales representatives or telemarketing staff. This method would be useful for high priced series or collections (encyclopedias, continuity series, or multi-volume reference works). It is also useful for sales to independent retail stores.

- **Offer free trials** – One of the most effective ways to sell expensive books is to offer a fifteen (or thirty) day free trial period. When a customer sends in his or her request, you send the book with an invoice. Upon receipt of the book, the customer then has fifteen days to either return the book if not satisfied or pay the accompanying invoice.

- **Supplement retail sales** – Harlequin uses direct mail to make sales they would not reach through retail stores. According to their president, Harlequin's direct sales do not cut into retail sales. This additive effect of direct mail sales has also been noticed in many other industries, such as the toy and gift industries.

- **Boost retail sales** – The publishers of Reader's Digest Books have found that many of the people they mail to actually buy the book at a retail bookstore rather than order direct by mail. Inevitably when they make a mailing on a backlist title, bookstore sales also increase.

- **Increase sales to libraries** – By increasing consumer demand via the mails, you also increase the number of people who go to libraries to request the book. Whenever there is a demand for a book, libraries will inevitably order the book. You can also stimulate college library sales by mailing to college instructors rather than direct to librarians.

- **Make special sales** – To reach potential volume buyers (for premium or catalog sales), direct mail followed up by telephone calls is the most cost-effective way to advertise.

- **Sell subsidiary rights** – One of the most cost-effective ways to sell licensing or other subsidiary rights is to reach potential buyers via direct mail and then follow up with telephone calls.

- **Publicize your books** – Most publicity is generated via direct mail, again followed up by telephone calls.

- **Maintain contact with key customers** – Direct mail can be used to send newsletters, updates, and other customer communications to help you maintain contact with your key customers. Such continuing contact can lead to better customer relations and, hence, to more sales.

- **Build your customer list** – One of the great advantages of direct marketing is that you can build up a list of buyers who are interested in the areas related to your specialty. Many direct marketers will even lose money on their first mailings just so they can build up their list – not only for their own future use but also to rent to others.

- **Conduct research** – You can use direct mail to do market research and surveys. Many published surveys, opinion polls, and other research is already conducted via this method.

- **Prepare new editorial material** – You can use direct mail to help you prepare your editorial content. For example, direct mail is the most cost-effective way to update directory listings.

- **Sell advertising** – If you publish directories or other reference books where advertising is accepted, you can sell advertising space by mail.

10:04 The 3 Fundamentals of Direct Mail

The following three elements are vital to the success of any direct mail promotions. If any of these are missing or inadequate, the chances of success are slim.

1. **The offer** – Your books must be worth the cost. Make an irresistible offer, and your chances of success are much greater than if either the book is inadequate or the price is too high (or low).

2. **The advertising copy** – The format of your direct mail is not nearly as important as its message. The copy must speak to the interests of the reader. The letter must stimulate the reader to act.

3. **The list** – You can have the best offer and the most irresistible copy in the world but, if you mail to the wrong list, none of that will have any effect. Hence, of the three fundamentals, many direct marketing professionals would insist that the list is the most vital.

10:05 How to Improve Your Offer

The most important element of your offer is the book. If the book answers a definite need, your offer may need little else to be effective. Nonetheless, here are a few other suggestions on how you can improve your offer to make it more enticing to the mail order buyer.

- **Offer a premium for buying the book.** As a publisher, an ideal premium would be another printed product (brochure, booklet, or book) related to the main book offer.

  When Ad-Lib first offered the *Directory of Short-Run Book Printers* for direct sale, we offered a choice of four reports for ordering early: 1) *20 Ways to Save on the Printing of Your Books*, 2) *16 Points to Consider When Selecting a Book Printer*, 3) *70 Full-Color Catalog and Brochure Printers*, or 4) *68 Books about Publishing and Self-Publishing – a Bibliographic Review*. We found the response to these free premiums to be so great that we included the first two reports in the Third Edition of the *Directory*. Whatever premium you do offer, be sure it has a high perceived value regardless of its actual cost.

- **Set a time limit.** If you limit the availability of the book or a special offer (such as the premium offer described above), you can increase the response. At the very least, most people will respond more quickly (which can be important if you require a faster inflow of cash).

- **Offer a discount** if they order within a certain time limit or if they order more than one book. For years now, Ad-Lib has offered a 10% discount to anyone ordering three or more books at the same time. And because of this offer, we seldom get orders for two books; when customers order more than one book, they invariably order three or more. Indeed, we have gotten many comments from customers saying that they couldn't resist the discount.

- **Offer payment options.** Allow payment by credit card, or check, or billing, or whatever. The billing option is almost an absolute necessity if you are selling to companies. Indeed, a credit or bill-me offer has been known to improve results by 50% or more. Installment payments, for items costing more than $25.00, can also improve results.

- **Make it easy for them to order.** Allow them to order by phone, or to call collect, or to call via a toll-free number. Provide a BRE (business reply envelope) to make it easier for them to send in the order.

- **Offer a free trial period.** The free trial period works particularly well for advertising in card decks where your advertising message is so limited by the available space that you almost have to offer people a chance to see the book itself if you expect them to buy it.

- **Guarantee satisfaction.** Offer a 30-day money-back guarantee, or a life-time replacement warranty, or some other form of guarantee that assures them you will stand by your product. Then stand by it.

- **Offer several versions of the product**, one higher priced and more exclusive, the other standard. For example, offer a limited edition of a book or an autographed copy or a hardcover/softcover option. In a mailing for the Third Edition of the *Directory of Short-Run Book Printers*, we offered both the standard book (for $13.00 postpaid) and a Deluxe MailMerge Edition (for $30.00 postpaid). About 15% of the resulting orders were for the higher priced edition.

  Generally speaking, you can never sell two items through one mailing package (unless your mailing package is a catalog), but you can sell two different versions of the same item—and make it work for you.

- **Make a special offer.** For example, send discount coupons to all your customers in celebration of your company's anniversary saying, "It's our birthday, but you get the present!" The coupon could, for instance, offer $3.00 off for any order regardless of size.

  Note: The more believable your special offer, the more likely it is that it will succeed.

- **Run a sweepstakes.** Sweepstakes can increase orders by 50%. For more on sweepstakes, see Section 11:29.

- **Offer rush service.** People appreciate fast service. If you offer special shipping, people will respond. Quick service is especially important when you are offering seasonal books such as holiday gifts or gardening books, or summer travel guides.

10:06 How to Design Effective Direct Mail

Although the format of your direct mail package is not nearly as important as the advertising copy itself, variations in format can have measurable effects on the response. Hence, in this section I will be describing not only how to write more effective advertising copy but also how to design your direct mail programs to produce greater response.

- **Sell the benefits.** Above all, write copy that sells the benefits that can be derived from reading the book. Don't leave any doubt about what the benefits are. And don't expect the readers to guess what the benefits are from a listing of the book's contents. Tell them. Spell it out in clear language that any bozo could understand.

- **Offer a benefit right away.** The first paragraph, indeed the first line should perk the interest of the reader, should inspire the reader to read on. You must capture the reader's interest right away, or the entire letter will fail simply because the reader stops too soon.

- **Use "you" copy.** Write in a personal, comfortable style. Don't use overly long sentences or paragraphs. Underline words to make a point. Vary the length of paragraphs. Ignore your high school English teacher. And even begin sentences with "and" or "or" or "but" or whatever. In short, write in a conversational tone as if you were writing to a friend rather than being graded by the queen's grammarian.

- **Remember the classic formula** for writing direct mail copy that sells: AIDA—Attention, Interest, Desire, Action.

  First, get the reader's attention.

  Second, once you have their attention, keep them interested by asking questions, answering questions, giving examples, and stating benefits.

  Third, stir their desire by demonstrating to them all the advantages of owning the book you are offering.

  And, finally, inspire them to act. Ask for the order. Make it easy to order. And don't let them delay.

- **Above all, ask for the order.** Make your offer clear to potential customers in simple, direct English. Repeat the offer again on your response card or order form.

- **Include a second order form** in your mailing package. This second order form could be printed in your brochure. Not only does a second form reduce the chance of a person losing the ordering information (price, address, etc.), but it also encourages pass-along orders.

- **Don't be afraid to be redundant.** Repeat if necessary. Say the same thing several times just to be sure that the reader has gotten the point. You don't have to repeat everything in the same paragraph, but you should repeat your main offer and the major benefits of the book several times in your mailing package — at least three times. Repetition helps to make your point clear and avoids any possible misunderstandings. You can even repeat the exact same sentence again later on in your letter. If it's a good sentence, it can bear repeating.

- **Use key words that people respond to.** Here are a few of those words: "you, your, free, new, bonus, satisfaction guaranteed, order now, success." There are many more, but these are among the most effective.

- **Print some teaser copy on your envelope.** One of the first barriers any direct mail letter faces is at the mailbox. Many letters are thrown away without being opened because the outside envelope did not inspire the recipient to open the letter. One way to avoid this is to print some teaser copy on the envelope that suggests a benefit that would interest the recipient. Here's the teaser copy used by SRDS for one of their directories: "Pros want it. Newcomers need it. You can test — FREE for 20 days!"

Another way to avoid having your envelope thrown away without being opened is to make the envelope look important — either by making it look like a telegram, like a bill, like a check enclosure, like a priority letter, like an important business letter, or like a personal letter.

A third way to get your envelope open is to use an unusual envelope. For instance, use an extra large envelope, an envelope with multiple windows, a flaming red envelope, a brown paper bag, or a mailing tube. Or use some special effects on the outside of the envelope — stickers, seals, commemorative stamps, tokens, cartoons, rub-offs, or embossing.

Here is a great envelope. Wouldn't you open it?

- **Use testimonials in your letter.** When we mailed out a letter offering the *Directory of Book Printers*, we included the following testimonial both as teaser copy on the front of the envelope and as the lead to our letter: "Without Kremer's *Directory* I paid $12,500 for the first printing of one book—and got plenty of production hassles. With the *Directory* I paid $4,500 for the identical job—and no problems!" That testimonial not only allowed us to sum up the two main benefits of the *Directory*, but it did it in an objective, yet very dramatic way.

- **End each page of a letter with an incomplete sentence** so the reader will turn the page. End the page by offering a special benefit or asking a question. Answer the question on the next page.

- **Highlight important points.** Besides underlining words, you might also circle certain words or write something in the margin (using legible handwriting). Don't overdo this, but use whatever seems appropriate to emphasize a point or make the letter more personal.

- **Direct your offer to the people reading the letter.** If you switch lists and the customer profile is different, you should rewrite your letter if necessary to appeal to the new audience.

- **Include a reply envelope** in your mailing, with or without return postage guaranteed. A pre-addressed reply envelope makes it easier for the person to respond. It's also more secure than a reply card by itself. Any time you ask for a check or credit card payment, you are better off including a reply envelope (note that American Express, as a security measure, requires any orders charged to one of its cards to be inserted in an envelope).

- **Print your name and address in many places** (at least once on each enclosure in the mailing package). First, this prevents the loss of an order when the customer misplaces the order form. Second, it adds a greater measure of credibility to your offer. If you were not proud of your product, you would try to hide your name.

- **Use actual stamps** (either precanceled bulk mail rate stamps or first class) rather than a printed bulk mail indicia. Or, if you're making a large mailing, use metered bulk mail rather than a printed indicia (bulk metered mail is not easily distinguished from first class metered mail; hence, it actually looks very businesslike). Or, finally, you could have a bulk mail indicia printed in red ink that appears exactly like metered mail (check with your post office to make sure you do this exactly according to specifications).

- **Write as much copy as you need to tell your story.** No more, no less. But note: Longer letters tend to pull better.

- **Add a P.S. at the end of your letter.** Time and again, a postscript has proven effective in increasing orders. Use it to restate the key benefit of your book, or to offer an added inducement, or to offer a guarantee. The P.S. is one of the most read parts of any direct mail letter.

- **Letters should look like letters.** Use typewriter type in your direct mail letters. It still works better than fancy laser typefaces — perhaps because it seems more personal and less high-tech.

- **Use involvement devices,** such as stickers, tabs, stamps, rub-offs, tokens — anything to get the reader involved. Such involvement devices almost always improve results.

  Graphics Arts Monthly enclosed a quarter with a request for reader feedback. They wrote, "There's no way we can pay for your time . . . perhaps the coin will help brighten the day of a child you know."

- **Break any of the above rules** if it makes sense to do so. However, if you do break a rule, make sure you thoroughly test your mailing promotion before you roll out to a large audience.

- **Keep a swipe file.** Save every direct mail package, catalog, flyer, ad, letter, or whatever that you find effective (whether because of its copy, its layout, its color, its graphics, or whatever).

- For more tips and ideas on writing and designing your direct mail packages, read my new book, *Mail Order Selling Made Easier*.

> Authors — Write a direct mail letter solicitation for your book. Make it benefit oriented. Sell, sell, sell. Writing such a letter will give you a new perspective on your book. At the very least, it should help you discover what benefits might be missing from your book. That's one good reason for you to try writing such a letter *before* you finish writing the book.

10:07 How to Get the Best Lists

Of the three fundamentals of direct marketing, perhaps the most important is the list. Put simply, if you mail to the wrong list, neither your offer nor your message will have any impact whatsoever. Here, then, are a few tips on how to generate, maintain, and select mailing lists that will produce the greatest results for your direct mail program.

- Since 20 to 30% of all addresses change every year, clean your house list at least every six months. To clean a list, simply print "Address Correction Requested" on the envelopes of any mailing to your list. The post office will charge for each address correction they return.

- Not only do individual consumers move with such regularity, but so do businesses and personnel. Job titles change, people get promoted or switch jobs (or companies), businesses expand, businesses move, businesses go out of business — these are all responsible for the deterioration of business mailing lists.

- Your own house list will usually offer the best return on any mailing, even when some of the buyers may have originally bought books unrelated to the book you are currently offering. Of course, buyers of previous titles in the same subject area are your best prospects of all.

- The next best list is buyers of similar books from another publisher. If your book is not directly competitive with the other publisher's books, you should be able to rent the list.

- Or, perhaps better yet, you might be able to arrange an exchange of lists with such a publisher. If you do exchange lists, make sure that the lists are as nearly equivalent as possible (in terms of average unit of sale, recency of list, number of buyers in relation to inquirers, number of names on the list, etc.). Ad-Lib has exchanged lists with Para Publishing, publishers of *The Self-Publishing Manual* and *Business Letters for Publishers*, and with McHugh Publishing Reports.

- When you have exhausted all lists of buyers of related titles, then test lists of buyers of items which are related to the title you are now offering. For example, if you have an organic gardening book, you might rent a list of buyers of organic pesticides.

No matter what your subject, there is a list out there somewhere that targets the audience for your book. Here, for example, are just a few of the different lists that are available for publishers of gardening books:

[ ] 60,000 subscribers to *Fine Gardening* magazine

[ ] 189,000 buyers of products from the *Smith & Hawken* garden catalog

[ ] 227,000 subscribers to *Horticulture* magazine

[ ] 50,000 subscribers to *Northern California Home & Garden* magazine

[ ] 150,000 buyers of home and garden products from Shar-Lane Industries

[ ] 99,000 buyers of items from the *White Flower Farm* catalog

[ ] 825,000 subscribers to *Home* magazine

[ ] 215,000 continuity buyers of My Green Gardens gardening cards

- In almost every case, a list of mail order buyers will out-perform a list of inquirers or a compiled list.

- Nevertheless, if no other buyers lists are available, your next best choice is a targeted compiled list. Ad-Lib, for example, regularly rents the R. R. Bowker list of U.S. book publishers, and this list has always performed well for us even though it is a compiled list.

- You can, of course, compile your own business mailing lists by going through the yellow pages of city telephone books. Many libraries have collections of the yellow page directories from most major cities. Some also have access to an Electronic Yellow Pages service.

- Membership lists of related organizations can also be superb sources of book buyers. Ad-Lib has used the COSMEP membership list which, next to our own house list, has been our best performer. Indeed, our own list now includes close to 70% of the COSMEP membership.

- Subscriber lists are also effective. Why? Because most newsletters and magazines are sold by direct mail. Also, of course, periodical subscribers are proven readers; hence, they are more likely to buy other reading material by mail.

- When selecting lists, get recommendations from three or four different list brokers. In such cases, you will undoubtedly receive duplicate recommendations from these brokers. These duplicate recommendations are likely to be the best lists to test first.

- When you are considering another list, try to get samples of direct mail promotions which have worked with the list. Ask the list owner to provide you with samples or to give you the names of some previous renters. The best samples to review are those from repeat renters of the list (no sane direct marketer would ever rent a list twice if it had not performed well the first time). When you do get samples, look for any similarities in appeals, or copy, or format which apparently worked in the past. These should give you some insight into how to best approach the list with your own offer.

- As part of your long range list research, try to get your own name on the lists which you might potentially use. Code your name so you will know when that list is used.

  You can, for example, code your name by using different initials for each list (J. L. Kremer for one list, J. A. Kremer for another, John F. Kremer for still another, etc.).

  How, then, do you get on other lists? Buy something, or make an inquiry, or ask for their catalog, or simply ask to be put on their mailing lists for their latest offers. Two of the main advantages of being on a list you might rent is that you will get a good idea of 1) how often the list is rented, and 2) what sorts of mailers rent the list.

  For example, I've been on some lists that are rented out four or five times a week—that's way too often to be effective for many promotions, especially ones for higher-priced items. I've also been on lists which, it turns out, were rented primarily to chain letter opportunists—again, not a list you'd ever want to use.

- To expand your own in-house list, offer a low-priced book or report that appeals to the same audience as the rest of your books. For example, to add names to our own list, Ad-Lib has offered several inexpensive reports and books including *70 Full-Color Catalog/Brochure/ Direct Mail/Card Printers* for $3.00 and *The Self-Publishing Book Review* (now incorporated into the new edition of *Book Publishing Resource Guide*) also for $3.00.

We offered these through press releases, small classified ads, and even as giveaways. Although in most cases we did not make money on these offers, we did add a good number of regular customers to our in-house list. These low-priced books, then, function the same as loss leaders: They bring in the customers, and once these customers discover all the other books we have to offer, they order more — enough, in the final analysis, to make the entire proposition pay off.

- Similarly, you could offer freebies to attract potential customers. Just be sure to offer a freebie that is related to your main line of books. Such free offers can bring in as many as 20,000 inquiries when offered in a magazine with national circulation (such as *Family Circle*).

- Add a section to your catalog order forms which give your current customers an opportunity to "Do a friend a favor." Ask them to give you the names of any friends who they think would like to receive your book catalog. This has worked well for a good number of mail order companies.

- For more details on how to build and maintain your own house list, how to find other appropriate lists, how to evaluate and select lists, and how to order and test such lists, read my new book, *Mail Order Selling Made Easier*. Not only will the book answer all your questions about mailing lists, but it will also provide you with a working knowledge of all the ins and outs, ups and downs, and nitty-gritty of running a mail order business. Look for the book in your local bookstore or order direct from the publisher by calling (800) 669-0773.

Authors — If you know of any targeted lists (associations, magazine or newsletter subscribers, catalog buyers, or other possiblities) that would be appropriate for your book, let your publisher know. They might not use the list, but it doesn't hurt to let them know it exists — and it may lead them to other lists that work even better.

10:08 How to Make Best Use of Card Packs

Card packs, those ubiquitous collections of loose postcards advertising from 30 to 150 offers, are one of the fastest growing areas of direct marketing. You can now choose from over 750 card packs, at least one for almost any audience you want to target (from engineers to doctors, from sales managers to craft store owners). Before you decide to use one, though, you should be aware of the disadvantages as well as the advantages of advertising in such response decks.

Disadvantages of Card Packs

• Since they are cooperative advertising vehicles, it is quite possible to have several of your competitors also advertising in the same pack. (Actually, this could be an advantage or a disadvantage depending on how your book measures up to the other books in price and offer.)

• Because of the small card size it is often difficult to sell books which require detailed explanation or extensive copy.

• Again because of the size limitation, it is often impossible to offer multiple order or payment options.

• You can't offer a business reply envelope (though you can offer a business reply card).

• Returns and bad debts tend to be higher among card pack buyers as compared to magazine advertising or regular direct mail.

• Since many packs are mailed only two or three times a year, they may not allow the best timing for your book promotions.

• Since card pack advertising may be more widely distributed than your own direct mail package, such advertising can tip off your competitors to your new offers.

• Response rates are low, anywhere from .1% to 1% are common.

Advantages of Card Packs

• Card packs offer one of the lowest costs for direct mail advertising ($17.00 to $20.00 per thousand as compared to $300.00 to $500.00 per thousand for your own packages).

• They are easy to use.

• Per inquiry or per order insertions are quite easy to arrange in many of the packs (especially with the recent oversaturation of the market).

• Card packs are superb lead generators.

• Card packs offer fast response. You can expect to receive half the response from your ad within 12 days of receiving the first response.

Questions to Ask Before Using Packs

1. What is the source of the list? (Make sure it's a reputable source.)
2. Is the list made up of buyers? (Mail responsive lists are better than compiled lists.)
3. If it is a list of buyers, how much did they spend on the product? (The price should be at least as high as the price of your book offer.)
4. How often is the list cleaned? (The more often it is cleaned, the better the list.)

5. How often is the pack mailed? (The better packs are mailed four to six times a year, thus allowing you more opportunities to follow up on the success of a card placement.)
6. Is it mailed to the same people each time, or to different lists? (Different lists are often better since they allow your offer to reach new prospects each mailing.)
7. Does the pack offer an A/B split for testing? (A/B splits allow you to mail one offer to half the list and another offer or format to the other half. Such splits enable you to test which offers/formats produce the best results.)

Tips on Using Packs

- Use packs that are sent to mail responsive names rather than to compiled lists. However, avoid hotline names which often represent current respondents only rather than paid buyers.

- Position is important. Some studies have shown that cards in the first half of the pack produce twice the results of cards in the second half of the pack. Hence, if you have to pay a premium for position, it may well be worth the extra payment.

- Free trial offers work better than direct credit card sales. McGraw-Hill has consistently found that 10-day free trial offers work the best for their books.

- If you do use such free trial offers, expect some debt collection problems and some returns (up to 13% or more of all orders). Factor these considerations into your calculations when figuring whether participation in the pack will pay off for your book.

- Note that offers for higher priced books are more likely to pay off for you as compared to lower priced books. Again, card packs are best for generating inquiries or leads that can be followed up with sales letters, telemarketing, or direct sales visits.

- One option that had worked well for Caddylak Systems was to offer three or four books on the same card. Although each book in itself was low priced ($9.95 to $14.95), multiple-copy orders usually made participation in the pack pay off. Note also that Caddylak publishes a line of some forty related books. Hence, any orders generated through the card pack usually resulted in additional sales from Caddylak's catalog which was sent as a bounceback with the original order.

  Recently, however, Caddylak has switched to offering higher priced books (usually $49.95 or higher) through card packs. Hence, while the lower priced offers may have helped them build up a good list of buyers, they were probably not making a profit for Caddylak.

- Always state the price of your book in the ad.

- Ask for a business card rather than having buyers fill out an order blank. Buyers with business cards are more qualified buyers. Also you can learn more about a buyer from a business card than you can from any information they fill out in an order blank. To encourage the sending of business cards, many card pack participants now print a light line saying, "Tape Business Card Here," over the coupon area.

- Use graphics or a photo of your book in the ad. Multiple colors also work better than a single color. Note that many card pack publishers will throw in a second color free to encourage you to test their pack.

- Lay out your offer in a horizontal format. Customers read the pack this way.

- Use headlines that will compel the casual browser to read on: FREE CATALOG! or FREE SAMPLE! or 50% OFF! or SAVE $10.00!

- Cards are one-second billboards. Most cards receive no more than a one-second glance from pack recipients as they flip through the deck. That one second is all you have to gain the attention of the recipient and earn a second chance to make a sale. Design your card with this one-second rule in mind.

- Many card packs accept per inquiry or per order advertising. Indeed, in many packs up to 30% of the cards are p.i. or p.o. ads. With per inquiry or per order ads, you only pay the card pack publisher for actual inquiries or orders you receive. For example, if you received 100 orders for a $19.95 book, you would have to pay the card pack publisher about $1000.00, or about 50% of your total income from orders you received. Similarly, you might have to pay $2.00 to $5.00 for each inquiry you received. When requesting a p.i. deal, make it clear to the pack publisher that if the results are good, you will be placing more ads.

- Some pack publishers will sell on a space available basis which could save you up to 50% of the pack cost. If you choose this option, you run the risk that the pack will fill up and your ad won't run.

- Other packs offer a 15% agency discount (for advertising agencies and card brokers). Many also offer such a discount for direct placement. Main Deck, for example, allows such a discount on the first placement.

- Note that many card pack publishers will also typeset, design, and even write the copy for your card. Many offer this service free to first time users (in the hopes, of course, that you will become a regular participant in their pack).

- Some book publishers who use card packs regularly have found that business (but not consumer) card packs have a huge pass-along readership.

- They also report no fall off of orders with larger packs (when packs go from 40 to 60 cards).

Card Pack Directories

To locate those card decks which would be most appropriate for your books, refer to the following directories:

- **1989 Card Pack Media Directory**, Solar Press, 1120 Frontenac Road, Naperville, IL 60566; (312) 983-1400; (800) 323-2751. This directory is free when you request information from this printer of card packs. It lists over 100 publishers of card packs.

- **SRDS Card Pack Rates & Data Directory**, SRDS, 3004 Glenview Road, Wilmette, IL 60091; (800) 323-4588. $95.00. Lists 650 card packs—with rates, frequencies, circulation, and more.

- **The National Directory of Postcard Deck Media**, Caddylak Systems, 60 Shames Drive, Westbury, NY 11590; (516) 333-7440. $49.95. Lists over 500 card pack publishers—with rates, frequencies, circulation, target markets, and more.

- **Book Publishing Resource Guide**, Ad-Lib Publications, 51 N. Fifth Street, Fairfield, IA 52556-3226; (515) 472-6617; (800) 669-0773; Fax: 515-472-3186. $25.00. Among other book marketing oppportunities, this directory lists over 317 card packs which feature books. Includes circulation figures, target audiences, and book subject categories.

Card Pack Inquiry Services

If you'd like to test card packs without spending a whole lot of money, you might want to try one of these card pack inquiry services. These companies will advertise a short listing describing your book (your book will be listed with 25 to 50 other products). They charge for each inquiry they generate (but they require an upfront deposit of $250 to $500).

- **Cata-List**, Venture Communications, 114 East 32nd Street #1700, New York, NY 10016; (212) 684-4800. Provides a 15-word listing of your brochure or catalog. You pay 50¢ for each inquiry you receive.

- **Computer Center**, Westwood International, P. O. Box 42640, San Francisco, CA 94101. They list about 9 products per card. Products range from books and audiocassettes to baseball bats.

- **Rayod House**, Attn: Free Information Service, 155 River Road, P. O. Box 520, North Arlington, NJ 07032; (201) 997-0880; (800) 526-1242. 55 character listing for any service or product. You pay $1.00 for each inquiry you receive.

- **SIE Sales Lead Program**, Select Information Exchange, 2095 Broadway, New York, NY 10023; (212) 874-6408. 10 to 15-word listing of your brochure or catalog. You pay 45¢ for each inquiry, and you can set a limit on how many inquiries you will accept.

Ad-Lib advertised our *PR Flash* database through one of these services. We received about 300 inquiries, but the sell-through was very poor.

10:09 Other Direct Mail Options

When using direct mail, you have a number of different formats you can use, formats which have proven successful for other companies. If any seem appropriate for your company, you should certainly test that format. Then, if it proves successful for your books, you might switch all or a large portion of your mailings to that format.

• **Classic letter package** — Perhaps the most common direct mail promotion is the classic letter package consisting of a letter (anywhere from two to twelve pages in length), outer envelope, BRE (business reply envelope), order form, and a lift letter, brochure, or both. Why is it so common? Because it works, time and time again.

If you use a **brochure**, here are a couple of hints for making it better:

1. A two-color brochure almost always outpulls a one-color brochure.
2. Put your selling message, the prime benefit, on the front cover. Most people never read past the front cover if it does not pull them in.
3. Make sure your brochure describes the complete offer. That way, even if the brochure gets separated from the rest of the mailing package, the customer can still place the order.

Lift letters are short letters usually printed on half-sheets of paper to supplement the sales story laid out in the longer full-size letter. When original, they can be effective in increasing results.

• **Card decks** — Rather than just mail one or two cards in another company's card deck, you could offer your entire line of books in card deck format, with one or two books offered per card. Mc-Graw-Hill and John Wiley offer several different card decks. Academic Press offers a separate deck aimed only at buyers of microbiology books.

St. Anthony Messenger Press replaced its Christmas gift catalog with a card deck to offer its line of religious books to over half a million customers. Results were "beyond anything else we've ever done."

Garden Way produces an ads-only periodical of direct response cards, called *Gardener's Marketplace*, to sell its line of gardening books and cookbooks. The *Marketplace* is mailed twice a year, in the spring and fall, to almost one million gardeners. This format has been effective for them, with one card alone bringing in over $40,000 in orders.

• **Catalogs** — Almost every book publisher uses this format once they've developed a list of books long enough to justify the cost. Many publishers, however, only send the catalogs to bookstores, wholesalers, and libraries. A growing list of book publishers are beginning to use catalogs to reach book buyers directly. Catalogs can produce excellent results if your own in-house list is large enough or your book list is specialized enough to allow you to target your catalog mailings to specific lists.

Why do people buy from catalogs? According to a recent Gallup survey, 36% of the respondents buy from catalogs primarily because they are more convenient than shopping in retail stores, while 19% like the variety that is available in a catalog, 17% like the lower prices, and 6% like the higher quality. Remember these percentages when planning and designing your catalog.

* **The Dover format**—Besides mailing special interest catalogs, Dover Publications also mails up to eight 11" x 17" flyers folded to fit inside a normal #10 business envelope. Each flyer features a separate line of about forty books (for example, paper dolls, crafts, graphic arts, or science). Although most books sell for under $5.00, Dover does well with these mailings because the average order is much higher, with most customers ordering three or more books.

* **Tabloid catalogs**—New Society Publishers prints their seasonal catalogs on tabloid-size newspaper stock which allows them plenty of room for describing and illustrating their new and backlist titles while being inexpensive to print.

* **Catalog in magazine format**—John Wiley has issued a catalog in magazine format, even giving it a fancy title, *Excel*, and volume and issue numbers. Their first issue was in the summer of 1985. I haven't seen any further issues, so the format may not have produced the results they had hoped it would.

    One advantage of the format, though, is that such a mailing format is more likely to be saved during the first sorting of mail—and it also has a better chance of being read. And a mailing that can produce those effects has a much better chance of making the sale than a mailing that gets tossed out without being opened at all.

* **Self-mailers**—Self-mailers are mailing formats which do not require an envelope. They come in many different sizes and formats—from simple folded leaflets to large folded brochures printed on card stock. Self-mailers offer several advantages:

    1. They are generally easy and quick to design and produce.

    2. Since they require no outside envelope, they are cheaper to produce.

    3. Because they are in one piece with no outside envelope, they require no collating and stuffing; hence, labor costs for preparing them for mailing are much lower.

* **Postcards**—Some publishers have used simple postcards to announce single titles. Postcards have a sense of urgency and informality which might be appropriate for some titles.

    Christine Adamec, author of *There are Babies to Adopt*, mailed out a simple postcard to some 400 radio stations to announce her availability as an expert available for interview. As a result, she was interviewed by over 15 radio shows (and still counting).

- **Broadsides or Posters** — These formats can be very effective for single titles with appealing graphics. Any use of broadsides or posters, whether for single titles or multiple titles, requires careful planning and graphic design.

- **Book jackets as brochures** — Book jackets or covers, printed on the inside with further details about the book, make excellent promotional brochures. They are especially effective when sent with press releases, with mailings to booksellers (who can then get a better picture of how the book will look on their shelves), and with special prepublication announcements.

- **Statement stuffers** — You can print small 8 1/2" x 3 1/2" flyers announcing new titles or older backlist titles to send out with your invoices and statements. These statement stuffers are cheap to produce and very effective in selling related titles.

  To promote their Boston guidebook, *In and Out of Boston (with or without) Children*, the Globe Pequot Press inserted statement stuffers in with the billing statements for the *Boston Globe*. As a result of this promotion and many others, they have thus far sold over 300,000 copies of the guide.

- **Stamps** — Little, Brown & Company uses a sheet of full-color stamps each bearing a cover illustration for one of their medical books. Recipients need only select the stamps for the books they'd like to receive, stick them on the order form, and send it in. Such offers work well if your covers are designed to sell your books and if you offer billing privileges.

- **Electronic bulletin boards** — Some publishers offer books on computer bulletin boards. Several publishers, including McGraw-Hill, Bantam, Rodale, and Mercury House, are now merchants in CompuServe's Electronic Mall. This videotext shopping service allows users to scan the offerings of many companies (not only book publishers) and to place orders using their credit card. The Mall now serves over a quarter million CompuServe subscribers (an upscale audience especially suitable for books on computers, technology, and business). To learn more about this service and how your company can be listed in the Mall, write to **CompuServe**, Attn: The Electronic Mall, 5000 Arlington Centre Boulevard, Columbus, OH 43220; (614) 457-8600. Note that there is a charge for such listings.

- **Videocassettes** — If you sell a high-priced book or series, you might try sending videocassette versions of your catalog to your top prospects. Not only will the videocassette attract people's attention, but it is also far less likely to be thrown out without being viewed.

  Royal Silk, a catalog of high-priced clothes for women, now offers a version of its catalog on videocassette. They charge $5 or $10 for it. They have found that people who order via the videocassette catalog spend an average of $20 more per order.

- **Newspaper clippings** — *Sales & Marketing Digest* encloses only one item in its direct mail letters: an ad that appears to have been torn out of the financial section of a newspaper. They've been using this format for several years, so it's apparently working for them.

- **Floppy disks** — Many major companies are now using computer floppy disks as a dramatic and often effective way to grab and hold people's attention. Here are just a few of the advantages of this new medium:
  1. They are still novel enough to attract attention.
  2. Computer disks are one of the greatest involvement devices. If designed well, they encourage interaction by involving recipients in answering questions, filling in the blanks, or making choices on what parts of the program to see.
  3. They can pack an incredible amount of information, with many options to choose from.
  4. Computer owners have attractive demographics: high income, college educated, home owners.
  5. You can create animated displays with great graphics.

  Here are just a few of the companies using floppy disks to market their products: General Motors received 300,000 requests for an interactive disk (for either IBM or Mac computers) that demonstrated one of its new Buicks. Ford Motor distributed 25,000 disks for its upscale sports sedan, the Merkur XR4Ti, with the following selling message: "Take a test drive on your disk drive." Chase Manhattan Bank sent out a disk to demonstrate its Electronic Funds Transfer service.

  If you would like to explore this new direct marketing format further, contact one of the following companies. Both specialize in designing interactive software for advertisers.

  E.A.S.I., J. G. Sandom, 530 West 23rd Street #232, New York, NY 10011; (212) 627-0970.

  The SoftAd Group, Paula George, 207 Second Street, Sausalito, CA 94965; (415) 332-4704.

- **Newsletters** — Because newsletters combine useful information with an advertising message, they can be one of the most effective ways to market books. Above all, they tend to be read — and that is always the first step towards selling anything by mail!

  The *Book Marketing Update* newsletter was begun as an advertising vehicle for Ad-Lib's books. The first two issues of the newsletter were sent to 20,000 publishers for a total cost of about $10,000. From those two issues we grossed about $35,000 in sales (with about a 4% response rate). From our experience, I would suggest these pointers:
  1. Keep the newsletter short.
  2. Publish monthly or bimonthly (repetition is important for creating the greatest impact).
  3. Start small. Keep testing till you find the right format and audience.

Many other publishers are currently using newsletters to promote their books, including Amacom Books, Backboard Press, Bantam (*Word of Mouth*, their consumer cookbook newsletter), Children's Book Press, Harper & Row (*Harper's Web*, their junior books group newsletter), New Riders Publishing (*The New Writer*), Nolo Press, Para Publishing (*Publishing Poynters*), Quality Press, Ransom Hill Press, and John Wiley (*Wiley Ideas*).

10:10 Marketing via Your Telephone

Within the next couple of years, most major companies (and many smaller ones) will be offering toll-free phone service for orders and customer service. The cost is now so low and the potential results so great (with proper promotion) that few companies can afford not to offer the service. For more details on the advantages of offering toll-free service, see Section 4:02 in this book.

While the installation of a toll-free number can have a great impact on your sales, you should not limit your telemarketing to passive order taking. As long as you have the customer on the phone, you should take the opportunity to make additional sales or to ask questions of the book buyers (to discover how they found out about your books and why they decided to order your book or books). If you prepare a standard script for your order takers, they can easily increase the sales of your books without any additional cost to you.

After you have organized an effective system for handling in-coming orders, you should consider establishing an out-going telemarketing effort as well. While some consumers resent the invasion of telephone sales calls into their homes (and rightly so), outbound telemarketing can still be an effective sales tool for your company. Here are a few ways to use outbound telemarketing to your advantage:

- **Test a list fast.** You can test a list of a thousand names within a few days by using your telephone. If the results are good, then you have reason to expect a follow-up mailing to a larger portion of the same list to produce similar results. Such a test is clearly not as reliable as a test mailing, but it can provide you with quick feedback on which of two or more possible lists is likely to produce the best results. According to one telemarketing expert, calls to 100 people will give a response equivalent to a direct mailing to 1,000 people.

- **Test an offer fast.** You can use telephone calls to test two alternative offers (for example, to test which of two premium offers will produce the most sales).

- **Follow up inquiries and leads.** For example, you could call instructors who have been sent examination copies of textbooks to check whether they will be using your book in their classes and, if not, why not.

- **Research your market.** For example, you might make phone calls to a sampling of doctors to see if they'd be interested in a book on gall bladder operations. Or perhaps, better yet, you could use the same phone calls to ask open ended questions that encourage the doctors to tell you what kind of information they do need. Then you can produce books that would fill that need.

- **Increase sales.** Telemarketing can increase the response to an offer by as much as five times. For example, if a list would normally yield a 5% response to direct mail, telemarketing might increase the response to 20 or 25%. Such increases may be attributed to the more personal nature of phone calls, to the greater opportunity for give and take in a phone conversation, and/or to the greater immediacy of phone calls.

- **Upsell.** When customers call to order one item, you can take that opportunity to sell them additional items, or sell them a higher-priced book in the same subject.

- **Collect delinquent accounts.** Probably more publishers use outbound phone calls for this reason than for any other.

- **Sell new editions.** Buyers of previous editions of reference books and manuals are the best prospects for new editions. You can make calls to your own in-house list of buyers offering a prepublication special.

- **Sell new titles to your in-house list.** Your in-house list is your best prospect for any new titles, especially ones related to the books previously bought by your customers. With a proper computer order entry and tracking system, you should be able to sort out those previous customers who are most likely to buy certain titles. You could then use telemarketing to produce enough prepublication orders to pay perhaps for the cost of producing the new title.

- **Open new accounts,** especially among booksellers and other key contacts. This application offers the greatest potential for producing profitable orders via telemarketing. You can use the phone not only to open new accounts but also to alert previous customers of new titles or offers.

- **Cut sales costs.** Telemarketing can be an inexpensive substitute for direct sales visits. Indeed, with bookstores which are located out in the boondocks, phone calls may be the only practical way to keep in touch with them. For smaller publishers who are not able to set up sales representatives, telemarketing offers a viable alternative, especially if it is used to supplement direct mail offers.

- **Create publicity.** Outbound phone calls, of course, are also an essential element in any aggressive publicity campaign. Phone calls are often the only practical way to follow up previous contacts. Also, since phone calls allow a certain give and take, negotiations for author interviews and appearances are much easier to conduct over the phone rather than through the mails.

- **Build good will.** A toll-free phone number demonstrates that you are responsive to the needs of your customers and open to their feedback. Answer your phone. Be open to calls from your customers.
- **Save customer time.** Not only can customers order faster over the phone, but they can also check on the availability of your books (especially backlist) and discuss any problems that might have come up in regard to any of their orders.
- **Answer questions.** You can answer questions over the phone that you could never answer in a print advertisement or catalog.
- **Provide customer service.** You can provide better customer service via the telephone than you can by mail.

10:11 Tips for More Effective Telemarketing

Telemarketing sales have grown to $161 billion in sales during 1987. Because telemarketing costs run high (anywhere from $1,200 to $2,000 per thousand names), response rates must also be high. While response rates for consumer telemarketing can range as high as 15% to 25%, you cannot expect such high response rates unless your telemarketing campaign is carefully designed.

Telemarketing, to be effective, must be highly organized. You cannot play it by ear. You must plan every step of the process if you hope to make efficient use of what is one of the most expensive and effective media for making sales. Here are a few tips to help you organize your outbound phone campaigns:

- **Use highly targeted lists.** Don't waste your phone time on general lists or random canvassing of phone books. Your own in-house list of buyers and inquirers or outside lists of buyers are your best prospects. Of all factors in any telephone marketing campaign, the list is the most important. Again, the offer and the audience must match.
- **Make a clear, specific offer** — one that can be easily stated in a few sentences. Make it easy for the listener to either say yes or no.
- **Have a definite script which your callers must follow.** Be sure to spend time training your callers to handle any customer questions or other responses. You should anticipate most questions in your script and have clear answers already prepared for the most prevalent ones.
- **Hire only phone callers who can handle rejection,** who can terminate a phone call politely and proceed right away with the next call. The best callers are those who can be casual in their tone and presentation while sticking to the script.
- **Accept purchase orders, C.O.D., or credit card sales.** Don't expect people to send checks in response to telephone sales calls.

- **Prepare a simple but complete order form** that allows your caller to record the order easily while continuing to talk with the customer.
- **Record responses.** Each phone conversation, whether resulting in an order or some other response, should be recorded in writing (whether on paper or in a computer database) and filed with your records.

  With outside lists, you might want your operators to check off a simple form recording the number of responses for each general category (orders, requests for more information, simple rejection, vehement rejection, hangups, no answers) rather than writing a complete memorandum.

- **Outbound sales calls can be more effective as followups to previous mailings than as cold calls.** Such a one-two punch can be more effective than phone calls or mailings made independent of each other.

  Enterprise Publishing uses outbound telemarketing to solicit feedback from previous customers. These outbound calls often result in further sales – about 10% of their sales come via outbound telemarketing.

- **Don't telemarket to any customer you have called within the previous three months.** For its encyclopedias, book clubs, and continuity programs, Grolier has a policy of not telemarketing anyone who has been called within the past three months. They also make an effort never to call anyone twice about the same product.

- **Make it as easy as possible for potential customers to reach you.** While continuing your outbound telemarketing, also work to make it easy for people to call you. Advertise your inbound numbers (both regular and toll-free numbers).

- **Whenever anyone calls you, try upselling** – that is, let them know what else you have to offer them. This upselling doesn't have to be agressive, but certainly it makes sense to let incoming callers know what else you have to offer. Whenever anyone calls Ad-Lib to order a book, we let them know that we publish an entire line of books on publishing and marketing.

- **Offer a special service.** To increase incoming phone traffic, you might want to offer a special service for those customers who are not ready to order anything. Then, when they call, offer them a limited-time special or tie-in merchandise.

  Banana Republic offers their catalog customers a Climate Desk phone service. Customers can call this toll-free number to find out weather information for their travel destinations. Information includes high and low temperatures for various seasons, average rainfall, political situations that might affect travel in that area, medical requirements, health precautions, State Department regulations, and clothing needs. Where appropriate, Banana Republic also suggests clothing or travel books that might be useful. Of course, any clothing or travel books that they recommend, they also sell. Customers may order right away.

- **Use call processing.** If you receive lots of incoming calls, you might want to use the new call processing technology, which functions like an automated receptionist. These machines automatically answer every call and, when the caller presses the appropriate touch-tone number, transfers the call to the right person or to another message. Here are just a few of the benefits this technology can offer you:

1. Answers all calls without your intervention, thus saving on the number of people you need to hire to answer your phones. All calls are answered by human voices (taped by you).

2. Automatically routes calls to the right department.

3. Can take orders right over the phone, with the callers leaving all required information by voice message or by punching the appropriate touch-tone numbers on their telephone pads.

4. Allows callers to leave messages for various people (so those people can always get their messages by just checking their telephone mail box).

5. You could program various sales messages that callers could access just by pressing the right touch-tone number. Hence, you could have separate sales messages for each title on your list. Or you could have separate messages for your sales reps, for booksellers, and for individual customers.

6. You don't have to provide a separate line for your fax or modem. Callers can access those machines by simply sending the correct touch-tone numbers to reach the appropriate extensions.

The Book-of-the-Month Club at one time installed call processing equipment on their lines — and it worked! When you called them, you could transfer immediately to the right person and leave that person a message (and know that he or she would receive it!). The great thing about their system was that their people did return their calls.

Since I wrote about their system in the second edition of this book, BMOC abandoned call processing. I'm not sure why. Though I suspect it might be because many consumers resent the impersonal nature of such systems. While my first experience with such a system worked very well, my experiences with call processing since then have been very frustrating. I much prefer a real person answering the phone and, I suspect, most other people do, too. If you use such a system, make sure you give callers a quick way to talk to a real person.

Authors — Your telephone can be one of your most potent marketing tools. If you do decide to help your publisher by calling major buyers or by conducting an outbound marketing test, be sure to coordinate your efforts with those of your publisher.

10:12 Advertising in Newspapers

While newspaper advertising outside of the book review sections is not used by many publishers, it has produced some fantastic results for publishers who have the money to commit to an extensive national campaign. Here are a few ways publishers have used newspapers to advertise their books:

● **Encourage bookstore sales.** Robert Ringer used newspaper advertising to market several bestsellers, including *Winning Through Intimidation, Looking Out for #1*, and *Crisis Investing.* His technique was quite simple: He wrote superb mail order copy, took out large ads in major newspapers, and then directed orders to bookstores rather than to his own publishing company. His aggressive advertising campaign combined with the cooperation of the major book chains pushed his books onto the bestseller lists and enabled him to sell mass-market rights for close to a million dollars.

Such techniques obviously won't work for everyone (if they did, you'd see many more publishers trying the same thing). His technique worked because his books were general enough to appeal to a wide audience and because he was a superb promoter, making good use of publicity to enhance the effect of his ads.

● **Sell books direct to consumers.** Some self-publishers, such as Ted Nicholas, Benjamin Suarez, and Joe Karbo, are all famous for their mail order promotion of books via national advertising in newspapers and magazines. In these cases, they usually went for the direct sale, with all orders coming to them.

● **Supplement book reviews** and other promotional activities. Most book publishers use advertisements to supplement book reviews. Hence, they tend to focus most of their advertising in the book review sections of major national newspapers.

● **Target specific audiences.** Other publishers advertise in sections targeted to a specific audience (for example, advertising a cookbook in the food section of a newspaper).

● **Advertise in the classified sections** of newspapers. Such advertising is only effective in newspapers where books are regularly advertised (such as the *Wall Street Journal* and the *San Francisco Chronicle* with its special book mart section). Some classified ads are made up only of words; others are small display ads in the classified section.

Hacker Art Books has advertised their sale catalog in the *Wall Street Journal* every year since 1952. Obviously they would not continue to do so if it did not pay off.

● **Advertise in specialized newspapers.** Don't overlook specialized newspapers such as those for army and navy bases, colleges, specific religions, ethnic languages, minorities, and so forth.

Ace Books, for example, advertised *The Specialist* by Gayle Rivers in armed forces newspapers.

● **Co-op ads with local booksellers.** Advertise through co-op ads with local booksellers. In such cases the publisher pays all or part of the costs of the ad if the bookseller buys a certain number of books. (See Chapter 12 for more details on offering co-op ads.)

● **Offer coupons.** In 1987, the Publishers Marketing & Couponing Group placed free-standing inserts in the *New York Times*. These inserts contained eight pages of coupons from major publishers, including Random House, Doubleday, St. Martin's Press, Scott Foresman, Lyle Stuart, and Rand McNally. Many New York area independent and chain booksellers participated by redeeming the coupons.

● **Offer free copies.** As part of their promotional campaign for the novel *Beaches*, Bantam placed ads in the *Los Angeles Times* offering two free copies to the first 2,000 people who wrote in (one copy for themselves and one copy for their best friend).

For Jonathan Kellerman's novel, *When the Bough Breaks*, New American Library placed direct response ads in seven newspapers (*Los Angeles Times, New York Times, Washington Post, Chicago Tribune, Boston Globe, San Francisco Chronicle,* and *Toronto Star*). In the ads they offered free copies of the book to the first 500 people to respond in each city. When NAL sent the free copy to each respondent, they also included a 30% discount offer for Kellerman's second novel, *Blood Test*. While NAL did not make any money on this special promotion, they did stimulate word of mouth for Kellerman's novels.

10:13 Tips on Advertising in Periodicals

Many of the tips given in Sections 10:05 and 10:06 for direct marketing also apply to any print advertising, but here are a few additional suggestions for improving the response to your ads:

● The most important element of most newspaper and magazine ads is the headline. The headline must offer a strong benefit, one strong enough or dramatic enough to get the attention of the reader.

● Consider using a second color. A number of tests conducted over a period of twenty years in the *Long Beach Press-Telegram* showed that two-color ads (one color plus black) outsold non-color ads by 64%.

● Use illustrations or other graphic elements. According to some studies conducted by McGraw-Hill, illustrations increase readership of ads. And increased readership will usually result in increased sales.

● Testimonials in the ad copy usually increase response. They are more believable than straight ad copy.

● Create a sense of urgency by putting a time limit on the offer.

- With smaller ads, the border becomes more important. It should clearly set the ad off from surrounding editorial matter or other ads and yet not distract the reader's attention from the ad's message.

- Advertisements which look like editorial copy have often proven to be more effective in producing sales.

- Put a coupon in the ad. Make it easy for the reader to order your book. Even Robert Ringer put coupons in his national advertising; in his case, though, the coupons directed the readers to the nearest chain bookstore. In general, ads with coupons pull better readership than ads without coupons.

- If you use coupons, place them on the lower outside corner where readers can cut out the coupon without having to ruin the entire page.

- Make sure your address and phone number are printed several times in the ad, once outside the coupon and once in the coupon itself. Thus, if someone has already clipped the order coupon, other readers can still find out where to send the order.

- For that same reason, your basic offer (the name of the book, the cost, and any special conditions) should also be repeated outside the coupon.

- Since Sunday newspapers usually have a higher circulation and a longer life, it's generally best to advertise in the Sunday editions as opposed to any daily editions.

- If you are using classified ads, make every word count. Don't be penny wise and pound foolish. If you need more words to describe your book adequately, then use more words. At the same time, don't waste words. You need to strike a balance between minimum word count (and, hence, minimum cost) and an adequate description of the benefits your book offers (and, hence, maximum sales results).

- Start small. Use smaller display ads before you place larger display ads. Indeed, many publishers have found that a series of smaller display ads will often outpull one large ad. Not only do smaller ads cost less, but a series of smaller ads can create multiple impressions that one larger ad cannot do.

- Maintain a swipe file. Whenever you see an ad with a good headline, or attractive layout, or well-written copy, or something else that attracts your attention, save that ad. Then, when you write your own ads, borrow the best ideas from the ads in your swipe file.

Authors — You, too, should maintain a swipe file of your favorite ads. Refer to it whenever you need some examples of good copy to stimulate your ideas when writing promotional copy for your books.

10:14 Advertising in Magazines

Magazines offer something most newspapers cannot offer, that is, targeted readership. There are magazines aimed at almost any audience you'd ever want to reach. Here's a checklist of a few samples:

[ ] animals (*Cats, Cat Fancy, Horseman, Ranger Rick*)
[ ] art (*Art and Auction, North Light, Graphic Arts Journal*)
[ ] business (*Business Week, Forbes, Inc., Income Plus, Entrepreneur*)
[ ] children (*Highlights for Children, Humpty Dumpty, Parents*)
[ ] clubs (*American Legion, Rotarian, Kiwanis, National 4-H News*)
[ ] computers (*Byte, PC, Personal Publishing, MacUser*)
[ ] crafts (*Crafts, Workbasket, Woodworkers Journal*)
[ ] ethnic/minorities (*Ebony, Jet, Scandinavian Times*)
[ ] farm (*Successful Farming, Farm Journal, Ohio Farmer*)
[ ] food (*Bon Appetit, Gourmet, Cuisine, Good Food*)
[ ] genre (*Fantasy & Science Fiction, Analog*)
[ ] health (*Prevention, Bestways, American Health, Longevity*)
[ ] home (*Better Homes & Gardens, House Beautiful*)
[ ] homemaking (*Good Housekeeping, Family Circle, Woman's Day*)
[ ] lifestyle (*Egg, Interview, Playboy, Cosmopolitan, Seventeen*)
[ ] literary (*New Yorker, Grand Street, Pig Iron*)
[ ] news (*Newsweek, Time, U.S. News and World Report*)
[ ] people (*People, Us, National Enquirer, Star*)
[ ] regional (*Mpls, New York Magazine, Houston Living*)
[ ] science (*Omni, Scientific American, Transpersonal Psychology*)
[ ] sports (*Golf, Running, Sports Afield, Sports Illustrated*)
[ ] trade (*Gift & Decorative Accessories, Playthings, Publishers Weekly*)
[ ] women (*First for Women, Savvy , Ms., Self, Working Woman*)

And many more, including alumni magazines, religious magazines, company publications, inflight magazines, scholarly journals, entertainment guides, Sunday magazine sections of local newspapers, gossip tabloids, and professional journals. For a complete list of such magazines, see the *Standard Periodical Directory, Ulrich's International Periodicals Directory, Gale's Directory of Publications and Broadcast Media,* or *SRDS Business Publication Rates and Data.* You should be able to find one or more of these directories at your local library.

The same basic rules apply to magazine advertising as apply to newspaper advertising. The one exception is that since you can target your audience more selectively with magazines, you can and should write more specific ad copy appealing to the special interests of the readers of each magazine.

Here are a few other tips on getting the most for your money through magazine advertising:

- **Advertise in regional editions of national magazines.** You can buy space in regional editions for much less than the cost of the entire national edition. One company ran a single ad in a regional edition of *Time* magazine and then used reprints of that ad for its window displays and direct mailings for the next five years. Hence, by advertising in the regional edition of such a well-known and respected magazine, the company was able to gain a level of credibility with its customers it could not have gained in any other way.

- **Arrange per order ads.** Many magazines will accept a per inquiry or per order arrangement for books which they feel will interest their readers. Similarly, some magazines will run an ad for free if you will dropship the orders for them. In this case, orders are sent direct to the magazine; then the magazine processes the order, takes its cut, and sends the order on to you (with their check) for dropshipping. In such cases you will be expected to give a discount of anywhere from 40% to 60% to the magazine.

  Globe Pequot provides ad slicks to special interest magazines that the magazines can use when they have unsold ad space. These ads (either full page or two-page spreads) offer Globe's books for sale through the magazine publisher on a per order basis. Not only does Globe get free advertising, but they are also able to go to bookstores and tell them that full-page ads appear regularly in major magazines.

- **Offer free excerpts from your books** to magazines in exchange for a tagline at the end of the article telling readers how they can order the book (your company name and address, the price of the book, and other ordering information).

  When an in-flight magazine contacted one publisher for permission to serialize a book on business management, rather than charge a fee for the serial rights, the publisher offered to let them run the excerpt for free as long as ordering information was listed at the end of the article. As a result, the publisher received over 1000 orders.

- **Buy remnant space.** Ask the magazine to let you know when they have unsold space, which can be bought at a fraction of the usual cost. Of course, when you rely only on remnant space, you have no way of controlling when and if your ads will appear. Hence, remnant ads are best used for titles which are not time sensitive.

- **Set up your own ad agency.** If your advertising budget is currently too small to attract an advertising agency, you might want to set up your own in-house agency so you can get the standard 15% agency discount offered by most magazines. It's not worth your time to do this, though, if you do not spend at least several thousand dollars in advertising each year.

Ad-Lib Publications has its own advertising agency, Ad-Lib Consultants, and thus saves 15% not only on the placement of many of its magazines ads but also 15% on the cost of many card deck placements and mailing list rentals. Our agency, however, is not an in-house ad agency, since we have offered consulting and promotional services to other companies for several years.

● **Use classified ads.** You may test some magazines by using classified ads. Not only are classified ads an inexpensive way to advertise, but they can often pull better than normal display ads. Classified ads are a superb way to compare the pulling power of different magazines.

The main disadvantage of using classified ads is that it is tough to sell books costing more than $5.00 through the classifieds. Why? There are two basic reasons: 1) the space limitation of classifieds may not allow a complete description of the benefits of your book, and 2) classifieds do not attract as affluent an audience as normal display ads.

There are, however, apparent exceptions to the rule. Jay Levinson used classified ads for many years to sell his self-published book *Secrets of Successful Free-Lancing* for $10.00. Why did his ad work where others didn't? Because he avoided the two main limitations of classified ads 1) by writing a long ad that described the benefits of his book in a clear and appealing way, and 2) by placing his ads in upscale periodicals such as the *Wall Street Journal* and several professional artist's and writer's magazines.

● **Use Selectronic printing to target readers.** Some magazines (including *American Baby, Farm Journal, Games*, and *Medicine*) are now offering Selectronic printing that allows an advertiser to target individual readers with personalized ads or messages. This personalization, of course, costs money, so this new technology should only be used for very specialized books.

● **Ask the magazines for their media kit.** When you write to magazines to request their advertising rates, ask for the following as well: a sample issue, rates for both display and classified ads, the names of their editors and book reviewer, their editorial schedule for the coming year, and copies of any reader surveys they have recently conducted.

For instance, a survey of *Crafts 'n Things* subscribers showed that 70% of their readers had purchased craft books in the past year. Moreover, 75% of their readers own more than 10 cookbooks and 50% had purchased books by mail. What a prime audience for books!

● **Use the magazine's support services.** Some magazines will prepare and typeset your advertisement for you — in the hopes, of course, that the advertisement will pay off for you so you will continue to advertise in the magazine.

When you advertise in some trade journals, they will provide you with a variety of other marketing programs. So be sure to ask them if they provide such programs. Here, for example, were a few of the marketing support services provided by *Target Marketing* to their advertisers:

List rental—You may mail to their entire list of 42,000 direct marketers (free one-time use of their list).

Market research—They will prepare a survey of 1000 of their readers for your company. They print, mail, and tabulate the survey for you free.

Research studies—All half-page or larger ads in certain issues are analyzed and studied for their effectiveness and recall by an independent research company.

Purchasing reports—They send confidential reports on their readers' projected buying plans.

Reader service—They forward leads to you when readers request more information about your ad by using the enclosed reader service cards in each issue.

Ad display mounts—They mount up to five of your ads for greater visibility at trade shows and exhibits.

Forbes ad—You could share space in *Target Marketing*'s full page ad in *Forbes* magazine at no extra cost.

Bonus distribution—Besides its regular subscriber mailings, *Target Marketing* is also distributed free at nearly 40 trade shows each year, giving you additional exposure to new buyers.

Special catalog ad rates—If you'd like to insert a four-page or eight-page catalog, you can do so for half what it would normally cost you.

Editorial support—When space is available, Target Marketing's editors make every effort to support your advertising with free publicity.

Other services that magazines might provide (either at cost or for free) include the following: reprints of articles, product sampling to prospective buyers, convention promotions, ad design and layout, and free directory listings.

Authors — You should write to magazines that cover the subject areas you write about. Ask for sample issues, ad rates, editorial schedules, and the names of appropriate editors. Not only will this information help you in planning promotion for your books, but it could also come in handy when researching and writing the book.

10:15 How to Advertise on Radio

Radio is not a common promotional vehicle for books. About the only books I've heard advertised on daily radio are mass-market paperbacks. For example, Dell conducted a national radio campaign of 60-second spots on late night and drive time network shows and major market radio stations for *Shattered Moon* by Kate Green.

Nonetheless, you might consider using radio even if you don't have mass distribution. For instance, you might advertise a regional title such as the *Boston Ice Cream Lover's Guide* on local stations. Or you might advertise a rock biography during a syndicated top 40 show or on serveral local rock stations. Or how about a religious title on a religious station? Or, perhaps best of all, market a Spanish-language book to an Hispanic audience via a local ethnic radio station or a national network (according to one source, 90% of all U.S. Hispanics listen to Spanish-language radio stations as compared to only 75% viewing Spanish-language television and only a little over 50% reading Spanish-language newspapers).

In each of these instances, you could advertise a specific title to a highly targeted audience. In such cases you would not need to have mass distribution as long as you had local distribution or offered to accept credit card orders via a toll-free number.

So you do not need to limit your advertising to national radio network or syndicated shows. You can also advertise on local AM or FM radio stations which have different audience profiles, from rock to country, from all news to easy listening, from sports oriented to religious oriented. Just select the audience profile that fits your books.

Here, then, are a few guidelines to follow if you do decide to test market your books on radio:

• **Rule one, as described above, is to match your books with the format** and, hence, audience profile of any radio stations you intend to use for advertising.

• **Advertise on a syndicated radio show** for the lowest cost for the widest possible reach. For instance, a 30-second spot on *Live from Gilley's* costs only $250.00. This show, which airs on 256 stations, has an estimated audience of 335,000 listeners.

• **Advertise on the radio networks.** Note that the major radio networks actually offer several possible divisions that enable you to target your audience more specifically. For instance, ABC radio offers the following networks:

ABC Contemporary — 262 affiliates (CHR and AC formats)
ABC Direction — 362 affiliates (AC and Country formats)
ABC Entertainment — 555 affiliates (Country and AC formats)
ABC FM — 133 affiliates (CHR and Urban Contemporary)
ABC Information — 622 affiliates (News, Sports, and Talk)

ABC Rock—80 affiliates (AOR, Rock, CHR)
ABC Talk—116 affiliates (Talk and Call-in formats)

• **Buy time through a media rep network.** Besides the major networks, you can also buy spot time on local radio stations across the country by working with a media rep network. For more information on some of the fifty media rep groups in the country, see SRDS's *Spot Radio Rates & Data* directory.

• **Try per inquiry ads.** Per inquiry ads are still available in some radio markets, but they are not that easy to find. If you'd like to try offering books direct to consumers via per inquiry radio advertising, work with one of the a media rep group. For instance, about 90% of Katz's direct response advertising placements are done on a PI basis.

• **Both radio and TV rate cards are negotiable.** Remember, if they don't sell the time, it is gone forever. Hence, if they have open time, they will be willing to negotiate a lower rate than the one stated on their rate cards.

• **The best time for running ads on radio are during its prime time hours,** the morning and afternoon drive times. Afternoon drive time has one plus over the morning drive time: As a rule, people are more relaxed and happier as they head home for the evening. Hence, they may be in a better mood for buying.

• **Radio requires frequent repetition for maximum effect.** Hence, you're better off concentrating your ads during a short period of time rather than stretching them out over a longer period.

• **As repetition of the commerical makes radio spots more effective, so does repetition within the commercial.** Repeat your main message at least three times (in different ways). And repeat the title of your book and name of your company at least twice.

• **30-second spots can sometimes work as well as 60-second spots** and are less expensive. Indeed, some studies indicate that people listen more attentively when an announcer speaks more quickly. Thus, you may find it more effective as well as cheaper to squeeze your message into 30-second spots.

• **Take time to make your lead-in effective.** With radio, you have about three seconds to attract the attention of the listener.

• **If you are asking for a direct order, you will also need to repeat the ordering information at least twice.** Don't try for a direct order unless you use a 60-second or two-minute spot. You simply would not have time to repeat your basic message and the essential ordering information in less than 60 seconds.

• **Listen to the tape of your radio commercial** on your car audio system. The closer you can get to stimulating how it will actually sound on ordinary car radio speakers, the more accurately you will be able to judge its effectiveness.

- **Use professional announcers and studio equipment** to make your commercials. Don't skimp on production.

- **Since radio is an audio medium, consider using appropriate music** to heighten the impact of your commercial. Or use other audio effects to enliven the presentation.

- **Here are a few of the advantages that radio offers over television:**
  1. Commercial time is significantly less expensive.
  2. Changes to the content of any commercial can be made more easily, more quickly, and less expensively than with almost any other media.
  3. Radio audiences can be pinpointed more specifically.
  4. Radio is a more pervasive medium. It can be heard in the home, in the office, on the beach, and while driving to and from work.

10:16 28 Ways to Advertise on TV

Television has a great advantage over radio: Not only can it be heard, it can be seen. Studies have shown that people's memories improve as much as 68% when they have a visual element to help them remember something. Hence, if your book lends itself to a visual presentation, you might find that television commercials will produce greater sales than radio commericals or print advertisements.

On the down side, of course, television costs more. To make it worth your while, then, your TV commercials must be effective. Publishers have developed a number of ways to increase the effectiveness of their TV promotions. Here are twenty-eight of them:

- Time-Life Books has used direct response commercials to sell various series of books on topics such as World War II, cooking, and home repair. The advantage of selling such continuity series is that the over-all sale (if the buyer continues with the entire series) is high enough to cover the cost of expensive TV time.

- Bantam advertised its series of Loveswept romances via TV ads and a toll-free 800 order line. They offered four romance novels (plus four additional free novels) for only $9.95 plus postage and handling. After the people paid for their first set of novels, they would be shipped four new novels each month for their approval. Anytime they wanted to stop receiving monthly shipments, all they had to do was send a request in writing to Bantam.

- Hal Lindsey's book *Countdown to Armageddon* was advertised via two-minute commercials asking viewers to order through a toll-free phone number. Within 90 days, they sold over 370,000 copies of the book via television ads.

• Mikhail Gorbachev's book *A Time for Peace* was also sold via two-minute commercials in smaller cities where the book would not otherwise be generally available. In this case, the TV commercials were used to supplement bookstore sales in major cities.

• Better Homes and Gardens used two-minute commercials to advertise its *Christmas Collection* book in the fall of 1988. The book sold for $21.95 plus $3.00 shipping and handling. Undoubtedly, when people ordered that book, they also received offers on other Better Homes and Gardens books.

• Dolphin got free 30-second spots on the syndicated show *Lifestyles of the Rich and Famous* to promote their book named after the show. The show, which is syndicated to some 200 stations across the country, ran the commercial each week for three months. If you have a book which is somehow tied into a TV series, you might try to arrange a similar promotion.

• Berkeley advertised the book *Return to Treasure Island* after each episode of the miniseries of the same name. The miniseries ran for ten weeks on the Disney Cable Channel. Berkeley, in this case, paid for the advertising.

• Morrow found that every time Jeff Smith's cable show *The Frugal Gourmet* moved into another market, sales for his book of the same name picked up dramatically. Morrow supported bookstore sales in these new cities by offering co-op advertising to local booksellers. Most booksellers, however, were reluctant to promote the book until the show came to the city. Eventually, though, as the show moved into more and more markets, the book became a national bestseller.

• Another TV tie-in, Knapp Press's *New York's Master Chefs*, sold over 110,000 copies through telephone sales generated by the show of the same name. Another 40,000 copies were sold through bookstores.

• New American Library promoted the *Weight Watcher's Quick Start Program Cookbook* through 30-second commercials in major cities. Ads were featured for two-week periods in each city. Both major bookstore chains found that sales of the book increased by over 40% during those two weeks, and that sales remained high for at least another week after the commercial stopped airing.

• Don't overlook local cable TV shows when planning your TV promotions. Local cable TV is still quite inexpensive as compared to local network TV. If your book can be linked in any way with a popular cable feature, you have a good chance of making the commercial pay for itself.

• Submit your books for sale via some of the home shopping shows. While they might not be open to selling a book by itself, they might sell a book combined with another product.

- While WTBS and some other major cable networks rarely accept per inquiry or per order ads anymore, local cable companies still accept them. When WTBS was accepting per inquiry ads, they required an advance payment of $50,000 to be placed in an escrow account (to assure payment of all monies due them and to assure fulfillment of all direct sales to viewers).

- The Beckley Group marketed its *Millionaire Maker Course* through one-hour shows in major and minor markets all over the country. They purchased the entire hour time period during which time they presented an informational seminar on how to get rich in real estate. Interspersed throughout the hour were commercials which presented the hard sell for the course. The advantage of this format is that the hour-long shows, which were packed with information of interest to the potential buyers of the course, presented the soft sell while the commercials closed the sale. Their courses sold for $295.00, and orders were taken via credit card, C.O.D., or check either by phone or through the mail. Using this method, they sold as many as 20,000 courses in one week.

  That sounds like lots of sales, and it is, but note that this is a high-risk way to sell anything. The Beckley Group had C.O.D. refusal rates as high as 30%. And, when they offered a later course on credit cards, they were also hit with a blizzard of returns. They have still not refunded all those owed a refund.

- Advertise on videotapes. If your book is tied in with a movie or other popular videotape title, you might arrange to advertise your book at the end of the videotape. Since many readers, after seeing a miniseries such as *Shogun* or a movie such as *Out of Africa*, buy the book to read, you may find a similar immediate response to popular videotape titles.

- Advertise in *TV Guide*. Although *TV Guide* is a print medium, it is so closely connected with TV viewing that you can reach much the same audience for a fraction of what it might cost to advertise on TV itself. Of course, the impact of a print ad is not as great as the impact of a TV ad.

- Advertise in the cable TV guides. Book-of-the-Month Club, Grolier, and Franklin Mint have all advertised in the *The Cable Guide* network of magazines serving 600 local cable systems (with a total circulation of over 5.5 million). Similarly, Doubleday, Grolier, and Encyclopedia Brittanica have all inserted direct response ads in *On Cable*, another network of magazines with a circulation of almost 1.5 million.

- Collins promoted their *Day in the Life* Series by televising documentaries based on the books as well as by organizing traveling exhibits of the photos included in the books. Carl Sagan's *Cosmos* and Kenneth Clarke's *Civilizations* both gained wide publicity and bestselling status as a result of their associated television documentaries.

- While it may be difficult to get your product featured in someone else's commercial, it sure beats paying for the commercial yourself. A summer 1986 commercial for Bartles & Jaymes wine coolers featured David Ogilvy's book, *Ogilvy on Advertising*.

- It is much easier to get your product given away on such game shows as *The Price Is Right*, *Wheel of Fortune*, or *Hour Magazine*. Here are two companies which, for a fee, will help you get your books or other products featured on TV shows:

  Game Show Placements, 7011 Willoughby Avenue, Hollywood, CA 90038; (213) 874-7818.

  Video Enterprises, 11340 Olympic Boulevard #365, Los Angeles, CA 90064; (213) 312-1500.

  While not all books would be appropriate for game show giveaways, many can be made appropriate when packaged with another product. For example, you could give away travel guides with a Mediterranean cruise, or an exercise or diet book with home exercise equipment, or a microwave cookbook with a microwave oven, or a dress for success book to accompany a new wardrobe, or a racy novel to accompany a fancy waterbed.

  If you use your imagination, I'm sure you can think of a prize to tie in with almost any book you publish. That way, although your book itself may not be that expensive, it would make a nice addition to a larger prize (just as they currently give away a year's supply of macaroni and cheese dinners with a new stove).

- A new video marketing tool is now being offered by PromoView. The company duplicates videos containing your advertising message, gift wraps them, and then ships them to targeted audiences. The advantages of video direct mail is twofold:
  1. It is perceived as something of value, so it is not likely to be tossed out without a second glance.
  2. Because recipients are involved with sight, sound, and action (and not sight alone) when viewing the tape, they are more likely to get involved with your message as well.

- **Financial News Network** offers space on its electronic ticker for paid headlines of PR announcements. The cost? $125 to run a headline across the screen four times. For more information, contact PR Newswire toll-free at (800) 832-5522.

- Per inquiry or per order advertising opportunities are not as available as they once were in television. With so many more advertisers using TV for direct response advertising, the demand has exceeded the available time. PI opportunities are currently more available on cable TV stations than on broadcast stations.

• The basic rule for how long your commercial should be is as follows: If you are asking for a direct order, use two-minute spots so you have enough time to adequately describe the book and to provide viewers with ordering information. If you are using the commercial to stimulate bookstore sales, then a 30-second time spot is plenty of time to make your point.

• Remember that television is a mass medium. Don't use it, therefore, if you don't have mass distribution (either through bookstores and mass market outlets or through a toll-free telephone order-taking system).

• If you are planning major TV exposure for direct sales via your own toll-free number, make sure you have enough operators to handle the response. According to one TV advertiser, you will need at least five lines to handle most local campaigns, even more lines to handle a larger regional or national campaign. If you are not prepared to hire and train operators and lease adequate phone lines to handle any response, then you should hire a professional telemarketing agency to organize and handle your phone orders.

• Many of the rules of print and radio advertising also apply to TV ads. Be sure you have a good offer, well-written copy, and an easy way for people to respond.

10:17 Tips on Producing Your TV Spots

While major TV commercials currently cost $70,000 or more per 30 seconds to produce, it is possible to create an effective TV commercial for much less. While you balance your budgetary constraints against your need for a quality production, don't try to do it all yourself. Use your in-house staff where your expertise is strong (for example, in the area of copywriting), but hire professionals where your expertise is weak (for example, in video production). As a guideline, remember that your audience is accustomed to high quality production values and will notice any commercials which are not carefully produced and edited (and will most likely not respond to such ads).

To help you in designing and producing your own television commercials, here are a few guidelines:

• The key to TV success, according to a number of regular TV advertisers, is your media buying skills. If you do not have knowledgeable media buyers, don't try to do the buying yourself. Use a professional agency. As noted above, radio and TV rate cards are essentially works of fiction—they are highly negotiable. Hence, make sure your buyers are highly skilled negotiators; the money you save could make the difference between profit and loss. The Beckley Group had as many as twenty buyers negotiating for media time whenever they rolled out one of their national TV campaigns.

- If you are working with a local TV station, let them provide all the technical production assistance (equipment, camera operators, lighting technicians, directors). Often they will provide such assistance for a minimum cost as long as you are buying time on their station. (In most cases, however, don't let them write your commercial unless you want it to sound exactly like every other local commercial on the station.)

- While many ad agencies use storyboards to lay out the story line of a commercial, you may not need one especially if your commercial is well-written, with all the action clearly described in the script. Storyboards can add from $200 to $500 to the cost of a commercial.

- Perhaps the best way to save money is to do most of your work at the preproduction stage rather than during the actual taping when costs can skyrocket if you have to stop to work out a problem. Hold preproduction meetings to make sure everyone understands the script and knows what to do. Check the scripting details, the lighting, the timing. Hold a dress rehearsal. Never go before a camera crew and other production assistants until you are sure that the production will go smoothly.

- Tape more than one commercial at a time. Since in most cases you will have to pay for a minimum amount of production time regardless of how much time you actually use (as well as travel and set up time), make the best use of the production time by taping two or more commercials or variations at the same time.

- When you plan the taping of your commercial, try to arrange the segments so that editing costs are kept to a minimum. Editing can cost anywhere from $250.00 per hour on up.

- Remember that TV is a visual medium. So be sure to create a strong visual message in your commercial. If the commercial can make its point even with the sound turned off, then you have a sure winner. Use music, sound effects, and words to enhance the visual impact not to replace it.

- If possible, show your book in use. If it is a cookbook, show someone using it to create a scrumptious meal. If it's a mystery, tease the viewers with a look at the unsolved crime.

- As with radio, commercials on TV must gain the attention of the viewer within the first few seconds. Make sure your commercials have a captivating lead-in.

- And, again, as in radio, don't be afraid to repeat.

Chapter 11

Offbeat Advertising and Other Promotions

While most books are advertised through direct mail, newspapers, magazines, radio, and TV, a good number of other creative methods have been used both by publishers and other companies to advertise and promote their products. This chapter presents a random collection of some of those methods.

When you consider using some of these offbeat advertising methods, don't just think of them as gimmicks. Rather, think of them as sales tools which should be integrated into your other advertising and promotional activities. Few of these methods will work alone; they must be part of a well-planned and well-executed advertising strategy.

11:01 Inserts in Shopping Bags

Some paper bag companies are now offering to insert advertising messages inside shopping bags at a relatively low cost per thousand. If you have a line of cookbooks, beauty and diet books, or romance novels, you might test this new method.

11:02 Printed Bags, Cartons, and Matchbooks

You might also test having your advertising message printed on the outside of grocery bags and other shopping bags where other people besides the recipient will see your ad. Some producers of milk cartons are also offering to print appropriate advertising messages on the outside of their cartons. And, of course, there are always matchbooks, a long-time advertising vehicle for correspondence courses which might also work well for do-it-yourself books or opportunity books.

11:03 Movie Theater Commercials

Theaters have begun interspersing commercials with movie previews before the main shows. Thus far I've seen ads for Wrangler jeans, GE radios, and O'Dell's butter (besides, of course, the popcorn and candy commercials produced by Coke, Pepsi, or Seven-Up). If you are publishing a book that ties into a movie, why not test an advertisement in movie theaters during the run of the movie? Indeed, you will probably find it just as effective to promote the book for several weeks before and after the movie as well as during the run of the movie.

How effective are such ads? While the same number of people will see a commercial in movie theaters during one month as will see an average commercial on television (about 30 million), one study reports that over four times as many people will remember the movie commercial the day after as will remember the TV commercial.

While such ads are effective, they are also expensive—as much as half a million dollars per minute. Perhaps a better way to expose your books to a movie audience is to participate in The Popcorn Report, a pre-movie short newsreel featuring four video news releases from sponsoring companies. For a fee of $17,500, your video news release will be featured in a minimum of 500 theaters across the country. For more details, write to **The Popcorn Report**, West Glen Communications, 1430 Broadway, New York, NY 10018; (212) 921-2800.

11:04 Ad Specialties and Premiums

When you advertise your books, you might offer a premium with the book—for example, a slide chart with baseball schedule for a book on baseball; or a calorie counter slide chart for a diet book; or a coupon clipper for a book of money-saving ideas.

You could also send ad specialties with your news releases and review copies to draw attention to your books. Or send them to key bookselling contacts to remind them to push your books. How about an imprinted coffee cup with a cookbook? Or matchbooks with a fire safety book?

Try to match the premium or advertising specialty to the contents or style of your book. Please don't send any more pens. But how about stickers, decals, buttons, balloons, memo cubes, note pads, rubberstamps, golf balls, calculators, paper clips, rulers, playing cards, yo-yos, thermometers, magnetic message holders, wine glasses, pot holders, key tags, ice scrapers, or any number of other items?

For more information about ad specialties, send for a free booklet, *Specialty Advertising: The Medium That Remains to Be Seen*. Write to **Specialty Advertising Association International**, 1404 Walnut Hill Lane, Irving, TX 75038; (214) 580-0404.

Authors — If your publisher offers a premium or advertising specialty with one of your books, ask the marketing department to provide you with a supply so you can hand them out to your contacts.

11:05 T-Shirts and Other Apparel

T-shirts are walking billboards. If you can convince people to wear your T-shirts (especially bookstore personnel), then you'll have a much better chance of getting your books noticed. Dell offered T-shirts imprinted with "It's Heaven ... and Heller" to promote Joseph Heller's book, *God Knows*. NAL offered T-shirts to promote Stephen King's *Skeleton Crew*.

How about baseball caps for a book on baseball, or sun visors for a book on golf, or muscle T-shirts for an exercise book, or bikinis for a diet book?

One way to distribute such imprinted apparel is to offer a free T-shirt with every order of ten or more books. Or give them away to a sampling of people at a public event (for example, imprinted baseball caps at a baseball game). Or give them to people who will wear them on crowded streets at lunch time (when many office workers do their shopping for reading material).

Remember that the main value of any imprinted item is to draw attention to your books and to act as reminder advertising. To accomplish these goals, the imprinted items must be seen. Hence, if you are using imprinted apparel, be sure get them into the hands of people who will wear them (or who will, in turn, give them to someone who will wear them).

Authors — If your publisher doesn't supply any imprinted apparel to promote your book, that shouldn't stop you from making your own—and wearing it wherever you go.

11:06 Calendars

Calendars are a superb way to advertise your books (of course, they are also a superb way to advertise your calendars). Send copies to all your main bookstore accounts and other key contacts.

Whatever you do, do not send generic calendars imprinted with your company name. Use photos or illustrations from one or more of your own books to enliven the calendar. One approach you might use is to print an illustration from a different book for each month—ideally from a book whose publication date is printed in large red numerals on that month's calendar (to do this, of course, you will have to schedule at least one new book for each month of the coming year and will have to commission artwork for that book ahead of time).

A calendar that would have great appeal for booksellers would be one with different promotional ideas outlined for each day or week or month of the year—a calendar similar to the promotional calendars now printed every four months in *American Bookseller*.

11:07 Party Kits

Bantam Books offers a Sweet Dreams pajama party kit free to anyone who requests one. The kit includes one of the latest novels in the Sweet Dreams romance series for young adults, menu ideas for the party, game ideas, and other items to enliven a pajama party.

How about a similar kit for a wine and cheese party to promote a cookbook or book on wines? Or a trivia party kit to accompany a book of lists, records, or ratings? Or a dance party kit to accompany the bio of a rock star?

11:08 Fan Clubs

Many authors already have fan clubs. If so, work with those fan clubs to promote new books or reissues from your authors. And, if there are no fan clubs, why not organize some by putting query coupons in new editions of your authors' books, especially those authors who have three or more books published by you? Fan clubs can be an effective way of starting the word-of-mouth bandwagon for a new book.

Of course, you don't have to organize fan clubs for authors only; you could also organize a fan club for your company or a special imprint. For instance, Scholastic offered a free Babysitter's Club starter kit in the back of their young adult novel, *Kristy's Great Idea*, one of four books in the Babysitter's Club series.

> **Authors** — If you have a fan club, be sure to let your book publisher know about it. If you don't have one, why not start one? If you're too modest to start one yourself, ask a friend or your publisher to start one for you. You deserve one.

11:09 Local Distribution of Flyers

If you have a local title (as, for example, the *Boston Ice Cream Lover's Guide*), why not print up some flyers and have them distributed in the local area by neighborhood kids or by a professional distribution service? Or how about distributing flyers about your new auto book under the windshield wipers of targeted cars in shopping centers or downtown parking lots?

11:10 Public Posters

Why not poster the town? Whenever I visit New York, I always see thousands of posters decorating construction sites announcing new plays or movies. Why couldn't a book be publicized in the same way? Especially in New York. I think such postering could be especially effective for celebrity bios and entertainment titles (rock music, movies, artists).

11:11 Samples

Another ubiquitous phenomenon I've noticed on New York streets are the people giving away samples (cigarettes, candy, whatever). Again, why not give away samples of a new book? Holt, Rinehart and Winston printed sample chapter brochures of Marek Halter's new novel *The Book of Abraham*. I don't know how these were distributed, but certainly some could have been distributed quite effectively on the streets of New York. What a marvelous way to get word of mouth going.

You could also distribute samples through participating bookstores, exhibits, conferences, book fairs, meetings, and other group events or public areas. Distribute samples, then, anywhere there are plenty of people who might be interested in the book being sampled. When you distribute samples, make sure your book is widely available in local bookstores so people can buy the book once their interest is sparked.

• Daytimers, through 1,500 trained counselors, has distributed over 750,000 samples of their products in one year. They have found sampling to be the best method to introduce their time schedulers to new audiences.

• Bantam distributed sample copies of *McDonald's: Behind the Arches* by John F. Love to many employees (and former employees) of McDonald's. Bantam also sent samplers of their Bantam Travel Guides to travel agents and airlines.

• Atheneum sent five postcard teasers (one each day for a week) to key book reviewers and booksellers for David Lindsey's novel, *In the Lake of the Moon*. The postcards featured excerpts from the book.

- When Globe Pequot Press discovered that they had the only *Guide to Eastern Canada*, they convinced the Canadian tourist information centers to stuff a brochure about the book in with their infopacks sent to travel inquirers. The tourist bureaus were happy to do it because the book promoted tourism in eastern Canada.

- Perigord Press sent advance reading copies (with a special wrapper and seal) of Joseph Wambaugh's novel, *The Blooding*, to the book trade, media, and top law enforcement professionals.

- When Warner Books published John Naisbitt's *Megatrends*, they sent sample copies to the chief executives of the 500 largest corporations in the country. As a result, they "created a groundswell of acknowledgement" for the book.

- If your book has a targeted audience, send samples to opinion leaders. On the other hand, if your book is a mass-market book, get copies into the hands of as many people as possible.

Authors − You can certainly help by giving away samples to key opinion leaders in your field (or by providing the names of these people to your publisher). And, if you are ever feeling adventurous, you can give away sample chapters of your books on the streets of New York, or Muncie, Indiana, or Valentine, Nebraska, or whereever appropriate.

11:12 Computer Bulletin Boards

Besides publishing your books or other information on electronic bulletin boards for a royalty, you could also just publish a sample chapter or two of the book to stimulate interest. That's what Leisure Books did with Jaron Summers's detective novel, *Safety Catch*. They posted the first chapter of this mystery featuring a computer detective on CompuServe and the Source. When they posted the first chapter, they also posted a notice offering $5.00 to anyone who will post the first chapter (and the $5.00 offer) on another bulletin board with at least 1,000 regular users.

This procedure provides a quick and easy way to offer many readers a sampling of your book. Other individuals have already offered similar samplings of science fiction works-in-progress, trivia books, and computer guides.

If your authors compose their manuscripts on computers, why not try a similar approach? A few months before you publish the book, post the first chapter (or another sample chapter) on one or more bulletin boards. It's a superb way to get word of mouth going.

Here are a few more ways you can use the new technology to promote your books:

- International Online Associates offers **SuccessMart**, an on-line store of inspirational business audiotapes, via Boston CitiNet. To access SuccessMart, computer users just call CitiNet at (617) 439-5699 via modem and type "GO $$$$." A subject menu comes up on their computer screen, followed by a listing and brief description of the 64 tapes currently available.

- Jeffrey Lant, author of *The Unabashed Self-Promoter*, has arranged to have his own forum on Boston CitiNet. Besides featuring articles on business development and promotion, he also posts book reviews and news releases. He will feature any product (especially information resources) that provide useful business development ideas. News releases and reviews should be sent to him on an IBM-PC compatible diskette in ASCII text. Send to JLA Associates, 50 Follen Street #507, Cambridge, MA 02138. If you'd like to see his forum, call CitiNet. When you are on-line, type "GO LANT."

  While CitiNet is currently available to 43,000 computer users in the Boston area, it will soon be available to users in New York and many other areas of the country. For more information about **CitiNet**, call (617) 439-5678.

- Pubtronix is offering a new way to buy (and even publish books). The service, BookMart, will allow computer users to order books on floppy diskettes. Here's how the service works:
  1. Authors or publishers pay $250.00 per year to list a book in the BookMart database.
  2. Computer users call **Pubtronix** and link to the BookMart database via modem.
  3. Users then scan through a list of available titles (both fiction and nonfiction) which include title, author, and five sample pages from the book.
  4. Once the users have selected which titles they want to order, they just indicate the selection and type in their credit card number.
  5. The books are then sent to users on floppy diskettes.

  To find out more about this program (and whether it might be suitable for distribution of your books), write to Pubtronix, Attn: **BookMart**, 2941 N.E. 23rd Street, Pompano Beach, FL 33062; (305) 946-3560.

- Eric Balkan, publisher of Packet Press, has organized another electronic experiment, BookScan, a form of computer shareware. He is putting together a diskette consisting of excerpts from some 30 to 50 books per diskette, with each diskette dealing with a specific topic. Each excerpt will be up to 11,000 characters long (or about six pages) and would include the publisher's name, address, and other ordering information so readers can order books that intrigue them.

This BookScan diskette collection would then be freely distributed through the standard channels for computer shareware (user groups, BBS's, and friends). Who would want such a diskette? Anyone interested in the subject focus of the diskette. For example, one of the most requested shareware diskettes covers Japanese origami, so shareware users do respond to specific topics.

There is no charge to participate in BookScan. Eric is currently putting together shareware diskettes on subjects that personally interest him (Asian history, movies, computers, tennis, psychology, and spy novels). To find out more about this opportunity, write to Packet Press, Attn: **BookScan**, 14704 Seneca Castle Court, Gaithersburg, MD 20878; (301) 762-7145.

Authors — Most of the computer distribution systems are very open to participation by authors independent of their publishers, so you need not wait around for your publisher to act. Indeed, I'm sure most of them would be only too pleased to have you explore these possibilities on your own.

11:13 Stadium Advertising

Berkeley used multi-media advertising in Yankee Stadium to promote Mickey Mantle's autobiography *The Mick*. Jove also used stadium ads for Jerry Kramer's football book, *Distant Replay*. Certainly, you could do the same with any book that would appeal to a sports audience or other public audience. You don't have to limit such advertising to baseball or football stadiums; you could also use basketball fieldhouses, boxing gyms, dance halls, or convention centers—wherever, again, an audience interested in the topic of your book might gather.

11:14 Blimps, Balloons, and Skywriting

Goodyear is probably better known for its blimp than for any other advertising it does. Currently a number of other companies are now flying blimps as well as hot air balloons to publicize the company name at public events. Although such extravagant advertising may not be appropriate for a single book, it might be appropriate for your company as a whole or for a series of books (for example, a series of adventure novels).

On the other hand, skywriting or banners flown from an airplane could work well for a single title. Since such advertising would also be expensive, your book would require mass-market distribution.

Random House had a plane fly over the beaches of Long Island on the Labor Day weekend carrying the following banner: "Get the new bestseller — *Through A Glass Darkly*." Why not use a similar banner to advertise one of your regional titles? For example, how about flying a banner over the beaches of Cape Cod announcing the *Boston Ice Cream Lover's Guide*?

As long as we're talking about high-flying promotions, how about trying to place one of your book characters as a balloon in the annual Macy's Thanksgiving parade? What are your chances? Not very good, but the exposure is so great that it could be worth the work. If Macy does select one of your characters, they build the balloon (and you share the construction costs with them). If interested, contact Macy's vice president of special productions.

11:15 Next Exit: Billboards

Billboards can be effective as reminder advertising to reinforce other forms of advertising or promotion. Dell, for example, has used billboards combined with national advertising and an author tour to promote Joseph Heller's novel, *God Knows*. Dell also used a billboard on Sunset Boulevard to advertise Kate Green's first novel, *Shattered Moon* (the setting for the novel was Hollywood and its environs).

Billboards work best for book publishers in areas where there is a high density of book buyers. You might try billboards in Silicon Valley, for example, to promote a series of books about computers. Or, if you publish a travel guide or atlas that is well distributed in gas stations, restaurants, or tourist spots, you might try billboards announcing that your guide is available at the next exit.

A few pointers: Use no more than six words in the ad. Motorists usually have the billboard in view for only a few seconds, so the message has to be simple and clear (hence, the book's message probably also has to be simple and clear). Try placing billboards where there is high foot traffic as well (as, for example, on Sunset Boulevard). Again, billboards are most effective when used as reminder advertising.

Here are a few more books which have been promoted on Sunset Boulevard billboards:

The Blooding, by Joseph Wambaugh (Perigord Press)

Max Headroom: The Picture Book of the Film, by Steve Roberts (Vintage)

Nice Guys Sleep Alone: A Survival Guide to Dating in the '80s, by Bruce Feirstein (Dell)

One More Time, by Carol Burnett (Random House)

Secrets, by Danielle Steele (Dell)

11:16 Display Billboards in Malls

Many shopping malls and airport terminals now offer space on their walls for billboard advertising. Why not test one of your major books (a general book that would appeal to an affluent audience) in a mall billboard, especially one near a chain bookstore?

- Day-Timers has found that its billboard advertising in airport terminals has yielded thousands of inquiries and orders every week.

- Avon advertised the mass-market edition of Spencer Johnson's *The One Minute Sales Person* in nine top-market airport terminals during the month of September, 1986. To complement these billboards, they placed a full-page ad in the Business Travel supplement of *USA Today*.

11:17 Transit Advertising

While not yet standard media for book advertisements, buses, subways, and taxis have been used to advertise books. If you do advertise any of your titles via such transit ads, try to include a "Take One" order pad attached to the ad so that interested commuters can easily remember the title of the book and where to buy it.

- A few years back one author, who was able to buy transit ads quite cheaply because of a family connection, filled the buses of New York with ads for his new novel. As a result, he received publicity in *Publishers Weekly*, the *New York Times*, and other major newspapers in the city. He also sold a lot of books to people who saw the ads in the buses. If I recall, he even got on a local bestseller list.

- New American Library also used transit advertising to promote the paperback edition of *Smart Women, Foolish Choices* by Connell Cowen and Melvyn Kinder.

Note that transit ads can appear on the outside as well as the inside. You might use outside ads on buses and taxis in the same way you might use a billboard ad. One advantage of transit ads over billboards is that the transit ad travels all over the city (that may also be a disadvantage if you are trying to target a specific district of the city).

Several services (such as Advan out of San Francisco, California, and Wheeler, Inc. out of Long Island City, New York) are now offering moving ads on delivery trucks. How much does it cost to place such an ad? About $9,000 per month. Advan claims to deliver 33,000 impressions a day—impressions which reportedly are quite effective in building a company's image. Again, if you are trying to make an impact on a local level (either for a mass-market novel or a regional title), such advertising might well be worth the expense.

A relatively new variation on the standard transit ad is known as moped advertising. In this case, a company pays a person on a moped to drive around (at a beach, in certain areas of the city, or at some public event) carrying a small billboard advertisement. Moped advertising has the advantage of allowing you to specifically target the areas and audiences you want to reach. You can also test advertise more cheaply than with other transit ads which usually require a minimum number of ads (whose cost, while cheap per advertisement, can add up quickly to become quite expensive).

11:18 Other Billboard Ads

A few other billboard-type ads which have been used include bench ads (at bus stops or park benches), sandwich boards carried around in heavy pedestrian traffic, picket advertising, parking meter ads, shopping carts, ski lifts, bumper stickers, and Johnny Ads (yup, you guessed it, these are ads in public toilet facilities).

• One way you might use such billboard advertising is to hire pickets to carry signs advertising one of your books in front of a major bookstore in a high traffic area. Before you do this, be sure you obtain the permission of the bookstore owner. Also, this type of advertising would probably be more effective if the advertising message were humorous or warmly appealing in some way.

• The *Denver Quarterly* has placed advertisements on bus benches in Denver which read, "Keep Denver literate. Read." The ads, which also feature their name and number, have proven to be quite effective in obtaining new subscribers.

• The sides of New York City bus shelters are now adorned with large full-color advertising posters which are protected by glass and illuminated at night. If you want to create an impression with the major media located in New York, you might want to place ads in midtown Manhattan. For more information, write to **New York Shelter Media**, 750 Third Avenue, New York, NY 10017; (212) 867-4700.

11:19 Business Cards

The use of business cards has already been discussed in Section 4:01. The only reason I mention them here is that you should think of your business cards as wallet-sized billboards and use them accordingly. Business cards can be one of your most effective promotional tools. Hence, be sure to remind your authors, editors, and marketing representatives to carry a few of their cards with them at all times. Business cards are great facilitators of networking opportunities.

11:20 The Yellow Pages

People rarely look at the Yellow Pages unless they are actively interested in buying something. Hence, advertising in the Yellow Pages may be a great opportunity for you to sell your books, especially if you publish a regional title that would be of interest to people who use the Yellow Pages to do their walking for them. For example, if you published a local restaurant guide, why not advertise the guide under the Restaurants section of the Yellow Pages? Whatever you do, don't list your company under books; list it under your subject specialty.

Indeed, you need not limit your advertising to the local directory. It is possible to buy space through a national network of Yellow Pages if you have a book that would interest a specific national audience.

For instance, we at Ad-Lib have been considering using the Yellow Pages in major cities to advertise our *Directory of Book Printers*. It would be a natural marketplace for our directory since most Yellow Pages do not carry a separate listing for book printers. Hence, if someone is searching for a book printer, they have to wade through all the quick printer listings under the Printing heading to find a company who prints books. Even then it is difficult to locate a quality book printer because they camouflage themselves as directory and manual printers. The only printers who advertise themselves as book printers are usually vanity presses. Our *Directory* would save the self-publisher much time in locating a reliable book printer.

If you have been thinking about advertising in any telephone directories, here are some resources to contact:

- **AT&T Toll-Free 800 Directories**, P. O. Box 6000, 44068, Jacksonville, FL 32231-4068; (800) 562-2255; Fax: (904) 636-1237.

- **National Yellow Pages Service Association**, 340 E. Big Beaver Road #500, ·Troy, MI 48083; (313) 680-8880. Send for their free 20-page booklet, *National Yellow Pages Advertising Fact Book*. Here are just a few of the facts cited in this booklet:

  76.7% of all adults refer to the Yellow Pages in a typical month.

  On a typical day, the Yellow Pages are referred to 49,000,000 times.

  50.0% of all Yellow Pages references result in a purchase of a
    product or service.

- The following two books will help you buy and design Yellow Pages ads that work:

  Advertising in the Yellow Pages, by W. F. Wagner — Harvest Press,
    15237 Sunset Boulevard, Pacific Palisades, CA 90272-9922;
    (213) 459-3824.

  Getting the Most from Your Yellow Pages Advertising, by Barry Maher
    — AMACOM, 135 West 50th Street, New York, NY 10020.

11:21 Other Directory Listings

Don't forget to get your books and company listed in any appropriate directories. Also, consider advertising in directory issues that are most applicable to your line of books. For example, if you publish craft books, you should certainly be listed in the periodic directory issues of *Creative Product News* — and you should also consider advertising in such issues. Dover Publications, Chilton Book Company, and Horizon Publishers all advertise in this trade magazine.

Note that *Book Publishing Resource Guide* lists many directories and bibliographies which feature books, authors, and publishers as resources.

Authors — You should be on the lookout for directories (and trade periodicals which feature directory listings) that might be appropriate for your book. Since you probably do more reading in your field than your publisher does, you are far more likely to spot such directories. When you do find some, ask your publisher to contact them for listing information and, if the budget permits, advertising rates.

11:22 In-Store Broadcast Ads

Some grocery stores and shopping malls now provide their own in-store background music programming. Often they also sell advertising on these broadcasts. Campbell Soups has used such in-store ads to build consumer interest in their LeMenu frozen dinners. Why couldn't a publisher of a series of romance novels use similar in-store ads to build consumer interest in their books?

Two major advantages of such advertising are that it reaches buyers *when* they are in a buying mood and *where* the product is readily available for purchase.

11:23 In-Flight Audio Magazines

W. H. Freeman had a segment from Linus Pauling's *How to Live Longer and Feel Better* featured on Eastern Airlines' Audio Magazine Program. I'm not sure if this segment was an excerpt from the book or a paid advertisement. Nonetheless, if you publish a book that would interest an affluent business audience, you should look into getting your book on similar programs (perhaps combined with an advertisement in the airline's in-flight print magazine).

11:24 Ads in Mail Order Catalogs

Some major mail order catalogs have begun accepting outside advertising in their catalogs. For example, *The Sharper Image* now carries four ads in each monthly issue of its catalog. Bloomingdale's carries as many as twelve ads in their catalog.

While advertising in these high-ticket catalogs is expensive, it might be appropriate for promoting an expensive limited edition title. You should also be on the lookout for other catalogs which might offer more affordable advertising rates and better demographics for your particular titles.

11:25 Multi-Level Marketing

Though multi-level marketing is both a method of advertising and a means of distribution, we can consider it here. Many books and reports (especially opportunity and home business titles) are already marketed through some form of multi-level marketing. Personally, though, I would be hesitant to use this method because the multi-level marketing industry still has a rather weak reputation. Too many fly-by-night operators are attracted to multi-level marketing programs. Besides, many of the programs themselves are too close to being pyramid schemes.

Multi-level marketing still hasn't developed its full potential. Perhaps someday someone will come up with a way to draw upon the strengths of multi-level marketing without incorporating its weaknesses. Until then, I cannot advocate it.

- Medallion Books, which made a concerted effort to promote general trade books via a multi-level marketing scheme, lost $4,500,000 during its year of operation. Among its titles were *The Chocolate Lover's Cookbook* by Billie Little, *Personal Power Program* by Bret Lyon (which sold 50,000 copies through multi-level marketing), *Immune for Life*, an illustrated Bible, and several novels. The company eventually went bankrupt.

11:26 Special Offers / Coupons

Coupons and other special offers have worked well for many book publishers. Certainly any cookbook publisher should be able to arrange cross-promotions for ingredients, cooking tools, aprons, or other kitchen utensils. How about offering free gambling tickets with a mystery novel set in Las Vegas? Or how about convincing tourist attractions to offer two-for-one specials to accompany a travel guide? Or, to accompany an investment guide, why not work with a reputable stock brokerage house to offer 10% discount coupons for brokerage services?

• Addison-Wesley arranged for special offers to be included with several of their books. In cooperation with the National Gardening Association, they offered a free subscription to the *National Gardening* magazine with any purchase of *Gardening: The Complete Guide to Growing America's Favorite Fruits and Vegetables*.

• For their updated edition of *The New Joy of Photography*, Addison-Wesley tucked in coupons worth $10.00 in film processing charges from Kodak.

• Bantam worked with Clairol to cross-merchandise their Loveswept romances and Clairol's Pazazz Sheer Color Wash. Each heroine in the *Delaneys of Killaroo* trilogy was described as having hair the color of one of the new shades being introduced by Clairol. To support sales of the novels, Clairol inserted 750,000 book samplers of the trilogy (provided by Bantam) in Pazazz displays that were placed in 10,000 food and drug stores. In addition, 50¢-off coupons for Pazazz were bound into every novel.

• To promote *Sprouse's Income Tax Handbook, 1989*, by Mary Sprouse, Penquin printed a coupon redeemable for a free copy of her $7.95 trade paperback, *How to Survive a Tax Audit*.

• As incentive for purchasing *The Birds Around Us*, illustrated by Robert Dawson, Ortho offered four reproductions from the book as frameable prints for only $6.95 plus the order form in the book.

• Better Homes and Gardens Books promoted several expensive books by offering coupons for free copies of less expensive, but related titles. They offered the $5.95 *Cooking with Whole Grains* free with purchase of the $24.95 *Better Homes and Gardens Eating Healthy Cook Book*. They also offered the $5.95 *Easy Bazaar Crafts* free with purchase of the $21.95 *Better Homes and Gardens Crafts to Decorate Your Home*.

11:27 Refunds and Rebates

Why offer rebates? Here are eight good reasons:

1. Booksellers are more likely to stock and feature your books if you offer some sort of promotion.

2. Consumers are more likely to buy your books if you give them some sort of incentive. According to one study, 65% of all consumers report that rebate offers do affect their decision to buy one product over another. In 1986, fifty billion dollars were offered in consumer rebate programs, yet less than 10% of that money was actually redeemed.

3. If you require customers to send in a receipt (or a coupon from the book) in order to get a rebate, you then get a chance to sell them additional titles on your list. When you send them their rebate check, also enclose information on related titles.

4. Of course, you should also add them to your mailing list so you can let them know about new titles you publish.

5. Rebates give you an opportunity to track book sales in different parts of the country (and in different markets). You can also conduct some market research at the same time—by asking the consumer to answer a few questions when they send in their request for a rebate.

6. Another advantage of rebates is that you can offer a discount on your books without hurting the bookseller's profit margin or causing other unnecessary administrative hassles (which would result if you offered direct cents-off coupons).

7. Rebates can be used to encourage readers to sample one of a series of books.

8. Rebates have also been used by other manufacturers to move surplus inventories. Perhaps publishers could use rebates to sell stagnant backlist titles or to remainder titles direct to consumers. Such rebates could replace the current attempts to remainder books in place.

Here are a few examples of how book publishers have used refunds and rebates to encourage sales of their titles:

- For a new series of gardening books, Houghton Mifflin offered a rebate to any reader who bought a second book in the series. All the consumer had to do was fill in a coupon and send it direct to Houghton Mifflin for a rebate.

- To promote its line of fourteen cookbooks from the California Culinary Academy, Ortho Information Services combined rebates along with cents-off coupons. Whenever a customer bought a book in the series, they received a $3.00 rebate coupon packed inside the book. When the customer mailed the coupon into Ortho, they were sent back a $3.00 rebate check as well as two bounceback coupons each worth $1.50 towards the purchase of other cookbooks in the series.

- Woodbine House offered a $1.00 rebate on the purchase of their $9.95 book, *The Catalog of Catalogs*. All the reader had to do was to clip the Proof of Purchase symbol on the back cover of the book, fill out the coupon on the last page of the book, and send both to Woodbine House. One drawback to this procedure: It is sure to discourage sales to libraries (since most would not appreciate users cutting out Proofs of Purchases from the covers of the book).

- Besides offering a $1.00 rebate coupon inside its $7.95 *1990 Road Atlas*, Rand McNally also included more than $700.00 in travel coupons, redeemable at various hotel chains, restaurants, and roadside attractions.

- Prentice Hall also offered an in-pack rebate as well as special coupons to promote *The 1989 Mobil Road Atlas and Trip Planning Guide to the United States, Canada, and Mexico*.

- To build up interest in *La Mattanza: The Sicilian Madness* by Charles Carmello, Paperjacks ran a big money-back ad in *USA Today* offering a $1.00 refund to anyone who mailed in the ad coupon, a cash register receipt, and the ISBN/UPC number from the book's cover.

- In the fall of 1986, Reader's Digest Books offered a $1.00 rebate to anyone who sent them a bookstore receipt proving that they had bought a Reader's Digest book. At the same time, they also invited bookstore customers to participate in one of the $6,000,000 sweepstakes offered by their mail order division.

- A **coufund** (a cross between a coupon and a refund) is a new form of refund that has yet to be tried by publishers. It's a standard coupon that is only valid after the customer glues three or four proofs of purchase on it. Like any other coupon, the coufund is redeemed at the cash register. Why not try offering a coufund for your books?

11:28 Sweepstakes

In a recent poll conducted by *Premium/Incentive Business*, over 96% of the companies which ran sweepstakes accomplished their goals. For these companies, sweepstakes helped to increase sales, public awareness, brand recognition, and/or store traffic.

Here are a few of the ways different publishers have used sweepstakes to promote their lead titles:

- For Pat Booth's novel, *Palm Beach*, Crown offered a free one-week vacation at the Breakers, a luxury resort in Palm Beach. An entry form, printed on the inside flap of the hardcover book, could either be clipped out or copied and then sent in to the sweepstakes office. To encourage bookstore promotion of this sweepstakes, Crown also offered to give the same vacation to the owner of the bookstore where the winner had obtained the sweepstakes information.

- Abingdon Press ran a "Win a Trip to the Holy Land" consumer contest to help promote William Gentz's *The Dictionary of Bible and Religion*.

- To promote the tie-in novel for the movie *Jewel of the Nile*, Avon ran a consumer sweepstakes with a grand prize of a trip to Morocco where the movie had been filmed. To draw attention to the sweepstakes, Avon provided bookstores and travel agencies with floor displays, brochures, and movie posters.

- Villard offered a $10,000 scholarship and ten personal computers in a "Dollars for Scholars" sweepstakes to promote *The Princeton Review: Cracking the System: the SAT*. Coupons for the sweepstakes were available at any store which displayed the "Dollars for Scholars" poster and shelf talker.

- Harlequin offered consumers a chance to have their "dreams come true" by winning a Rolls-Royce or a trip to Paris in their First Class Sweepstakes. The sweepstakes was announced on the covers and in four-color inserts of all fall releases in Harlequin's romance novel series. Harlequin also provided stores with posters and shelf talkers to draw attention to the sweepstakes. Entry forms were available in each book as well as on point-of-purchase coupon entry pads.

- Bantam sponsored a sweepstakes to promote its series of books featuring Disney characters. The prize? A free trip to Disneyland for a family of four.

- New American Library received 250,000 responses when they gave away the car used in the movie, *Christine*, in a sweepstakes promotion for the mass-market paperback reprint of the Stephen King novel.

- NAL sponsors about 20 promotions annually for the 450 books they publish each year. In one case they calculated that they sold 21% more books than they would have without a promotion. In another case, they received about eight times more floor displays in stores because of a sweepstake.

- For Clark Howard's novel, *Quick Silver*, NAL/Signet offered an instant win sweepstakes with a grand price of $1,000.00 and 100 second prizes of $25.00 each. Each copy of the novel contained a bound-in "Quick Silver" scratch-off card. To help promote the sweepstakes, NAL provided stores with an eye-catching 36-copy floor display.

Sweepstakes are an excellent way to spur interest in one of your books, especially one which you are backing with a major advertising budget (because sweepstakes work best with highly visible titles). Sweepstakes can also boost response to direct mail promotions by as much as 50%.

If you decide to offer a sweepstakes, you should hire a company which specializes in managing sweepstakes and other contests. The legal requirements for sweepstakes are so exacting that you shouldn't even try to offer one without advice from an experienced consultant. Besides helping you to meet the legal requirements, such companies can provide creative development, prize selection and acquisition, judges, and fulfillment. They are well worth any additional cost.

For more information write or call one of these companies (which all have excellent reputations):

D. L. Blair, 1051 Franklin Avenue, Garden City, NY 11530; (516) 746-3700.

D.-J Associates, 77 Danbury Road, P. O. Box 2048, Ridgefield, CT 06877; 203-431-8777.

Ventura Associates, 1350 Avenue of the Americas, New York, NY 10019; (212) 586-9720.

11:29 Other Contests

Another way to generate interest in your books is to sponsor contests which are in some way connected with the contents of your book or series of books. Unlike sweepstakes, these contests could be tests of knowledge, skill, or some other capability.

- For instance, Bantam sponsored a cover-girl contest to help promote its Sweet Dreams series of novels. Bantam also sponsored a Choose Your Own Adventure writing contest to help promote its series by that name; the winning manuscript, in this case, was published by Bantam as part of the series.

- In the back of book #12 in their Sweet Valley High series, Bantam printed two dozen questions based on the first twelve books of the series. Bantam received over 20,000 entries. Winners were randomly chosen from those who answered all the questions correctly. The prizes included a trip to New York City to meet Francine Pascal, creator of the series, as well as tickets to a Broadway show and a visit to the set of *All My Children*. The contest had its desired effect. Sales of backlist titles increased considerably.

  As an added benefit, Bantam was able to develop a list of teenage romance readers. Since the contest, Bantam has sent these readers newsletters and announcements of new series that might also interest them.

- Perhaps more than any other publisher, Bantam uses contests to promote its series. To promote Marcia Leonard's *Eating*, one of four titles in their What I Like series, Bantam sponsored a baby photo contest targeted at parents. The winner received $1,000 towards their child's education.

- John Magel, author/illustrator of *Dr. Moggle's Alphabet Challenge* published by Rand McNally, offered a set of alphabet blocks enclosed in a handmade cherry case as a prize to the reader who correctly identified two hidden words which he had designed into the book's illustrations. Besides identifying the two words, the winning reader also had to explain in 40 words or less the significance of those two words.

- Morrow, publisher of *Who Killed the Robins Family?* by Thomas Chastain and Bill Adler, offered a $10,000 prize to the reader who submitted the best answer to the title question.

- To promote its line of Ramona Quimby young adult novels by Beverly Clearly, Morrow sponsored a Ramona Quimby Look-alike Contest in 1984. Contestants had to go to bookstores to fill out the entry blank and submit a photo. Winners were chosen by a random drawing.

- To promote Arnold Lobel's *The Book of Pigericks*, Harper & Row invited children to write their own limericks about pigs.

- Putnam ran two contests to promote Eric Hill's *Spot's First Easter*, one of nine books in their Spot Lift-the-Flap book series. First, they ran a Draw Spot Contest for children, ages 3-10. Then, they ran a window display contest for bookstores displaying the drawings. In this way, they were able to promote both consumer and retailer awareness of the entire book series.

- Houghton Mifflin and five Twin Cities bookstores ran a Curious George Word-Search Contest for children through a full-page ad in *Minnesota Monthly*, the member magazine for donors to Minnesota Public Radio. Houghton Mifflin provided 75% of the $1,200 ad cost through co-op monies due the five bookstores; the bookstores each paid $60.00 as well. All the participating bookstores reported increased sales of Curious George titles plus a large mail order response to the contest. The prizes for the contest were children's dictionaries.

- Avon Books sponsored a Howard Cosell sound-alike contest for Cosell's *I Never Played the Game*. They backed up the contest with full-size color posters of Cosell, in-store displays, co-op advertising, radio contest promotions, and national broadcast and print publicity.

- During the summer of 1990, Llewellyn sponsored a book review contest in which previous customers were invited to write a 500-word review of a Llewellyn title. Those who wrote the best reviews of any title received a $20.00 gift certificate good for other Llewellyn titles.

11:30 Brandstanding

Brandstanding is the linking of special events with specific brands or products. For instance, Budweiser and Pepsi sponsor a number of different sports events each year. Millers sponsors golf games. Virginia Slims sponsors tennis tournaments. Why couldn't a publisher of an exercise book help to sponsor a run-for-fun event?

- When Bantam launched its Sweet Dreams line of young adult novels, it tied into the nationwide fashion shows sponsored by *Seventeen* magazine.

- How about sponsoring an attempt to break a world record? If the record were broken, the chances are that your company name or book title would be mentioned in *Guinness*, which currently sells over one million copies every year. That's a lot of free advertising.

- Bridge Publications sponsors an Indianapolis 500 race car (driven by 4-time winner, Al Unser, Sr.) to promote *Dianetics*, a self-help title. They promoted this sponsorship with a front cover ad in *Publishers Weekly* and other trade magazines.

If you publish books about sports, recreation, or even travel, you might consider sponsoring a sports event as a means to gain more recognition for your books.

11:31 Co-Op Ads

Co-operative promotions allow publishers to share mailing and labor costs while promoting their titles to specific markets. Because co-op mailings are so much less expensive and time-consuming than doing your own promotions, they allow you to promote to marginal markets that you might not otherwise approach.

Here are a few of established co-op marketing programs that you might want to use:

• **Author/Expert Interview Service** — Mailed three times a year, this file folder full of flyers is sent to 1,300 radio and television talk show hosts. Write to Para Publishing, P. O. Box 4232, Santa Barbara, CA 93140; (805) 968-7277; (800) 727-2782. Para Publishing also runs the following co-op promotions: **Reviewer's Choice** (sent three times a year to 3,000 in-house and corporate magazines), **Journalist's Resource** (sent twice a year to 1,500 freelance writers), and **Products on Review** (sent twice a year to 3,000 catalog buyers).

• **Leading Edge Review** — A four-page newsletter that features New Age titles, it is distributed free to 10,000 bookstore customers. The book publisher pays to have a book featured; the bookstore pays to have its name imprinted on the copies it distributes to customers. For more information, contact Leading Edge Review, P. O. Box 5010, St. Cloud, MN 56302; (612) 259-6364.

• **PMA Co-op Mailings** — Publishers Marketing Association sponsors many co-op programs every year (to libraries, bookstores, reviewers, and target markets). For more information, write to Publishers Marketing Association, 2401 Pacific Coast Highway #102, Hermosa Beach, CA 90254; (213) 372-2732.

• For other co-op marketing opportunities, read the COSMEP and PMA newsletters every month.

11:32 Book Fairs

Participating in local book fairs is an excellent way to introduce your books to new readers. Most of the people who come to such book fairs are avid readers who, if they like one of your books, will very likely order others as well. Make sure everyone who passes your booth gets a brochure or catalog.

Some of the best-known book fairs include the New York Is Book Country fair (October), the Great Midwestern Book Show in Minneapolis (September), Miami Book Fair International (November), San Antonio Inter-American Book Fair (October), and other fairs in San Francisco, Boston, and Seattle.

- Miami Book Fair International attracts over 100,000 readers every year and many major authors. Publishers have reported sales of $5,000 to $10,000 during the book fair.

- The Marin Self-Publishers Association sponsors a fair every year to exhibit books published by its members. The fair, usually held in September, draws a good number of book buyers as well as some media attention.

- The Philadelphia Publishers Group donated $3,000 worth of books to a city-sponsored literary celebration called Philadelphia Ink. The celebration included a book fair, seminars, and book readings, plus drawings for seven free collections of books.

- At the Great Midwestern Book Show in 1985, Ad-Lib sold over $600 in books. A number of other smaller presses did even better — so good, in fact, that they had to close early because they had run out of stock on most of their titles.

11:33 Other Festivals and Fairs

Besides participating in book fairs, seek out other fairs or festivals which might offer a market for your books. For example, if you publish books on crafts, why not exhibit at some local craft shows? Or, how about exhibiting your books on automobiles at a car show? Or books on sailing or fishing at a boat show?

- When Signe Carlson exhibited her book *North of Skarv Island* at Scan-Fair in Portland, Oregon, she sold 52 copies of the book in one day.

- Redbird Productions, as noted earlier, sold over 27,000 copies of their self-published book, *Cream and Bread*, by exhibiting at any festival which might be attended by people of Scandinavian heritage.

Chapter 12

Getting Distribution

The key to bookstore sales is two-pronged:
1. You have to get your books into the stores (distribution).
2. You have to get them out of the stores (advertising, publicity).

You won't make any bookstore sales if you do not have your books in the stores when your advertising and publicity hits the public; hence, you need to get distribution. But once you get distribution, you must be sure to promote your books so that they move off the booksellers' shelves into the hands of readers rather than back into your warehouse as returns.

No sane bookseller will carry your books for very long if you do not provide advertising and other promotional support that will help him or her sell your books. The average turn at retail for bookstores is somewhere between three and four times a year—that means that booksellers, in effect, replace their entire inventory of books about every three or four months. Booksellers cannot afford to stock books on their shelves which do not have sufficient demand to turn at retail within six months at the very latest. For the sake of completeness, they might carry a few titles just to fill out a special section but, even then, they will not tolerate slow moving books for long.

How do bookstores get the books they stock? In one recent survey of independent bookstores, 51% of the booksellers said that they used publishers as their primary source of supply, while 12% bought primarily from one wholesaler, 23% bought from more than one wholesaler, and 14% gave no response. Of course, many of the booksellers who used publishers as their primary source also bought from wholesalers as their secondary source.

The rest of this chapter reviews the various ways publishers can get their books distributed to bookstores.

12:01 Why Bookstores Buy from Wholesalers

Bookstores have a number of good reasons for buying from wholesalers or distributors rather than direct from a publisher. Here are just a few of them:

1. By combining a number of smaller orders, they can usually get a higher discount from distributors.
2. By consolidating orders with one distributor or wholesaler, they save a lot of time by eliminating the paperwork necessary to deal with many small orders. Not only do they save time in ordering, but they also save time when paying bills. It's far easier for them to keep track of one bill than many bills.
3. If a book doesn't sell, they can use their credit on returns to buy other books from the distributor. In the case of a one or two-book publisher, they could be stuck with no options for using the credit.
4. Distributors and wholesalers tend to be more reliable. They usually ship books faster than a publisher. Even major publishers are two to three times slower than wholesalers in shipping books.

12:02 Distributors and Wholesalers

Because there is such a wide variety of wholesalers and distributors in the book trade, the distinction between the two is not always clear. In this book, however, and in our *Book Publishing Resource Guide*, we do make a general distinction between the two functions.

A **distributor** stocks books, reps the books to its accounts, handles all fulfillment, and pays for the books on consignment (i.e., only when they are actually sold).

A **wholesaler**, on the other hand, functions essentially as an order taker for its accounts. Wholesalers generally do little promotion outside of a catalog, order books as the need arises or in small stock quantities, and pay for the books under normal terms (usually net 30 or net 90).

12:03 Distributing through Distributors

Why, then, use a distributor to represent your books when you could simply sign up a number of wholesalers to carry your books or do it yourself? Here are a few reasons why other publishers use distributors:

- Distributors have sales reps and other active means of promoting your books.
- Since they have established marketing channels, they can often move more books than you could on your own.

• Because they tend to represent fewer books than wholesalers and often specialize in certain kinds of books, they are more likely to promote the titles they carry.

• The major chain stores no longer buy directly from smaller publishers; hence, you need a distributor or established wholesaler to fulfill any chain store orders.

• They handle all the fulfillment and collection. What a relief!

The main disadvantages of using distributors is that they stock books on consignment (usually paying 90 days after they've sold the books), and they usually ask for a hefty discount (effectively, as much as 65-70%).

Distributors vary widely in their ability to cover the book trade or any other outlets. Hence, you should avoid signing an exclusive deal with any distributor unless they can demonstrate to you that they do offer full coverage of the book trade. At the very minimum, they must have sales representation in all major areas of the country, must make regular visits to the key chains and wholesalers, and should offer other means of promotion (such as catalogs and other mailings).

Here are the names of a few leading distributors. For a complete list (with names, addresses, phone numbers, territories served, subject interests, and other details), see the companion directory to this book, *Book Publishing Resource Guide*:

• **General distributors:** Independent Publishers Group, Kampmann National Book Network, Publishers Group West, Publishers Marketing Services, Seven Hills Books, Slawson Communications, and Talman Company.

• **Library distributors:** Quality Books and Unique Books.

• **Literary and small press distributors:** Consortium Book Sales, Independent Literary Publishers Association, Small Press Distribution, and Sun & Moon Press.

• **Religious distributors:** Genesis Marketing Group and Spring Arbor Distributors.

• **Specialty distributors:** African-American Book Distributors (books by and about African-Americans and Third World peoples), Ardic Book Distributors (travel), The Best Sellers (cookbooks), Children's Small Press Collection (children's books), Cogan Books (cookbooks), Horizon Publishers and Distributors (crafts), Royal Publications (health, new age), and Samuel French Trade (movie/theater books).

12:04 Selecting a Distributor

When selecting a distributor for your books, be sure to ask each of them for the following information which will allow you to make a reasonable choice:

1. **The discount they require from you** — Be sure to verify how they figure the discount. Get a firm idea what the resulting average discount will be (since many require a discount on net sales, the actual figure you pay them can vary depending on the net sale price). Most distributors ask for a discount of 15% to 30% of the net sale (which may, in turn, be discounted 30% to 50% from the retail price).

2. **Their terms** — How often will they pay? How often will they report sales? How soon after sales are made will they pay? Generally speaking, most pay 90 days after the sale.

3. **Their territory** — Are they asking for exclusivity? If so, what territory do they cover? What markets do they serve? Is the exclusivity only for a certain territory or market, or for the entire book trade?

4. **Insurance** — Do they insure your books while on consignment in their warehouse? If so, for how much?

5. **Their sales expectations** — Ask them how many of each title they expect to sell. Are they enthusiastic about your titles or only lukewarm?

6. **Other contract provisions** — Ask to see a sample contract. Check to see what the duration of the contract will be. If need be, how can the contract be terminated? What are your responsibilities? What are the responsibilities of the distributor?

7. **References** — Ask for the names, addresses, and phone numbers of other publishers they distribute. Phone these references, and check to see how well the distributor has served them. How many books did the distributor sell? Did they pay on time? Any problems? Any dramatic successes?

8. **Customer references** — As long as you are checking references, you should also ask for the names of some of their accounts. How well do they service their accounts? What kind of reputation do they have? Obviously you would not want a distributor who has a dishonest, sloppy, disorganized, or otherwise unhealthy reputation.

9. **Financial statements** — If you have any questions about the viability of a distributor, ask to see their financial statements to verify that they are sufficiently well-financed. You don't want to tie up your stock with a distributor who is teetering on the edge of bankruptcy.

When you do choose a distributor, remember one thing: The distributor cannot sell your books without your help. You must be prepared to back up their sales efforts with your own advertising and publicity campaign. Don't expect them to perform miracles without your help.

Furthermore, once you have signed up with a distributor, keep in touch with them. Let them know about your upcoming titles. Send them review copies as soon as they are off the press. Get their feedback on the cover designs, titles, and contents of your books before you go to press. Also, get their feedback on your promotional plans. Let them help you help them. The more you communicate with them, the more they can sell.

12:05 Distributing through Wholesalers

Instead of distributing your books exclusively through distributors, you might want to set up your own accounts with major wholesalers. In this case you would make your own sales presentations to the wholesalers (either by mail, over the phone, or through direct visits), take their orders, and handle all fulfillment and collection on your own.

Wholesalers can often provide you with as much distribution to the book trade as can a distributor. More bookstores order through Ingram and Baker & Taylor, the two largest bookstore wholesalers, than through any other distributors or wholesalers.

The advantages of using wholesalers rather than distributors are:

1. Wholesalers usually require a smaller discount (typically 46% to 55%).
2. They pay by invoice usually within 60 to 90 days, rather than stock books on consignment (though some wholesalers are now asking for consignment terms).
3. They do not require exclusive contracts. Instead, they will stock any books for which there is customer demand.

The disadvantages of using wholesalers rather than distributors are:

1. Wholesalers tend to be passive order takers. Although they usually publish a catalog of titles they stock and will often do some telephone marketing, few of them have sales representatives who regularly call on bookstores to promote new titles.
2. Since they carry so many more titles, they cannot promote your individual titles as aggressively as can a distributor who has fewer titles to offer.
3. Wholesalers do not offer complete fulfillment services for publishers.

Since wholesalers do not require exclusivity, you should try to set up accounts with as many as possible. Ingram and Baker & Taylor, of course, are essential for any general books, but if you publish highly specialized titles, you should also seek out those wholesalers who specialize in your subject area.

When approaching wholesalers, you will need to show them your catalog of books, your upcoming list, your promotional plans, your terms and discount schedule, and your returns policy. If you can demonstrate to them that you are producing quality books with general appeal, offer standard terms, and are well enough capitalized or committed (so that you will still be in business when — and if — it becomes necessary to return titles to you), you should have no trouble selling your books to them.

To help you understand the best way to approach wholesalers, here are the results of a survey we conducted in late 1986.

How Do Wholesalers Find Out About New Books

Here are the ways that 200 major wholesalers report that they find out about new books (note that they gave multiple answers to the question):

142 Direct mail from publishers
127 Reviews in trade magazines
124 Advertisements in trade magazines
119 Sales calls from representatives and/or word of mouth
82 Telephone calls from publishers
65 Reviews in newspapers
36 Advertisements in consumer magazines and newspapers
14 Other (bibliographies, conventions, authors)

From this survey, it is obvious that wholesalers do pay attention to their direct mail—and respond by buying. Reviews and advertisements in trade magazines are also effective in getting their attention. Direct contact through sales reps or phone calls are also effective (though not as effective as direct mail or trade magazines).

What Influences Wholesaler's Decision to Stock a Title

Once you get a wholesaler's attention, you must still convince them to stock your book. How can you influence their decision to stock a title? Here are a few ways:

72 The book fits their subject interest and/or market
27 Sales potential of the book
21 Customer requests or demand
18 Author's reputation and/or sales history
15 Price
14 Promotional plans and publisher support
12 Terms and discounts
11 Past sales of similar titles
10 Cover design
3 Timeliness

In our survey, this question was open-ended (fill in the blank). The above numbers summarize the wholesaler's answers to this question.

From this survey, obviously the most important criterion to most wholesalers is whether the book fits their subject interest or market. Hence, above all, you must match your promotions to the interests of the wholesalers. When you send them your catalog or a new title for consideration, be sure to point out how your book or books are appropriate to their markets.

Other factors enter in, but they play a more important role for certain types of wholesalers. For instance, mass-market jobbers are influenced by the author's reputation, the cover design, and publisher's promotional plans, while library wholesalers are more influenced by customer requests.

12:06 Working with Ingram Book Company

Ingram is the largest wholesaler to independent bookstores. They serve over 18,000 retail booksellers and libraries with a stock of 100,000 titles from 900 publishers. In 1988, they shipped over 60 million books.

Because Ingram offers a large selection of books, toll-free ordering, fast shipping, and easy returns, many booksellers would prefer to order through them rather than go direct to the publisher. As a result, if you want to penetrate the independent bookstore market, you need to get your books into Ingram's system.

If you are a small publisher or new to Ingram's system and want to get your books stocked by them, send your catalog, terms and discount schedule, and a short letter outlining your publishing and promotional plans to **Ann Mogensen, Ingram Book Company, 1125 Heil Quaker Boulevard, Lavergne, TN 37086; (615) 793-5000.**

Ingram takes an active role in promoting the books they carry. Here are just a few of the services they offer to bookstores:

* **Monthly magazines** — In their monthly magazines *Advance* and *Paperback Advance*, which are mailed to about 9,000 bookstores, Ingram lists the major new titles they have begun to offer. As a publisher, you may buy advertising in these magazines to help promote your books.

* **Microfiche** — ReadyStock is a weekly microfiche service listing all titles currently in stock in Ingram's three warehouses. By using this service, booksellers can special order any title in stock for their customers and expect shipment within days (rather than weeks or months which seems to be the standard when they order direct from the publisher).

* **Telephone promotions** — Ingrams offers telephone promotions of titles with wide appeal. When bookstore customers call in, they are asked if they would like to hear about some interesting new titles. If yes, then the telephone operators describe the new titles being promoted that week. Some publishers have reported sales increasing by 600% during the week they paid Ingram to promote one of their titles.

* **Bestseller lists** — Ingram publishes its own bestseller lists, both for general hardcover and softcover books and for specific areas like computer books, inspirational titles, cookbooks, how-to books, and so on. Booksellers use these lists as guides for ordering titles.

* **Ingram Books in Print Plus** — Ingram, in conjunction with the R. R. Bowker Company, has developed a database of over 800,000 titles on a CD-ROM laser disc. This database allows booksellers and librarians to identify and acquire almost any book still in print.

* **Bookshelf** — Ingram issues a monthly full-color consumer buying guide which they provide to bookstores at their cost ($5.00 per 100). The guide lists bestselling books as well as potential bestsellers.

- **Special catalogs** – Ingrams produces special interest catalogs, some aimed at consumers (such as their gift and computer book catalogs) and some aimed at booksellers for title selection (such as their guide to business and economics books). In every case, you may buy advertising space in the catalog to promote your titles in that category.

- **A.I.D.** – Ingram provides an Automatic Inventory Distribution program which allows booksellers to automatically receive a certain number of copies of any new title selections made by Ingram's own buying staff.

- **ROSI** – Ingram also provides a Recommended Opening Store Inventory selection service for new or expanding bookstores. ROSI is a computerized printout of bestselling titles by subject categories based on the popularity of those titles in a particular region. The bookseller can then edit the printout to their own needs and return it as an order.

- **Statement stuffers** – Ingram will insert your advertising flyer into their microfiche and statement mailings. The cost? About $1,000.00.

- **Other services** – Ingram also offer inventory control systems, co-op advertising summaries, audio/video and software stock, and many other services that aid booksellers in their business. Indeed, non-book product (software, audiotapes, and videotapes) accounted for 54% of Ingram's total business in 1986).

Because Ingram offers so many services to booksellers and because many of these services rely on their in-house selection of book titles, you should make a special effort to get your books stocked by them.

12:07 Working with Baker & Taylor

Baker & Taylor is the other major wholesaler to booksellers (and an even larger wholesaler to libraries). To get your books listed with Baker & Taylor, write to **Publishers Contact Services, Baker & Taylor, 652 East Main Street, P. O. Box 6920, Bridgewater, NJ 08807; (201) 218-3865**. Or fill out their Vendor Profile Questionnaire (write to them for a copy or photocopy the one on page 128 of *Book Marketing Made Easier*) and return it to them.

Whenever you complete your Advance Book Information forms for listings in the *Books In Print* database, send a copy to Baker & Taylor as well. Also send any other information about the book (brochures, copy of the cover, etc.) that will aid them in their title selection.

When your books come off the press, send a review copy to Baker & Taylor right away. These review copies will be evaluated by their staff of librarians for selection in their Final Approval Program. If your books are selected, the opening order would be for about 100 copies. Three factors affect their selection of a book:

1. sustained demand for your books,

2. the viability of your company (how long has it been in business, how actively does it promote its books, etc.), and

3) whether you offer normal terms of doing business.

Baker & Taylor is especially strong with libraries. If you are a new or small publisher, you can expect that as many as 75% of your library orders will be placed through Baker & Taylor. Here are just a few of the services that Baker & Taylor offers its customers:

- **Final Approval Program** — Some libraries order every title that is selected by Baker & Taylor for inclusion in this program.

- **Cataloging** — Baker & Taylor catalogs all new titles they stock. The cataloging of these titles encourages library and school orders because it makes the books more accessible and easier to process.

- **Special orders** — Baker & Taylor offers one-stop buying to its customers. Hence, even if your books are not stocked by any of its four centers (in New Jersey, Georgia, Illinois, and California), they will still order books from you when a customer requests your books. Such orders trickle in (one or two copies at a time) until such time that the demand warrants a larger order.

- **Bookfinder Microfiche** — They offer a weekly microfiche listing of the books in their inventory as well as their *Tradeweek* magazine on microfiche (which provides current information on new books, major buys, publicity campaigns, author tours, and a cross-check of bestseller lists.

- **FIRSTcall II** — They offer an electronic ordering system for bookstores with computers.

- **Journals** — Baker & Taylor publishes two bibliographic journals which they send to libraries to encourage orders. *Forecast* goes to 17,000 public libraries in the United States and Canada. *Directions* goes to about 7,000 academic and special libraries. Your books will be listed in the appropriate journal or journals if selected for the Final Approval Program. Plus, you can also advertise in either journal.

- **Book Alert** — Baker & Taylor also publishes a catalog of new titles which it sends to over 4,500 booksellers and 4,000 libraries. Advertising is also accepted in this catalog.

- **Library bestseller list** — Each month *Library Journal* lists those fiction and nonfiction titles which are most in demand by libraries from Baker & Taylor nationwide. Baker & Taylor also advertises that all new titles reviewed in *Library Journal* may be ordered through them.

- **Exhibits** — Baker & Taylor exhibits selected titles at overseas book fairs, including the Moscow and Frankfurt book fairs.

- **Overseas representation** — Their Feffer & Simons division is one of the major representatives of American books in European markets.

● **Other services** – As with Ingram, Baker & Taylor offers telephone solicitation of selected titles, statement stuffers, approval programs, and other special services.

As with Ingram, all these services mean that Baker & Taylor has developed a loyal following of booksellers and librarians who will not order a book which is not available through their programs. Hence, it would be worth your while to spend some time to get your books selected for Baker & Taylor's Final Approval Program.

12:08 Golden-Lee Book Distributors

According to one source, over half of all retail book sales pass through six major book buyers: the three major chains (B. Dalton Booksellers, Waldenbooks, and Crown) and the three major wholesalers (Ingram, Baker & Taylor, and Golden-Lee Book Distributors).

While not as large (yet) as Ingram and Baker & Taylor, Golden-Lee is growing fast. They recently opened a third distribution center in Atlanta, Georgia to complement their current distribution centers in Brooklyn, New York, and Los Angeles, California.

For more information or to submit your titles for consideration, write to the appropriate buyer (hardcover, mass-market, or trade paperback), **Golden-Lee Book Distributors, 1000 Dean Street, Brooklyn, NY 11238-3393; (718) 857-6333; (800) 221-0960**. Note that some publishers have reported collection problems with this wholesaler.

12:09 Working with Other Wholesalers

While courting the big three wholesalers, you should not overlook the good number of other regional and special wholesalers who offer great service to booksellers and librarians. For instance, Bookpeople is well-known as a wholesaler of books from independent publishers, especially on the West Coast. Gordon's Books, which covers the Rocky Mountain region, is another strong regional wholesaler.

To attract these regional and special wholesalers, you must woo them the same way you woo Ingram and Baker & Taylor: Produce great books. Offer standard terms. Let them know about forthcoming books early enough so they can have them in stock before publication date. And support your books with sufficient advertising and promotion.

Here are the names of a few of the best known wholesalers (again, for more detail, please see the *Book Publishing Resource Guide*):

● **General and regional wholesalers** – Bookazine, The Bookmen, Book-people, Dimondstein, the distributors, Gordon's Books, Inland Book, Koen Book Distributors, and Pacific Pipeline.

- **General library wholesalers** – Blackwell North America, The Book House, Brodart, Eastern Book Company, Emery-Pratt, Yankee Book Peddler, and those listed above.

- **Academic and special library wholesalers** – Academic Book Center, Ambassador Book Service, Ballen Booksellers, EBS Book Service, Midwest Library Service, Scholarly Book Center, Scholium International, and Siler's Library Distributors, among others.

- **Medical wholesalers** – Login Brothers Books, J. A. Majors Medical Book Company, Matthews Book Company, Rittenhouse, and others.

- **Law book wholesalers** – Fred B. Rothman Company, Thomas Law Book Company, Weidner & Associates, and others.

- **Religious wholesalers** – Riverside Book and Bible, Spring Arbor Distributors, and others.

- **New age wholesalers** – DeVorss Book Distributors, Moving Books, New Concepts, New Leaf Distributing, Samuel Weiser Inc., Starlite Distributors, Wishing Well Distributing, and others.

In dealing with wholesalers, remember the following key points:

- Don't give away the store. Make them earn their discounts. Don't offer them higher discounts unless they buy in quantity. For instance, don't offer more than 20% discount for orders of 1 or 2 books. Offer 50% discount only if they order at least 25 or 100 copies.

- Offer net 30 terms. Don't let any wholesaler ever go beyond 90 days in paying their invoices.

- When receiving orders from new wholesalers, check their credit carefully. Ask them to prepay orders until their credit is established.

- Keep your wholesalers informed of new developments with your books and authors.

12:10 ID's – Independent Distributors

Independent distributors (otherwise known as ID's or paperback jobbers) are responsible for the distribution of most mass-market paperbacks and magazines. These jobbers are local agencies which distribute to booksellers, schools, drug stores, food stores, airport news outlets, newsstands, and other paperback outlets. Most of them get their stock from national distributors such as Kable News Company, Select Distributors, and Simon & Schuster Mass Merchandise Company rather than direct from the book publishers.

Although most of their business involves magazines and mass-market paperbacks, some of these local jobbers also carrying hardcovers and trade paperbacks, especially bestsellers and regional titles. Some will also represent textbooks to schools and colleges.

If you publish regional titles which might interest these jobbers, you should check to see if your local jobber handles anything other than magazines and mass-market paperbacks. You might find a willing helper for your local distribution.

Tom and Marilyn Ross met with the truck drivers of their local jobber, San Diego Periodical Distributors, to promote their book on *Creative Loafing*. This meeting helped them to get greater local distribution for the book than they could have accomplished on their own time.

And, as mentioned previously, Jacqueline Susann was famous for her breakfasts with such truck drivers, working to convince them to give her books the best positions in the paperback racks.

12:11 Distributing through Other Publishers

Many major book publishers also distribute other publishers' lines. If you've developed a line of books and are looking for distribution to the trade, you could contact another publisher whose publishing philosophy you admire. You might find them amenable to taking on distribution of your line.

Most publishers who do distribute other publishers's books require a hefty discount to do so, as much as 25% of the net price of the book. In turn, they take care of all sales visits, distribution, fulfillment, and collection. Meanwhile, you would still be responsible for editing and producing the book, plus all advertising and promotion.

What are the advantages of distributing through a larger publisher? Besides the benefits of sales representation, fulfillment, and collection, distribution via a larger publisher provides your line of books with more credibility and clout. It also provides your company with instant access to the major trade accounts.

What are the disadvantages? First, a larger publisher will always give first priority to their own line and only then focus on the other publishers they represent. Second, few larger publishers will distribute smaller book publishers unless they are producing at least three or four new titles each season (spring and fall).

Here are a few major publishers who distribute other publishers' books. Note that most of the smaller publishers listed here have been distributed by major publishers for at least three years, so it must be working for them.

- **Farrar, Straus, & Giroux** distributes AARP Books, Aperture, North Point Press, PAJ Publications, and Soho Press.

- **Harper & Row** distributes Beacon Press, Crossroad/Continuum, Garden Way Publishing, Inner Traditions, and Kodansha International, among others.

- **Little, Brown & Company** distributes Atlantic Monthly Press, Boston Museum of Fine Arts, M. Evans and Company, New York Graphic Society Books, and Oxmoor House, among others.
- **Random House** distributes Readers Digest Books, Sierra Club Books, and TSR Inc.
- **Rizzoli International** distributes Eridanos Press, Hudson Hills, PBC International, Timken, and Vendome Press (all publishers of art).
- **St. Martin's Press** distributes Jeremy P. Tarcher and Prima Press.
- **Simon & Schuster** distributes Meadowbrook Press and Paris Review Editions.
- **W. W. Norton** distributes Dembner Books, The Ecco Press, New Directions Books, Pushcart Press, Saybrook Publishing, Taunton Press, and Thames & Hudson, among others.

An alternative to being distributed by a larger publisher is to join with a group of other publishers to form your own distribution. That's what the Independent Literary Publishers Association and Wisconsin Authors and Publishers Alliance have done. Other regional book publisher associations have also experimented with temporary distribution arrangements.

For Expo 86 in Vancouver, The Mountaineers Books and Sasquatch Books organized a group of 25 small presses in the Pacific Northwest and put together a catalog of the best travel books for the region. This *Expose Yourself to the Pacific Northwest* catalog was distributed at the Expo and to all the bookstores in the region. Pacific Pipeline, a regional wholesaler, handled fulfillment. Not only did the presses receive many orders as a result of the catalog, but they also received lots of publicity.

Many smaller and mid-size publishers, such as Bob Adams, Writer's Digest Books, and Voyaguer Press, have begun to distribute other publishers books. Indeed, such mid-size publishers may offer the best alternative distribution setup for startup publishing companies.

Recently Ad-Lib Publication signed up with Voyageur Press to handle our distribution to the book trade. So far, it's working out well. They are small enough to give us individual attention yet large enough to command the interest and respect of the major chains and wholesalers.

12:12 Selling to Chain Stores

Rather than go with a distributor, you could handle your own distribution through wholesalers, chain stores, and direct sales to independent booksellers. In that case, you would have to make your own sales to the major chain stores. The three major chain stores (B. Dalton / Barnes & Noble, Waldenbooks, and Crown) account for almost 30% of all retail bookstore sales. Hence, you can hardly afford to ignore them if your books are of general interest.

Here are a few guidelines and suggestions on how to sell your books to chain stores:

- The major chain bookstores have all cut back on the number of vendors they will buy from. Hence, in the beginning, you will not be able to sell to them direct. If they like your book or books, they will order through one of the major wholesalers or distributors.

- Later, if they begin to sell $100,000 of your books every year, they may take you on as a vendor. There are exceptions to this rule, but not very many.

- In most cases, the chains are looking for publishers who can offer a steady flow of new books of broad general interest each season.

- They are more likely to take on a book from a small publisher if the book fills a need.

- The books from smaller publishers that are finally chosen for the major chains' backlist often start off as good sellers in some of their local stores.

- Most chains have central buying offices that do most of the buying for all the stores in the chain. In some cases, individual stores may also buy regional titles or other books of special interest to their customers.

When Aaron Silverman and Molly Maguire self-published the *Raymond Chandler Mystery Map of Los Angeles*, they sold the map to the local B. Dalton and Crown stores. The Hollywood B. Dalton store sold 20 copies in five days, while ten Crown stores each sold ten copies in ten days. Of course, they all reordered.

- The best way to begin contact with the major chains is to call and ask for the name of their buyer who would be the most appropriate person to send your materials to. Then, on a regular basis, send that person information about your forthcoming books.

- Once you have books in hand, send them a copy of the bound book before you call to ask for an order. Especially with new or unknown publishers, they would prefer seeing a finished copy of the book so they can verify for themselves that the book is of high quality in both production and contents.

- Keep your key contacts informed. Let them know about any major rights sales, publicity, new promotions, and author appearances. Especially inform them of any strong local promotions you'll be doing so they can order books for their local outlets.

For example, as part of their promotion of the new edition of *The TM Book*, Fairfield Press worked with Waldenbooks to do a special co-op advertising test in a number of major cities.

- Be cautious about selling too many books to the chains. Note, for one thing, that returns from chain stores average about 25% as compared to about 10% from independent stores.

- A recent study indicated that 38% of the chain store buyers found out about new titles by reading direct mail promotions sent by the publishers themselves. In another study of smaller chain stores conducted by the *Huenefeld Report*, over 90% of the respondents reported that catalogs and flyers were the most effective way (other than personal visits) for publishers to keep them informed. Hence, don't be hesitant to mail information about your new books to these buyers.

- Work with the editors of chain newsletters such as Walden's *Xignals* (sent bimonthly to 250,000 science fiction book buyers), *Crime Times* (for mystery fans), *WaldenCooks* (for cookbooks), *Fiction Finds* (first novels and midlist titles), and *Walden Journal* (for business titles). For example, when books are promoted in *WaldenCooks*, sales have sometimes increased by as much as ten times.

  Knopf claims that a B. Dalton newsletter (with its enthusiastic rave reviews) almost single-handedly put their cookbook, *The Vegetarian Epicure*, on the bestseller lists.

- Finally, don't put all your eggs in the same basket. While the major chain stores may have a significant impact on retail sales, don't overlook the smaller regional chains and the great number of independent and specialty stores.

  For the names and addresses of almost 300 bookstore chains as well as 150 top independent booksellers, see *Book Publishing Resource Guide*.

12:13 Distributing through Independent Sales Reps

If you decide to handle your own distribution, you could assign certain regions of the country or certain markets to sales rep groups. Or you could have representatives handle all your sales calls, from visits to the major chains and wholesalers to regular trips to see independent booksellers.

To set up your own network of sales reps groups, consult the list of sales representatives in *Book Publishing Resource Guide*. Write or call those who look like they could fill your needs. To cover the entire country, you will probably have to contact six to ten groups since few of them cover more than ten states. When you do write to them, send them the same information you would send to a wholesaler or chain store.

Most sales rep groups ask for a commission of 10-15% on all retail sales and 5% on all wholesale sales in their area, irrespective of whether they made the sale or not. Generally, they will visit most larger bookstores in their area twice a year (spring and fall). The main advantage of having sales reps is that many booksellers still respond better to sales visits than to direct mail. The main disadvantage of having sales reps is that they only sell; they do not handle warehousing, fulfillment, and collection as distributors do.

One caution on setting up independent sales reps: Check their references as thoroughly as you would for distributors. When I was consulting in the gift industry, one of the companies I was working with hired a new rep without checking his references very carefully. At first, everything seemed fine. He sold many new accounts and, hence, seemed to be doing a good job. Unfortunately, he sold most of those accounts by telling them that they didn't have to pay for 90 to 120 days and if they hadn't sold the product by that time, they could return it for full credit. Meanwhile, he collected his commissions. Only when we began having problems collecting these accounts did we discover what he had done. Since he would take no responsibility for the situation, the company ended up losing close to $10,000 in bad debts.

12:14 Hire Your Own Sales Reps

Many major publishers hire their own network of sales reps to cover the entire country. Having your own reps is, perhaps, the best of all distribution alternatives. The only difficulty with hiring your own reps is that you need to have at least $350,000 in net annual sales to the book trade before you can justify the cost of hiring even one rep. With salary, travel expenses, and other costs, each sales rep will cost you anywhere from $30,000 to $60,000 per year.

If you do decide that you can afford to hire a rep or two, start small by hiring one or two to cover your own region first. In that way you can keep their travel expenses down while you test the effectiveness of having reps for your line of books.

12:15 Handle Your Own Distribution

As an alternative, you can test the effectiveness of hiring reps by first asking some of your regular personnel (sales manager, editors, or yourself) to handle the local sales calls. In this way you can get experience on what works best for your company before you commit your time and money to organizing a separate department for sales representatives.

Another advantage of handling your local sales in this way is that you give your sales manager and editors experience in the field. Prentice-Hall requires that all new employees begin by going on the road for three years before they are allowed to edit or market books. A number of other companies also encourage this policy. Only by going out into the stores can you see what kind of books are actually selling, what kind of merchandising actually works, and what sort of people buy your books. Moreover, being out in the field is one of the best ways to get ideas for new books.

If you do decide to use your other employees part time as sales reps, train them well before you send them out. Make sure they know your list of new titles, not only the names of the books but also why the bookstore should carry them—why, for instance, these new titles will interest the bookstore's customers. Also, be sure they are familiar with your backlist—which titles are selling best, what other titles might interest a particular group of people, any titles you are offering at a special discount, and so on. Finally, have them memorize your company's payment terms, discounts, returns policy, co-op advertising terms, and any other promotional programs you offer.

Don't send out anyone who you do not feel will represent your company in a professional manner and in keeping with the image you want to project for your company. And don't force anyone to go out who really does not want to go.

To supplement your own direct sales, you could also use direct mailings and telemarketing to cover the bookstores, wholesalers, and other buyers. The next chapter on Working with Bookstores goes into more detail on how to handle your own distribution through bookstores.

12:16 Why Exhibit Your Books

One of the most effective ways to get your books known to booksellers is to exhibit your books at their conventions. Not only can you show your books to as many as 8,000 booksellers, but you can also attract new distributors, corporate buyers, and subsidiary rights buyers.

The major book show in the United States is the American Booksellers Association (ABA) Convention which is generally held the first weekend in June. It is held in different parts of the country each year. In 1991, it will be held in New York City. For more information about this show, contact the American Booksellers Association (address on p. 35).

Other major shows include the Frankfurt Book Fair (held in October at Frankfurt, West Germany), the Bologna Children's Book Fair (held in the spring in Bologna, Italy), the Christian Booksellers Association Convention (July), the American Library Association Convention (July), the Canadian Booksellers Association Convention (July), and National Association of College Stores (April). Major international shows are also held in London, Barcelona, Cairo, Jerusalem, and Moscow. Many of the regional booksellers associations hold book shows in September.

When planning your book exhibits, don't forget other trade shows. For example, if you publish children's books, you might want to exhibit at the toy show in February. Or, if you publish craft books, exhibit at some of the annual craft shows (Dover Publications exhibited at Quilt Market '85). Or, for travel books, you might try an exhibit at the International Travel Industry Expo in mid-April.

If you publish academic books, you should consider exhibiting at professional conferences such as those sponsored by the American Institute of Biological Sciences, the American Sociological Association, or the American Political Science Association.

Besides selling books, here are a few other reasons why you should attend at least one of these shows or conferences every year:

• Your number one reason, of course, should be to sell books. That means you should be prepared to take orders right at the show, to offer special discounts for orders placed at the show, to staff your booth with sales oriented people, and to have catalogs and brochures ready to give out to all who attend the show.

At the 1988 ABA in Anaheim, the Crossing Press took orders for 5,000 books. They lured booksellers to their booth by offering food samples from their new cookbook, *Street Food* by Rose Grant.

At the 1986 ABA in New Orleans, Basil Blackwell wrote almost $12,000 in business while the University of Chicago Press sold $60,000 worth of books. Not that all publishers do this well. Many publishers, especially smaller ones, are quite pleased if they sell $2,000 to $5,000 worth of books.

At the National Association of College Stores convention, Berkley wrote orders for more than 40,000 units.

In 1985, 17% of all bookstore orders from Christian publishers were placed at the CBA Convention in Dallas.

• Use conventions to display new books to the trade and to any media in attendance at the show. Book shows are superb times to give away samples of your books to opinion makers – especially booksellers.

At the 1988 ABA Convention, Algonquin Books gave away 1,600 sample copies of Clyde Edgerton's *The Floatplane Notebooks*. At the same convention, Ad-Lib Publications gave away 1,500 reading copies of *Tinseltowns, USA*.

For the ABA Convention in Anaheim, California, Avery Publishing Group gave away a bound sample chapter from their *Guide to Natural Food Restaurants*. The chapter listed those natural food restaurants in the southern California area.

Chase Communications gave away a brochure excerpted from *TV PR* by Wicke Champers and Spring Asher. The brochure listed ways that publishers and booksellers could use *TV PR* to sell books.

• Rather than place an emphasis on book sales, you may choose to use shows to establish your company name and image more firmly in the minds of booksellers and the media. Book shows are one of the best ways to gain such exposure.

At the various ABA Conventions, I've met media contacts for the CBS *Morning Program*, *New York Times Book Review*, *USA Today*, the *Tonight Show*, and many radio and TV shows around the country.

- You will be able to make valuable marketing contacts. In many cases you will have an opportunity to meet with buyers for major chain stores, wholesalers, distributors, and corporations. At no other events would you find such a concentration of buyers.

  At the 1988 ABA Convention, Coffee House Press found foreign reps for their books in Holland, France, and Germany.

- Such conventions provide a superb learning opportunity—to see how others display and merchandise their books, to network with other publishers to discover new ways to market your own books, and to meet booksellers face to face to learn what more you can do to fill their needs.

- Many major rights deals are made at conventions. Not only can you sell rights to your books, but you can also pick up the rights to other people's books. Even smaller publishers can get into the act.

  I know of a good number of smaller publishers who have obtained English language rights to books by attending the Frankfurt show and other shows.

- Conventions can be a concentrated form of market research. In just two to three days, you can get a detailed overview of the industry, discover what sorts of books other publishers are promoting, and learn what new lines your competitors are bringing out. You may even uncover an emergent trend that you can exploit before others follow suit.

- Conventions are also an excellent place to meet new and established authors and to come up with ideas for new books. This book grew out of my experience at the 1985 ABA convention in San Francisco. Almost every smaller publisher I talked to at that convention had one question to ask me: "How do I get my books into the hands of the people who can use them most?" This book, I hope, provides a few answers to that question.

- Bring your authors to the major book shows. If possible, try to get them booked as one of the major speakers at the breakfast meetings with booksellers because these meetings (more than any other event at the ABA Convention) are the major showcases for authors.

  Since only a few authors and celebrities will be invited to speak at the meetings, you should also try to get your authors a spot in the autographing booths (where you can give away 200 copies in half an hour).

Authors — You, too, should attend these major trade shows, Indeed, some 1,000 authors attend the ABA Convention every year. If you would like to share the spotlight with fewer authors, ask your publisher to send you to the regional booksellers convention nearest you.

12:17 How to Exhibit Your Books

To mount a successful exhibit, you must plan ahead. Not only should you design your booth, but you should also decide which of your books you will display (and which will get the limelight), what promotions you will run, who will staff the booth, and how the booth will be shipped, set up, maintained, dismantled, and shipped home.

To help you plan your exhibit, read *Book Fairs* by Dan Poynter and *Exhibit Marketing* by Edward Chapman. Also, to ensure that you cover all the necessary steps in preparing and packing for a book exhibit, use the Exhibit Planning Checklist in *Book Marketing Made Easier*.

Here are a few other pointers on how to exhibit your books:

● If there are certain people you want to be sure to meet during the convention, contact them in advance to arrange an appointment to see them during the show. Don't expect that you will be able to just drop by their booth and meet them. Chances are that they will be out on the floor just like you. So be sure to make appointments ahead of time with any major buyers or other key contacts that you want to meet. Then confirm those appointments the first day of the convention by dropping your card off at their booth with a short message confirming the time and place of your meeting.

● In his *Book Marketing Handbook*, Nat Bodian summed up the best way to work a show:

1. Make the booth accessible.
2. Make your books accessible.
3. Make yourself accessible.

● Arrange your booth so people can get in and out easily. Have your books, catalogs, and other sales literature readily available so that people can reach them without having to run an obstacle course.

● Hire a professional to design your booth (or, at least, make it look like it was designed by a professional). It should be attractive, open, and inviting. It should project an image compatible with the one you want for your company.

● Arrange your books so that they are easy to find—either by subject, title, or author. Display new titles up front where they will get the most attention.

● Give away samples of your books—either advance review copies or at least sample chapters. This is one of the best ways to get people talking about your major titles months before their publication dates.

● Staff your booth with friendly, knowledgeable salespeople. The people in your booth must know your line of books well enough to talk intelligently about any title. They must also know your company's terms and discounts, upcoming promotions, and other policies.

- Make sure you have enough people to staff the booth. Staffing a booth can be tiring, especially after four days, so be sure each person in your booth has enough time off to rest between work periods. Also, make sure each person has some time to scout the convention.

- Train the people who will staff your booth so they are comfortable staffing the booth. They should be ready to answer any questions that might come up (and they should be aware that if they cannot answer a question, they should write it down and be sure to get an answer or follow up with a letter after the convention). They should be alert and willing to help any passersby. They should not smoke in the booth.

- Have them make notes of those books which attract the most attention from browsers and buyers. These notes might come in handy in planning future exhibits or sales promotions following the convention.

- Have them also make notes of any questions, comments, inquiries, or other conversations which might come in handy for future promotions.

- If you cannot afford to rent a booth on your own, then join in a cooperative exhibit. Several of the publishers associations, including COSMEP, the Publishers Marketing Association, NAPRA, and the Rocky Mountain Book Publishers, offer cost-effective group exhibits at the major shows.

   Publishers' Book Exhibit and Conference Book Service also offer group exhibits at many conferences, association meetings, regional library meetings, and smaller book fairs which you might not otherwise be able to attend.

- When considering your costs for exhibiting at a show, remember that the booth rental represents perhaps as little as 25% of your total cost. Other costs include travel expenses, housing and food, staff salaries, booth design and construction, promotional materials, shipping, and miscellaneous booth charges.

Again, remember that the most important function of any exhibit is to sell your books. Keep that purpose in focus, and all the minor details will fall into place, making your job easier and more enjoyable.

12:18 How to Attract People to Your Exhibit Booth

When you have spent so much money on designing and staffing a booth, you don't want to leave it empty. While most of the attendees will pass by your booth sometime during the convention, many of them will probably pass by without much more than a glance — unless you provide them with some incentive to pause.

- **Display good books.** Of course, the best way you can ensure that they will stop to look is to have something worth looking at. If you publish good books (and people know it), people will stop by.

- **Advertise show specials.** Give a larger discount, or offer free freight, or announce some other special for any order placed at the show.

  At the 1988 ABA Convention, Krause Publications offered a 50% discount on selected titles, plus free freight on domestic orders over $300.00. Many other publishers also offered similar terms.

  Prior to the 1987 and 1988 ABA Conventions, Chilton Book Company placed an advertisement in *American Bookseller* offering a 10% discount to any bookseller who placed an order at the show and brought along the coupon in the ad. Anyone who placed an order was also entered into a drawing to be made at the end of the show—to win the order they placed during the show.

  In 1969, Lyle Stuart gave away $10.00 bills to the first 1,000 booksellers ordering at least 10 copies of their new title, *The Rich and the Famous*.

- **Hold a drawing.** To encourage more people to leave their business cards, hold a drawing each day for a free prize. Place a basket (or some other container) at the front of your booth so people can enter the drawing. It's a perfect way to get the names and addresses of convention goers so you can send them more promotional material after the convention.

  Perhaps the most attractive prizes given away in these drawings are free trips. To promote its new series of travel guides, Viking Penguin held a drawing for a free one-week trip for two to Italy. To highlight its *Escape in Style*, Inner Traditions offered a week at a private villa in Jamaica. Several publishers also offered free trips to the next year's ABA Convention.

  Many publishers also hold drawings for free books. At the 1988 ABA Convention, Woodbridge held a drawing for $1,000 worth of its books. Mustang Books and Indiana University Press gave away $500 worth of their books, while Moving Books and Steve Davis Publishing gave away $100 worth of their books.

  Little, Brown and Company gave away an alligator purse as part of their promotion of the novel, *The Lady with the Alligator Purse*.

  To promote *Prove It All Night: The Bruce Springsteen Trivia Book*, Mustang Press gave away an autographed copy of Bruce Springsteen's *Born in the USA* album.

  At the 1987 ABA Convention, Caedmon held drawings for three compact disc players. Indiana University Press raffled a VCR. The Better Baby Press gave away tuition for the "How to Multiply Your Baby's Intelligence" course. Bowker drew for an Hitachi CD-ROM drive. Four or five publishers gave away bottles of wine.

- **Give away something attractive.** Many publishers give away advance reading copies of their books, posters, bookmarks, buttons, book bags, and other attractive gifts.

Cliff Notes, for instance, gave away free stuffed penguins to promote their new advertising slogan: "Our product line is dressed to sell."

Advocacy Press gave away roses to all the women booksellers who came by their booth at the 1985 ABA convention. The roses were very much in keeping with the floral cover design of her book *Choices*, which is aimed at helping young girls make choices.

At the 1983 ALA Convention, Festival Publications gave away over 12,000 signs with humorous messages such as, "Ever meet a librarian who wasn't all booked up?" Each sign, of course, also carried a short sales message and ordering information for Festival's publications.

• **Give away a tie-in to your books** — especially your lead title. To promote Sara Shannon's *Diet for the Atomic Age*, Avery Publishing Group gave away personal radiation detectors.

• **Provide a service to the attendees.** If you can provide some service to the attendees, something they could really use, they'll flock to your booth. Staff members of the Lotus Light / Auroma International booths provided foot and back massages to anyone in need. Healthy Alternatives also gave free neck and shoulder massages. Ashley Books provided an electric foot massager. At the Triad Publishing booth, Deborah Caplan, author of *Back Trouble*, gave advice on how to make your back feel better.

• **Leave promotional literature where it can be seen.** If the convention has set aside a place where you can offer free literature, use it. At the 1985 ABA convention in San Francisco, several tables were placed outside the convention hall where publishers could place free literature and announcements of any special promotions. I saw many booksellers sifting through the material to select items of interest to them. Such free material, especially if it has your booth number on it, might help to draw more people to your booth.

• **Leave promotional items where people congregate.** To attract more people, publishers have placed napkins imprinted with their sales message and booth number on the counters of the coffee areas in the hall.

One enterprising small publisher placed fortune cookies near the press room coffee pot. Each fortune asked a question and listed the publisher's booth number as the place to go to get the answer. Cable News Network and several other reporters followed up on the story.

• **Hold a special promotion.** At the 1985 Canadian Booksellers Association convention, McClelland & Stewart offered a free Macintosh computer to the bookseller who came closest to guessing what the total sales would be for the major M&S titles through December 1985. As part of the contest, they also asked the booksellers to estimate how many of each title they expected to sell. This contest not only helped to draw booksellers's attention to M&S's major titles, but it also gave M&S a breakdown of the sales expectations of the booksellers.

12:19 Get Listed in Trade References

To aid booksellers in finding you and your books, make sure you are listed in all the major trade reference books. The references used most often by booksellers include *Publishers' Trade List Annual*, *Books in Print*, *Publisher's Weekly* spring and fall announcement issues, the *ABA Book Buyer's Handbook*, and the *NACS Book Buyer's Manual*.

For a listing of all the major directories of publishers, see the *Book Publishing Resource Guide*.

● *Publishers' Trade List Annual* is a multi-volume collection of the catalogs of most major publishers. You must pay to get a listing in this publication, but the cost is quite reasonable for the circulation it provides for your catalog. In a recent survey by the publisher of *PTLA*, 84% of the bookstores and over 90% of the libraries indicated that they used *PTLA* for ordering books.

● In a 1982 membership survey, 97% of the respondents said that the most valuable service provide by the American Booksellers Association was the *ABA Book Buyer's Handbook*. Hence, it is reasonable to conclude that the handbook is a vital source for them when they are ordering books.

● Besides advertising in *PTLA* and *Publishers Weekly*, you might also consider advertising in *Forthcoming Books*, the bimonthly update of the Books in Print series. Over 15,000 booksellers, librarians, and wholesalers use *Forthcoming Books* to help them locate and order new titles.

Listings in these major reference books will not only help you to get additional sales from booksellers and librarians, but should also help you in gaining distribution and representation. If you hope to gain maximum distribution of your books in bookstores, you must do at least some advertising in trade publications as well as in consumer publications.

Chapter 13

Working with Bookstores

According to a Gallup survey conducted in 1985, 55% of all book purchases are made in bookstores, 9% from supermarkets, 8% from department or discount stores, 7% from book clubs, 6% by direct mail, 4% from drug stores, 1% from newsstands, and 10% from other sources. Since bookstores are the primary source of books for most people, you would do well to serve them well.

Once you have a method of getting your books into the bookstores, you must still work to see that your books move out of the bookstores. Besides promoting your books to the general public via advertising and publicity, you can also work with the bookstores to see that your books are properly displayed and merchandised. This chapter, then, will describe different ways to work with bookstores to increase the exposure and sale of your books.

13:01 Setting Priorities

To get the most out of your sales calls to bookstores, you must make your priorities clear. Not only must you decide exactly what you want to accomplish with each visit, but you must also decide which of your accounts you should visit first. Here are some guidelines to help you in setting your own priorities:

• Remember the old 80/20 rule. 80% of your business will come from 20% of your accounts, so be sure to place your greatest emphasis on keeping in touch with these major accounts. At Bantam, they have a core group of experienced salesmen who handle only four or five accounts each. Since 25 major accounts make up almost 60% of their business, they give them extra special service and support.

- You or your reps should visit each major account at least twice a year, preferably more often. At the very minimum, you should call on your key accounts to show them your spring and fall lists. Your key accounts would probably include several major wholesalers, the biggest chains, and perhaps a few independent stores.

- If you are a smaller company without your own sales force or distributor, then you should certainly contact these key accounts by mail or by phone at least twice a year, or whenever you are bringing out a major new book.

- If many of your titles are regional in content, you should place more emphasis on stores in your own area. In such a case you could even visit the stores once a month or once every two months, thus providing them with far better service than they will ever get even from major publishers. New England Press does this with bookstores within the New England region.

- As long as you are already in an area visiting a major account, you might also visit some of the independent stores in the area at the same time. For example, if you were in Minneapolis to visit the regional B. Dalton buyers, you could also call on The Bookcase, Gringolet Books, Hungry Mind Bookstore, and Odegard Books, among others.

- Contact by phone or mail your promotional material to those stores and other accounts which you or your sales reps cannot visit directly.

13:02 Getting the Most from Your Sales Calls

In making sales calls to independent bookstores, smaller publishers have several advantages over major publishers. First, they can offer titles to the independent bookseller that most of the big chain and discount stores do not carry. Second, they can give more personal service to each store they visit.

Here are just a few suggestions for making your sales calls to the independents more effective.

- How do you find booksellers to call on? Here are some basic ways:
  1. Check the yellow pages of each city you visit.
  2. Go to the local library. Ask them if any new bookstores have started up. While there, also leave them one of your catalogs.
  3. Consult the *American Book Trade Directory*.

- When you visit booksellers, approach them as friends and co-workers. You can work with them to offer the best books to the reading public. Let them know you are there to help them.

- Expect to make full sales calls to two or three bookstores each day (four maximum when visiting a larger city). Prentice-Hall expects its sales representatives to visit about 80 bookstores four times a year.

- Start your visit with some chitchat about books. Ask them how their business is going? Who are their customers? Have they noticed any new trends?

- Prepare a sales book which features your new titles. Start with your lead titles. The sales book should include a cover of the book, catalog copy (with one or two points highlighted), any prepublication reviews or testimonies, and the major benefits of each book.

- Prepare effective sales literature that you can leave with the stores when you visit them. Always leave something behind. Give them your catalog, flyers or brochures describing your new titles, a price list with your terms and policies, and any other literature that will aid them in making a decision on which books to buy. For all your new titles, have extra cover samples printed up so you can show the booksellers what the books will look like on their shelves. Better yet, carry the actual books with you.

- If possible, travel with a carload of books so you can stock the store immediately. Since they often have to wait three to six weeks to get books from major publishers, booksellers will appreciate the immediate response. Plus it will save them shipping costs and will save you the time you would otherwise have to spend in packing and shipping them later.

- Give actual samples of your major new titles to your regular accounts. Not only will they appreciate this special service, but they are far more likely to order more copies of the books if they have read them.

- Work with them to prepare an adequate order for your titles. Don't push them to stock too many, but do let them know which titles you will be promoting most heavily so they can stock up on those titles.

- Before you leave, set up your next appointment with them. Tell them when you will return and then write it down on your calendar in front of them. Confirm that the day and time will suit them.

- When you come back for a return visit, check their remaining stock of your titles and prepare a proposed reorder that takes into account which of your titles sold best in *their* store.

Above all, when you or your sales rep visit a store, be sure you are prepared to talk about your books. Reps who have read the books they represent and can communicate their enthusiasm for a title will have an easier time selling to booksellers. Besides knowing your books, you should also know enough about the booksellers you visit to know which of your titles will go best in their stores.

When the Viking rep made a sales call at Just Books, he didn't talk about print runs. Instead, he talked about the books he'd read and recommended which ones he thought would go well at Just Books. As a result, the owner read two of the books and, in turn, recommended them to his customers—who bought over 200 of each title.

13:03 Make an Offer They Can't Refuse

Whenever you approach bookstores (whether in person, via telephone, or by mail), offer them something special which will encourage them to place an order or to increase their order for your titles. Here are a few offers that have worked successfully for other publishers:

- **Grant them larger discounts on non-returnable orders.** Because such discounts will allow bookstores to make more profit on the sale of each book and because they cannot return the books, they are more likely to promote your books in their store. Hence, not only will the bookstores tend to sell more copies of such titles, but you will also save time and money by not having to process returns. Thus, the larger discounts will often pay for themselves.

  Ad-Lib Publications offers a 50% discount for orders of ten or more books on a non-returnable basis.

  On selected backlist children's titles, Macmillan offered a 55% discount plus free freight for orders placed on a non-returnable basis.

- **Pay postage** on all orders of ten or more books (or some other limit you set). Free freight is one of the most requested items on the wish lists of bookstores.

  On orders for ten or more books from accounts which are paid up, Globe Pequot Press pays all freight charges that exceed 3% of the net invoice.

- **Offer a freight pass-through plan.** With such a plan, you price your books so that the discount is taken after the freight has been subtracted. For instance, if your suggested retail price for a book is $9.95, you could invoice your discounts on the freight pass-through price of $9.45 (allowing an average of 50¢ in shipping costs per book).

  Addison-Wesley suggests the following freight pass-through price to booksellers: "Add 4% to the invoiced list price and round to the nearest nickel. List price of $25.00 or more, add $1.00 to list price."

  Houghton Mifflin determines freight pass-through prices by adding the following amounts to the invoiced list price: For books retailing for $34.00 or more, add $1.00; $10.00 to $33.95, add 50¢; $5.00 to $9.95, add 25¢; under $5.00, add 15¢. Hence, for a book that they invoice at $9.50 retail, they would suggest the bookseller set the price at $9.75.

- **Participate in the Single Title Order Plan** (STOP) and let booksellers know that you do. This may result in a trickle of single title orders in the beginning, but once a store has become accustomed to ordering from you (and have found your service to be fast and reliable), they will be more likely to place larger orders from you when you do approach them with titles that suit their customer profile.

- **Offer white sales.** Run special sales on some of your slower moving titles to encourage bookstores to stock up on those titles.

Houghton Mifflin runs semi-annual white sales offering discounts of up to 85% on selected titles (all in mint condition). They require a minimum order of 25 assorted books on a non-returnable basis.

If you were going back to press on some backlist titles (and will be raising the prices of the books), you could offer a "Buy before the price increase!" promotion.

- **Offer a special anniversary discount.** If you are celebrating a company anniversary, a book anniversary, or an author's birthday, you might want to extend special discounts on certain titles.

To celebrate their first five years in business, Free Spirit Publishing offered booksellers a $5.00 certificate good toward their next purchase of $50.00 or more. Orders of $100.00 or more received a $10.00 certiif-cate. They limited this offer to one certificate per customer.

- **Offer delayed billing** on prepublication orders for major titles. Rather than invoice the bookstore at net 30 (which means they must pay in 30 days), you offer them net 60 or net 90 days.

To encourage larger stocking orders on its new edition of *The New Doubleday Cookbook*, Doubleday offered delayed billing on any order of ten or more copies.

For major fall titles, some publishers are now offering to delay billing until after the holidays. Booksellers, of course, love this practice since it not only eases their cash flow problems, but it also means that they have one less thing to worry about during their busiest selling season.

For their fall 1986 stock offer, Thomas Nelson Publishers offered Christmas dating *or* free freight on any order of 100 or more books. On any order of 500 or more books, they offered both Christmas dating *and* free freight.

New American Library offered a choice of either delayed billing or an extra 1% discount on any backlist order of 250 or more books.

- **Set up an agency plan** with new accounts. If you have a backlist of ten or more books within a specific subject area and publish three to four new titles each season in that same subject area, you might want to develop an agency plan that ensures that each participating store carries a minimum quantity of each of your current titles.

With such plans, a store usually is required to order a minimum of five or ten copies of each title, guarantee that they will maintain a stock of at least two to three copies of each title (and reorder when the stock runs low), and put in a standing order for five or more copies of each new title you release. In exchange for such guarantees, you would offer them a 5% or greater bonus discount over your normal schedule.

Agency plans are often used by professional and technical publishers who usually sell to booksellers on a short discount (a discount of no more than 20%).

- **Set up an In-Store Merchandising Program** (IMP) similar to the one set up by Houghton Mifflin. IMP offers booksellers incentives for stocking and displaying specific categories of Houghton Mifflin titles. The incentive package includes delayed billing, co-op money, rebates, plus a merchandising kit with materials for preparing special displays. Houghton Mifflin also offered prizes to the booksellers who set up the most effective displays. Over 400 independent stores plus a number of smaller chains took part in the first year of IMP programs.

- **Organize a remainder-in-place program.** Again, Houghton Mifflin organized a Houghton Mifflin Markdown Program (HMP) whereby the publisher and bookseller shared the cost of reducing prices on certain titles. Each book that was sold at a reduced price had to be clipped. The clippings then had to be submitted on a worksheet to Houghton Mifflin so the bookseller could get credit for the greatly reduced price. Waldenbooks, which participated in this program, noticed that sales went up dramatically for some discounted titles and several sold out.

- **Offer a returns incentive plan.** Berkley offers a retail incentive plan, whereby direct retail accounts which keep returns under 25% during a year can earn an additional 1% discount if their net dollar sales increased 5% to 7.9% over the past two years, or an additional 2% discount if their net increase was between 8 and 11.49%, or as much as an additional 4% discount if their net increase was over 13.5%.

- **Grant them a 5% discount for cash payment with the order.** You can afford to give a 5% discount to prepaid orders since you will save billing and collection costs on such accounts. Plus, of course, you will get the money several months earlier.

- **Give one free copy with a minimum order.** This promotion is most commonly used when a publisher wants to place a counter-top display in stores. Publishers also use the free-copy offer to promote new titles at the ABA Convention or for fall stock offers.

  To encourage booksellers and other retailers to stock the counter-top display for *Tinseltowns, U.S.A.*, Ad-Lib Publications offered a baker's dozen—one free copy with an order of a 12-copy counter-top display.

- **Promote backlist titles.** Offer special discounts or billing options to encourage booksellers to stock selected backlist titles.

  As a fall stock offer, Workman gave a 55% discount on a minimum order of five copies each of selected backlist titles; one order per store. Watson-Guptill offered a 50% discount or delayed billing on a minimum backlist order of 50 books and 25 titles per ship-to locations.

  Schocken Books offered a 43% discount on backlist orders of 25-49 books and 10 titles or a discount of 48% on backlist orders of 100 books and 25 titles, plus delayed billing of 90 days end of month. In addition, backlist quantities combined with frontlist quantities to maximize the frontlist discount.

- **If all else fails** to entice a prospective account to order your titles, offer to let them have the books on consignment—that means, they pay for the books only after they've sold them. For a sample consignment agreement which you should have the bookseller sign, see page 140 of *Book Marketing Made Easier*.

  When Renny Darling of Royal House Publishing published her first cookbook, *The Joy of Eating*, the book sold few copies until she went down personally to the Beverly Hills B. Dalton store and left five books on consignment for 90 days. Two days later the store ordered fifteen more copies; two days after that, another 30; a few days after that, several cases of the book. Her husband, seeing those results, took to the road and began peddling copies of the book in all the bookstores up and down the state of California. The book has now sold a half a million copies in the past ten years, and Royal House has gone on to publish seven more books. It all started, though, with that first small consignment.

13:04 The Importance of Service

Once you have gained an account, the best way to keep that account ordering your titles is to provide them with fast and friendly service. Make it easy for them to work with you, and they will remain loyal to you. Make it tough, and they will find someone else who can provide similar titles (even if those titles are not as good as yours).

- **Fill orders promptly.** If possible, ship the books the same day you receive the order. Ad-Lib has had a same-day shipping policy from the beginning, and we continually get rave reviews (and more orders) from our customers because of our prompt response to orders.

  If you can't offer same-day shipment, at least aim to ship all orders out in three days or less. Booksellers will love you if you do.

- **When billing, send legible invoices.** More than one bookseller has complained because of the sloppy business habits of some smaller publishers. A bookseller will always choose to work with a company which is well-organized and efficient over one that is not. And, as one bookseller noted, the ones who are organized are the first to be paid.

  Invoices (and packing lists) should include the following information: ISBN, title (unabbreviated), author, price (if the price has changed, note the price change), discount, invoice date, invoice number, purchase order number, freight charge, and retail total.

- **Provide alternative ways to transmit orders.** More and more booksellers are asking for alternative ways to order—by telephone, by fax, by computer. Independent booksellers are especially looking for ways to serve their customers better. If you provide them with ways to place orders more quickly, they will be more likely to order from you.

- **Pack your books carefully.** Avoid using styrofoam peanuts because they are messy to unpack. Booksellers prefer heavy folded paper or confetti (shredded invoices will do) or, better yet, shrinkwrapping. If you want a model, look at any shipment from Ingram.

   Also use a sturdy box. If shipping multiple boxes, number them (1 of 4, 2 of 4, etc.). Make sure the customer's purchase order number is on the mailing label.

- **Listen to booksellers.** First, of course, talk to them. Learn what their concerns are. Find out what you can do to make their job easier. And when they request a special service or an exception to the way you are accustomed to doing business, fill their request if it is reasonable.

- **Send thank you notes** to new accounts and to old accounts who have placed especially large reorders.

- **Support your books** by advertising and publicizing your books. No bookseller would want to carry a book which does not have the support and commitment of its publisher.

- Follow all the other suggestions contained in Chapter Four on how to serve your customers best.

13:05 Keep in Touch with Your Accounts

As part of your overall service to your accounts, you should have some means of maintaining contact with them between actual sales calls. You can use the phone, direct mail, catalogs, or newsletters to help you keep in touch with them. The following points provide a few suggestions on how to use each of these means to help you keep in touch with your bookstore customers.

13:06 Reach Out and Touch Someone

One of the best ways to keep in touch with your bookstore customers is to call them regularly. While this may not be practical if you have a large customer list, you can still use phone calls to keep in touch with your major accounts and other key contacts.

- Again, as I've mentioned before, installing a toll-free 800 number will encourage your customers to call you with new orders, questions, inquiries, suggestions, and other matters of importance to your relationship with them. When they do call, take the time to listen to them.

- Use outgoing calls not only to speed collection of past due accounts, but also to clarify any problems you might have encountered in fulfilling the order. For example, if the address is illegible or the purchase order number is missing, don't ship the order until you've called the bookseller and confirmed the order.

- Outbound sales calls preceded by a mailing of your catalog or other sales literature can increase your orders by as much as 60% (in the experience of at least one publisher).

- You can also use outbound phone calls to encourage orders from bookstores which have not previously ordered from you.

- Use the phone to communicate with your sales reps. A few days before Abigail Van Buren mentioned Rhoda Levin's book for cardiac spouses, *Heartmates*, in her column, she called the author and told her to "tell those Prentice Hall sales reps to get the book into the stores." Because Prentice Hall had established a digitized telephone message center, the author was able to leave a message for all sales reps with just one call. Since each sales rep checks into the message center every day, the word got out right away. That same day, the reps placed 1,000 orders for her book.

For more pointers on using telephones in marketing your books, see sections 10:10 and 10:11 of the chapter on advertising earlier in this book.

13:07 Sell by Direct Mail to Bookstores

Direct mail can be an effective way to reach the person responsible for buying new titles at bookstores. As mentioned in the last chapter, surveys have shown that chain store buyers relied on brochures and flyers as a major means for finding out about new titles. Review the first part of Chapter 10 for general pointers on using direct mail. Here, though, are a few specific tips for using direct mail in your trade promotions.

- Mail to the book buyer. Unless specifically requested to do so (or you have the names of subject-specific buyers in those stores), do not send your catalogs or other sales literature to more than one person at each store.

- For mailing lists, use your own list of bookstore buyers or rent lists from R. R. Bowker (publisher of the *American Book Trade Directory*), American Booksellers Association, Christian Booksellers Association, National Association of College Stores, or Association of Booksellers for Children. The association lists tend to be better because they are made up of active members (and the lists are more up-to-date).

  You could also use the lists of specialty bookstores, top independent booksellers, and chain stores in the *Specialty Booksellers Directory* and the *Book Publishing Resource Guide*. Targeted mailing lists are also available on pressure-sensitive labels or on computer disks for you to do your own mailings to these booksellers. For more information, call Ad-Lib Publications at (800) 669-0773.

- Mail regularly. Establish a certain schedule, two to four times a year (or more frequently for your best customers), so that booksellers begin to anticipate your mailings.

- Establish a recognizable format so that booksellers can easily recognize your promotions. This, again, will help to establish your company in the minds of the booksellers.

- When you send out invoices and statements, always include some announcement regarding one or more of your titles. Use these statement stuffers to offer special sales or promotions.

Authors — You can also make effective use of direct mail to promote your book to booksellers. As a member bookstore of ABA, I've received numerous promotions from authors. For example, to promote his novel, *Rush to Nowhere*, Howard Lewis Russell sent the following postcard to booksellers:

Dear Bookseller,
Enough about The Mysteries of Pittsburgh. Here's a mystery of New York: how do I make sure my book keeps selling? There's nothing sadder than a book that starts to sell well but doesn't catch on *because stores don't reorder*.
My book, **Rush to Nowhere**, has been in stores for two or three weeks now and, by all accounts, it's selling well.
So: please reorder my book. I'd hate for the three years I spent working on it to become a **Rush to Nowhere**.
Thanks for your support.

HOWARD LEWIS RUSSELL   124 East 91 Street NYC 10128

P.S. It's available from Ingram, Baker & Taylor, and my publisher, Donald I. Fine.

[Notice how he personalized the postcard with his address.]

13:08 Sell Via Catalogs

Your catalog is probably your best sales tool, other than your books themselves. Hence, you should design your catalog so that it effectively sells your books. You should design and publish a new catalog with each new list (usually in the spring and fall). To help you in designing your catalog, here are a few suggestions that might work for your books:

- **Mail your catalog only to your own house accounts** and other major prospects. Mail flyers or brochures to other marginal prospects offering them the complete catalog upon request.

• **Don't be stuck on one format for your catalog.** You can design your catalog for easy filing, or feature only frontlist titles, or make it so it stands out in the crowd—whatever works for your titles *and* the image you want to project for your company.

Stoller Publications' catalog for its line of calendars is a calendar itself with sample full-color pages from each of its major calendar titles. Not only is the catalog appropriate for its contents, but it also stands out from the crowd. Many booksellers undoubtedly put the beautiful calendar on the wall above their order desk, where it would be readily available for ordering.

Both Random House and Ballantine/Del Rey/Fawcett have put their frontlist catalogs on floppy disks to make it easier for computer-literate booksellers to find the books they need. With these floppy disks, booksellers will be able to select titles and transfer them directly to their own computerized databases for order entry.

• **Organize your catalog so every title is easy to find.** Provide a table of contents and a cross-referenced index by author, title, and subject (if appropriate).

• **Include all appropriate bibliographic information** so it will be readily accessible to anyone wanting the information. Include the title, subtitle, author, price, ISBN number, LCCN number, number of pages, trim size of book, type of binding(s), and the type and number of illustrations, indexes, appendices, and other information. Also describe the audience for the book, something about the contents and benefits of the book, and any other promotional information that will encourage booksellers to stock the book.

• **Make it easy to find the order form,** easy to detach from the catalog and mail, and easy to use to place an order. Include one or two extra order forms so that the catalog doesn't become obsolete after the first order is placed.

• **Include a clear and concise statement of your terms** and discounts, returns policy, and any other information a bookseller might want to know before placing an order with your company. If you offer co-op advertising money or other merchandising programs, promote these programs in your catalog so the booksellers know that you back your books with advertising support.

• **List the addresses of your sales representatives** or any distributors and major wholesalers who handle your book. Not only will this list make it easier for bookstores to consolidate their order for your books with other orders, but it will also encourage the wholesalers to stock more copies of your books. Be sure to send the wholesalers copies of your catalog so they are aware that orders may be coming their way.

• **Provide a return envelope** (whether prepaid or simply self-addressed is up to you) to make it easier for them to order.

- **Promote the use of your order phone number** (whether a standard line or an 800 number) so bookstores can easily find the information if they need to order quickly.

- **Describe the shipping information**—how you ship the books, what the charges will be, and what your usual turnaround time is. Of course, if your turnaround time is unimpressive, don't mention it until you have taken steps to improve it.

- **If you publish a catalog for direct sales to readers, don't send that catalog to booksellers.** Prepare a separate one for them, one that addresses their needs and concerns.

Don't offer better discounts in your consumer catalog than you give to booksellers. Don't laugh. Some publishers have.

Better yet, design your consumer catalog so it encourages bookstore sales. For instance, the order form of Picture Book Studio's consumer catalog features the following words: "Look for Picture Book Studio Books at Fine Bookstores Everywhere" — a line that many publishers have used. But Picture Book Studio went one step further. They added the following phrase: "and at These Special Dealers," and went on to list the names, addresses, and phone numbers of 250 bookstores! These special dealers had agreed to stock a minimum of 28 titles (for a total order of 84 books) and display Picture Book Studio books in a section by themselves.

13:09   Promote Via Newsletters

One of the best formats you can use to communicate regularly with your major accounts is a newsletter format. Newsletters can be more personal, newsy, and informal than catalogs. Plus, since newsletters do not require extensive graphics or design, the cost of producing a newsletter (both in terms of time and money) will usually be less than the cost of producing a catalog or other direct mail package.

Use your newsletter to let your key accounts know about new titles, upcoming promotions, updates on previous promotions, recent subsidiary rights sales, reprints or new editions, changing trade terms, and any other information that may be of use to them in selling your books. At the same time, however, be sure to keep the tone of the newsletter low-key and personal.

To encourage readership of your newsletter, add informative features on how to set up a display, or how to run a book fair, or other how-to items which would make life easier for the bookseller.

Finally, you could also include short camera-ready articles that booksellers could reprint in any newsletters or other mailings that they make to their own customer list. This copy could feature a special theme or subject (travel, cooking, or back to school) and excerpt material from one or more of your books. In this way you would be helping booksellers to find good material for their newsletters while promoting your books at the same time. When you offer such material, make it clear to the booksellers that they have your permission to reprint the material in their promotions.

- Scribners publishes a quarterly newsletter featuring new titles from their line of mystery books. The newsletter also describes any other recent successes with previous titles. This newsletter is mailed to their house list of bookstores, agents who might buy subsidiary rights, individual readers who have requested to receive the letter, and to Baker & Taylor's 18,000 library and bookstore accounts.

- Pocket Books published a similar newsletter directed at science fiction and fantasy readers. At the World Science Fiction Convention, they offered a free subscription to anyone requesting one. Since the people who attend such conventions are among the most active and influential readers in that genre, Pocket Books was able to create significant word-of-mouth advertising by mailing its newsletter to these people.

- To educate bookstores on how to merchandise audiotapes more effectively, Audio Renaissance Tapes publishes *New Audio Age*. This newsletter features retail marketing ideas, industry stats, marketing tips, and a letters section where retailers can share ideas and concerns.

- Henry Holt lists six purposes for their bimonthly *Hooters* newsletter, which is sent to the book trade:
  1. To bring into closer perspective marketing, publicity, and sales objectives for new titles on each seasonal list.
  2. To stimulate consumer sales by coordinating in advance promotional plans with booksellers.
  3. To offer sales incentive programs.
  4. To bring retailers in close touch with the direction, development, and performance of Henry Holt and Company's publishing programs, order fulfillment, and customer service.
  5. To gauge sales performance factors through booksellers' input and response.
  6. To keep the trade current on special promotions and events that impact sales.

- Random House sends out their *Kids' News* newsletter to children's booksellers and media as a follow-up to their seasonal catalogs.

- To promote their children's books, Dell sends the *Carousel* newsletter to 8,000 booksellers, librarians, educators, and media.

- Bantam publishes their *Dateline* newsletter to keep wholesalers and jobbers informed of new developments in their adult and children's lines. They also publish the *Rooster Crows* newsletter, which is sent to children's booksellers.

- The quarterly *Mysterious News* features stories from authors as well as excerpts from book reviews and a calendar of upcoming events.

Authors — You can write and mail your own newsletter not only to your fans but also to booksellers and jobbers. For instance, Julie Garwood, author of *The Lion's Lady*, offers to send a copy of her newsletter to anyone who writes to her.

13:10 Advertise in Trade Magazines

Another major way of keeping in one-way communication with your accounts (and other prospective customers) is to advertise your books in the major trade journals such as *Publishers Weekly, American Bookseller, Library Journal,* and some of the wholesaler and chain store publications. If you do not have a large ad budget but yet want to promote your books to the trade, your first priority should be to promote your new lists in the spring and fall announcements issues of these magazines.

Along those same lines, you should exhibit at the major book trade conventions whenever possible. Such conventions offer a superb opportunity to meet your customers face to face and to discuss with them how you can better serve their needs and desires.

13:11 Support Your Independent Bookseller

Do whatever you can to help booksellers sell more books (whether your own titles or books in general). Provide them with display materials, promotional literature, or any other services that will make their job easier and more productive.

Here are just a few of the things you can do for them:

- **Provide bookstores with camera-ready copy for their newsletters.** Since their regular customers enjoy the informative sales format of newsletters, many bookstores have found newsletters to be their most effective advertising media. Any help you can give them to make their newsletters better will certainly be appreciated.

- **Provide materials for bookstores who want to host open houses or book fairs** for librarians and school teachers. Let bookstores know that you are willing to supply them with giveaway items that would interest teachers and librarians — items such as bookmarks, bookplates, stickers, display materials, and other giveaways.

- **Prepare audio or video excerpts** of some of your books and send them to booksellers who host local radio or TV book programs (such as Penguin Bookshop's weekly *From the Bookshop* show on cable TV). You could also send such excerpts to other radio/TV book reviewers.

Such videos can also work as in-store ads. For instance, Gulf Publishing promoted its book, *Know your Rights*, via in-store videos featuring author interviews interspersed with ads for the book. Preliminary results from a number of other book publishers indicate that video promotions work best for midlist nonfiction titles.

- **Provide support for reading programs.** Houghton Mifflin, for example, underwrote a special issue of *Instructor* magazine which focused on helping schools to establish educational partnerships with local businesses and community groups. Their suggestions included establishing an after-school read-aloud program, donating a library of special titles to a retirement home, and giving free book coupons to students who help to tutor fellow students to read.

If you would like to support such programs, you could provide stores with cents-off coupons redeemable for those of your titles which would appeal to young readers.

- **Arrange readings by your authors.** While readings are most effective for poetry and fiction, they can also work for nonfiction.

Black Oak Books in Berkeley, California, sponsors from four to ten in-store events each month. While some of these events include autograph sessions, photography exhibits, and benefits, their most popular events are author readings. They feature not only fiction authors (such big names as Ursula LeGuin, Elmore Leonard, and E. L. Doctorow), but also nonfiction authors in such disciplines as psychology, philosophy of science, and mathematics. From 35 to as many as 500 people attend these readings.

Authors — If you'd be willing to do readings from your book, let your publisher know. Also, don't be afraid to contact local bookstores yourself to arrange such readings. Just be sure to coordinate such contacts with your publisher.

- **Arrange special demonstrations** linked to your books.

For a cookbook featuring Virginia seafood recipes, GB Publishing arranged for a chef to give cooking demonstrations at local bookstores. As part of the demonstration, they also gave away seafood samples. Helen Rathbone of Powell's Books for Cooks says that such in-store demonstrations are one of the best ways that they have found to promote a book. As she points out, not only do such demonstrations give people a chance to sample recipes from the book, but they also make the bookstore staff more familiar with the book.

Similar demonstrations could be arranged for craft books, how-to books, and even travel guides (with tips for travelers about how to pack), among other topics.

The Children's Bookstore in Chicago, Illinois, has sponsored such diverse in-store events as booktalks for parent groups, small pet show-and-tells (in honor of a visit from Stephen Kellogg), child development workshops for parents, dance workshops, writing contests, bilingual story hours as well as performances by storytellers, musicians, clowns, puppeteers, theatre groups, magicians, and dancers. Do you have any books or authors that would be suitable for such performances?

Authors — If you have an idea for an in-store demonstration, let your publisher know what you can do and when and where you would be available. If you work up a demonstration, make it lively, visual, and educational.

• **Sponsor any author events** that come your way, from autograph sessions to readings to demonstrations to special weeks.

For example, Colorado Governor Roy Romer proclaimed October 23 to 29, 1988, as Colorado Authors' Week. Over 150 authors participated in the week's events, including a reception at the Governor's Mansion. If any of your authors ever have an opportunity to participate in such events, give them your whole-hearted support.

During the week of November 5 to 12, 1988, the Chesapeake Regional Association of Booksellers sponsored Chesapeake Regional Authors Week. Member stores throughout the region presented book signings, readings, children's events, and more. Again, if you have an opportunity to participate in such a week, do so.

Authors — If you hear about any such upcoming weeks, especially local ones, let your publisher know about them as soon as possible so they can sponsor your participation *and* so they can ensure that your books are stocked in all stores in the region.

• **Provide bookstores with flyers and brochures** which can be imprinted with their name and address. Such promotional literature will be most effective if it is targeted at a specific audience (such as school teachers, craft people, corporate accounts, or travellers).

Gulf Publishing provides brochures and fliers with a blank space for an address for those bookstores who want to mail to their own customers or who would use the pieces for statement stuffers, bounce-back offers, or as counter pieces to solicit special orders.

- **Keep them up-to-date on your successes.** One year (or some other suitable time period) after publication of important titles, send extra covers of the book printed on the inside with the book's sales history and any other important information.

- **Support other bookstore outreach programs.** Besides providing material for school book fairs, check for any other audiences which bookstores might want to tap—such as corporate accounts, senior citizens, fundraising organizations, churches—and offer to provide the stores with material appropriate for that audience.

- **Encourage bookstores to sample your books.** The more they know about your books, the more likely they are to recommend your books to their customers. So send them advance reading copies of special books. While such advance reading copies might not carry that much weight with booksellers, when they *ask* for a galley copy from you, be sure to send it. If you want to ruin your reputation with booksellers, there is no quicker way than to ignore their requests for advance reading copies.

  M. Evans offered booksellers a chance to see galley copies of their new book, *The I-Like-My-Beer Diet*. With the galley copies, they offered a free case of beer to any bookseller willing to try out the diet.

  Newmarket Press offered to send booksellers, librarians, and teachers a review copy of *Lynda Madaras Talks to Teens about Aids* if they sent their request on their letterhead plus included $1.00 for shipping.

- **Offer bookstores a lamp** so they can highlight your book. Studies of bookstore browsers have shown that they tend to gravitate to those parts of the bookstore which are lit best. In other words, a light sells books. While you cannot make this offer to all bookstores, you sure can test it out in one or two of your local booksellers.

- **Conduct market research.** In researching the market for their *Country Inns of New England*, Globe Pequot Press visited various inns to find out who stayed at the inns. As a result, they discovered that the largest number of visitors to New England inns were coming from California. Armed with this information, they approached Waldenbooks and convinced them to test the guidebooks in their California stores. When the books sold out, Waldenbooks bought more. Now the California Waldenbooks stores are steady customers for the book (which has sold over 500,000 copies in ten editions).

- **Sponsor in-store contests.** Times Books sponsored a "Win a Great Meal" contest to publicize *Mariani's Coast-to-Coast Dining Guide*. Winners, chosen in a random drawing, were given dinners for two at selected restaurants featured in the book. Several winners were chosen in each of fifty major cities. Free dinners for two were also given to the bookstores where the winners had picked up their entry blanks for the contest (these free dinners were incentives for the bookseller to promote the contest).

To encourage bookstore personnel to read David Sandison's *Once Upon a Christmas*, Barron's held a contest to name the rock stars hidden in the book's artwork. The contest was only open to bookstore personnel. The winner received $1,000 worth of stereo equipment.

Morrow Junior Books offered retailers an opportunity to sponsor their own Encyclopedia Brown Mystery Contest when they placed a minimum order of Donald Sobol's *Encyclopedia Brown and the Case of the Treasure Hunt*.

• **Participate in holiday catalogs.** Over 800 stores and 55 publishers participated in the 1985 ABA *Time* magazine insert which promoted buying books for gifts. 90% of those bookstores participating in the insert were satisfied with the results. The 1986 insert, which cost publishers almost $7,000 to participate (with a photo and short description of one book), ran not only in *Time* but also in the *New York Times* and *New Yorker* magazine.

In 1986, five regional bookseller associations sponsored holiday catalogs. The New England Booksellers Association's catalog was sent to 2,000,000 people through inserts in twenty major Sunday papers. Publishers were charged $2,000 for a listing in the catalog.

The combined catalog of the Mountains and Plains Booksellers Association and the Intermountain Booksellers Association was inserted in seven Sunday papers with a combined circulation of 1,200,000. Listings cost $950.

The 1986 holiday catalog for the Pacific Northwest Booksellers Association was produced by Pacific Pipeline, a regional wholesaler. The catalog was distributed to 1,105,000 people through newspaper inserts, bookstore mailings, and distribution in the stores. Listings cost $1,200 per book (with regional titles costing only $850).

Instead of being inserted in newspapers, the 1986 holiday catalog for the Upper Midwest Booksellers Association was mailed to 300,000 customers on the combined mailing lists of member stores, plus 65,000 copies were inserted in the December issue of *Minnesota Monthly* magazine. Publishers paid to $850 per book for a listing.

13:12 Co-op Advertising

Perhaps the best promotional support program you can offer a bookseller is co-op advertising. Under such arrangements, you would rebate a portion of the bookseller's total purchase of eligible titles to be used by the bookseller to advertise your titles in local media. A typical rebate percentage would be about seven or eight per cent of the net dollar amount of the bookseller's order. Manufacturers of all types now set aside more than $10 billion a year in co-op advertising funds (of which about 70% is actually used).

Here are a few guidelines to follow in setting up a co-op advertising program to support your booksellers:

- If you offer co-op advertising to one bookseller, you have to offer the same terms to other booksellers. Not only is this the fair thing to do, it is an FTC regulation. So set your terms, and then stick to them.

- Both the chains and independent booksellers are open to such co-op advertising. Few booksellers will refuse such help.

- Offer co-op advertising only for your titles which have wide distribution. Be selective. Titles of wide general appeal are best for national co-op advertising programs; titles of regional appeal are best for regional co-op advertising programs.

- One drawback to co-op ads is that some booksellers may stock up heavily on your co-op titles in order to get a larger co-op advertising allowance and then end up returning most of the books. In such cases, there is no way for you to get any of the co-op money back. To limit your risk, set an upper credit limit for such co-op ads.

- Alternatively, you can award co-op moneys based on the bookseller's total buy for the previous year (rather than tie it to specific titles) and allow booksellers to choose which titles they advertise.

  Dial/Dutton makes available to bookstores 10% of their net order on a seasonal basis; they also offer 20% of the net sales on books sold during an autograph session.

  Harper Junior Books Group gives stores co-op ad credit worth 5% of the stores' previous year's dollar volume. Houghton Mifflin makes available 10% of the previous year's buy. Macmillan offers 8% of the store's net buy from the previous season. Oxmoor House gives 10% of retail on co-op ads with a supporting order for all trade titles. Viking Penguin allows 5% of the net value of one order per season.

  Booksellers, of course, like this option because it gives them the opportunity to push titles that they are enthusiastic about and which they find most suitable for their market. Most booksellers find it a pain to be restricted to one or two titles.

- Provide booksellers with appropriate copy for co-op advertisements, preferably camera-ready ad slicks which can be inserted with the bookstore's logo and address (or prerecorded tapes for radio ads).

- Allow booksellers to use the co-op money for alternative advertising promotions as well as the usual newspaper and radio ads. For instance, if they want to feature your titles in their direct mail literature, newsletters, or catalogs, work with them to arrange a co-op ad that satisfies both of you.

- Keep your co-op policy simple. Booksellers often complain about the paperwork involved in co-op ad programs. If you make yours simple to use, they will be more likely to work with you to promote your titles.

- Perhaps the best way to deal with co-op fund requests is to credit the bookstore's account after they provide you with a copy of the appropriate supporting invoice and a copy of the applicable ads.

- For more details on how to create a co-op advertising policy, see the sample statement of terms on page 141 of *Book Marketing Made Easy*. You may adapt this standard policy to suit your own needs.

- As an alternative to offering co-op ad funds to booksellers, you could offer co-op advertising opportunities in which you list the stores in your major consumer advertisements if they purchase a minimum quantity of the advertised titles.

  For instance, in a recent ad in *Parents* magazine, Macmillan promoted six of its books for children and listed 20 member bookstores of the Association of Booksellers for Children.

  Basil Blackwell placed a four-page center spread in the *New York Review of Books* in which they displayed 50 titles and featured the names and addresses of 74 bookstores. The booksellers qualified for the free listing by ordering at least 40% of the chosen titles, with no minimum quantity. Also, by listing so many bookstores, the publisher qualified for the lower retail ad rate.

  Both the Northern California Booksellers Association and Southern California Booksellers Association offer publishers an opportunity to advertise a book in the major regional newspapers (the *San Francisco Chronicle* and *Los Angeles Times*, respectively) at the lower retail rate if they list a local bookstore in the ad. To find out more about these programs which have been successful in producing bookstore sales of advertise titles, call or write the appropriate newspaper. Ask for their Bookline advertising program.

13:13 Point of Purchase Displays

As many as 50% of all bookstore customers have no specific purchase in mind when they first enter the store. Because such a large percentage of readers come to browse and window shop, you should do everything you can to encourage impulse sales of your books. There are any number of point-of-purchase (POP) sales aids which you can provide bookstores to help them sell your books. Here are just a few of them:

- **Bookmarks**—Supply bookstores with attractive bookmarks featuring your lead titles. Since many readers collect bookmarks, such giveaways will help to attract buyers into the store while at the same time bringing their attention to your books. Bookstores like to give them away.

  To promote Leo Buscaglia's *Bus 9 to Paradise*, Morrow distributed approximately 100 bus-shaped bookmarks to each bookstore receiving Ingram's monthly *Advance* magazine.

- **Book covers as billboards** — Above all, the covers of your books should be designed to sell books. When designing the covers, think of them as billboards which must attract the attention of the casual bookstore browser (and then make the sale).

- **Posters** — If your cover is well designed, blow it up and provide a copy for bookstores to use in their window displays. For instance, provide free posters with any order of ten or more books. Posters can be especially helpful in promoting children's books and science fiction books or, for that matter, any other books which are valued for their cover designs or interior illustrations.

  Arbor House, Delacorte, Harper & Row, and Random House, among others, all provide big blowups of book covers if a bookstore is sponsoring an autograph party. Bantam also supplies such blowups for bookstores to use in creating window displays.

  To promote the tenth anniversary of the Arthur series of children's books, Atlantic Monthly Press gave away "Happy Birthday, Arthur" posters.

- **Shelf-talkers** — Shelf-talkers are promotional cards, tags, or labels which help to draw attention to books on the shelf.

  For example, Crown used tent cards to promote a number of its cookbooks as lifestyle books. When the cookbooks are promoted in this way, they sell far faster than they would if shelved along with many other cookbooks.

  Avon provides booksellers with folding cards which announce that a book is by a local author.

  To promote its *The New Doubleday Cookbook*, Doubleday provided a shelf talker with a pad of tear-off recipe cards which had a cookbook comparison chart on the back side. Guess whose cookbook came out on top in the chart?

- **Bag stuffers** — Doubleday provided the same recipe cards in loose sheets as well so booksellers could place the cards into the bags of any book buyer who purchased a related title.

- **Book bags** — You can help bookstores save money by providing them with book bags advertising your books (and, if practical, imprinted with the store name). One advantage of imprinted bags is that they expose your advertising not only to the book buyer but also to the general public.

  Avon provided imprinted shopping bags to promote Gail Godwin's *The Finishing School*. Dell did the same for Richard Adams's *Maia*.

- **Door hangers** — To promote *Merry Christmas, Amelia Bedelia* by Peggy Parish, Greenwillow Books gave away door hangers that announced, "Do not disturb — I'm reading." A great promotion to give to children. Not only does it attract them to the book being advertised, but it also reinforces that reading books is a special activity.

- **Buttons**—Send the bookstores buttons advertising one of your books. Their employees can wear these buttons, or they can give the buttons away to customers.

  NAL used buttons to help promote the mass-market edition of *Smart Women, Foolish Choices*.

  To promote the *Amelia Bedelia Five-Volume Set* by Peggy Parish, Harper & Row provide "Thank you from Amelia Bedelia" buttons for the bookstores to give away to children.

- **Window streamers**—NAL also sent stores window streamers to help promote *Smart Women, Foolish Choices* as well as Robin Cook's *Mindbend*. Since most bookstores have only a limited amount of space to devote to window streamers, don't use them for any but your major books which you will be advertising and promoting extensively.

- **T-Shirts**—Provide imprinted T-shirts for each employee of your major bookstore accounts. Encourage them to wear the shirts on (and off) the job.

  To promote its book *Boomerang*, Workman handed out T-shirts that read "I Am the Thrower" on the front and "I Am the Catcher" on the back. Whenever you do provide imprinted items to bookstores, be sure that the imprint has some connection to the book you are promoting.

- **Coupon pads**—Along with the free poster for display in the bookstore, you could provide a coupon pad which would allow any consumer to order a free copy of the poster with the purchase of any of your books. Again, such offers would be especially suited to any books which are valued for their cover designs or interior illustrations.

- **Mobile displays**—Tyndale House not only supplied shelf talkers and full-color posters to promote their Campus Life series; they also provided a full-color mobile. Such active displays are more likely to attract attention.

  To celebrate Clifford's 25th birthday and to promote *Clifford's Birthday Party* by Norman Bridwell, Scholastic provided a 2-color mobile, posters and red and white birthday balloons.

- **Floor displays**—Anytime you can get the bookseller to give you some space all for your books, the better chance you have of attracting the attention of browsers and impulse buyers. Floor dumps or risers are an effective way to convince booksellers to give you that space. Note, however, that booksellers are not likely to give up such space except for titles expected to be bestsellers.

  If you can combine copies of previous titles from the same author in the display with his or her newest bestseller, then you'll have a good chance of increasing sales of those backlist titles. Random House combined Robert Ludlum's latest bestseller, *The Bourne Supremacy*, with copies of his previous bestsellers.

To promote John G. Jones novel, *The Supernatural*, Tudor provided retailers with a full-color, motorized, traffic-stopping display. The motor turned the header card to reveal three different posters.

Delacorte designed a pagoda-type floor display to promote Robert Duncan's novel, *China Dawn*. The bottom consisted of a corrugated cardboard base imprinted to look like wicker. The base could hold ten copies of the book. The display was topped off with a large red umbrella imprinted in bright gold lettering with the novel's title.

● **Counter displays** — Counter displays have one great advantage over almost any other sort of display: They can be placed right next to the checkout counter to encourage last minute impulse sales. Such counter displays work best for inexpensive humor and novelty books.

Klutz Books was able to get prominent display of its instruction books on how to juggle and how to use hacky sacks by providing stores with ready-to-use counter packs of ten books each.

The best displays are those which get the customer involved. Ingram Audio prepared a special display of audio tapes which included a personal tape player so bookstore browsers could listen to samples of the tapes featured in the display. Such a display not only got customers involved, but it also allowed them to sample the tapes before buying.

Philomel's counter display for Eric Carle's children's book, *Have You Seen My Cat?*, included a riser and a mobile to draw attention to it.

If you want to test counter displays for your books, you can order white corrugated displays in small quantities from Ad-Lib Publications. We stock counter displays for 6" x 9" and 8 1/2" x 11" books. For more information, call toll-free (800) 669-0773.

● **Window displays** — By encouraging booksellers to display your books more creatively, you will help them increase their sales at the same time you increase the sales of your titles.

For your main titles, provide special display materials to any bookseller ordering ten or more copies. Addison-Wesley supplied booksellers with a watering can and other gardening paraphernalia to promote the sale of its new book, *Gardening*.

Wilshire Books provided booksellers with copies of the sheet music from Tommy Boyce's most famous songs (*Last Train to Clarksville*, *Come a Little Bit Closer*, *I Wanna Be Free*, and *Valerie*) to accompany display copies of his book *How to Write a Hit Song and Sell It*.

To draw attention to his book about two famous San Franciscan dogs, *Bummer and Lazarus*, Malcolm Barker of Londonborn Publications had a designer prepare a display for his booth at the 1985 ABA convention. Because these two dogs were said to be so close to one another that their "tails wagged as one," the display was designed to show two dogs with their tails wagging in unison. After the ABA convention, Malcolm offered the display to a local bookseller who put it into his window. Not only did the display help the bookseller sell ten copies of the book every week, but it also drew people into the store. The bookseller loved the display so much that he refused to give it up.

Friendly Press offered bookstores "touring" window displays for two of its titles. They provided an expensive antique kimono to use in designing a window display for *Once Upon a Time: Visions of Old Japan* and blowups of filmstrips to promote *The Most Beautiful Place in the World: Impressions of Ten Master Photographers*. Friendly coordinated the window display tour. Each bookstore was expected to ship the display materials on to the next bookstore on the list after their week or two of the tour was up.

- **Window display contests** — To encourage booksellers to use the materials you provide or to develop their own displays for your books, offer a prize for the bookseller who puts together the best display.

   Pantheon Books offered a two week vacation in Paris for the bookseller who came up with the best display for its *Hachette Guide to France*. In this case, Whole Earth Provision Company of Austin, Texas, won the prize by setting up a temporary outdoor cafe offering French food and music.

   To promote *The Mollen Method* exercise book, Rodale Press offered a free four-day Caribbean cruise to the bookseller who put together the best display for the book. Rodale supplied a fitness display kit including a gym bag, T-shirt, ankle weights, sweatband, jump rope, and poster to be used in putting the display together.

- **Costumes** — Provide bookstores costumes based on some of your book's characters that they can use for special promotions.

   To promote the children's book, *D.W. All Wet*, Little, Brown and Company made available a costume of Arthur (the brother of D.W.).

   To celebrate The World of Beatrix Potter (and their large backlist of Beatrix Potter titles), Viking Penguin and Frederick Warne provided department stores with a kit containing posters, streamers, bookmarks, balloons, buttons, and more. Plus, they made available costumes of many of the characters.

- **Boutiques** — As part of its 50th anniversary celebration, Penguin offered booksellers a 47% discount on any order of ten or more books if they would establish a permanent Penguin boutique consisting of a wall section or floor fixture given over solely to Penguin titles. Penguin also offered a 50% discount on all orders of ten or more books to any bookseller joining their 2500 Club, which requires that the bookseller commit to stocking all 2,500 Penguin titles (and buy at least three copies of each new Penguin title).

- **In-store video ads** — Fleming H. Revell provided bookstores with videotapes of Zig Ziglar in action to help promote his new book, *Top Performance*.

Chapter 14

Selling through Other Retail Outlets

According to publisher David Godine, only 32% of the population of the United States has ever been in a bookstore, much less bought a book there. Whether his figure is accurate or not, there is certainly a large proportion of people who do not visit bookstores regularly. Hence, if you want to reach these people, you have to get your books into the places where these people will see them.

In Los Alamos, New Mexico, there are two full-service bookstores — and 28 other stores in the town that sell books. Nationwide, there are about ten times as many non-bookstore retail outlets as there are bookstores — over 200,000 such outlets. These retail outlets currently account for about half a billion dollars worth of book sales every year. That's a market worth pursuing.

14:01 The Advantages of Other Retail Outlets

The major advantage of distributing your books in non-bookstore retail outlets is that you can get your books before people who would not otherwise enter a bookstore. That means, if David Godine's estimate is true, that you could triple the number of people you reach by getting your books into other retail outlets. Here are a few other advantages of distributing your books through these outlets:

- Your books do not have to compete with as many other books. Bookstores carry anywhere from 500 to 25,000 titles in stock; how many of your books could possibly stand out in such a crowd? On the other hand, most other retail outlets usually carry only a few other books (as few as three or four to as many as 100), thus giving your books a better chance of attracting the attention of casual browsers.

• You can target your audience much more sharply by distributing through specialized retail outlets. For example, you are far more likely to sell books about fishing in a sports shop than in a bookstore.

• Your books are more likely to be displayed prominently in non-bookstore outlets. In many stores, they will be given space right next to the cash register.

• Many special retail outlets have greater in-store traffic than most bookstores. This is especially true of tourist spots, stationery stores, drug stores, and supermarkets.

• Your books can be sold just about anywhere. New England Press, for example, sells its Vermont titles in cider mills, wood-products stores, pottery shops, T-shirt shops, country stores, drug stores, lodges, and even the ferries which cross Lake Champlain.

• In many ways, these alternative markets are easier to break into. For instance, because there are no wholesalers in the gift industry and because the gift industry thrives on novelty, retailers are more accessible to anyone with a fresh idea.

14:02 Alternative Retail Outlets: Some Examples

Because books provide information, instruction, and entertainment applicable to just about every field of life, they can be sold in almost any type of retail outlet. Here are a few examples of how other publishers have approached getting their books into alternative retail outlets.

• **Supermarkets** — There are some 150,000 grocery stores in the U.S.; about 30,000 of them are supermarkets. Supermarkets currently account for about 8% of all books sold each year. While most of their sales are mass-market paperbacks, a number of publishers have been very successful in selling hardcovers through supermarkets.

  Before the rise of the major chain bookstores, HP Books sold almost all their books through supermarkets. To make it easy for the supermarkets to offer their books, HP designed spinner floor racks which could display a range of their cooking, crafts, and gardening titles. HP also pioneered the use of cross-merchandising in selling books to other retail outlets. For example, they supplied wire racks that would allow their pasta cookbooks to be displayed right next to the boxes of noodles and spaghetti. Finally, they offered supermarkets highly competitive terms including far better discounts than they were accustomed to getting from most other suppliers.

• **Home improvement centers** — According to the *National Home Center News*, 30% of all how-to books on home repair and interior decorating are sold through home improvement centers. Because how-to books teach customers how to do their own home improvement work, these centers encourage the sale of such books.

About 21,000 retail outlets (hardware stores, decorating shops, and home centers) service this market. Besides home repair books, these outlets often carry books on cooking, gardening, decorating, crafts and architecture.

Ortho Information Services publishes an entire series of gardening and cooking books, all with first print runs of 50,000 copies. Using the 250 sales representatives of its parent company, Chevron Chemical, Ortho makes over half its sales through garden centers and hardware stores.

* **Gourmet shops** — Besides the independent gourmet shops, many gift shops and cookware departments in major department stores also feature cookbooks. Regional and specialty cookbooks are big hits in these retail outlets.

  Barron's has over 40 reps selling their cookbooks to gourmet shops alone. 101 Productions has set up their own distributorship network to sell their cookbooks to gourmet and gift shops.

* **Food stands** — Garden Way sold *The Apple Cookbook* and *Simply Strawberries* in orchards and at roadside fruit and vegetable stands. A Good Thing Publishing sold *The Florida Citrus Cookbook* at citrus stands across the state. The book made a perfect tourist item — and an extra sale — for these stands. Globe Pequot sold its *The Bluefish Cookbook* through fish stands and stores up and down the Atlantic Coast.

* **Shoe stores** — New England Press sold its autobiography of running great Clarence DeMar in the Bill Rodgers chain of athletic shoe stores. It was their only title to sell in those stores, but because it tied in so well with the main line of those stores, the book sold well.

* **Toy stores** — In 1984, over 142,000,000 books were sold through toy stores for a total value of $188 million. There are about 8,000 toy stores in the country. If you want to sell in this market, you should produce full-color story or learning/activity books which can retail for less than $8.00 (most titles sell for prices ranging from $1.00 to $5.00). You'll have a better chance of placing your books with toy stores if you offer them sets or series of books.

* **Record stores** — Wilshire Books sold more copies of *How to Write a Hit Song and Sell It* in record stores than they did in bookstores. Here's another case where matching the book to its potential audience allowed a publisher to open new markets.

* **Auto supply stores** — With 40,000 outlets, this is a large and virtually untapped market. Currently, some of them do carry books on auto repairs, tune-ups, and other do-it-yourself subjects.

  But don't overlook other possible topics for sale to this market. Other male-oriented topics, such as sports, home repair, and electronics might also sell well. And how about a novel? *The Body in the Volvo*, a mystery novel by K. K. Beck, was carried by the local Volvo dealer.

- **Pet shops**—Pet care and training books have always sold well in pet shops. For instance, Green Turtle Publications has sold over 55,000 copies of the *Marine Aquarium Handbook*. Most of those sales were made through pet stores.

  T.F.H. Publications, probably the world's largest publisher of pet and animal books, started out selling small pamphlets through pet shops. While most of their sales are still through pet shops, seven of their books are now on the ABA Basic Book List (a list of recommended titles which every bookstore should stock).

- **Drug stores**—There are some 45,000 drug stores and pharmacies in the U.S., of which about half are chain stores. Drug stores currently account for about 3% of all consumer book purchases. While most of their book sales are mass-market paperbacks, some do carry hardcover and trade paperbacks as well.

  For example, Afcom Publishing's *The Complete Guide to Home Remedies* has sold well in pharmacies and drug stores.

- **Camera shops**—Through a network of sales representativess who sell to camera shops across the country, Amherst Media has sold over 45,000 copies of *Basic 35mm Photo Guide for Beginning Photographers*. To encourage sales in non-bookstore outlets, they provide free counter-top displays with the purchase of twelve or more copies. Besides its own titles. Amherst also distributes about 30 other books on photography.

- **Gift shops**—Blue Mountain Press has sold over 10,000,000 copies of Susan Polis Schutz's poetry books as well as 200,000,000 greeting cards. One of their hardcover books, *To My Daughter with Love*, sold out its first printing of 70,000 copies in just one month. Since, however, most copies of the book were sold in gift and card shops rather than bookstores, the book never showed up on any bestseller list.

14:03 Alternative Retail Outlets: A Checklist

Use the checklist below to aid you in locating other possible outlets for your books. For example, if you publish cookbooks, you could sell to appliance stores, campgrounds, candy shops, Christmas stores, coffee houses, cookware stores, doctor's offices, fish markets, fitness centers, food stands, garden supply stores, gift stores, grocery stores, gourmet shops, health food stores, hospital gift shops, houseware shops, marinas, supermarkets, and tourist shops.

Of course, out of this list you would have to select those shops which are most appropriate for your particular cookbook titles. A regional cookbook could be sold in gift shops, campgrounds, and tourist shops while a natural foods cookbook would be most appropriate for health food stores and fitness centers. Here then is a checklist of alternative retail outlets for your books:

[ ] **art supply stores** — graphics, art, architecture

[ ] **appliance stores** — house & home, how-to, cookbooks

[ ] **automobile dealerships** — automobiles, how-to, travel, recreation

[ ] **barber shops** — sports, recreation, novelty, humor

[ ] **beauty shops** — beauty care, fashion, diet, exercise

[ ] **camera shops** — photography, art, travel, coffee-table books

[ ] **campgrounds** — recreation, sports, travel, novelty, regional books

[ ] **candy shops** — cookbooks, diets

[ ] **chain stores** — general, mass-market, novelty, celebrity bios

[ ] **children's stores** — juveniles, games, humor, child care

[ ] **churches** — religious, family life, inspirational

[ ] **clothing stores** — fashion, beauty care, diet, exercise

[ ] **coffee shops** — cookbooks, poetry, general

[ ] **college stores** — textbooks, general, literature, novelty, music, art

[ ] **cookware stores** — cookbooks, diets, health

[ ] **computer stores** — computers, business

[ ] **craft stores** — crafts, how-to, hobbies, cookbooks

[ ] **discount stores** — general, remainders, mass-market, biographies

[ ] **doctor's offices** — health, diet, cookbooks, recreation

[ ] **dress shops** — fashion, beauty care, sewing, diet, exercise

[ ] **drug stores** — general, mass-market, novelty, beauty care

[ ] **fabric shop** — sewing, crafts, fashion, beauty care

[ ] **fish markets** — seafood cookbooks, recreation, sports

[ ] **fitness centers** — health, diet, recreation, cookbooks

[ ] **florists** — gardening, how-to, crafts

[ ] **food stands** — cookbooks, gardening, how-to, regional books

[ ] **garden supply stores** — gardening, crafts, cookbooks
[ ] **gas stations** — travel, atlases, humor, novelty, regional books
[ ] **gift stores** — coffee-table books, humor, novelty, hobbies
[ ] **golf clubs** — sports, recreation
[ ] **gourmet shops** — food, cookbooks, diet, crafts
[ ] **grocery stores** — food, cookbooks, diet, crafts
[ ] **gun shops** — sports, recreation
[ ] **hardware stores** — crafts, how-to, sports, recreation
[ ] **health food stores** — cookbooks, diet, health, alternative lifestyles
[ ] **hobby shops** — crafts, hobbies, how-to, games, novelty
[ ] **home improvement** — house & home, how-to, crafts, design
[ ] **hotel gift shops** — travel, novelty, coffee-table books, regional
[ ] **hospital gift shops** — cookbooks, diets, humor, health
[ ] **houseware shops** — cookbooks, crafts, how-to
[ ] **law offices** — business, law, politics, social issues
[ ] **marinas** — seafood cookbooks, recreation, sports
[ ] **maternity shops** — juveniles, child care, education, diet, exercise
[ ] **military PX's** — general, military, adventure, recreation
[ ] **movie theaters** — celebrity biographies, movies, entertainment
[ ] **museum shops** — coffee table books, art, literature, juveniles, crafts
[ ] **music stores** — music, celebrity biographies, entertainment
[ ] **newsstands** — local titles, general, novelty, mass-market, genre novels
[ ] **novelty shops** — humor, games, novelty, recreation
[ ] **office supply stores** — business, humor, novelty, computers
[ ] **pet shops** — pet care, animals, recreation, gardening, hobbies
[ ] **print shops** — graphics, art, novelty, business
[ ] **prison commissaries** — general, literature, self-help
[ ] **record shops** — music, celebrity biographies, novelty
[ ] **religious stores** — religion, family life, general, inspirational
[ ] **school supply stores** — education, juveniles, crafts, how-to
[ ] **shoe stores** — fashion, beauty care, running, exercise
[ ] **specialty shops** — novelty, regional, entertainment
[ ] **sports shops** — sports, recreation, games, humor, novelty
[ ] **stationery stores** — novelty, humor, calendars, business, careers
[ ] **supermarkets** — cookbooks, mass-market, juveniles
[ ] **tourist shops** — travel, regional titles, novelty, humor
[ ] **toy stores** — juveniles, child care, novelty, games, sports
[ ] **travel agencies** — travel books, regional titles, recreation
[ ] **video stores** — movies, entertainment, games, novelty, biographies

14:04   Tips on Marketing to Other Retail Outlets

To work with other retail outlets, you must first learn what their standard operating procedures and expectations are. Few other stores operate in the same way as bookstores. For example, grocery stores operate on a 20% discount for many food items (they make up for the low discount with much higher volume), though they've come to expect and appreciate higher discounts for non-food items. Gift stores, on the other hand, buy almost all products at a 40 or 50% discount (they have a lower volume, higher risk business where fads and heavy promotions play an important role in their success or failure).

These differences in operating procedures and expectations are governed by a number of factors: the type of product the store normally sells, the average price of items sold, the volume of sales, the type of customer, the distribution network for that industry, and tradition.

If you are not aware of these differences, learn them. Ask local retailers how their industry works, who they buy from, what kind of discount they get, what their expectations are, and any other questions that will help you to sell your books to other similar stores.

Here, then, are a few other tips on how to market your books to other retail outlets:

• **Many other retail outlets are accustomed to buying direct from manufacturer's sales representatives** (perhaps even more so than in the book industry where many bookstores have now become accustomed to buying through major wholesalers or direct from publishers). To locate commission sales reps for these other outlets, go to the various trade shows for that industry, read their trade magazines, ask your local retailer who their favorite reps are, and visit showrooms of reps in the nearest major city.

In the gift industry, reps are accustomed to commissions of 12% to 20%. Many reps won't even take on a new item unless they get at least a 15% commission. So your pricing formula must be able to support the larger commissions and larger discounts of the gift industry if you hope to sell to that market.

To facilitate their book sales to specialty outlets, Globe Pequot Press has four sets of sales representatives: 1) for the book trade, 2) for library sales, 3) for the gift and stationery trade and 4) for the gourmet trade. The Mountaineers has separate sales groups for both the book trade and the outdoor trade.

When you are ready to sign up commission sales reps to represent your line, be sure you get a signed agreement that outlines their responsibilities, territories, and markets. To help you design an agreement that meets your needs, you may use the sample sales representative agreement on pages 133 and 134 of *Book Marketing Made Easier*.

- **Attend the trade shows for that industry,** especially when you are first starting out. Trade shows are the best place to get an overall view of the industry as well as an education in the detailed policies and procedures of that industry. Later, if your sales in those retail outlets are good, you might consider exhibiting at the trade shows.

  To give you an idea of the variety of trade shows that are held every year, here are a few that might be appropriate for books (for a more complete list, see the resources listed on page 37):

  World Sports Expo, in mid-October
  World Souvenir Show, in late November
  Consumer Electronics Show, in early January
  National Automobile Dealers Association Convention, in January
  International Travel Industry Expo, in April
  National Stationery Show, in mid-May
  International Cat Show, in early March
  National Sewing Show, in early March
  National Hunting, Fishing, and Camping Show, in mid-March
  Natural Foods Expo West, in mid-March

  WRC Publishing and Garden Way Publishing both exhibited special cookbooks at the San Francisco Gourmet Products Show. Among their titles, WRC displayed *Chocolate Truffles* and *Knowing Beans About Coffee*, while Garden Way displayed *Simply Strawberries*.

- **Read the trade magazines in that field.** Again, in the gift industry, this means reading *Gift and Decorative Accessories*, *Giftware Business*, *Giftware News*, and *Gift Reporter*. In the toy industry, the two major trade magazines are *Toy and Hobby World* and *Play-things*. These magazines will not only give you a good idea of what is currently happening in the industry, but they will also provide you with many key contacts (such as sales representatives, wholesalers, and retail stores).

- **Learn where to go for distribution.** You will discover that there are many book distributors who can already provide you with distribution into these other markets. For example, Cogan Books and The Bestsellers both provide distribution into cooking stores, gourmet shops, and other cookbook outlets. Riverside Book and Bible and Spring Arbor Distributors both distribute to religious stores.

  On the other hand, you will find that in some industries you will be better off working within their distribution system. This is especially true in the drugstore and toy markets, where major wholesalers dominate many local and regional markets (just as the national distributors control much of the distribution for mass-market titles in the book industry). Again, you can learn who these major wholesalers are by asking your local stores, going to trade shows, and reading the trade magazines. Also, if you've set up a rep network, they will undoubtedly take care of these contacts for you.

Besides working with sales reps or distributors, you could work with another company to arrange distribution in a special market.

Kartes Video signed an agreement to have Hanes distribute their videos to 90,000 chain stores, supermarkets, drug stores, convenience stores, and other retail outlets where Hanes sells their L'Eggs panty hose. Hanes sales representatives not only installed the video display racks, but they also checked the racks regularly, restocked them, and removed tapes that were not selling.

- **Set your discount schedule and terms to suit the industry.** In the gift industry, this means often giving 50% discounts for packaged deals (such as a prepack display of ten or more books). In most cases you will not need to offer a returns policy. Let your sales reps and local retailers help you to set a reasonable discount schedule and statement of terms. As a caution, always verify any advice you get from one source by checking with another source.

- **Design packaged programs** that make it easy for other retailers to order, stock, and display your titles. Since many retailers may not be set up to display books, be sure to offer a display with your books. The easier you make it for them, the more likely they will buy from you.

  Again, if you'd like to test an inexpensive counter-top display in other retail outlets, Ad-Lib Publications stocks white corrugated counter top displays for books. You can order a sample display and shipping carton for only $5.00. Or you can order in quantities of as few as twenty-five. For more information, call toll-free (800) 669-0773. Or write to Ad-Lib Publications, 51 N. Fifth Street, P. O. Box 1102, Fairfield, IA 52556-1102; (515) 472-6617; Fax: (515) 472-3186.

- **When you send out display packages, always include reordering instructions with the display.** You might put these instructions in front of or inside of the last copy in the display. If you hope to get reorders, you have to provide some procedure such as this to make it easy for the retailer to place the reorder.

- **When you approach stores, you must convince them that they can make an easy profit,** that your title or titles will sell well. Perhaps the best way to accomplish this is to demonstrate how well other stores have done. If you can tell them how often your books turn at retail (how often other stores have to reorder), or can demonstrate the profit potential of your books (how many dollars in sales they can expect to make per square foot per year), then you have a chance to make the sale.

- **Better yet, show them how well your titles fit into their product mix,** how your titles can help them to sell other products. One way to convince them is to show how your books can serve as easy reference guides for their customers.

Aris Books was able to place *The Grilling Book* in hardware stores and *The California Seafood Book* in fish markets because both books were superb guides to using the products of those markets.

● **Show stores how they can cross-merchandise your books with their product line.** Barron's offers dumps to supermarkets so their seafood cookbooks can be placed near the fresh fish and their salad cookbooks near the fruits and vegetables. They have also packaged dessert cookbooks with baking trays so the books could be sold in cookware departments of stores.

Similarly, 101 Productions has recommended to stores that they package a few tools with their book about kitchen tools.

The Rotation Diet was highly promoted and cross-merchandised with many recommended food products in supermarket chains across the country. As a result, it has sold well over half a million copies.

● **Publish special editions for some markets.** For example, pop-up and other special effects books sell better in toy stores than do books with no play value.

To make their booklet *Key to North American Waterfowl* more usable by hunters and bird watchers (who could easily drop the book in a lake or swamp), Schroeder Prints printed the booklet on special waterproof paper which actually floats. Because of its unique design, the book has sold well in sporting goods stores where it is often displayed submerged in a pail of water.

● **Don't overlook a store just because it doesn't sell books when you approach it.** Perhaps no one has ever shown them how they can make money selling books.

The Los Angeles representative for Prentice Hall approached a store that sold goo, smoke, and scum for use in special effects. That's all they sold. Their market was solely people from the movie industry. So why would they be interested in selling books? Well, the Prentice Hall rep convinced them to sell science books for adults and kids. And the books sold. Indeed, they sold so well that now the store sells goo, smoke, scum, and books.

● **Make a commitment.** Don't think that opening special markets is something you can do on a lark. It must be seen as a long-term commitment, because that is what it takes to be successful.

Bonus Books sells many books to such chains as K-Mart, Osco Drugs, and Toys R Us. How do they do it? Generally, they start by calling the chain to find out the name of the buyer. Then they send a review copy of the book. Then they start the round of follow-up calls. Sometimes it takes as many as 20 calls to the same person before they get an order. The key here, of course, as in most special sales is to be persistent. It's the only thing that works.

> **Authors** — You can help your publisher open up new retail
> outlets by doing some of the preliminary research for them.
> If, for example, you think your book would do well in sporting
> goods stores, visit some of your local stores and ask the
> manager some of the basic questions. See page 61 for a list of
> appropriate questions. Then follow up on the information
> yourself or pass it on to your publisher.

14:05 Some Key Contacts for Other Retail Markets

Here is a sampling of key distributors, directories, and organizations
that can be helpful to you when you are researching and selling to special
retail outlets. This list is nowhere near complete. For a more complete
list, refer to the *Book Publishing Resource Guide*.

- **Alpenbooks**, P. O. Box 761, Snohomish, WA 98290; (206) 672-9316.
  This book publisher wholesales about 700 sports and recreation titles
  to outdoor recreation and bicycle shops.

- **Wellton, Inc.**, 109 Baldwin Lake Circle, P. O. Box 6066, Folsum, CA
  95630; (916) 988-4116. This publisher is looking for other cookbooks
  and gift titles to distribute via their network of gift and gourmet sales
  representatives.

- **Royal Publications**, Michael Van Meter, Buyer, P O Box 5793, 790 W
  Tennessee, Denver, CO 80223; 303-778-8383. This wholesaler distributes books and other supplies to natural food stores around the
  country. They also have a mail order division, Aurora Books.

- **Specialty Retailer**, 7628 Densmore Avenue, Van Nuys, CA 91406-
  2088; (818) 782-7328. This magazine serves giftshops at hospitals,
  hotels, resorts, and colleges. You might want to advertise in this
  magazine's Marketplace department or rent its list of subscribers.

- **Sports Market Place**, P. O. Box 1417, Princeton, NJ 08542. This annual directory lists suppliers, associations, magazines, and other media
  which cover the world of sports.

- **Toy and Hobby World**, 4637 Seventh Avenue #202, New York, NY
  10018; (212) 594-4237; Fax: (212) 563-1415. This is one of the major
  magazines serving the toy trade.

- **National Home Center News**, Lebhar-Friedman, 425 Park Avenue,
  New York, NY 10022; (212) 371-9400. This magazine serves the home
  center trade.

- **Museum Store Association**, 501 S. Cherry Street #460, Denver, CO
  80222; (303) 329-6968. This association sponsors an annual convention
  in May and publishes a quarterly magazine, the *Museum Store*.

- **Toy Manufacturers of America**, 200 Fifth Avenue, New York, NY 10010; (212) 675-1141; Fax: (212) 633-1429. Write them for more information about the Toy Fair (held every February in New York) as well as regional toy shows.
- **National Office Products Association**, 301 N. Fairfax Street, Alexandria, VA 22314; (703) 549-9040; Fax: (703) 683-7552. Their annual convention is in mid-October.

14:06 Discount Stores and Warehouse Clubs

Discount and department stores currently account for about 10% of all book sales. Meanwhile, the 325+ warehouse clubs are having a growing impact on book sales, especially the higher priced coffee-table and reference books which can be discounted more deeply than lower priced books. Sales through warehouse clubs now total over $100 million yearly. While it is a limited market (few warehouse clubs stock more than 200 titles), when they do buy, they buy big (from 10,000 to 50,000 copies).

Here are a few major buyers and wholesalers of books to the mass merchandisers and warehouse clubs:

- **Target Stores**, Ed Erickson, Book Buyer, 33 S. 6th Street, Minneapolis MN 55420; (612) 370-6365.
- **Advanced Marketing Services**, 5880 Oberlin Drive #200, San Deigo, CA 92122-9653; (619) 457-2500. This wholesaler services many mass merchandisers and warehouse buying clubs. They have a new division that serves the office products warehouses.
- **Computer Book Service**, 4201 Raymond Drive, Hillside, IL 60162-1786; (708) 547-4400. Another wholesaler that services discount stores and warehouse clubs.
- **Handleman National Book Distributors**, 500 Kirts Boulevard, Troy, MI 48084; (313) 362-4400. The third major book wholesaler to discount stores and warehouse buying clubs.

14:07 The Military Market

As Nat Kornfield, the advertising director of *Army Times*, recently noted, "The military is the only market in the country that has no recession, no unemployment, and no pay cuts." How big is the market? It consists of over 2,200,000 active-duty personnel plus their dependents, 1,200,000 civilian employees, and 1,500,000 retirees. With a combined total income of over $160 billion, it is a significant market.

To help you reach that market, here are a few resources:

• **Stars and Stripes Book Department,** APO San Francisco, CA 96503-0110; (03) 401-8928. With buying offices in Japan, the book department operates 25 full-line stores as well as 500 book departments in military exchanges overseas.

• **M. J. Daniel Company,** 1000 Beltline Road, Carrollton, TX 75006; (214) 245-3600. This sales rep group sells to military exchanges around the world.

• **Army and Air Force Exchange Service,** Mark Moody, Book Buyer, AAFES Headquarters, Department PD-C, P. O. Box 225590, Dallas, TX 75222-5590. Write to the Public Affairs Division of the Information Services Branch for a free copy of their *AAFES Facts for Vendors*, a book that tells you how to sell to military bases.

• **American Passage,** 6211 W. Howard Street, Niles, IL 60648; (312) 647-6860. These media consultants can help you to place ads in a network of base weeklies covering most of the U.S. military bases.

Chapter 15

Selling to Schools and Libraries

Schools and libraries form a larger market than retail bookstores. In 1986, U.S. sales of school textbooks amounted to about $3.0 billion, while sales to libraries were almost $1.4 billion—that's more than 40% of all U.S. book sales. Hence, if you are looking for new markets for your books, look into selling to these two major book markets.

15:01 School Textbooks: How to Get Adopted

Textbooks make up the major portion of book sales to schools and colleges. The best way to get your books adopted for classroom use is to get samples of your books into the hands of the instructors who make the adoption decisions. And the best way to reach these instructors is through direct mail. To obtain lists of schools and teachers, contact one of the following mailing list suppliers:

- **Advanced Publishing Systems**, 403 Grand Central Avenue, Lavallette, NJ 08735; (201) 793-5600; Fax: (201) 830-1029. Provides lists of college professors.

- **College Marketing Group**, 50 Cross Street, Winchester, MA 01890; (617) 729-7865. Perhaps the largest supplier of college mailing lists, their lists are broken down into about 3,500 course offerings. They can also supply you with department heads, departmental library representatives, and library decision makers (subject area specialists).

- **Consolidated Mailing Service**, P. O. Box 495, St. James, NY 11780; (516) 584-7283. Probably the least expensive source for elementary and secondary school mailing lists, Consolidated charges only $18.00 per thousand. Because their lists are compiled, you won't be able to get the actual names of contacts or subject specializations.

- **Education Mailings Clearing House**, 601 E. Marshall Street, Sweet Springs, MO 65351; (816) 335-6373. Lists of schools, teachers, and other lists.
- **Market Data Retrieval**, 16 Progress Drive, Shelton, CT 06484; (800) 243-5538 or (203) 926-4800. Besides college lists, they also supply lists of elementary and secondary schools, teachers, libraries, and day care centers. Lists can be supplied as labels, directories, printouts, Rolodex cards, and computer floppy disks.
- **Mike Wilson List Counsel**, 12120 Washington Blvd., Los Angeles, CA 90066; (800) 445-2089; (213) 398-2754. Lists of schools, teachers, colleges (faculty, department heads), libraries, medical professionals, day care centers, family buyer lists, and much more.
- **Patterson's Mailing Lists**, P. O. Box 199, Mount Prospect, IL 60056. Provides directories of schools.
- **PCS Mailing List Company**, 85 Constitution, Danverse, MA 01960; (508) 777-3332; (800) 532-5478. List compiler and broker of many lists.
- **Quality Education Data**, 1600 Broadway, 12th Floor, Denver, CO 80202-4912; (800) 525-5811; (303) 860-1832. One of the major suppliers of school names: day care centers, schools, colleges (department heads and program directors), and public libraries.
- **School Lists Mailing Corporation**, 1710 Highway 35, Ocean, NJ 07712; (201) 531-2212. Lists of schools.
- **Willowood Lists**, P. O. Box 1846, Minot, ND 58702; (701) 838-0579. Lists of schools, libraries, and college English departments.

If the number of instructors in a particular discipline is very small, you could send them review copies of your books right away. In most cases, however, you will want to pre-qualify recipients to make sure that they are responsible for making the adoption decision. Hence, when you send them your direct mail package describing your new textbook, enclose a reply card that allows them to request a complimentary examination copy (also known as a teacher's desk copy). On the card, ask them to answer the following questions:

1. Instructor's name,
2. Department and school where course is taught,
3. Address of school (where book should be shipped),
4. Title of course,
5. Current and/or previous textbooks used in the course,
6. Age and grade level of students taking the course,
7. Estimated number of students in the course,
8. Date course will begin,
9. Office phone number and office hours, and
10. Author and title of book they'd like to review.

Not only will requesting this information weed out casual inquirers, but it will also provide you with some valuable marketing data for future promotions. When you send the review copy, enclose a review slip which asks the instructors to give you feedback on why they did or did not select your title for adoption. This feedback will be helpful in producing future textbooks and marketing promotions.

For reproducible copies of an Examination Copy Request Form and a Complimentary Book Acknowledgement form, see pages 123 and 124 of *Book Marketing Made Easier*.

15:02 How to Deal with Requests for Comp Copies

To sell college textbooks, you have to offer complimentary copies to faculty members so they can review the textbook before assigning it for a course. Unfortunately, many college professors have gotten into the habit of requesting review copies for any book that might remotely interest them—even if they have no intention whatsoever of assigning the book for a class. Indeed, many college professors sell these complimentary copies to used-book wholesalers who, in turn, resell them to college bookstores which, in turn, resell them to students. It is estimated that the resale of these comp copies cost publishers $80 million dollars per year in lost sales. How can you cut these losses? Here are a few suggestions:

- **Don't give away comp copies at all**. One publisher of a scientific reference textbook reports that they "would go bankrupt if we gave away books to potential buyers. Professors who write asking for a free desk copy are sent a polite note with advertising material."

  Another small publisher has sold over 2,000 *examination* textbooks to teachers who otherwise would have asked for a free copy. Whenever he publishes a new book, he sends teachers a sales leaflet with the following offer:

  Send for your professional sample now. The price is $12.50, but for a limited time you'll receive 20% off and free shipping—total $10.00. Please enclose payment—no invoicing. Sorry, no free copies. Of course, if you don't like the book, we'll gladly send a refund. But if you like it enough to assign it to your students, you'll receive a double refund of $20 upon any order of 15 copies or more.

- **Invoice for examination copies**. Many small publishers are now invoicing professors for examination copies. As in the example above, they might offer a 20% professional discount, but they require that if the professor is not going to adopt the book, then he or she must pay the invoice within 30 or 60 days. If they do not return the book or pay the invoice, they are put on a "book grabber" list.

- **Charge a processing fee**. Globe Pequot Press charges a $3.00 processing fee with every request for an examination copy.

- **Require a license agreement.** Either send the license agreement with the review copy or, better yet, require that a teacher sign the license agreement before they receive a comp copy. The license agreement should specify restrictions on its use (i.e., for examination purposes only, not for resale, etc.).

- **Use a special book design for examination copies** that indicates the book is free (under the assumption that students will refuse to pay for something marked free). Scott Foresman and St. Martin's both use such examination copy designs.

- **Pay for book returns.** To make it easy for the professor to return a comp copy, accompany the book with a prepaid return envelope.

15:03 Factors Affecting Textbook Adoptions

When instructors review books for possible adoption, the most important factor influencing their decision is the quality of the text. The book must provide a reliable and comprehensive treatment of the subject. Here, though, are a few other factors that could influence their decision:

- **The timeliness of the information** — The book must be current; it must reflect the trends of the time. As a result, you should consider updating a textbook at least every three or four years.

- **Author's reputation** — The author's reputation is not that important for elementary textbooks or, for that matter, for introductory college-level texts, but it can be crucial for upper-level textbooks. In such cases, the author should be a recognized expert in the field.

- **Suited to the teacher's style** — The book must suit the teaching style of the instructor who will be using it in the classroom. If the instructor is uncomfortable with the format, style, or content of the text, she will not use it unless there are no comparable texts on the market.

- **Special features** — If the textbook includes quizzes, exercises, review questions, or other material that makes the teacher's job easier, it is more likely to be selected. Also, if you provide an accompanying teacher's handbook, transparencies, tests, and other teacher's aids, your textbook will have a better chance of being selected.

- **Binding** — Because they tend to take more abuse and last longer, hardcover bindings are preferred over paperback bindings. This can be a crucial factor in school districts which provide textbooks for their students. It is not so important at the college level where the students have to buy their own texts.

- **Price** — Price is much more important to school districts which must pay for their own texts than it is for colleges where the students must pay the price. At the college level, the quality of the text is given primary consideration.

- **Graphic design** — The design of a book is rarely a factor in the decision. The only time the design might come into play is when two textbooks are equally matched on all other points but one is more graphically appealing than the other. Hence, the increased use of graphics in introductory textbooks.

15:04 The El-Hi Textbook Adoption Market

The el-hi textbook adoption market is complicated by the varying standards and requirements set by state departments of education. Some states restrict teachers's options to only those books approved by the state; others allow more flexible purchasing.

At present, the following states restrict purchases to a select list of books deposited in or consigned to a state depository: Arkansas, Florida, Georgia, Louisiana, Mississippi, New Mexico, Oklahoma, Oregon, Tennessee, Texas, and Utah.

The following states maintain an official adoption list but do not require publishers to consign copies with them: Alabama, California, DC, Hawaii, Idaho, Indiana, Kentucky, Nevada, North Carolina, South Carolina, Virginia, and West Virginia.

While the following states maintain no adoption list, they do require publishers to register with them and/or meet other requirements (such as price guarantees): Arizona, Illinois, Missouri, Montana, North Dakota, and Ohio.

All other states currently have no requirements or adoption lists. For more information, write to the appropriate state agencies. Check your local library for the addresses of the departments of education in the various states.

Remember that states with approval plans do not necessarily review new titles every year. California, for instance, approved reading language arts programs in 1988 and history books in 1990.

15:05 Other Sales in the El-Hi Market

Breaking into the el-hi textbook market could be difficult against the dominance of the already established textbook publishers, but there are other ways to sell books to schools. Here are a few examples of how smaller publishers are selling books in the school market:

- Instead of aiming for textbook adoptions, **publish workbooks, practice guides, and other supplemental texts** which do not have to be approved by the state agencies and which may be purchased from supplemental funds.

- **Go regional.** Instead of trying to compete with the major textbook publishers for national adoptions, publish regional books that might be adopted by your state or states in your region. For instance, why not publish a language arts book based on stories from regional authors? Or publish a state history book. Or a social studies program featuring regional problems, organizations, companies, and governments.

- **Sell your books through the school supply stores** where teachers go to buy teaching aids and other supplies to enrich their lessons. To learn more about this market, read *Educational Dealer*. Write to **Educational Dealer**, P. O. Box 1080, Geneva, NY 14456: (315) 789-0458.

  Or attend one of the two major trade shows for this industry. Here are the addresses and convention dates for the school supply associations:

  Educational Dealers & Suppliers Association, 711 West 17th Street, Suite J-5, Costa Mesa, CA 92627; (714) 642-3986; (800) 654-7099. The EDSA convention is held in April.

  National School Supply and Equipment Association, 2020 N. 14th Street #400, P. O. Box 17005, Arlington, VA 22216; (703) 524-8819; (800) 395-5550. The NSSEA convention is in November.

  Not only does Music in Action sell its books to public school music teachers via direct mail, but it also works through a network of 75 educational music dealers.

- **Organize book fairs.** For example, Gryphon House sells preschool centers sample copies of their books which the schools can then display at book fairs. The schools then take orders for additional copies which they, in turn, buy from Gryphon at a 20% discount.

- **Form a book club.** Again, Gryphon House mails a tabloid listing about 100 of its titles to over 10,000 preschool centers. The teachers at these schools, in turn, consolidate orders received from parents and send them on to Gryphon House for fulfillment. Gryphon processes the combined order and ships the books to the schools where the books are distributed to the students. Under this program, the schools get to choose free books for their libraries, the number of books dependent on the amount of orders which were placed by the parents.

  If you don't form your own book club, work to get your books carried by the other book clubs that specialize in serving elementary schools. Here are two of the major ones:

  Scholastic Book Services, 730 Broadway, New York, NY 10003; (212) 505-3000. Operates the See Saw Book Club (grades K-1), Lucky Book Club (grades 2-3), Arrow Book Club (grades 4-6), and Teenage Book Club.

  Weekly Reader Book Clubs, Field Publications, 245 Long Hill Road, Middletown, CT 06457; (203) 638-2400. Operates Buddy Books (grades K-1), Goodtime Books (grades 2-3) and Discovering Books (grades 4-6).

- **Work through catalogs.** A number of companies distribute books to schools and teachers through direct mail catalogs. To locate some of these companies, check with your local school teachers. They will be able to show you the catalogs they receive.

  For example, *Paperbacks for Educators* is a catalog featuring books on careers, children's books, education, child development, family life, psychology, and counseling. To submit your titles for consideration, write to **Paperbacks for Educators**, 426 W. Front Street, Washington, MO 63090; (800) 227-2591; (314) 227-2591.

- **Offer your books to school fundraisers.** Student clubs, bands, sports teams, and even the PTA might be willing to sell some of your titles in order to raise funds for their programs. For example, sports teams could sell your fishing guides or other sports books to help raise money for special team trips. Look into any student function that might tie into one or more of your titles. Then send information on your fundraising programs to the faculty advisors at those schools which you feel would be most open to such fundraising. Before committing a lot of time or money into such a program, however, first test it with some local schools.

- **Sell site licenses.** George Moberg of The Writing Consultant offers site licenses to schools. His offer reads as follows:

  For a small fee, your school or district can now create (in your duplicating room or at a local printshop) as many legal copies of the student text Writing on Computers *as needed for your classes. This is money-saving even for as few as 30 copies (for your lab or one class). At list price they would cost $435, whereas your Share-Text / Site-Licence, plus original copy, would come to only $117.00 — a nifty savings of about $300 to $400, depending on duplicating costs.*

  Because this program has increased his cash flow, he has offered similar programs for school districts and even states.

- **Sell to adult education programs.** Because teachers of adult education programs usually have much more flexibility in choosing which textbooks they use for their courses, you might be able to establish your new textbooks first through these programs. Sales to these programs might be enough to support the development and marketing of your textbooks until you are able to work your way through all the ins and outs of the school adoption processes in various states.

  Dobry Enterpress sells their instructional drapery textbooks to home economics programs, extension services, and continuing education programs.

- **Promote to the home schooling movement.** There are hundreds of active organizations across the country now promoting home schooling as an alternative to public and private schools. Many of the people involved in this movement are actively looking for alternative textbooks as well.

• **Have your author tour schools and libraries.** Author appearances at schools and libraries have always been a part of the children's books marketing programs of many major publishers. Why not make it a part of yours? Even if you don't have the time or money to arrange author appearances at schools and libraries yourself, at the very least, support your authors when they are able to arrange such appearances.

Authors — If your publisher is not able to put much attention on arranging appearances for you at schools and libraries, you can arrange your own. Arrange to read during one of their children's book hours, or to answer questions on what it is like to write a book.

Don't be concerned that reading at a library or school will cut down your book sales. Indeed, the opposite is more likely to be true. Just as children like to see a movie again and again, they also like to read their favorite stories again and again. If they hear you read from your book (and your book tells a good story), they are likely to want a copy of their own to take home to read again and again.

• **Sell your books to school libraries.** While school libraries may buy only one copy of each title, there are so many school libraries (over 100,000 public, private and parochial school libraries on the Bowker lists) that even one copy per library could make your books bestsellers.

15:06 Other Sales to the College Market

In 1984, college textbooks accounted for over $1 billion in sales (1986 sales were over $1.4 billion). Unfortunately for the smaller publisher, over two-thirds of those sales were made by the twelve largest publishers with the largest publisher alone accounting for almost 18%. Nonetheless, one-third of $1 billion is still a huge market.

Besides the textbook market, the 12 million college students also represent a $20 billion market for non-school related items, from cars and clothing to records and movies to magazines and books. According to one study, the average college student spends $121 a month on consumer and entertainment items. They report buying over half a billion dollars worth of books from college stores and bookstores.

The major way to reach the college textbook market is to get your books into the hands of the instructors who make the adoption selection. Here, however, are a few other things you can do to sell more of your books (both textbooks and regular trade books) in the college market:

- **Direct mail to faculty members** is still the best way to reach this market. Whether you want to sell textbooks, supplemental readings, or reference books to colleges, instructors are still the people who make the major adoption decisions.

- Nonetheless, when you do send direct mail to faculty for books that might merit library acquisition, **enclose a library routing slip** that will make it easy for the faculty members to recommend your titles to their libraries. If you want to sell to the 3000 college and university libraries, you need to bring your books to the attention of the librarians. Faculty members can help you to do that if you make it easy for them. For a sample routing slip that you may use in your promotions, see page 125 of *Book Marketing Made Easier*.

- Look for ways to **adapt your trade titles as supplemental readings** for college courses. You may find it easier to compete against the major publishers by going after these supplemental sales.

- **College travelers (sale representatives) can help to bring your books to the attention of faculty members**. While fewer publishers are currently using such representatives, you might test using reps in certain regions (or try doing your own repping in your local area).

- To bring your books to the attention of specific faculty, **exhibit your books at academic conferences and conventions**. For example, exhibit your city planning texts at the American Society of Public Administration, the Urban Affairs Association, or the Population Association of America.

  Conference Book Service offers cooperative exhibit services for several hundred conferences each year. Write them for their schedule: **Conference Book Service**, 80 South Early Street, Alexandria, VA 22304; (703) 823-6966.

- **Get reviews in the appropriate scholarly journals**, especially those which are most applicable to your specific titles. If the reviews bring good results, then test an advertisement in subsequent issues to capitalize on that interest.

  Of course, you should also try for reviews (and advertise) in the book review media appropriate for college level books—*Choice*, *Library Journal*, and *Reference Quarterly*, among others.

- **Advertise** in *The College Store Journal* to bring your books to the attention of the college store book buyers. These bookstores carry not only textbooks and supplemental readings, but also other general trade titles that they feel will interest college students. According to one study, students spend an average of $248 per year in these stores, of which $33.70 is spent on books.

  For more information on advertising in the *Journal* and exhibiting at their convention, write to the **National Association of College Stores**, 528 East Lorain St., P. O. Box 58, Oberlin, OH 44074; (216) 776-7777.

- **Mail directly to college bookstores.** Robert Oman offers a list of 1,900 college or college-related bookstores for $120.00. For more details, write to **Robert Oman**, 204 Fair Oaks Park, Needham, MA 02192; (617) 444-7455.

- **Sell to the college chain stores.** One of the larger chains is Follett College Stores, which operates several hundred stores on college campuses around the country. Besides textbooks, they also buy trade books (and tee-shirts, coffee mugs, and other paraphenalia). Send your catalogs to **Follett College Stores**, Director of Trade Books, 400 W. Grand Avenue, Elmhurst, IL 60126; (708) 279-2330.

- **Use a card pack.** Magna Publications mails a card pack that reaches 60,000 student affairs personnel, general administrators, and faculty at colleges across the country. For more details on this card deck, write to **Magna Publications**, 2718 Dryden Drive, Madison, WI 53704-3006; (608) 249-2455.

- **Mail your catalog direct to students.** According to a recent survey, 55% of all college undergraduates have bought by mail or telephone during the past year. Of those who did, 45% bought books.

- **Advertise in magazines aimed at students.** Here are the names of just a few of the magazines which are published for college students: *The Black Collegian, Campus USA, Campus Life, Campus Voice, College Outlook, College Preview*, and *Panache. Newsweek* and serveral other magazines also publish special college editions.

- **Promote on campus.** MarketSource is one company that makes available campus promotions for various products. Their promotions range from trial packs and sampling to a Term Planner advertising publication and Campus Source billboards. For more information, write MarketSource, 10 Abeel Road, Cranbury, NJ 08512; (609) 655-8990.

15:07 The Importance of Sales to Libraries

Since libraries buy over $1.4 billion worth of books every year, they represent a major market you should not ignore. Library sales are especially crucial for the over 2,000 children's titles published every year, the majority of which are still bought by schools and libraries. Libraries offer several other advantages to book publishers:

- You can sell books to libraries at little or no discount. While some publishers offer a 10% to 25% courtesy discount to libraries, most offer no discount at all on single copy orders.

- You don't have to offer a return privilege to libraries. They seldom return a book.

- The greatest advantage of library sales, though, is that they often result in further sales. If your book is the kind that readers would want to refer to again and again, those readers who first discover your book in a library will often order the book direct from you rather than continue to check the book out of their local library. Personally, I've bought many books in just this way.

In one study of technical book buyers, it was discovered that 2% to 3% of all such buyers bought the book because they had first seen the book in a library.

15:08 The Diversity of the Library Market

The library market is not a homogeneous whole. Instead, it is made up of many smaller markets, each with its own special audiences and interests. Of the $1.4 billion in annual sales, 23% of those sales are made to public libraries, 33% to el-hi school libraries, 27% to college libraries, and 17% to special libraries.

There are well over 150,000 libraries in the United States, including almost 9,000 public libraries, 3,000 college libraries, over 100,000 el-hi libraries, 1000 governmental libraries, almost 2,000 business libraries, over 2,000 medical libraries, 1,000 law libraries, and over 1,000 formal church libraries (and an estimated 50,000 smaller church libraries). Plus almost every organization in the country has its own small collection of books.

- Most of these figures are taken from the mailing list catalog of R. R. Bowker and Company, the major supplier of library mailing lists in the country. For more information, write to **R. R. Bowker Company**, Mailing List Department, 249 West 17th Street, New York, NY 10011; (212) 337-7164; (800) 537-7930.

- Other major sources for lists of public libraries are noted in point 15:01 above.

- For lists of Canadian libraries, write to **Micromedia**, 158 Pearl Street, Toronto M5H 1L3, Ontario Canada; (416) 593-5211.

- For special libraries, write to the **Special Libraries Association**, 1700 18th Street N.W., Washington, DC 20009; (202) 234-4700.

15:09 Why Libraries Buy from Library Jobbers

According to several studies, anywhere from 65% to 75% of all library orders are placed through wholesalers. Of these wholesalers, Baker & Taylor is far and away the most significant for library sales. As many as 50% of all library sales for smaller publishers will come through Baker and Taylor. Other major library wholesalers include Brodart, Blackwell North America, Midwest Library Service, Eastern Book Company, Emery-Pratt, as well as a good number of specialized wholesalers such as J. A. Majors (medical books), Riverside Book and Bible (religious books), Maxwell Scientific International (reference books), Bilingual Publications Company (Spanish books), and Small Press Distribution (literary and poetry books).

Why do libraries prefer buying from these wholesalers rather than direct from publishers? Here are just a few reasons:

- Library jobbers provide many more services, such as cataloging cards, book processing, and special bindings.

- Jobbers offer a greater selection than any one publisher can hope to offer. In essence, they offer the library one-stop shopping.

- There is less paperwork and check writing involved in placing a large order from one source as compared to placing many smaller orders from a number of sources.

- There is also less work in processing the books when they are received as one shipment.

- Jobbers usually offer equal or higher discounts than those offered by publishers, especially on larger orders (which the library can place when it consolidates orders for books from many different publishers).

- Jobbers, in general, offer faster and more reliable service than publishers. We as publishers should not be proud of this fact, but a fact it is.

- Jobbers tend to publish more frequent catalogs and other announcements of new titles. Many publish monthly, thus enabling the librarian to keep up to date on all new titles.

- Many jobbers offer continuation, standing order, or on-approval plans for specific subject areas. Because most publishers do not publish enough books in any one subject area, they cannot possibly compete with jobbers in offering a comprehensive standing order plan for specific subjects.

15:10 How to Appeal to Libraries

To make it easy for librarians to order your books, you must provide them with the information they need to make informed decisions. Do not clutter your sales literature with hype. Instead, provide them with the following information in a clear and simple presentation:

- **ISBN and LCCN numbers** – State the ISBN and Library of Congress Cataloging numbers for every title listed.

- **Publication dates** – List the publication dates for your new and forthcoming titles so librarians can be sure when the books will be available; then be sure to meet those publication dates. List the month and year of publications for your backlist titles as well; librarians like to know how current the information is in any book they order.

• **CIP data**—If you participate in the Library of Congress's Cataloging in Publication program, be sure to indicate this. The CIP program provides ready-to-use cataloging information which any library may use. Libraries are more likely to order a book if they know that catalog card information will be readily available even prior to a book's official publication date.

• **Prices**—Indicate the prices for each and every edition of your books. Librarians must have prices if they are to prepare book orders within their allotted budget. Librarians rarely choose on the basis of price alone, but if your book is less expensive than another equivalent book on the same subject, most librarians would undoubtedly order yours. The key word here is "equivalent." If one book has gotten better reviews, even if it is more expensive, librarians will almost always order it. Quality of content and format is far more important to them than is the price alone.

• **Edition statement**—Whenever one of your titles has been published in a new edition (or as part of a continuing series), make that fact clear. Many libraries which have been satisfied with previous editions of a book will order new editions of the book to keep their collections as current as possible.

• **Contents**—Give the librarians some idea of what your books contain. Either reprint the table of contents, print a short representative excerpt, or write a short descriptive statement.

• **Reviews**—Quote any favorable pre-reviews from leading library journals or from endorsements provided by people who are well-known in the book's field. These outside testimonials carry far more weight than anything you can write about the book.

• **Supplementary material**—State the number of pages, number of illustrations (photographs, drawings, tables, forms, graphs, etc.), and what other additional information the book provides—especially whether it provides any appendices, a glossary, bibliography, index, and so on.

• **Author credentials**—If the author is an expert in the field or has other credentials that make him or her particularly suited to writing the book, be sure to state these facts.

• **Physical qualities**—Indicate whether your books are available in both hard and softcover versions and, if so, at what prices. Also indicate any editions with special library bindings or acid-free paper which make for a more durable, longer-lasting book.

• **Availability**—If your book is available through library jobbers, list the names of the most prominent ones.

In short, provide libraries with any information that (1) demonstrates the benefits of your books for readers, (2) makes it easier for the librarian to place an order, (3) indicates that your books will stand up to heavy library use, and (4) shows that your books are readily available.

15:11   Some Tips on Selling to Libraries

Libraries are really quite easy to sell to if you publish books that fill a need, whether it be entertainment, information, or instruction. Once you've produced a book of quality, all you have to do is to let the librarians know about the book.

Perhaps I make it sound too simple but, nonetheless, it is easier to get the attention of librarians than it is to reach booksellers or consumers. The main point to remember is that librarians are information specialists. They are continually and actively seeking new titles which can help them better serve their library patrons. Hence, you don't have to overcome as much sales resistance as you would with consumers or booksellers who have many other activities demanding their attention.

Here, then, are a few ways you can attract the attention of librarians to your books:

• First, and perhaps foremost, **you must work to get reviews** of your books in the major library review media such as *Publishers Weekly*, *Library Journal*, *Booklist*, *Kirkus Reviews*, *Choice* (for books of interest to graduate and undergraduate libraries), *Horn Book* and *School Library Journal* (for children's books), *Small Press Book Review* and *Small Press* magazine (for small press titles), and *New Pages Press* (for alternative press publications), as well as in the general review media which librarians rely upon (such as the *New York Times Book Review*).

Since they don't have time to read every book that is published, librarians must rely on reviews from respected media to help them make informed buying decisions. A review in *Library Journal*, for instance, can result in orders for 1,000 books or more.

What are your chances of getting a review in these journals? Well, here are a couple of sobering facts: *Library Journal* reviews 4,000 books per year, while *School Library Journal* reviews 5,000. Yet these two journals receive 600 books and galleys every week—that's over 30,000 new books every year. As a result, your chances of getting a review in one or both of these journals is somewhere between 1 in 6 and 1 in 8.

• **Get other notices in these journals.** For example, in each issue *School Library Journal* publishes a listing of new award recipients. Hence, if your authors or books receive any awards, send information to the library and other book trade journals.

The August 1988 issue of *School Library Journal* listed the following awards: Detroit Public Library's Author Day Award, Dorothy Canfield Fisher Award (voted by Vermont children in grades 4-8), Paul A. Witty Award, Iowa Children's Choice Award, Judy Lopez Memorial Award (for pre-teen books), National Jewish Book Awards, Young Reader's Choice Award (Schaumburg Public Library), and others.

Both *School Library Journal* and *Library Journal* also feature free or inexpensive posters, pamphlets, calendars, bibliographies, and other library resources in their monthly Checklist departments.

My *Independent Publisher's Bookshelf* (now the bibliography of the *Book Publishing Resource Guide*) was featured in *Library Journal*. As a result, we received many direct orders from libraries for the book.

Pueblo Stories and Storytellers, a children's paperback book costing $9.95 (from Treasure Chest Publications), was featured in the Checklist department of the August issue of *School Library Journal*.

- **Advertise in these journals**, especially in *Library Journal* and *Choice*. Librarians like to know they are dealing with reputable and reliable suppliers. Ads in these journals help to reinforce your company image and also indicate to librarians that you are seriously pursuing their market.

- **Send your catalogs and other seasonal announcements to libraries.** Arrange your catalogs by subject area, then by author. Clearly indicate any new or forthcoming titles with the month and year of publication. Use simple, clear layouts with wide margins (for making notes). Provide an easy-to-use order form arranged by subject.

- **If you want libraries to order direct from you, provide some incentive for them to do so.** Offer sale prices on certain titles, or prepayment discounts, or free postage. Be sure to set a time limit on these sales to encourage the libraries to order right away and to prevent orders from trickling in for years (which could cause all sorts of problems in your fulfillment department). At the same time, though, since many libraries have rather elaborate purchasing procedures, allow ample time for ordering; hence, set a deadline that is at least 60 to 90 days from the date you will be mailing the promotion.

- **Direct mail does work.** In one survey of librarians (in England), the most oft-cited source of information used in making acquisition decisions was direct mail from publishers.

Twin Peaks Press has continued to sell their book, *All about Sewing Machines*, to libraries via direct mail and still gets lots of reorders even though the book was originally published in 1970.

One note of caution. In the January 18, 1988 issue of *Library Hotline*, one librarian shared the following "time-and-money saving idea" with his fellow librarians. At his library they have their mail clerk automatically throw out all mail with a bulk rate or non-profit mail insignia — without even opening it. As he puts it, most of it is of little interest to the library anyway. Since this rather dubious "great idea" was shared with about 2,000 other librarians, you might want to reconsider using bulk rate for your mailings to libraries.

- **Offer standing order plans** for annuals, series, or subject areas where you publish many books (such as poetry books or children's books).

- **Refer readers to their local library.** Librarians are especially sensitive to the needs and requests of people who use their library and will often order a book simply because one or two people request the title.

  Melvin Powers of Wilshire Books often sends readers of his advertisements to their local library to check out his books before they buy them. Not only does this allow readers to preview the books before they buy them, but it also increases the demand at local libraries which, in turn, will order extra copies if the demand persists. He claims to have sold thousands of copies in this way.

- **Work with the major library wholesalers.** Send them information on your forthcoming titles in plenty of time for them to place orders before they, in turn, receive purchase orders from libraries. Remember that as much as 75% of your library sales will come through these jobbers so make it easy for them to work with you.

  Baker & Taylor, the largest library wholesaler, runs a four-page ad in every issue of *School Library Journal*. This ad lists all titles reviewed in that issue with a blank space to allow librarians to enter how many copies of each title they want to order. All books reviewed in that issue are available through B&T.

- **Provide libraries with display materials.** Almost every library has one or two display areas which they change every month or two. If you provide them with posters, extra book jackets, or other display material, they are more likely to order your book *and* feature it in one of their displays. Indeed, you might just include an extra copy of the book jacket in with any direct orders from libraries.

- **Provide libraries with library cards.** If your primary market is libraries, you might want to offer library cards with your books. This makes it easier for librarians to catalog and shelve your book.

  You can order cards from the Library of Congress. Just send them your LCCN (Library of Congress Cataloging Number) and 65¢ for each set of 8 cards you want. They only sell cards in sets of 8 (main entry cards only). Before ordering from them, write for complete information. Write to the **Cataloging Distribution Service**, Library of Congress, Washington DC 20541; (202) 707-6100.

  Of course, once you have a complete sample, you could also print your own cards locally.

- **Exhibit your books at the major library association meetings**: the American Library Association convention in mid-summer, their midwinter meeting, and the conventions of the Special Library Association, the Association of College and Research Libraries, and the many regional associations. If you cannot afford to exhibit on your own, join one of the cooperative exhibits (Conference Book Service, Publishers Book Exhibit, COSMEP exhibit service, Publishers Marketing Association exhibit service, and others).

- **Join cooperative mailings to libraries** such as the ones provided by the Publishers Marketing Association, Twin Peaks Press, or Direct Mail Promotions. Many publishers have reported superb results using these inexpensive promotions. For a more complete list of such co-op marketing plans, see *Book Publishing Resource Guide*.

- **Arrange distribution in special subject catalogs** such as those issued by North Carolina Biological Supply, Social Studies School Service, Ross Book Service, or Gryphon House. Some of these are cooperative ventures; others are catalogs issued by publishers who also distribute other publishers' books.

- **Get listed in the standard reference works** used by librarians to place orders, such as *Books in Print*, *Small Press Record of Books in Print*, and *Publishers Trade List Annual* (addresses for obtaining listings in these bibliographic reference works are listed in *Book Publishing Resource Guide*). Few librarians will track down a publisher who is not listed in these standard reference works if there is another publisher who is listed and who can supply a similar title. Moreover, such listings can lead to many direct sales since librarians use these books not only to locate publishers but also to locate books of special interest.

  Davis Publications found that most of the library sales for Carolyn Hall's *Soft Sculpture* were attributable to the fact that it was the only book listed in the title volume of *Books in Print* under "soft sculpture."

- **Hire sales representatives.** Generally speaking, this step would not be cost-effective unless you publish many new titles each year for the library market.

  Doubleday has a special sales force which represents their line of science fiction hardcovers (and other titles) to libraries and institutions, which sign up for a year's worth of books at a special discount.

- **Sign up with a library distributor.** For many smaller publishers, this option has provided a significant jump in sales. Currently, there are two active distributors of small press titles to libraries.

  Quality Books, 918 Sherwood Drive, Lake Bluff, IL 60044-2204; (708) 295-2010; Fax: (708) 295-1556. Write for a copy of their New Title Submission Form.

  Unique Books, 4200 Grove Avenue, Gurnee, IL 60031; (312) 623-9171.

  While most library wholesalers do not go out of their way to promote your titles (but, instead, passively process the orders they receive from libraries), Quality Books actively distributes non-fiction adult books to libraries throughout the country. They exhibit at the major library conventions, have field sales reps which cover the entire U.S., offer standing order plans, telemarket, mail catalogs, and do whatever else they can to sell small press titles. And they have been successful: They have sold over a million small press books. Besides that, they are easy to work with and pay on time. What more can you ask for?

Chapter 16

How to Sell Subsidiary Rights

The sale of subsidiary rights is now a major source of income for trade book publishers. Indeed, if it were not for subsidiary rights income, many publishers would lose money on their lead titles as well as on their midlist titles. For this reason, many major publishers have established a separate department of three or more people whose sole responsibility is to arrange sales of subsidiary rights.

Given the potential for income, you too should seriously consider establishing your own subsidiary rights department or at least assign someone to spend a portion of each day pursuing sales of subsidiary rights. Nick Lyons Books, a small New York City publisher, has set up such a department which brings in $6,000 to $12,000 a year just from the sale of serial rights. If you publish five or more titles of general interest every year, you might well discover that an organized pursuit of subsidiary rights sales will more than pay for itself.

16:01 6 Benefits of Subsidiary Rights Sales

While subsidiary rights sales are a great source of income for any publisher, there are many other reasons why you should pursue the sale of subsidiary rights. Here are six of them:

1. First and foremost, of course, the rights income itself will help to pay for the printing and promotion of your books. Such sales are especially useful in helping to pay for an increased advertising budget which can, in turn, mean increased sales in the retail stores.
2. Prepublication rights sales can increase the visibility of your titles and, hence, can lead to larger bookstore orders and more prominent displays and, thence, to greater sales.

3. Rights sales increase the credibility of any book. A rights sale, in effect, says that at least one person has sanctioned the book as something worth being excited about.

4. Rights sales beget other rights sales. For instance, a first serial sale to a major magazine can spark interest in the book from the major mass-market reprinters or from independent movie producers.

5. The exposure given a book by a first serial in a magazine can increase bookstore sales significantly. For instance, the serialization of Erich Segal's *Love Story* in *Ladies Home Journal* caused such a positive reaction from the readers that most went right out and bought the book. The excerpt thus helped put that book on the road to bestseller status.

6. The sale of movie or TV rights can create a second wave of book sales when the movie plays in the theaters or the TV show is aired. This second wave of sales can sometimes be greater than the first wave.

16:02 Tips on Selling Subsidiary Rights

To make subsidiary rights sales, you must be well-organized, persistent, and attentive to details. Here are a few steps you can follow to increase your effectiveness in selling subsidiary rights:

• Before you do anything else, do your homework. Above all, this means developing a contact list for each major subsidiary right you might sell. Hence, you should have a separate list for serial rights sales, another for dramatic rights, another for reprinting, another for book clubs, and so on. In addition, each list should be broken down by category—for instance, those interested in fiction, or biography, or science, or whatever categories you specialize in publishing so you can match your new titles to each potential buyer.

Such a database should be quite easy to develop with a computer. As a starting point, you could begin with the *Book Marketing No-Frills* and *PR FLASH No-Frills* data files from Ad-Lib Publications. Among other listings, these data files include almost 7,000 major newspaper and magazine editors, their addresses and phone numbers, whether or not they buy serial rights (or do book reviews), and the topics they are most likely to buy (or review). It also lists 180 book clubs, mass-market rights buyers, and other rights buyers. The listings can be selected by name, zip code, subject category, and a number of other criteria.

• Once you've developed a list, keep these key contacts informed of any forthcoming books. Send news releases to them the moment you have signed an author for a new book and have set a proposed publication date. Send them your catalogs, noting especially those titles which would most interest their audience. Finally, once you have a manuscript in hand, send a letter to each of your key contacts offering them a preview galley copy or photocopy of the manuscript.

- Send out review copies (either copies of the manuscript or galley copies) as soon as you receive requests. The quicker you send them out, the less chance the editor or buyer will have to lose interest in your book. In most cases, these review copies must be in the hands of major rights buyers at least six months before publication date so they have plenty of time to make a decision and schedule their use of the rights they buy.

- When you send out the review copies, be sure to include the following vital information:

  1. A letter or memo outlining why the book should interest their audience,

  2. A biography of the author, and

  3. A fact sheet highlighting the contents of the book and your promotional plans for it.

  4. If you have prepared a mockup of the cover of the book, send that also.

  5. Finally, be sure to note the publication date.

- Don't be afraid to approach more than one rights buyer at a time; it's standard operation procedure at the major publishing houses. As a courtesy, though, let the buyers know that others are also being approached. The advantages of such multiple submissions are that 1) you can approach more potential buyers in a short period of time, and 2) if more than one buyer expresses an interest in your book, they might well bid against each other thus raising the final price for the rights.

- Some rights buyers prefer to be telephoned first so they can screen a title. Others prefer to have some promotional literature or a review copy in hand before you call. Here's a general guideline of how to decide whether to call first and mail later or mail first and call later: If you are unsure whether or not a rights buyer would be interested in a particular title, call him or her and ask; on the other hand, if you are sure that the book will interest him or her (because the book is highly targeted to his or her audience), then send the book or promotional literature first and follow up with a call.

- Regardless of whether you call first and mail later or mail first and call later, always be sure to do some sort of follow-up on every contact you make. Don't assume that just because they have not contacted you that they are not interested. There could very well have been some foulup in shipment or receipt that caused your contacts not to receive their review copy. So always follow up your initial contacts.

- When you do get an offer or expression of interest from one buyer, don't sell that particular subsidiary right until you have heard from other potential rights buyers who've received a review copy. If the others haven't contacted you, call them and ask if they are interested in the book as well.

- If more than one rights buyer expresses a strong interest in one of your books, you could hold a **rights auction**. To hold an auction, set a closing date for bids, lay down the basic rules for the auction, and set the minimum opening bid you will accept. You may offer the "floor" to any buyer who will guarantee payment of that minimum opening bid. In exchange, that buyer usually gets the right to sit out the bidding and to top the last bid by 10% or some other agreed upon figure.

  You can ask for written bids to be submitted by the closing date, or you can accept telephone bids on the closing date. In either case, once the auction date has arrived you should review all the bids and then call the lower bidders to see if any of them want to top the highest bid. Continue this procedure until every bidder but one has dropped out. Then sell the rights to that highest bidder.

  If someone has the floor, call them back at the end to see if they'd like to top the final bid by the agreed upon percentage. If they'd like to, then they gain the rights. If not, the highest regular bidder gains the rights for their bid price.

  When Conari Press announced a rights auction for Daphne Kingma's *Coming Apart: Why Relationships End and How to Live Through the Ending of Yours*, nine out of ten mass-market publishers responded. Conari set the lowest acceptable advance at $50,000.. The bidding by telephone went on for ten rounds over two days. Ballantine eventually bought the rights for an $85,000 advance.

- While the best policy is to pursue rights sales in an organized way, there have been a number of cases where rights buyers discovered the book rather than the publisher discovering the rights buyer. Sometimes this has occurred even several years after the original date of publication. So don't give up. If you have published a worthwhile book and it is selling well, the subsidiary rights buyers will come to you sooner or later if you don't find them first.

- If your book is rejected once, it doesn't mean you can't later offer the book to the same rights buyers again. If your book goes on to gain great reviews, large sales or some other sort of notoriety, you would certainly be justified in resubmitting the book for consideration.

  Quality Paperback Book Club, for instance, often buys backlist titles once they have established some sort of track record. They have even succumbed to other convincing arguments. After QPBC first rejected the *Greystone Bakery Cookbook* by Helen Glassman and Susan Postal, Shambhala Publications sent the club editor a chocolate cake (made from a recipe in the book). Not only did QPBC rethink its decision and buy the book club rights, but so did the Cooking and Crafts division of Book-of-the-Month Club.

- If you want to attract the attention of other rights buyers, be sure to send a notice of any rights buys to Paul Nathan, the Rights columnist at *Publishers Weekly*.

That's how Conari Press first attracted the attention of mass-market publishers. When Literary Guild made *Coming Apart* one of their selections, Conari immediately sent a note to *PW*. Soon after the *PW* notice, Ballantine inquired whether the mass-market rights were available. As a result, Conari ran their auction.

● Another way to attract the attention of rights buyers is to build on any other publicity that ties into the book. Again, Conari's auction worked even better than expected because the author appeared on the *Oprah Winfrey Show* just days before the auction.

Similarly, just before the Naval Institute Press was to hold an auction for the mass-market paperback rights to *Flight of the Intruder* by Stephen Coonts, one of their people noticed the galley copy of *Flight* on President Reagan's desk (in a photo that appeared in *Fortune* magazine). The Press rounded up five copies of the magazine and air expressed them to the five publishers bidding for the rights. By the time the auction was over, Pocket Books bought the mass-market rights for $341,000.

● If you don't want to sell the rights yourself, work through an agent. Here are the names of two literary agents who specialize in making subsidiary rights sales for independent book publishers.

Mary Jane Ross, 85 Sunset Lane, Tenafly, NJ 07670; (201) 568-8739.

Writers House, Inc., Karen Wallace, Subsidiary Rights Manager, 21 West 26th Street, New York, NY 10010; (212) 685-2400.
Handles subsidiary rights sales for 11 smaller publishers.

Other literary agents may also handle subsidiary rights sales for smaller publishers. If you'd like one of these agents to represent your company, send them your catalog. You should not have to pay agents to represent you; they will generally work for a percentage of the sale (plus expenses). Generally, their percentages would be as follows:

Book club rights — 10%
Mass-market reprint rights — 10%
Movie/TV rights — 15%
Serial rights — 20%

When Libra Publishers needed help selling rights, they turned to Mary Jane Ross. She sold book club rights to *Hidden Bedroom Partners* to three different book clubs, mass-market reprint rights to Pocket Books, and first serial rights to *Glamour*.

Authors — If you have retained most subsidiary rights, you can sell them yourself or work with your literary agent to sell them. Even if you have assigned these rights to your publisher, you can still help if you have some prime contacts.

16:03 The Subsidiary Rights Contract

While many subsidiary rights buyers have their own contract which they require you to sign when they buy rights from you, you may also want to develop your own contract. To ensure that all points are covered in such a contract (whether theirs or yours), you may want to use the sample subsidiary rights license on page 151 of *Book Marketing Made Easier.*

Here are the major points which need to be covered in any subsidiary rights agreement:

- **Title and author of book** — Be sure that the title, edition, and name of author are spelled out correctly in the agreement.

- **Rights being granted** — State exactly what rights are being granted. Be as specific and as clear as possible. Make sure that both parties clearly understand which rights are involved.

- **Territory covered** — State whether the rights are for North America only, or the English language only, or whatever territorial restrictions might apply.

- **Duration of rights** — State the term of the assignment of rights. For example, most mass-market paperback rights are sold for a term of five to seven years. Other rights might be sold for the life of the copyright. Others, such as serial rights, are only sold for one-time use.

- **Use of the book material** — If there are any questions about how the rights may be used, spell them out clearly. Can the rights buyer change or edit the material? Are there any restrictions on how they may advertise or promote their version of the book?

- **Amount to be paid** — The amount to be paid should be clearly spelled out, including any advances and royalties. Due dates for payments and methods of accounting also need to be delineated in detail.

- **Other limitations** — For certain rights you might want to include some other limitations. For example, in selling mass-market rights, you will undoubtedly want to require a limitation stating that no such edition can be published until at least one year after the publication date of your hardcover edition. That will give your hardcover edition a decent chance to sell out before the mass-market edition is published.

> **Authors** — Make sure your contract with your publisher specifies which rights you own and which rights you assign to your publisher — or what percentage of any rights sales you and your publisher share. Generally speaking, unless you are a well-known or well-connected author, it is to your advantage to let your publisher handle these rights sales.

According to *Entertainment Industry Contracts*, the split of subsidiary rights between author and publisher is generally as follows:

50/50   Mass-market paperback rights (author/publisher)
50/50   Book club rights
75/25   First serial rights
50/50   Second serial rights
90/10   Movie or TV rights
80/20   Foreign rights
50/50   Licensing or merchandising rights
50/50   Audio, video, or filmstrip rights

The above percentages should only be taken as guidelines. All such percentages are negotiable.

16:04 First Serial Rights

First serial rights are the rights sold to magazines and newspapers to excerpt part (or sometimes all) of a book before its date of publication. While most first serial rights are sold for anywhere from $400 to $5,000, they have gone for as high as $200,000 (*Woman's Day* paid that much for exclusive rights to excerpt Rose Kennedy's autobiography *Times to Remember*).

Aside from the income such sales can generate, the other main benefit of first serial rights is the exposure they provide for new titles. This exposure can sometimes make or break a book. For example, Lee Iacocca's autobiography was launched through a pre-publication excerpt and interview in *Newsweek*. This cover story was all the publicity Iacocca did for his book, and yet it was enough to create the word of mouth which made his book one of the first mass-market hardcover bestsellers. *Newsweek* has since provided similar (though less effective) sendoffs for Geraldine Ferraro's biography and David Stockman's *The Triumph of Politics*.

Since first serial rights can be so important to launching any major title, here are a few guidelines on how to handle such sales:

• To place first serial rights, contact the book editors (or whoever is responsible for buying serial rights) at magazines which you believe would be interested in the subject of your book. Send them a copy of the manuscript at least six months in advance of the book's publication date. For a highly illustrated book (such as a travel guide or photography book), it is better to send a copy of the finished book if at all possible, or quality photographs with the manuscript if no finished book is available.

In general, the other basic procedures for handling serial rights sales and contracts are similar to those outlined above for any other subsidiary rights sales.

- First serial rights can be sold on a non-exclusive basis. That means that you can sell excerpts from different parts of the book to as many buyers as are interested.

  For example, Patricia Breinen, rights director at Holt, Reinhart & Winston, made ten first serial sales for Louise Erdrich's episodic novel *Love Medicine*. She sold chapters from the book to *Ms.*, *Atlantic*, *Mother Jones*, *Kenyon Review*, *North American Review*, *North Dakota Quarterly*, *New England Review*, and two excerpts to *Chicago*.

  Stanton & Lee, a regional publisher out of Madison, Wisconsin, sold 34 separate serial rights to their book *Haunted Heartland*, a collection of 150 "true" stories of the occult by Beth Scott and Michael Norman. Because these purportedly true stories take place in 108 different locations in the Midwest, Stanton & Lee found it quite easy to sell first serial rights to 34 Midwestern newspapers including most of the major ones. Because of the attendant publicity, the first printing of the book sold out the day after publication.

  Three magazines bought first serial rights to *How to Make Love All the Time* by Barbara De Angelis. *Cosmo* paid $1,000 for first North American rights only. *Family Circle* paid $4,000 for world rights to its excerpt. And *McCall's* paid $1,500 for a four-page quiz.

- Note that you can also sell exclusive first serial rights to various categories of publications.

  For example, Marcia Chellis's agent sold exclusive newspaper syndication rights for her book, *Living with the Kennedys*, to the New York Times Syndicate for $30,000 and sold exclusive tabloid rights to the *National Enquirer* for $75,000, for a total first serial sale of $105,000.

- First serial sales can be made to newspapers, magazines (both consumer and business), tabloids, and syndicates. Plus, within each category you can make sales to any number of publications. For example, if you have a health book, besides selling first serial rights to *Prevention* or *Today's Health*, you might also be able to sell rights to sports magazines such as *Running*, women's magazines such as *Self* or *New Woman*, alternative magazines such as *Mother Earth News*, and business magazines such as *Inc.* — all dependent on how appropriate the contents of the book are to the different audiences. Don't overlook potential sales just because a magazine has never used such material in the past. Editorial trends are always changing. Keep up with them, or even ahead of them.

- To obtain the higher bids for serial rights sales, you generally have to get some of the major bidders interested in the book. Some of the major bidders include *Redbook*, *Cosmo*, *McCall's*, *National Enquirer*, *Ladies' Home Journal*, and *Self*.

- If the major magazines are not interested, try the Sunday supplements to the local newspapers in the author's home state (or your own home state). Your author should be able to help you make contacts.

• When negotiating book contracts with your authors, try to get a 50/50 split on the income from serial rights sales. While some authors (or their agents) insist on an 90/10 or 80/20 split, you should try to convince them to go for a more equitable split — one which would make it worth your while to pursue such sales. The income generated from such rights sales should at least pay for your costs in obtaining such sales, and that usually requires at least a 50/50 split, especially on second serial rights sales.

> **Authors** — If you decide not to handle your own serial rights sales (by yourself or through your agent), give your publisher an adequate share of the rights sales so they can afford to pursue such sales. Remember: The more such rights sales your publisher can afford to make, the better off both of you will be — not only because you will both be getting more income but also because of the attendant publicity (which will mean greater sales for the book itself).

16:05 How to Determine a Fair Price

With first serial rights going for as much as $200,000 and for as low as $400, you should carefully consider what price to ask for such rights. You don't want to price your book out of the market, but at the same time you do want to get a fair price for the book — the highest possible fair price. Here are a few guidelines to use in determining a fair price:

• What is the circulation of the periodical? The higher the circulation, the more the periodical can generally afford to pay. Hence, while *Playboy* can afford to pay $3,500 or more for first serial rights to a story, a magazine such as *Fantasy and Science Fiction* could hardly afford to pay more than its going rate per word which would result in a far smaller payment.

• What does the periodical normally pay for such rights? And what is the maximum amount it has been willing to pay in the past? Here are a few examples of high prices paid by some of the major buyers of first serial rights:

Redbook — $44,000 for *Breaking Point* the story of John Hinkley written by his parents and $30,000 for an excerpt from Carol Botwin's *Men Who Can't Be Faithful — How to Pick Up the Pieces When He's Breaking Your Heart.*

Good Housekeeping — In the upper five figures each for both Eddie Fisher's autobiography *Eddie: My Life, My Loves* and *The Pritkin Diet.*

Ladies' Home Journal—$120,000 for Betty Ford's autobiography *The Times of My Life*, $100,000 for Sophia Loren's autobiography *Sophia*, and $87,500 for Gail Sheehy's novel *Pathfinders*.

Woman's Day—$200,000 for Rose Kennedy's autobiography *Times to Remember*.

Family Circle—$100,000 for Lauren Bacall's autobiography *By Myself*, $75,000 for Richard Simmon's *Never Say Diet Cookbook*, and $35,000 for Nancy Sinatra's *Frank Sinatra, My Father*.

National Enquirer—$37,000 for the *I Love Lucy Book* by Bard Andrews, $27,000 for *The Duke: The Life and Times of John Wayne* by Donald Shepard and Robert Slatzer, and $70,000 for a four-parter from Shirley Temple Black's autobiography, *Child Star*.

- How much of the book do they want to excerpt? The more they want to excerpt, the more they should pay. For example, *Family Circle* paid $125,000 for five installments of Marjorie Craig's exercise book *10 Minutes a Day Shape-up Program*.

- Does the publication want exclusive rights to the entire book or to just a part? You would, of course, have to charge more for exclusive rights since you are giving up the possibility of any other income.

  Good Housekeeping paid $90,000 for the exclusive right to use a 2000 word excerpt from Bill Cosby's book on *Fatherhood*. That's $45.00 per word, far higher than normal for such rights.

- If they do want exclusive use of all or a part of the book, how long do they want such exclusivity? The longer they want such exclusivity, the more they should pay.

- How badly do they want the book excerpt? Again, the more they want the excerpt, the more you can charge for it. Probably the only way, though, that you will ever be able to tell how much they want it is if some other competitor also bids for the rights. Of course, the more competition there is for the rights, the higher the price will go.

- First serial rights are worth more than second serial rights because of their "scoop" value. The buyer of first serial rights is paying for the opportunity to give the world its first look at a new book.

- Syndication rights should sell for more than first serial rights to one publication. Remember that most syndicators are going to make back whatever they pay for the rights by reselling the rights to syndicate members.

  For example, the Los Angeles Times Syndicate paid almost a $100,000 for the syndication rights to Anthony Summer's biography of Marilyn Monroe, *Goddess*. Within 48 hours they had recouped their investment by reselling the abridgement to 17 newspapers.

- Celebrity biographies, as a rule, tend to draw the highest bids for first serial rights. Other books usually have to settle for earning smaller first rights sales.

- When pricing the first serial rights to your books, remember these two points: 1) Most first serial rights go for less than it would cost the magazine to commission an article from a freelance writer. 2) A book excerpt is easier to edit than an original article (which saves the periodical both time and money in editorial costs). So don't hesitate to ask for a fair price for such rights.

16:06 Second Serial Rights

Second serial rights are those serial rights which are sold after a book's publication date. Since the printing of excerpts from a book after its publication does not have the exclusive "scoop" value of excerpts prior to publication, second serial rights are usually sold for a lot less than first serial rights. Standard payment for second serial rights can range from $50 to $2,000, depending primarily on the circulation of the publication and the number of first and second serial rights which have previously been sold. Nonetheless, payments for second serial rights can sometimes rival those made for first serial rights.

- The *National Enquirer* paid almost $20,000 to reprint portions of Robert Lenzner's biography of John Paul Getty, *The Great Getty*.
- In an auction for second serial rights, *Redbook* paid $25,000 for Judith Krantz's novel, *Till We Meet Again*.

Why would magazines buy second serial rights? Besides the fact that such rights are cheaper, the magazine gets the benefit of the book's publicity and other promotion. Plus, the editor can work from a finished, completely edited and proofread book, thus making his or her job easier. Finally, before buying such rights, the editor has a chance to gauge readers' response to the book and, hence, can better decide if the book would be appropriate for the magazine's readership.

When you do approach periodicals about buying second serial rights, let them know of any previous first and second serial rights sales. Not only is this common courtesy, but it also demonstrates to the prospective buyers that the book has material that lends itself to being excerpted.

16:07 Freebies, Adaptations, and P.I. Deals

Rather than sell second serial rights, you may decide to give away excerpts of one of your books in order to increase the book's exposure to its major audience. These freebies benefit the periodical by providing it with solid editorial material, and they benefit your book by increasing its visibility at no cost to you. These freebie deals can be arranged in at least four different ways:

- Offer free excerpts of parts of the book to any magazine or newsletter that expresses an interest. Stipulate that they may reprint the excerpt free as long as they provide a statement at the end of the article describing how the book may be ordered. That statement should include the title and author of the book, the name and address of your company, and the price of the book, plus any other appropriate ordering instructions.

  Ad-Lib has offered excerpts of several of its books to the newsletters of some of the smaller publishers associations. These associations rarely have a budget for such articles, yet their members would clearly be interested in the information contained in our books and would be likely to order our books if they had a chance to sample the contents of the books. Hence, we look on these freebies as samplers which we are able to get into the hands of prime prospects at no cost to us.

- Offer such freebies in trade for advertising space. Since the advertising space you get will often have gone unsold anyway, the article doesn't cost the magazine anything; and since you would not have otherwise sold serial rights to the magazine, you are able to get a free ad which will reinforce the article's impact and increase direct sales of your book. Since the ad is yours to do as you please, you can have the orders come direct to you.

  A number of business opportunity and trade magazines regularly participate in such exchanges. So do many limited circulation magazines and newsletters.

- If the magazine will not trade advertising space, you could offer them a per inquiry (P.I.) or per order deal. Under such an arrangement, they not only run an excerpt of your book, but they also run an advertisement or bingo card which allows readers to order the book through them. The magazine then sends the orders to you for fulfillment (after taking their cut, which may be anywhere from 40% to 60% discount, depending on the discount you've negotiated).

  For its *Office Purchasing Guide*, Lowen Publishing permitted a chain of twenty regional purchasing management magazines to run a year-long series of articles excerpted from the book in exchange for monthly P.I. ads for the book. This arrangement gives double exposure for the book to its prime market.

- Finally, rather than excerpt part of the book, you could adapt material from the book to create new articles. These articles, in turn, could be sold in the same way as any other freelance article or could be given away under one of the above arrangements.

  I adapted part of *The Independent Publisher's Bookshelf* for an article about publishers associations which I then sold to *Small Press* magazine. The payment I received for that one article paid for my expenses in preparing the entire bibliographic review.

The one disadvantage of giving away freebies is that such arrangements make it harder to sell second serial rights for your other books. Magazines, which previously have gotten articles for nothing, are not likely to want to pay for excerpts of new books if they can still make other arrangements. Perhaps the best policy, then, is to offer freebies only to limited circulation magazines or newsletters who cannot afford to buy serial rights in the first place. All others pay cash.

> **Authors** — Once any serial rights sales have been made, you can explore these other options. Before you do, however, coordinate any efforts with your publisher so you don't interfere with their on-going publicity or rights sales.

16:08 Mass-Market Paperback Reprint Rights

Here's where the big money is. Paperback rights have gone for as high as $3.2 million (that's what Bantam paid for Judith Krantz's *Princess Daisy*). Even reprint rights for midlist titles will often sell for $25,000 to $100,000 or more. Hence, of all subsidiary rights, these reprint rights are probably the most important. So you would do well to research this market carefully. Find out who the major players are, what categories of books they buy, and how much they are willing to pay for major titles. To give you a beginning, here are a few brief notes about some of the major mass-market publishers:

- **Avon** — A member of the Hearst Group (which includes Morrow and Arbor House), Avon has previously paid $1.9 million for Colleen McCullough's *The Thorn Birds*, $1.5 million for Collins and LaPierre's *The Fifth Horseman*, and $1.5 million for Woodward and Bernstein's *The Final Days*.

- **Ballantine** — Owned by Random House, this house publishes both general fiction and non-fiction. Its Del Ray line publishes some of the best science fiction and fantasy novels. Fawcett is also now owned by Random House. Ballantine has previously paid $1.9 million for Marilyn French's *The Bleeding Heart* and $1 million plus for Erich Segal's *Man, Woman and Child*.

- **Bantam** — Besides being a major publisher of hardcover bestselling biographies, Bantam is also known for its paperback bestsellers, including its two lines for young adults, Sweet Dreams and Sweet Valley High (which do not currently buy reprint rights). Besides paying $3.2 million for Krantz's *Princess Daisy*, Bantam has paid $1.8 million for E. L. Doctorow's *Ragtime*, $3.0 million for James Herriott's *The Lord*

God Made Them All (along with the renewals for three previous titles), and $1.9 million for Cynthia Freeman's *No Time for Tears*. Dell, another major buyer, is now a division of Bantam Doubleday Dell.

- **Berkley** — Part of the Putnam group which includes Jove, Ace, and several other lines, Berkeley publishes general fiction and non-fiction. Berkeley paid $825,000 for Gerald Browne's *Stone 588*.

- **New American Library** — Part of the Viking-Penguin group, NAL also has its own hardcover line, as well as the Signet line of paperback classics. NAL has paid $2.6 million for rights to Robin Cook's *Brain* and *Sphinx* and over $3 million for two new Cook novels. NAL has also paid $2.2 million for Mario Puzo's *Fools Die* and $1.5 million for Irma Rombauer's *The Joy of Cooking*.

- **Pocket Books** — Part of Simon & Schuster, Pocket Books publishes in most fields including a separate science fiction line, Tapestry romances, and Washington Square Press high-quality paperbacks. Pocket has paid over $2 million for John Irving's *Hotel New Hampshire* and $1.6 million for Judy Blume's *Smart Women* and a renewal of her *Wifey*.

- **Warner** — A division of Time Warner, Warner Books publishes contemporary fiction and general non-fiction. Warner has paid $1.2 million for Judith Rossner's *August*. They have also paid $2 million for Richard Nixon's *Memoirs* and $2 million for Woodward and Bernstein's *All the President's Men*.

- Other mass-market paperback lines include Baen, DAW, Harlequin, Leisure, Lynx, Tor, Mysterious Press, Pageant, Paperjacks, Penguin, Questar, Revell, Scholastic, St. Martin's, Tudor, and Zebra. Many of these lines specialize in various genre of fiction.

Once you've located those paperback houses who you think would be most interested in your titles, send them a copy of your book for consideration. Reprint rights can be sold at almost anytime — at the time of signing the hardcover edition (a joint hard/soft deal), prior to hardcover publication, or anytime after publication.

What are your chances of selling reprint rights to your titles? Very good if your book is fiction, since nearly 3/4 of the 4,000 mass-market paperbacks produced each year are fiction titles. While many of those 3,000 fiction titles are original paperbacks, perhaps as many as a quarter are reprints of the 2,000 hardcover or trade paperback fiction titles published each year. That would mean that about 1/3 of all fiction titles are sold for paperback reprinting each year.

For nonfiction titles, however, the prospects for mass-market reprint rights sales are not that good. Each of the 35,000 hardcover and trade paperback nonfiction titles published each year in the U.S. must compete to be one of approximately 1,000 mass-market nonfiction titles produced in the U.S. each year. Since a number of those 1,000 titles are originals, the opportunities are even more limited.

Here are the odds for a number of categories (based on entries in the *Weekly Record* and *Paperbound Books in Print* databases for 1981 and 1982): For cookbooks and juveniles, about an 8% to 10% chance. For sports and recreation titles, about a 15% chance. For biographies, about a 4% chance. For all other titles, about a 1% to 2% chance.

If you do make a sale, the basic terms of the contract would be about the same as for any other subsidiary rights. Royalty rates range anywhere from 6% to 10% (and higher for a few brand name authors). The term for such rights is usually five to seven years. Most contracts also stipulate that the mass-market edition may not be published within a year of the hardcover edition (this allows the hardcover a decent life span).

16:09 Trade Paperback Reprint Rights

If you do not publish your own trade paperback editions, you could sell such reprint rights before you sell mass-market rights. In this way, a book can have three full lives — as a hardcover, as a trade paperback, and as a mass-market paperback. *The Joy of Cooking*, for example, has been a bestseller as a hardcover (over 10 million), a trade paperback (over 1.5 million) and as a mass-market paperback (over 5 million).

Trade paperback reprint rights usually sell for a royalty of between 6% and 10%. Other provisions of the contract are similar to mass-market rights and subsidiary rights in general.

16:10 Selling to Book Clubs

Besides the extra income that book club sales generate, there are a number of other advantages to such book club sales:

1. If the book club joins your print run, you could save 10% or more on the production costs of your own copies.
2. Book club sales rarely eat into normal trade sales or other sales by mail. They are, in effect, add-on sales you probably would not have gotten in any other way.
3. The promotional exposure provided by book club magazines helps to support your own promotional efforts and often leads to more bookstore sales.

Royalties for book club sales are usually around 10% of the club's list price (which itself is often 70% or less of the book's original list price). The royalty decreases to 5% if the book is used as a premium. The average advance against royalties offered by the major book clubs for a main selection is between $95,000 and $200,000 (to as high as $1,000,000). For featured alternates, the advance is generally around $25,000; and for other selections, advances can range from $4,000 to $10,000.

If they are doing their own print run, the smaller book clubs usually offer an advance of half the royalties expected to be earned based on the club's initial print run. If they buy copies from your stock, they will generally want to pay manufacturing costs plus a royalty of 10% to 15%.

The term for most book club contracts is two to three years, during which time the book club has the right to distribute the book to its members as they see fit. Generally, the major book club licenses require exclusive book club rights. Most smaller ones do not require exclusivity.

When submitting books to various book clubs for consideration, don't pass by a book club just because it has never offered a similar book in the past. If you believe that their members would be interested in one of your titles, send them a copy. Don't rule out any club; let them make the selections. For example, M. Evans sold Rodale's Prevention Book Club (which normally features health and nutrition books) Julia Grice's *How to Find Romance After 40*. Although the book is clearly not a health book, it still has a natural appeal to the club's members, most of whom are over 40.

Below is a list of various categories of book clubs. For a complete list of book clubs, their addresses, phone numbers, and interests, see the *Book Publishing Resource Guide*.

- **General-interest hardcover book clubs** — Book-of-the-Month Club and Literary Guild are the two major ones.

- **General-interest paperback book clubs** — Quality Paperback Book Club, a subsidiary of Book of the Month Club, is the major paperback book club. They are interested in backlist as well as frontlist, hardcover as well as softcover. Troll Book Club is the other major club.

- **Book Condensations** — Reader's Digest Condensed Books are the leaders in this field. While book abridgements and condensations are not technically book club sales, we list them here because in most ways they are similar. *Reader's Digest* paid $40,000 to abridge *The Judgment* by Howard Goldfluss. In June, 1989, they started a nonfiction condensed book club that features history, biography, and other general interest nonfiction books.

- **Professional book clubs** — McGraw-Hill and NewBridge both offer a number of different specialized book clubs for professionals, from engineers and computer programmers to doctors and architects.

- **Book clubs for teachers** — Early Learning Book Club and Instructor Book Club are two that serve teachers. Recently, Bright Ring Publishing sold rights to both of these clubs for its *Scribble Cookies and Other Independent Creative Art Experience for Children*.

- **Children's book clubs** — Field Publications (with their Weekly Reader, Buddy Books, Discovering Books, and other book clubs), Scholastic (with their Arrow, See-Saw, and Teen Age Book Clubs), and Grolier (with their Beginning Readers' Program and Disney's Wonderful World of Reading) are the major companies in this field.

- **Special interest book clubs** — There are a good number of special interest book clubs offering books for almost any interest, including writing (Writer's Digest Book Club), science fiction (Science Fiction Book Club), cooking (Cookery Book Club, as well as the cookbook division of Book of the Month Club), military (Military Book Club), and gardening (The Garden Book Club), among others.

- **Religious book clubs** — There are a good number of book clubs in this field for Catholics, Protestants, Evangelicals, and Jews.

- **Subscription book clubs** — Franklin Mint, for example, offers a fifty-volume series on Great American Fiction. The Easton Press offers a limited edition collection of the Masterpieces of Science Fiction.

- **Alumni book clubs** — Several universities, including Notre Dame and Marquette, have book clubs that feature books by alumni and/or faculty of the university (or other books that might interest the alumni). Books are featured in and sold through the alumni magazine.

> **Authors** — Check to see if your university has such a book club. If so, let your publisher know so they can send a review copy of your book to the university book club. Also, if you know of any special interest book clubs that you think would be appropriate for your book, tell your publisher.

16:11 Motion Picture Rights

Except for mass-market reprint rights, sales of movie and TV screenplay rights probably generate more excitement than any other sale — primarily because they usually involve more money. Options can go for anywhere from $500 to $100,000, with an average of about $10,000. Pickup rights go for anywhere from $25,000 to $2.5 million (that's how much United Artists paid for rights to Gay Talese's *Thy Neighbor's Wife*). The average pickup prices for movie rights are between $75,000 and $150,000.

Options allow movie producers to gain exclusive rights to a book while they arrange for financing of the movie, assemble the necessary talent (screenwriters, directors, actors, and other necessary personnel), and explore the feasibility of making a movie based on the book. The term of most options varies from 90 days to 1 year. Option payments are non-refundable. That means that the author and/or publisher keeps the money even if the option is not exercised (i.e., the movie is not produced). If the option is exercised, the option payment is applied to the purchase price of the movie.

Besides the pickup or purchase price, brand name authors can sometimes negotiate for a percentage of the profits after the pickup price has been covered. In any movie or TV rights contract, there should be a provision allowing for the reversion of rights to the author if the movie or TV series is not produced within so many years (for instance, five years).

While most books are optioned for movies as the result of sustained publicity efforts by the publishers and the work of special TV/movie agents (most of whom are based in California), happenstance can also play a role in which books are chosen for production as movies. For example, Calvin Floyd of Producers Enterprises recently optioned Judith Richards's 1978 novel *Summer Lightning* after his Swedish-born wife happened to pick up a Swedish translation of the novel while they were visiting in Stockholm.

Besides selling original screenplay rights, here are three other ways that you could sell movie rights to a book:

- **Novelizations and movie tie-ins** – In recent years, there has been a turnabout in book/movie rights. Now, not only do movie producers buy screenplay rights to books, but publishers buy novelization rights to screenplays. Novelizations of *Rocky*, *Return of the Jedi*, *Raiders of the Lost Ark*, and *E.T.* have all become bestsellers as a result of their tie-ins to the original movies.

  On the other side, previously published novels such as William Styron's *Sophie's Choice*, Tom Wolfe's *The Right Stuff*, and Isak Dinesen's *Out of Africa* have all become bestsellers for a second time after the release of a movie by the same name. Because the one media helps to spur sales in the other media and vice versa, both book publishers and movie producers benefit from the sales of such rights.

- **Sequel rights** – If the movie producer decides to produce a second movie based on the book, the purchase price is usually about 1/2 of the pickup price for the original movie. Of course, if the original movie was a real blockbuster, sequel rights could sell for a lot more.

- **Remakes** – Payments for remakes are usually less than the payment for the original version (unless, of course, the original version was made many years ago). The 1960's musical movie *Shangrila* was a remake of the 1930's movie *Lost Horizons*, which was based on the novel by James Hilton.

16:12 Television Rights

Often TV rights are sold at the same time or in lieu of motion picture rights. In general, the option and pickup prices for prime time TV movies are about the same as those for movies. However, while TV movie rights might sell for anywhere from $25,000 to $75,000, miniseries rights sell for about $20,000 to $40,000 per two-hour segment.

Besides rights to adapt a book to a TV movie or miniseries, there are several other rights which can be sold to television:

- **Specials** — Rights can be sold to produce a special based on a book. Motown bought rights to produce a show about weight loss and fitness based on Harvey and Marilyn Diamond's *Fit for Life*.

- **Series** — The ABC series *Spenser: For Hire* is based on Robert B. Parker's series of novels about a detective named Spenser. Rights for a television series go for about $1,000 per episode for a half-hour show and about $1,500 or more per episode for a full hour show.

  The Ramona Quimby series of young adult novels by Beverly Cleary was produced as a TV series for PBS in the fall of 1988. To tie into this series, Yearling reissued the novels with new covers announcing the series. Morrow Junior Books also published a book about the production of the seris, *Beverly Cleary's Ramona: Behind the Scenes of a Television Show* by Elaine Scott.

- **Reruns** — Reruns pay about 20% of the fee for the original show.

- **Cable TV** — Rodale Press has begun producing special shows on gardening and other how-to subjects for distribution to cable TV stations. Since cable is still a rather new field, no standards have been set for payment, terms, or other conditions of sale.

- **Cable networks** — Home Box Office (HBO), other movie channels, and specialized cable networks are all potential buyers of TV rights to books. For instance, in the fall of 1988, HBO produced a documentary based on *My Book for Kids with Cansur*, written by eight-year-old Jason Gaes when he was a cancer patient. The book was published by Melius & Peterson.

  A number of bestsellers have come out of original HBO programming. For instance, Rich Hall's bestselling trade paperbacks, *Sniglets* and *More Sniglets*, came out of HBO's *Not Necessarily the News*. Similarly, Xerox sold over 50,000 copies of an activity book tied into HBO's *Brain Games* series created by Jim Henson of Muppet fame.

- **Videotapes** — Probably the fastest growing area of TV rights sales at the present time is the area of video rights (rights to reproduce books as videotapes for direct sale or rental to consumers).

  MGM/UA Home Video recently paid a $50,000 advance against a 20% royalty for video rights to Stuart Berger's *Dr. Berger's Immune Power Diet*. While that is a higher advance and royalty than most books will get, the field is wide open.

  By 1995, it is estimated that 90% of all American homes will own a videotape player. Again, since this is such a new market, no standard terms have been set. Since many book publishers have begun forming their own videotape publishing departments to take advantage of this growing trend, sales of these rights may be pitched to other publishers as well as to movie and TV production companies.

Videotapes have had a secondary effect on the sale of movie tie-ins and novelizations. Since videotapes usually do not go on sale until after the original run of the movie (and often not for a year or two after the original movie), they can create a secondary burst of sales for tie-in books.

Scholastic didn't even publish its novelization of *The Karate Kid* until after the film, yet the book sold so well that they published a sequel. Similarly, just before the release of the videotape two years after the movie, Tor published a novelization by Richard Mueller of the movie *Ghostbusters*.

When selling movie and TV rights, don't overlook nonfiction books. Certainly biographies, histories, and current events stories such as *All the President's Men* are all adaptable to the screen. Plus feature films and TV movies have been made of such prosaic titles as *How to Succeed in Business Without Really Trying*, *Everything You Always Wanted to Know about Sex*, and *Sex and the Single Girl*. Plus, of course, some of the biggest selling videotapes have been nonfiction titles such as *Jane Fonda's Workout*.

16:13 Tips on Selling Movie/TV Rights

Most rights sales to movie and TV producers are made through literary agents who specialize in this field. You can find the names of many of these agents in *Literary Market Place*. To get you started, here are four such agencies:

- **The Gersh Agency**, 130 West 42nd Street #2400, New York, NY 10036-7802; (212) 997-1818. LA offices: 232 N. Canon Drive, Beverly Hills, CA 90210-5385; (213) 274-6611.

- **International Creative Management**, 40 West 57th Street, New York, NY 10019-4070; (212) 556-5600.

- **Triad Artists, Inc.**, 888 Seventh Avenue #1602, New York, NY 10019-0076; (212) 489-8100. LA offices: 10100 Santa Monica Boulevard, 16th Floor, Los Angeles, CA 90067-4107; (213) 556-2727.

- **William Morris Agency**, 1350 Avenue of the Americas, New York, NY 10019-4864; (212) 586-5100.

If you'd like to handle your own rights, you have several options on how to proceed:

- You can hope for an act of God or lucky happenstance (with a little push from you). That's how Naiad Press sold the movie rights of Jane Rule's novel, *Desert of the Heart*, to Donna Deitch, an independent producer. The publisher gave a copy of the book to a friend who, in turn, happened to meet the producer at a party one evening. The rest, as they say, is history.

- You can work through scouts. These people work for producers or production companies scouting for literary properties that might be suitable for making into movies. Here are several such scouts:

  Act III Communications, 401 Park Avenue South, 7th Floor, New York, NY 10016; (212) 545-5100. Pamela Walker and Rosalie Siegel are literary consultants for Act III, the production arm of TV producer Norman Lear.

  Marie B. Campbell Associates, 31 West 57th Street, 6th Floor, New York, NY 10019; (212) 888-2700. Literary consultants for Steven Spielberg's Amblin Entertainment.

  Scott Rudin Productions, Ruth Pomerance, Columbia Pictures, 711 Fifth Avenue, New York, NY 10022-3195; (212) 702-6042.

- Work with an IndieMogul (which is a combination of an independent producer, personal manager, financier, studio, and film distributor). Among the developing IndieMoguls are Carolco Pictures, Weintraub Entertainment Group, Lorimar, and Management Company Entertainment Group.

- To locate independent producers and other influential people in the entertainment industry, review one of the following directories. At least one of them should be available at your local library:

  The Acquisitions and Development Directory — published by ADD, 12021 Wilshire Boulevard #459, Los Angeles, CA 90025; (213) 460-2544.

  Film Producers, Studios, and Agents Guide — published by Lone Eagle Publishing, 9903 Santa Monica Boulevard #204, Beverly Hills, CA 90212-1671, (213) 471-8066.

  The Hollywood Reporter Studio Blu-Book Directory — published by The Hollywood Reporter; available from Samuel French Trade, 7623 Sunset Boulevard, Hollywood, CA 90046; (213) 876-0570.

  Who's Who in Entertainment — published by Marquis Who's Who, 3002 Glenview Road, Wilmette, IL 60091; (800) 621-9669.

  Who's Who in Television — published by Packard Publishing Company; available from Samuel French Trade (address above).

16:14 Other Subsidiary Rights

There are any number of other subsidiary rights that you can sell, everything from audio rights to merchandising (or licensing) rights to dramatic rights to other print rights. Indeed, you can sell rights from books for almost any product or service that uses words or illustrations — tee-shirts, clothing, stuffed animals, food, toys, home furniture, and so on. Just use your imagination. To help your imagination, though, here are a few of the other subsidiary rights that are regularly sold:

• **Audio rights**—Besides those already mentioned, these rights are the most important and can bring in significant royalties. For instance, Warner Audio paid a $37,000 advance for exclusive audio rights to *The IBM Way* by Buck Rogers (which it recouped by sublicensing audio rights to several companies selling to non-retail markets).

Nightingale-Conant paid an advance in the high five figures for George Burn's two bestsellers, *How to Live to Be 100 or More* and *Dr. Burns' Prescription for Happiness*.

Audio or recording rights can be sold separately for audiotapes, records, and the new compact discs. The standard royalty is around 5% to 10%. The term of such recording rights is usually two years with automatic renewals until one or the other party serves notice.

You can even sell audiotape rights more than once—for unabridged rights and for abridged rights. In 1986, *The Collected Stories of John Cheever* were available in three different audiotape packages: as an eight-cassette unabridged package from G. K. Hall ($49.95 retail), as a two-cassette package from Listen for Pleasure ($13.95), and as a one-cassette Audiobook from Random House ($7.95).

Audio rights can also be divided between direct marketing rights (for tapes to be sold only by mail order or telemarketing) and retail rights (tapes to be sold only through retail outlets). They can also be sold separately for excerpt rights and dramatization rights.

Finally, audio rights can be sold to audiotape subscription services such as Soundview Executive Book Summary, which features audio-cassette summaries of business books.

• **Radio broadcast rights**—The right to broadcast a recording of a book via radio can be licensed separately. There are a number of such programs currently run on both public and commercial networks. Among other books, Jeffrey Archer's *Kane and Abel* and a number of James Herriott's books have been broadcast on radio.

• **Dramatic rights**—Books are sometimes made into stage plays before or even after they have been made into movies. These dramatic rights may be for amateur or professional productions, on Broadway or off, for serious drama or musical comedies. Since few books are made into plays, prices can range from as little as $1,000 on up.

Sam Gallu, a playwright, paid a $2,000 advance for rights to adapt Curtis Bill Pepper's *An Artist and the Pope* for the Broadway stage. If the play was actually produced, he would pay more.

Broadway plays have been produced from *A Bell for Adano*, *The King and I*, *Les Misérables*, *Mister Roberts*, *My Sister Eileen*, *Phantom of the Opera*, *South Pacific*, and *Teahouse of the August Moon*. All were later made into movies (for which separate movie rights were paid).

- **Ballet or Opera** – Although such rights are rarely sold, choreographer John Butler prepared a ballet trilogy based on stories by Southern authors. The ballet, commissioned by the public TV station in Jackson, Mississippi, was aired in 1987.

- **Filmstrips, microfiche, microfilm, transparencies** – These rights rarely bring in much money. Such rights are used primarily in preparing educational support material for schools, government programs, and business training programs.

- **Computer software** – These rights could develop into a significant source of income for book publishers as home computers develop more capability at less cost.

  Random House licensed its dictionary and thesaurus to be used in the computer spelling check programs of *Reference Desk* and Borland's *Turbo Lightning*.

- **Electronic database** – A number of publishers have already sold rights to reference books to be used on electronic databases available from such computer services as the Source, CompuServe, and NewsNet. This field has yet to develop a strong market and may well be usurped by the CD-ROM technology now available for computers. Meanwhile, if you publish reference books, these rights could be a significant source of additional income.

- **Interactive novels** – Spinnaker currently publishes a series of interactive crime detective novels for home computers. Recently Spinnaker paid a five figure advance against royalties for the right to adapt an Ellery Queen novel to this format.

- **Computer games** – Software rights can also be sold for computer games. For example, Roger Zelazny's *Nine Princes of Amber* has been licensed to Telarium Corporation for its role-playing game available on the Apple, Commodore, and IBM computers.

- **Board and role-playing games** – TSR has brought out a board game version of Tom Clancy's *The Hunt for Red October*.

  Victory Games has bought rights to produce a role-playing game based on the James Bond books by Ian Fleming. A number of other books, especially in the fantasy and science fiction fields, have also been licensed for role-playing games.

- **Card games** – Sapiens Press sold game rights to U.S. Games Systems for its three Enjoyable English card games, *Challenges*, *Winning Words*, and *Fool 'Em*.

- **Merchandising rights** – Also known as licensing rights, these rights can cover any commercial reproduction of words, illustrations, or characters from a book (or movie, or whatever). Almost any product can be – and has been – licensed, from T-shirts to coffee mugs, from greeting cards to rubber stamps, from dolls to toys, from carpets to salad dressing.

Wendy's Restaurants, for instance, licensed the rights to *The Rotation Diet* by Martin Katahn for its Rotation Diet salad and dressing.

Viking Penguin licensed its Little Chef series of books to Riegal Textiles for a book/apron combination package.

Acropolis Books licensed rights to *Your Colors At Home* by Lauren Smith and Rose Bennett Gilbert to the following companies:

Ex-Cell Home Fashions—shower curtains, bath ensembles
Linde Company—decorative pillows, chair pads
Ceramic Fashions—vases
National Ceramics—lamps

Acropolis also actively looked for *Your Color At Home* licensees in the following product areas: at-home wear, blankets, broadloom carpet, ceramic tiles, china, closet accessories, drapes, floral arrangements, plumbing fixtures, soap, wallpaper, and window treatments.

- **Permissions**—If another publisher wants to use a short section, chapter, or larger unit of one of your books in one of their books, they must request permission from you to reprint. You will then have to decide how much to charge for such permission. Permission rates range from token charges for shorter quotes to charges comparable to second serial rights for anthology selections.

- **Limited editions**—It is possible to sell rights to another publisher to produce limited editions of your books. For example, both Phantasia Press and Underwood-Miller publish autographed, numbered and slipcased editions of books by well-known science fiction authors (such as a $50.00 autographed edition of Roger Zelazny's *Trumps of Doom* or a $40.00 autographed edition of C. J. Cherryh's *Cuckoo's Egg*). These higher priced editions rarely compete with standard hardcover or paperback editions since they are issued in limited runs of 250 to 1,000 copies and are sold primarily to collectors.

- **Library editions**—Some publishers like Gregg Press specialize in publishing library editions of books whose hardcover editions have gone out of print.

- **Large print editions**—As the mature market has grown, large print editions have also sold more copies—and brought higher prices for rights. Thorndike paid $36,000 (in an auction against G. K. Hall) for large print rights to Anne Tyler's novel, *Breathing Lessons*. Large print rights for Toni Morrison's bestselling novel, *Beloved*, went for $7,500. Both of these sales were unusually high for such rights; most such sales go for less than $5,000.

- **Syndication**—The New York Times Syndication company syndicated the *Legal Question & Answer Book* published by Reader's Digest in a weekly column.

Entertainment News Service syndicated questions from John Kremer's *Tinseltowns, U.S.A.* in 70 newspapers across the country.

Chapter 17

Selling Your Books Overseas

For a smaller publisher with a limited list of titles, the best way to sell books overseas is to sell the translation rights rather than the books themselves. Translation rights require no shipping, warehousing, distribution, or customs clearance. Even then, translation rights sales are not likely to make you rich. Not only do translation rights usually sell for less than a $5,000 advance, but your payment can also be reduced by agent fees, taxes, exchange rates, shared translation costs, and the author's share of the sale (usually 75%).

Besides translations rights, there are a number of other ways to arrange distribution of your books overseas. This chapter will outline these strategies in brief.

For more information on selling your books overseas, see *Marketing Books and Journals to Western Europe* by Pamela Spence Richards (published by Oryx Press). Or subscribe to the *International Publishing Newsletter* which reports on worldwide book trade news, foreign exchange rates, international copyright concerns, and other matters of interest to publishers. For subscription information, write to the **International Publishing Newsletter**, 80 S. Early Street, Alexandria, VA 22304.

17:01 Two Kinds of Foreign Rights

You have two basic options when you sell foreign rights: You can sell reprint rights (such as British Commonwealth rights) or translation rights (e.g., French language rights). In each case you can divvy up these rights into certain territories. For example, you can sell English language rights to the entire British Commonwealth or to Great Britain only (thus allowing you to sell separate rights to Australia, India, and other countries).

Reprint rights allow a foreign publisher to reprint the English language edition of the book and market it in certain territories. The most common English language reprint rights are for British Commonwealth rights (exclusive of Canada), Canadian rights, and Australian rights.

- Crown sold British rights to Payne Harrison's technothriller, *Storming Intrepid*, for $105,000. The Atlantic Monthly Press sold British rights for Rian Malan's *My Traitor's Heart* to The Bodley Head for $38,000.

- Collins Harvill paid almost $480,000 for the British rights to two novels by Martin Cruz Smith. Italian rights sold for $125,000 and Japanese rights for $100,000.

Translation rights permit a publisher to translate the book into another language and then sell that book in any country speaking that language. Because of the cost of making good translations, translation rights are rarely divvied up into smaller territories. As a result, the buyer of Spanish language rights may sell the translation not only in Spain, but also in most Latin American countries.

- Japan is a growing market for American books. Recently, Japanese publishers have paid $40,000 for Payne Harrison's *Storming Intrepid*, $30,000 for *Raymond Chandler's Philip Marlowe*, and $80,000 for Daniel Burstein's *Yen! Japan's New Financial Empire and Its Threat to America*.

- Other strong markets for U.S. books include France, Germany, Spain, Italy, the Scandanavian countries, and Holland. Because these markets are often smaller, translation rights go for less than English language reprint rights. For instance, Permanent Press sold U.K. rights to Philip Metcalfe's *1933* (an account of Hitler's rise to power) for $25,000, while Dutch rights went for $6,600 and Swedish rights for $6,000.

17:02 Advantages of Selling Foreign Rights

When you sell foreign rights, you give away most of your control over how your books are to be packaged and marketed in those countries. Nonetheless, if you are careful in your selection of which publishers you sell rights to, the advantages to selling foreign rights far outweigh the disadvantages. Here are a few of the advantages:

- You don't have to deal with the vagaries of selling your books in a foreign country. Foreign publishers are much better prepared to deal with the laws, customs, and changing tastes of their own countries.

- With the sale of foreign rights, you don't have to arrange customs clearances, shipping, distribution, and fulfillment.

- You receive payment for the rights up front. Most advances for rights go for about $1,000 to $5,000, with a royalty of 8-10%.

• You can draw on the experience of these publishers to sell not only to the direct market, but to a number of related countries. For example, by selling British Commonwealth rights to a British publisher, you not only get distribution in Great Britain, but also in Australia, New Zealand, India, South Africa, and other members of the British Commonwealth. In most cases the British publisher will also handle distribution of English language books to other European countries, Africa, and Asia.

• Sales of a translated edition can also spur sales of the English language edition, especially among libraries and scholars.

17:03 How to Sell Foreign Rights

Out of almost 52,000 titles published by West German publishers in 1984, slightly over 4,000 (or about 8%) were translations from English. Similarly, out of over 32,000 titles published by Spanish publishers in 1982, almost 4,000 (or about 12%) were translations from English, while 10% of Italy's book production of 20,000 plus titles for that year were translations from English. In general, then, if we allow for duplication, anywhere from 5,000 to 8,000 English language titles are bought for translation each year. Since as many as half of these titles were originally published in Great Britain, the total annual market for translation rights of American books is probably about 3,500 titles—or about 8% of all titles produced in the U.S. each year.

What all this means is that each new book has about one chance in twelve of selling any translation rights. Since a good number of the books produced in the United States have a limited foreign market, your chances of selling translation rights to your books increases even more. Indeed, your chances of selling foreign rights are probably greater than your chances of selling mass-market reprint rights or any dramatic rights.

To help you in arranging a sale, here are a few tips and suggestions for working with foreign publishers:

• The most important thing you can do to sell foreign rights is to get reviews and distribution in this country. If the book sells well here and has a potential market overseas, you'll be contacted.

• You have four basic choices in selling foreign rights:

1. **Contact foreign publishers on your own.**

2. **Hire a U.S. literary agent** who specializes in foreign rights sales. For a list of such agents, see *Literary Market Place*.

3. **Commission foreign agents** who handle English language rights sales in their own country. Some can be found in *Literary Market Place*; even more are listed in *International Literary Market Place* (both published by R. R. Bowker).

4. **Contact scouts** (U.S. representatives of foreign publishers). These, again, are listed in *Literary Market Place*. Send these people your catalog regularly. While they will not represent your books, they might be interested in buying titles for the foreign publishers they represent.

- The main advantage of using agents when you are first starting out is that they know the market better than you could possibly get to know it without devoting full time to the project. Agents are well worth the 10% to 20% fee that they charge.

- If you do hire agents, keep them up to date on what you are publishing. Send them copies of your major titles, supporting material, and copies of any major reviews. Work with them the same way you'd work with any key contact.

- While it is possible to find an agent or to sell rights direct to publishers via phone calls and letters, the most practical way to make the necessary contacts is to attend the major international book fairs.

  While some contacts can be made at the annual ABA convention, the major international trade event of the year is the Frankfurt Book Fair, held every year around the beginning of October in Frankfurt, West Germany. Almost 200,000 people representing about 6,000 different firms from around the world attend this fair every year.

  Other major international book fairs of importance to general trade publishers are the Bologna Children's Book Fair held in early April in Bologna, Italy, and the London Book Fair held in mid-April. Other fairs are held either annually or biennially in Jerusalem, Barcelona, Cairo, Quebec, Mexico City, Brussels, Stockholm, Belgrade, Warsaw, Moscow, and New Delhi, among other cities.

- If you cannot afford to display your books on your own, you can join one of the cooperative exhibits put on by Publishers Marketing Association, Independent Publishers Services, and others. They offer a relatively inexpensive way to expose your books to foreign publishers.

  Some wholesalers, among them Baker & Taylor and Bookpeople, have also mounted group exhibits at international book fairs.

- Whether you have your own display or participate in a cooperative exhibit, you should definitely attend one of these book fairs yourself if you are at all serious about pursuing overseas sales of your books. Attending such fairs, especially the Frankfurt fair, will enable you to make invaluable contacts, learn firsthand how foreign rights are sold, and perhaps even buy some translation rights from others (to expand your own list of titles here in the U.S.).

- Before you go to an international book trade show, write letters and send your catalog to those publishers or agents you'd like to meet. Use the *International Literary Market Place* to locate their names and addresses. Try to make appointments beforehand.

Because the Frankfurt fair is spread over six buildings and thousands of exhibits, it is almost impossible to meet with anyone unless you have already made an appointment prior to the fair.

- When you send out information to prospective rights buyers, include a fact sheet which describes the book, its author, its audience, and what rights are available. This fact sheet should provide all the information a rights buyer would want to know in a clear and concise format.

- Be persistent. If the first publisher you approach is not interested in your books, ask them what publishers they think would be interested in your line of books. These references can be the most valuable leads you will receive.

- Remember the bandwagon effect. Once you make one foreign rights sale, publishers from other countries are more likely to jump on the bandwagon as well. One rights sale often leads to another which leads to another until you've signed up five or six or more countries.

- When selling rights, don't just take the first offer or the highest advance; look for the publisher who can best market the book. Check out the publisher. What other titles do they offer? How are their sales? What is their reputation in their market? Look for publishers you'd like to work with. Try to establish long-lasting working relationships with them.

- Don't overlook the third world countries. While they might not have that much money to spend, they can be a continuing source of sales for your other titles. The third world is still a wide open market, hungry for knowledge.

- Try a listing in *Rights from USA Review*. This semi-annual newsletter is sent to 300 selected book publishers in England, Europe, Japan, New Zealand, and Australia. A listing costs $60.00 and includes the following information: title, author, bibliographic data (ISBN, size, number of pages, price), list of rights available, name and address of publisher, and 100-125 words describing the contents of the book, the sales history of U.S. editions, and why the book would cross over or translate well. For more information, contact **Rights from USA Review**, Hunter House, P. O. Box 847, Claremont, CA 91711; (714) 624-2277.

17:04 Other Ways to Sell Overseas

While selling translation rights may be the quickest and easiest way to get your books distributed abroad, it is not always the most financially rewarding. Moreover, you do lose control over the presentation and marketing of your books. If you decide you'd rather market the books yourself, there are a number of arrangements you can make: direct sales, co-publishing, export sales agents, agency arrangements, bookselling distributors, U.S. exporting distributors, and subsidiaries.

Before going on, however, here are a few resources that may help you in your exploration of the various options for selling your book overseas:

- *A Basic Guide to Exporting*. This basic guide is available free from the International Trade Administration of the Department of Commerce. Contact one of their 47 offices across the country. Or you can get if from the Superintendent of Documents, U.S. Government Printing Office, Washington, DC 20402 for $8.95.

- *The Exporter's Guide to Federal Resources for Small Business* is a 125-page guide to all federal export-assistance programs. Available for $3.50 from the Superintendent of Documents.

- **Export-Import Bank of the United States.** (800) 424-5201. This bank is chartered to facilitate export of U.S. goods through loans, guarantees, and insurance programs.

- **Export Now!**, U.S. Department of Commerce, Suite 1500, North Lobby, 1331 Pennsylvania Avenue, Washington, DC 20004-1703. A joint program of the federal government and private business.

17:05 Selling Direct to Overseas Customers

In 1982, U.S. publishers exported $641.3 million worth of books, which represents a little over 8% of all U.S. book sales for that year. These figures indicate that foreign markets represent a significant market for English language books. For direct sales, the bestselling American titles are in the fields of business, science, technology, and reference books.

- The major markets for direct sales of American books are Great Britain, continental Europe, Japan, and Australia. Smaller markets for STM (scientific, technical, medical) titles exist in almost every country.

- Mailing lists to reach these overseas markets are available from the following companies:

    IBIS Information Services, 152 Madison Avenue #803, New York, NY 10016-5424; (800) 433-6226; (212) 779-1344. The major source of library and professional lists for European markets. IBIS also provides a number of international co-op mailing opportunities for publishers.

    Mailing List Marketing, Medical Economics Company, 680 Kinderkamack Road, Oradell, NJ 07649; (201) 262-3030.

    Dillon Agnew Marton, 12 West 18th Street, New York, NY 10011; (212) 255-6102.

    Mailing Lists Asia, 9/F Nin Lee Commercial Building, 45 Lyndhurst Terrace, Central, Hong Kong 5-430556.

- Another source of targeted mailing lists of international book buyers
  are the foreign subscribers of U.S. magazines. The *Harvard Business
  Review*, for example, has more than 30,000 foreign subscribers.
  Foreign members of professional associations would also be prime
  prospects for books in their areas of interest.

- Besides direct mail promotions, you could test advertisements in leading overseas journals. For periodicals that might reach the same audience as your books, check *Ulrich's International Periodicals Directory*
  (available in most libraries) or *Benn's Media Directory* (available from
  Benn Business Information Services, Sovereign Way, Tonbridge, Kent
  TN9 IRQ, England.)

- The main advantage of direct sales is that you are in total control. The
  main disadvantages are the expenses of mailing promotions overseas
  and the problems with collecting payments with changing foreign currency rates. The best way to avoid the second problem is to request
  payment in U.S. dollars (with a check drawn on a U.S. bank).

- To cut your costs for mailing promotional literature and packages
  overseas, look into using the U.S. Postal Service's International Sur-
  face Air Lift (ISAL). To use this service, you must have enough
  volume to be able to ship in bulk. Plus, you need to be near an ISAL
  airport (most large cities). Write to the **U.S. Postal Service**, Customer
  Service Department, Room 5520, 475 L'Enfant Plaza WSW,
  Washington, DC 20260-6342; (202) 268-2000. Or contact the customer
  service representative at your local post office.

- To learn more about the international direct mail market, subscribe to
  the *Publisher's Multinational Direct* newsletter (12 issues for $195.00).
  This newsletter covers everything from how to find the best international advertising media to the least expensive ways of mailing, plus it
  provides many tips for working with companies in other countries. For
  more information, write to **Publisher's Multinational Direct**, 150 East
  74th Street, New York, NY 10021; (212) 861-4188.

17:06 Co-Publishing

When two publishers agree to share the costs of acquiring, producing,
and marketing a book, this arrangement is known as co-publishing. Such
arrangements are usually made between two English-language publishers
since the main benefit of co-publishing is the savings in typesetting and
production costs. Co-publishing offers a number of advantages:

- The two publishers can share the costs of production. Sometimes one
  publisher simply joins the print run of the other publisher so each
  gains from the reduced costs of a larger print run. In other cases, the
  originating publisher provides camera-ready copy to the other publisher, thereby eliminating duplicate typesetting and preparation costs.

- They can share marketing costs as well, especially when exhibiting the book at international book fairs and when selling translation rights.
- Promotional efforts by one of the publishers will often spill over into the other publisher's marketing area. For example, advertisements or reviews in *Publishers Weekly* or the *New York Times Book Review* will benefit other English-language publishers of the same book since many international buyers read these publications.

17:07 Export Sales Agencies

Export sales agencies are U.S. organizations which act as distributors of books by American publishers in overseas book markets. They function in much the same way as an American distributor:

1. They represent the titles of a number of different publishers (anywhere from ten to one hundred publishers).
2. Their sales representatives call on the book trade (booksellers, schools, and libraries) in each country they serve.
3. They handle all distribution and collections.
4. They handle most of the promotion of the titles they carry in the markets they serve.

If you are a smaller publisher who wants to avoid all the hassles of marketing to the book trade overseas and would rather not have to worry about the details of distribution, fulfillment, and collection, an export sales agency will serve you well. On the other hand, if the overseas market is a significant source of sales for your books and you'd like to market your books more aggressively, you would probably be better off seeking other arrangements. Since an exports sales agency may be serving as many as a hundred different publishers, you can't expect your books to get the royal treatment.

Export sales agencies expect a discount and commission structure similar to many U.S. distributors (40% to 45% discount with a 15% commission). They pay quickly with checks drawn on U.S. banks. Most export sales agencies do not warehouse books, but rather place orders as they receive orders through their sales visits and other promotions in the countries they serve.

Here are two of the major export sales agencies in the U.S.:

- **Baker & Taylor,** 1114 Avenue of the Americas, 5th Floor, New York, NY 10036-7794; (212) 819-7474. Formerly called Feffer & Simons, this subsidiary of Baker & Taylor is the largest export sales agency in the United States. They represent all countries.
- **Worldwide Media Service,** 115 East 23rd Street, New York, NY 10010; (212) 420-0588.

17:08 Agency Arrangements

An agency is a company (either another book publisher or a sales representative) which stocks books, fulfill orders, and handles billing and collection for other publishers. Some agencies will also handle marketing functions, including sending out review copies, mailing promotions, advertising in journals, exhibiting at conferences and book fairs, and visiting stores and jobbers. Exactly what services they offer is determined at the time you sign a contract with them. Their services can be either exclusive or non-exclusive.

The main advantage of agencies is that they stock books in the countries they represent. Hence, you can refer orders from overseas customers direct to a distributor in their own country. This saves them time and money, as well as saving you the hassle of handling such orders. Plus the agencies know the markets and media in the countries they represent and can therefore often do a better job than you could in promoting your books in these countries.

The disadvantages of such agencies are:

1. Agencies may be not be able to offer the kind of marketing service you'd like because they are representing too many other companies.

2. Since they take books on consignment, they may tie up stock that you could be selling.

3. They may not cover all areas of their market territory as well as you or another agent might do.

4. They are expensive. As a rule of thumb, you should have at least $50,000 in sales to those countries served by the agency in order to justify the expense of such arrangements (especially the cost of shipping the books to them on consignment).

The actual terms for such arrangements vary depending on the services provided and the territories covered. As a general rule, agencies expect a discount between 45% and 55%. They handle all costs of shipping, insurance, warehousing, trade discounts, fulfillment, and promotion.

The best place to make agency arrangements is at an international book fair such as Frankfurt or London. If that is not possible, then locate another publisher who works through an agency and see if their agency would be willing to take your line on as well. Of course, be sure to ask the other publisher if they are happy with the agency before making an initial contact.

• The overseas subsidiaries of John Wiley and HarperCollins both act as agents for a number of smaller U.S. publishers.

• General Publishing of Toronto acts as an agent for U.S. publishers in Canada.

17:09 Bookselling Distributors

You can also distribute your titles overseas by using library jobbers, booksellers who also act as distributors, and academic booksellers (such as Blackwell's). Most such distribution arrangements, like those with library jobbers in the U.S., are non-exclusive. Such distributors will usually stock your books, take orders, bill, and distribute for a 20% to 30% discount. If these distributors also do major advertising and promotion, the discount would go up to 40% or 50%.

17:10 U.S. Exporting Distributors

A number of U.S. library jobbers and wholesalers also offer export services to other countries. Among these are Baker & Taylor (which exports to all areas of the world including the Soviet Union and the People's Republic of China) and Ballen Booksellers International. You might want to check with these companies to see if they would like to participate in any joint promotions of your titles.

17:11 Establishing Your Own Subsidiary

One final way to distribute your books in other countries is to establish your own subsidiary in that country. The subsidiary would not only distribute your books but also acquire and publish original editions in that country. Such arrangements are not for small companies. To justify the costs of establishing a subsidiary, you would have to have a million dollar a year market potential in the area served by the subsidiary.

While a number of U.S. publishers have Canadian subsidiaries, only a few have established subsidiaries elsewhere. The prime other market area for U.S. subsidiaries is Great Britain. Here are a few U.S. publishers who have established foreign subsidiaries.

• John Wiley has established subsidiaries in Canada, Great Britain, Singapore, and Latin America.

• HarperCollins has offices in Great Britain, the Netherlands, Australia, Mexico, and Brazil.

• Bantam, itself a subsidiary of the giant Bertelsmann Group of West Germany, has subsidiaries in Canada, England, Australia, and New Zealand.

• McGraw-Hill has subsidiaries in Australia, Brazil, Canada, Colombia, France, Great Britain, India, Japan, Mexico, New Zealand, Panama, Portugal, Singapore, South Africa, Spain, and West Germany.

17:12 Selling Books to Mainland China

As part of its modernization effort, China is rapidly becoming a major market for English language books (English is already the second most popular language in China). Over 30,000 book buyers were attracted to China's first international book fair held in Shanghai. The market is wide open to small publishers as well as large publishers, especially publishers of scientific, medical, and technical books.

Here are a few pointers on how to get your books distributed in China:

• Several national book import agencies are currently active in seeking out new titles from American and Canadian publishers. Send them your catalog on a regular basis. Also let them know about your new titles. Since they are more likely to respond to publishers whose names they recognize, make sure you keep sending them material on a regular basis.

• When the import agencies receive your catalog, they review it very thoroughly, select those titles which would most interest Chinese readers, clip out the information from the catalog, publish a collection of these clippings grouped by subject, and send the resulting catalog to bookstores, libraries, and universities around the country. A network of foreign-language bookstores receive the orders from these institutions, send them on to the import agencies who then order the books from the appropriate American or Canadian publisher.

• The first and largest of these import agencies is the China National Publications Import and Export Corporation. They buy books from every subject category. Send your catalogs and other correspondence to **China National Import and Export Corporation**, Box 88, Beijing, People's Republic of China (cable: PUBLIMEX BEIJING; telex: 22313 CPC CN).

They also have a subsidiary in the U.S. for handling shipping of the books to China. Their address is **Beijing Book Company**, 701 E. Linden Avenue, Linden, NJ 07036; (201) 862-0909.

• The other major agency handles only books in the humanities and social sciences. Write to **China Book Import Centre**, Box 399, Beijing, People's Republic of China (cable: CIBTC BEIJING; telex: 22496 CIBTC CN).

They also have a subsidiary to handle fulfillment. Write to **Cypress Book Company**, 49 West 39th Street, 4th Floor, New York, NY 10018; (212) 768-3850.

• A relative newcomer is Shanghai Book Traders, which acts as both an importer and a distributor (through its chain of Shanghai Foreign Language Bookstores). They request that you send your offer of terms (discount schedule, payment requirements, freight arrangements) along with your catalogs for review. If they feel your titles are appropriate for their audience, they will ask you to send sufficient catalogs and other promotional material on a regular basis so they can, in turn, distribute them to their prospective book buyers. They currently only distribute in the immediate region around Shanghai. Their address is **Shanghai Book Traders**, Box 234, Shanghai, People's Republic of China (cable: SHANBOT; telex: 33355 SBT CN).

● A mailing list of 2,500 institutional book buyers of scientific, technical, medical, engineering, and professional books in China is available from James Chan, a consultant on selling books to China. For more information, write to **James Chan**, 2014 Naudain Street, Philadelphia, PA 19146; (215) 735-7670; Fax: (215) 735-9661.

Chapter 18

Special Sales: Special Opportunities

Special sales are those sales made outside the normal book trade and retail channels. Some standard special sales outlets include corporate sales, premium uses, catalog items, fundraisers, and remainders. Nonetheless, you need not be limited to these outlets. Because books both inform and entertain, they can fulfill almost any need and appeal to almost any audience. Hence, in reality, the range or extent of your special sales are limited only by your imagination.

The great incentive for pursuing special sales is the real possibility of making high volume sales in a single stroke. It is not unusual for a single key contact to result in sales of thousands of copies of a book.

The other great advantage of special sales for smaller publishers is that the major publishers do not—and cannot—have a stranglehold on the distribution and sales network (since, in fact, there is no such network). For that reason, it is possible for a small unknown publisher to compete for the biggest sales in this area.

18:01 How to Make Special Sales

Since special sales are—as their name implies—special, there are no standardized channels for making such book sales. Nonetheless, there are certain steps you can take. Here are a few of them:

- **Work directly with people, not titles.** When you contact a company to make a sale to their sales division or personnel division, get the name of the sales manager (or personnel manager) and then call them direct. If they seem interested, then send a sample book and appropriate sales information. As with most key contacts, follow up with a phone call within a few weeks after sending out the book.

• Again, as with other key contacts, **keep in touch.** Cultivate a lasting relationship with these people. Even if they do not buy your first book, or second, or whatever, continue to approach them. Sooner or later, if you have done your research and your books do meet their needs, they will place an order with you.

• In the case of most special sales (especially catalog and premium sales), **be prepared to wait** as long as six months or more before any final decision is made. Even then, it may be another three to six months before you receive the order. Most catalogs, for instance, work with at least a nine-month lead time.

• When approaching these special contacts, **make a clear and direct connection between your book and their needs.** Don't assume they'll make the connection. Point out the benefits of your book to their target audience (whether it be consumers, salesmen, or buyers).

• **Prepare a merchandise data sheet** or other fact sheet which provides all the details about your book at a glance. Refer to page 175 of *Mail Order Selling Made Easier* for a standard data sheet that provides all the information these buyers would want to know.

• If the deal has the potential of being really big (25,000 or more unit sales), **offer them exclusive use** of the book within their market. Otherwise, it is not necessary to offer exclusives.

• Some special markets will insist on a discount as high as 60% or 70% (sometimes even more). If you are not prepared to give discounts that high, then you should reconsider whether you want to invest the time and money to enter this market. Note, however, that you should not offer high discounts unless they, in turn, are prepared to order large quantities. **Arrange your schedule so that higher discounts are available only if they order sufficient quantities to make it worth your while.**

To give you an idea of what kind of discount to offer, here are the discount schedules of two publishers.

The following discount schedule was offered by Rayod House for the trade paperback edition of *In Search of Excellence*, which sold for $8.95 retail. Note that Rayod House is not the publisher; hence, the publisher is probably offering even a deeper discount.

Copies	1-11	12-239	240-499	500-999	1000-4999	5000+
Price	$4.95	$4.50	$3.95	$3.25	$2.95	$2.50
Discount	45%	50%	56%	64%	67%	72%

Here is a representative discount schedule offered by Time-Life Books for premium sales:

Copies	50-199	200-1999	2000-4999	5000+
Price	$9.72	$8.97	$8.22	$6.73
Discount	35%	40%	45%	55%

• **Most special markets will require some sort of assurance that you can fulfill their order.** This means that you must be able to prove to them that you either have the manufacturing capacity, stock on hand, or reputation to be able to handle whatever volume they require.

• **For some special markets, there are sales representatives or distributors who can do most of your selling for you.** For example, the premium/incentive field has premium rep groups, jobbers, wholesaler distributors, and premium promotion houses who provide many businesses with prearranged premium programs.

• You can also **exhibit at appropriate conventions** such as the annual Premium/Incentive Show or the Licensing Show. If nothing else, you should attend such shows to learn more about the industry. Plus, of course, they provide great opportunities to make connections with sales reps, wholesalers, distributors, and buyers.

   A number of publishers, such as Viking Penguin and Warner Books, have exhibited at the New York Premium Incentive Show. At the 1986 show, Viking exhibited *The Essential Wine Book*, *Lyn St. James' Car Owners Manual for Women*, and *Fitness after 50*—all superb candidates for incentive programs.

• In some cases you can also **advertise in appropriate magazines.** In the case of premium sales, you could advertise in *Potentials in Marketing* or *Premium/Incentive Business*. Warner Books, Addison-Wesley, Hammond, Viking Penguin, Random House, Time-Life Books, Western Publishing, and Rand McNally, among others, have advertised in these magazines. You could also advertise in other sales and marketing magazines (if you are offering a book as a sales incentive) or in personnel or training magazines (if you are offering a book for training programs).

• **Use consultants.** Crisp Productions has been successful approaching personnel consultants to sell their *Retirement Planning Book*. The advantages of using such consultants are that:

   1. They already have established clients.

   2. They know the needs of their clients.

   3. Their clients will usually have confidence in their recommendations.

   For the consultants, such sales offer two benefits: 1) they are able to provide an additional service to their clients, and 2) they are paid a commission on the sale. One consultant working with Crisp Productions sold 800 copies of their *Retirement Planning Guide* to Monsanto.

   Here are two consultants for special markets:

   Arthur Schwartz & Company, P. O. Box 434, New York, NY 10028-0004; (212) 794-9012. Product development and special market sales.

   Elizabeth Tyler Consultants, 76 Highland Road, Glen Cove, NY 11542. Consultant for sales to non-bookstore markets.

18:02 Premium and Incentive Sales

In 1987, American businesses spent over $23.1 billion dollars on premiums and incentives. Of that amount over 50% was spent on incentives (20.6% for dealer incentives and 31.5% for sales incentives). Business gifts made up 12.6%, self-liquidators another 12.5%, continuity programs another 7.9%, and all other programs the remaining 15%.

Of the $23.1 billion dollars in premium sales, about half a billion was spent on books. Books can be used in many different ways as either premiums or incentives. You should be aware of these different ways so you can adapt your promotional literature so it clearly addresses the needs of companies and other organizations who buy premiums.

Books have a number of advantages over other premiums. They have a high perceived value. The premium buyer does not have to worry about styles, colors, sizes, breakage during shipping, or service problems afterward. Plus, books are available to suit almost any need, for any audience, at any price range. Finally, of course, books can be imprinted with almost any message.

Here, now, are just a few of the ways that companies might use your books as premiums:

- **Dealer incentives** – Such incentives reward retailers and other dealers for displaying a manufacturer's wares prominently and/or for selling a significant amount of those wares. While most dealer incentives are for larger gifts such as trips, appliances, and gift certificates, books can supplement or augment other dealer promotions.

  Coors Beer bought 100,000 of *The Colorado Scenic Calendar* from Westcliffe Publishers to give to their distributors who, in turn, gave them to their retail accounts. While these calendars were a small gift, they did help to keep Coors's name in front of their key accounts.

- **Sales incentives** – To encourage salespeople to better their previous sales records, companies often give them prizes (the greater their sales, the larger the prize). Again, most sales incentives involve higher priced prizes such as trips or appliances. Nonetheless, books could be used to spur the salespeople along during the middle of a competition.

  For example, a travel guide book for France could be offered to any salespeople meeting a minimum sales goal. Not only would such a prize give a boost to their sales enthusiasm during the middle of a contest, but it could also be tied into a grand prize trip to Paris and, thus, as the salespeople read the guidebook, they would be inspired to work that much harder to win the trip.

- **Employee incentives** – Such incentives are given to employees who meet certain goals (other than sales goals), for example, increasing production or setting new safety records.

For example, *In Search of Excellence* by Tom Peters and Robert Waterman or another business bestseller such as Lee Iacocca's biography would make a suitable incentive for employees who come up with suggestions that save time or make the business environment a better place in which to work.

• **Business gifts** — To show their appreciation to their major customers, businesses often give gifts during the holiday season. While in many cases, these gifts involve food for the body, there is no reason such gifts could not involve food for the mind. Why not encourage businesses to give holiday bestsellers instead of food? Or a beautiful four-color coffee-table book that employees could enjoy for years to come.

Warren Cassell of Just Books promoted *An Island Garden*, a beautifully illustrated reprint of an 1894 book, as a corporate gift. Indeed, as part of his promotion, he gave 25 copies to CEOs to encourage them to think of books as gifts.

Besides giving books to major customers, businesses can also give books to their employees for birthdays, weddings, illnesses, deaths, retirements, promotions, or other major events.

• **Company celebrations** — Upjohn celebrated its 100th anniversary by having the Benjamin Company prepare a history of its first 100 years, which it gave to its employees and customers.

To celebrate its 100th anniversary, Pet Foods offered consumers a cookbook using recipes from Pet products. The book, *Celebration of Cooking in America*, sold for $8.95.

• **Opening celebrations** — A Santa Barbara bank celebrated the opening of a new branch by giving away 5,000 copies of Judy Dugan's self-published book, *Santa Barbara Highlights and History*, to every customer that came in during the first week.

• **Giveaways** — One small publisher sold a book on dental care to the American Dental Association which, in turn, provided the book to its members.

• **Publicity** — The Benjamin Company produced a *Consumer's Buying Guide* for a number of Better Business Bureaus who, in turn, sold them to various utilities and banks to be used in their public relations programs. The Benjamin Company produced a similar book for banks on *How to Manage Your Money*.

• **Increase name recognition** — As part of its continuing promotion to the youth market, Coors bought the exclusive rights to Edward J. Rogers's *Getting Hired: Everything You Need to Know about Resumes, Interviews and Job Hunting Strategies* to distribute free to the college market. The first year Coors distributed 165,000 copies of the book on college campuses. The man who put this deal together, Jeff Herman, notes that such a promotion need not be a one-time thing since every year there is an entirely new crop of graduating seniors.

- **Traffic builders** – Bamberger's department store chain gave away 50,000 copies of Hammond's *A Taste of German Cooking* to promote the store restaurant during its Octoberfest celebration.

- **Attention-getters** – To reinforce its image as an air cargo service, United Airlines shipped a book case, magnifying glass, and *Doubleday Dictionary* to 1,700 freight forwarders and commercial shippers. Later, they also sent copies of the *Hammond Almanac*, *Guinness Book of Records*, and *Hammond World Atlas*. Each book had a specially printed jacket outlining United's services. For example, the Guinness book carried the following legend: "Who holds the record for serving the commercial shipper? United Airlines Cargo."

- **Bonus premiums** – To encourage subscriptions to its magazine, *Working Woman* gave away copies of *Boss Lady*, the autobiography of advertising executive, Jo Foxworth, as a bonus to new subscribers. The response rate to their direct mail promotions increased by 25% as compared to other giveaways they had been using.

  Reader's Digest Condensed Books gave away 750,000 copies of Judith King's *Greatest Gift Guide Ever* as a premium for joining.

- **Self-liquidators** – Many cereals and other food products offer special items for sale at wholesale with a small payment plus proof of purchase. Life cereal offered a *Rand McNally Road Atlas* for $3.50 and two UPC symbols. Post Grape Nuts, to reinforce its natural image, offered a free copy of a *Rand McNally Nature Guide* for three box tops or one box top and $2.00. Total cereal offered a *Reader's Digest Do-It-Yourself Manual* for $1.30 and two UPC symbols. Bran Chex cereal offered three books (*The New Aerobics*; *Dr. Abravanel's Body Type Program for Health, Fitness and Nutrition*; and *Running for Health and Beauty*) for two proofs-of-purchase plus 50¢ postage and handling for each book ordered.

  Gerber baby foods offered a Rand McNally *Travel with Baby* manual for 50¢ and 24 UPC symbols.

  Grosset & Dunlap sold over a million Nancy Drew and Hardy Boys books when they were offered as a self-liquidating premium on 20 million boxes of Post Raisin Bran cereal. Not only do such on-pack offers sell a lot of books, but they also provide incredible exposure to your books. Sales of the Nancy Drew and Hardy Boy titles in retail bookstores increased during this same promotional period.

  To promote its Ziplock storage bags, Dow Chemicals gave away 250,000 copies of a 22-page, four-color recipe collection excerpted from Dom DeLuise's new book, *Eat This – It'll Make You Feel Better*. Since DeLuise was the TV spokesman for Ziplock bags, the promotion was a perfect tie-in for Ziplock. Simon & Schuster, publishers of the book, also benefited – not only for the money they earned from the excerpt, but also because the excerpt promoted the book for five months before its publication date!

- **In-packs** — With in-packs, the premium is offered inside the package. When the customer buys the product, they get the premium.

  Alka-Seltzer has used excerpts from several books as in-packs to promote its "relief-giving" properties. During tax time, they gave away *Tax Relief*, an excerpt from *J.K. Lasser's Your Income Tax*. In another promotion, they gave away *Hot & Spicy Favorites* recipes excerpted from various Better Homes and Gardens cookbooks.

- **On-packs** — With on-packs, the premium is offered on the outside of the package. Most on-packs are short quizzes, puzzles, or other items that can be printed on the package (for instance, a follow-the-dots drawing on a box of cereal).

  Kraft Foods offered an unusual on-pack premium for their frozen cocktail sausage rolls. They packaged the sausage rolls with one of 30 different romance novels from Mills & Boon, a British publisher of mass-market romance novels. With more than 30 titles to choose from, Kraft didn't have to worry about consumers ignoring the offer once they had collected one premium. As a result of this promotion, sales of the sausage rolls exceeded projections by 50%.

- **Educational promotions** — Dorsey Laboratories in cooperation with Random House developed a children's book, *The Care Bears Help Chase Colds*, to help promote the sale of their Triaminic cold care product. Not only did this promotion help them to sell 2 million units of Triaminic (each with a free book), but it also helped them to get better display space in stores.

- **Introduce new products** — When O. M. Scott introduced its new line of lawn care products, it decided to use a book that would appeal to the same audience as its products. Hence, it offered a free copy of *How to Watch Pro Football on TV* prepared by The Benjamin Company. During their promotion, they gave away almost one and a half million copies of the book.

- **Promote product use** — Meredith Publishing prepared a special *Best You Can Bake Chocolate Desserts* cookbook for Nestle. This 32-page booklet was given away free to 2 million people who bought Nestle's Tollhouse Morsels. Western Publishing put together an even fancier cookbook for Hershey's called *Hershey's Chocolate Treasures*.

- **Sweepstakes prizes** — Any company offering a grand prize of a trip in a sweepstakes promotion could use a travel guide to the trip's destination as third or fourth prizes to be given away at the same time. Since sweepstakes tend to work better when there are more prizes to be awarded, such low-cost yet valuable prizes can add considerably to the perceived value of the sweepstakes.

- **Frequent buyer programs** — One of your travel books, for instance, could be used as a premium in a frequent flyer program for one of the airlines — especially if it featured one of the airline's destination.

- **Door openers** – A company could offer one of your books as a free gift to prospects who will listen to their sales presentation. For instance, an insurance saleswoman could give away a tax guide to everyone who listens to her sales pitch.

- **Establish customer relationships** – As a means of establishing a continuing relationship, salesmen can give away a volume from a series each time they call on a client.

- **Referral premiums** – A company could give away a book each time one of their customers refers a friend to their products or services. The book should tie-in somehow with their product or service and be something the customer would value.

- **Dealer promotions** – Time-Life Books offered a display loaded with various 32-page booklets (excerpted from its series of do-it-yourself books) to manufacturing companies who could, in turn, offer the display to home centers, lumber yards, and other places that would sell their product to consumers. Included in each booklet, which sold for $1.00 each, were coupons from the manufacturer.

You won't have to look far for companies interested in premiums and incentives. They are all around you. To help get you started, here's a "short" list of some of Hammond's premium clients:

Allied Chemical, American Cyanamid, American Express, Amoco Oil, AT&T, Audubon Society, Avis, Avon, Award Lines, Bank of the South, Barclays Visa, Bell of Pennsylvania, Bendix Corporation, Bloomfield State Bank, BMW, Book of the Month Club, Bristol-Myers, Burger King, Britches of Georgetown, Byron Broadcasting, Cadillac, Chemical Bank, Citibank, Coca-Cola, Contadina Foods, Crown Life Insurance, Diamond Shamrock, Doubleday, ESPN, Exxon, Farmers & Merchants Bank, Farrell Lines, Firestone, Fortune Magazine, Ford, GAF, Gallo Winery, General Motors, GEO Magazine, Glendale Federal S&L, Goya, Green Giant, Gulf, Honda, IBM, Indiana University Alumni Association, Ingersoll-Rand, International Playtex, J. C. Penney Life Insurance, Johnson & Johnson, J. P. Stevens, Kavco Marketing, Kawasaki, Keystone Automobile Club, KLM, Korea Shipping, Leathersmith of London, Lever Brothers, Liberty National Life Insurance, Lumbermans Mutual Insurance, Mazda, Media Networks, Mercedes Benz, Merrill-Lynch, Mister Doughnut, Money Magazine, Morris County Savings, Mother's Trucking, Myron Manufacturing, Nabisco, New York Life, Paine Webber, Parents Magazine, Parke-Davis; Peugeot, Pfizer, Pitney Bowes Credit, Pontiac, Prudential, RCA, Reader's Digest, Royal Crown Cola, Sandoz, Seagrams, Sea-Land Service, Shell Chemical, Standard Commercial Tobacco, Stanley Tools, Sunshine Specialties, Texaco, Time Magazine, Travel Masters, Truckstops of America, TWA, Union Pacific, United Technologies, U.S. Air Force Academy, U.S. Golf Association, Volkswagen, Volvo, Warner Brothers, and Warner Lauren.

18:03 Some Premium/Incentive Resources

How do companies select premiums and travel incentive sites to use in their promotions? According to a study in *Premium/Incentive Business*, here's how:

25.1%   while brainstorming with management
18.7%   from seeing ads in trade magazines
12.5%   during trade shows
10.7%   through manufacturers' representatives
8.3%   because of the popularity of past awards
8.0%   from incentive house suggestions
7.2%   by reading new product announcements in trade journals

Since trade magazines and trade shows play such an important part in their selection process, if you are serious about the premium field, you should read at least one of the following magazines and attend one of the two major trade shows held every year.

Magazines

Besides reading one of the following magazines, you should also send them your publicity and test an advertisement for your premium offers.

• **Incentive**, Bill Communications, 633 Third Avenue, New York, NY 10017; (212) 986-4800.

• **Potentials in Marketing**, Lakewood Publications, 50 S. Ninth Street, Minneapolis, MN 55402-3165; (612) 333-0471.

• **Premium/Incentive Business**, Gralla Publications, 1515 Broadway, New York, NY 10036; (212) 869-1300.

Trade Shows

Besides the two major trade shows listed below, you might also want to attend the Specialty Advertising Showcase.

• **National Premium/Incentive Show**, Hall-Erickson, 150 Burlington Avenue, Clarendon Hills, IL 60514; (800) 752-6312. Held in Chicago in late September.

• **Premium Incentive Show**, Thalheim Expositions, 42 Bayview Avenue, P. O. Box 4200, Manhasset, NY 10030-4200; (516) 627-4000. Held in New York in early May.

• **Specialty Advertising Showcase**, Specialty Advertising Association International, 1404 Walnut Hill Lane, Irving, TX 75038; (214) 580-0404. Held in various parts of the country during early August.

Sales Consultants / Organizations

• **Sales Aides International**, 7425 Old York Road, Melrose Park, PA 19126; (215) 782-9090. A premium company which specializes in bringing together suppliers and potential buyers.

18:04   Other Corporate Sales

Besides premiums and sales incentives, corporations and other organizations can use books to aid their other departments. Here are just a few of the other approaches you can use to sell your books to corporations:

* **Training programs** — Corporations and governmental units spent $60 billion in 1984 to train their employees. Why shouldn't they be using your books as resources in their training programs?

Addison-Wesley has a separate sales force that calls only on businesses. One of their trade bestsellers, *Born to Win*, originated in a Bank of America training program. Since expanding that book to the trade market, they have sold almost two million copies (plus sold the mass-market reprint rights for just over $1 million).

Roger Von Oech sold many copies of his self-published book, *A Whack on the Side of the Head*, to corporations who used them in training their creative staffs. IBM bought 2,000 copies, Hewlett Packard 700 copies, and Control Data 600 copies.

Jossey-Bass Publishers sold 4,000 copies of *The Empowered Manager* by Peter Block to Sears and over 2,000 copies to AT&T to use in their manager development programs.

* **Health care programs** — In order to promote the health and well-being of their employees, many companies have established health care programs. To support these programs, companies often buy books to give their employees to help them understand how to take better care of themselves.

Over the years, Addison Wesley has sold 3 million copies of D. M. Vickery and J. F. Fries's *Take Care of Yourself*. 450,000 copies of the book were sold in 1985 alone, yet the book never showed up on the bestseller lists because over 90% of those copies were sold to corporate health care programs.

To promote employee health awareness, the Texas Medical Association and the University of Texas have offered copies of *The American Medical Association Family Medical Guide* to their employees. Random House reports some companies buying as many as 75,000 copies of the book at $7.25 each — that's a half a million dollar sale!

* **Retirement planning** — As mentioned previously, Monsanto bought 800 copies of Crisp Production's *Retirement Planning Guide* to give to its employees to help them with their retirement plans.

* **Sponsorships** — As part of their public relations programs, some companies will sponsor worthy causes and special publishing projects related to those causes.

Weyerhaeuser donated $25,000 worth of paper to Melior Publications for the publication of *Washington: Images of a State's Heritage* to celebrate the state's centennial in 1989.

Collins used corporate sponsors to help underwrite the costs of producing their *Day in the Life* series of books. Sponsors have included Kodak, Canon, American Express, and Apple Computers, as well as many hotels and airlines, plus some nonprofit associations and governmental agencies. Every sponsor is given credit in the front of each book. One of the corporate sponsors, Petro Canada, offered a free copy of *A Day in the Life of Canada Road Atlas* to patrons of its gas stations just prior to the publication of the larger book, *A Day in the Life of Canada*. Not only did this provide income for Collins from the sale of the atlas, but it also provided some of the best prepublication promotion the book received.

* **Public service** — DC Comics produced a Supergirl comic promoting car safety for Honda who, in turn, gave the comic away free to driver's education classes around the country.

* **Bundling** — Apple Computer bundled Addison Wesley's two books about the PostScript programming language along with every Laser-Writer it sold. A number of other laser printers bundled the books with their machines as well.

   Wham-O bundled Para Publishing's *Frisbee Player's Handbook* with many of its frisbees. Minolta offered Lowen Publishing's *Office Purchasing Guide* with its office machines. And Hayes Microcomputer bundled St. Martin's *The Complete Handbook of Personal Computer Communications* with its modems.

* **Examples of their work** — McNaughton & Gunn, printers of Dan Poynter's third edition of *The Self-Publishing Manual*, gave a free copy of the book to each new publisher who requested a quotation from them. Delta Lithograph did the same thing with Poynter's *Business Letters for Publishers* which they printed. Xerox bought 1,000 copies of Poynter's *Word Processors & Information Processing* book for which they did the typesetting — again, to show as samples of their work.

* **Company connections** — When Prentice-Hall published Eddie Rickenbacker's autobiography, they offered to print a special edition for Eastern Airlines (Rickenbacker had been chairman of Eastern's board of directors). Eastern bought 15,000 copies of the special edition.

* **Editorial mentions** — Earlier in the book I recommended that you edit your books for promotional clout. As an example, I suggested that if you were editing a gardening book, why not list specific seed and tool companies as resources in the appendix? Not only do such lists benefit the reader, but they also provide you with potential premium sales.

   That's what Warner Books did with the resource directory in the back of Howard Ruff's bestselling book, *How to Prosper During the Coming Bad Years*. They mailed a copy of the directory to each company on the list with a note suggesting that they might offer the book to their customers. They received many orders as a result of this promotion. One dehydrated food company ordered 1,000 copies every month.

When they published *The Best of Everything*, St. Martin's Press did a similar promotion. As a result, they sold a premium edition of the book to Sylvania, whose nineteen-inch color TV had been voted the best in the field.

• **Corporate libraries**—Many corporations have business or technical libraries to support their administrative, marketing, or research personnel. Some of your initial contacts with corporations could result in orders trickling in from these libraries even if you don't make a direct premium or corporate sale.

> **Authors** — If you or your book have connections with any companies, be sure to let your publisher know so they can explore various sales possibilities. You might want to make some contacts yourself. Indeed, you might be a more effective salesperson than someone from your publisher. But before making any personal contacts, coordinate your activities with your publisher's marketing department.

18:05 Selling to Associations

Besides selling to corporations and small businesses, you can also sell to associations, clubs, and other organizations. Just as companies need premiums, employee gifts, and training guides, so do associations. Don't overlook them. They can lead to significant sales.

Fundraising Sales

Schools, churches, clubs, and other organizations often sell books as a means of raising money to support their activities. For example, schools sponsor book fairs to raise money for their libraries. Churches often have book sales tables where they sell books after church services.

• Advocacy Press, the publishing arm of the Girls Club of Santa Barbara, has sold over 100,000 copies of *Choices*, a career planning workbook for teenage girls, and *Challenges* (for boys). Both of these titles are used as fundraisers for other girls' clubs, YMCAs, and Boy Scout troops.

To reach groups which might be interested in using books as fundraisers, advertise in appropriate media (such as a magazine for church leaders or a journal aimed at faculty advisors of school clubs). You might also use direct mail aimed at such church leaders or faculty advisors. The standard discount schedule for such sales is a 20% to 40% discount on sales of 25 or more books.

Educational Sales

When you do approach associations, be sure to emphasize the educational value of your books as well as their sales value. Books are far more likely to tie in with the group's purposes and activities than are other standard fundraising items such as cookies, candy, or magazines. Indeed, some books might actually be used in their educational activities.

• King County Rape Relief sells many copies of *He Told Me Not to Tell* and *Top Secret* to PTAs, state agencies, schools, scouting organizations, doctor's offices, and counselors.

• New Society Publishers has sold their books on social change to the Seneca Women's Peace Encampment, the San Diego Peace Resource Center, New England Greenpeace, the Resource Center for Nonviolence, the Maine Nuclear Freeze Campaign, the National Fellowship of Reconciliation, and the Women's Division of the Methodist Board of Global Ministries. These associations have used the books for both educational and fundraising work.

Membership Training

Besides educating people about the values and purposes of an organization, books can also be used to train or inform members of the organization itself.

• When they published the story of the CanSurmount cancer patient program, *I'm a Patient, Too*, Nick Lyons Books sold 5,000 copies of the book to the CanSurmount organization and even more copies to *Cope*, a new magazine for cancer patients.

Other Ways to Work with Associations

Besides selling books directly to associations, you can also work with them to promote your books direct to their members, either by renting their lists, by advertising in their journals or newsletters, by joining in with them for a mailing or other promotion, or by giving them books for their libraries (in the hope that members will see your books in the library and want to buy copies for themselves).

Resources

Here are a few resources to help you explore the association market:

• **American Society of Association Executives**, 1575 Eye Street N.W., Washington, DC 20005; (202) 626-2723.

• **National Associations of the U.S.**, Gale Research Company, 835 Penobscot Building, Detroit, MI 48226; (313) 961-2242; (800) 877-4253; Fax: (313) 961-6083. Lists 19,700 associations.

• **National Avocational Organizations**, Columbia Books, 1212 New York Avenue N.W. #330, Washington, DC 20005-3920; (202) 898-0662. 2,500 sporting, hobby, and cultural organizations.

> **Authors** — Again, if you are a member of any associations or if you know of any associations that might be interested in offering your book as a premium, fundraising item, educational guide, or whatever, tell your publisher. If you are a member, you might be the best person to contact the association about selling your book. If you are not a member, let your publisher make the contacts.

18:06   Selling to the Government

Just as corporations and associations can use books for premiums and other special purposes, so can various governmental units. For instance, Graphics Arts Center sells many of its regional pictorial books to state governments to be used as honoraria for visiting dignitaries.

As a $200 billion dollar market for supplies and services, the federal government is a large potential market for your books. If you are interested in exploring other options for selling to government, read the following resource books and magazine:

- **Government Product News**, Penton Publishing, 1100 Superior Avenue, Cleveland, OH 44114. This magazine is sent to government executives, administrators, engineers, and purchasing officials. The July, 1987, issue of the magazine featured *Facts about Aids*, a book from Evergreen Publications.

- *Doing Business with the Federal Government*—This 48-page booklet tells how to bid on government procurements, market products to federal agencies, and other useful guidelines for dealing with government procurement agencies. Available for $2.50 from the **Consumer Information Center**, P. O. Box 100, Pueblo, CO 81002.

- *Getting Started in Federal Contracting*—While much of this book is aimed at companies providing construction or manufacturing services to the federal government, some of it might be of use to those of you who want to offer consulting services. Available from **Panoptic Enterprises**, P. O. Box 1099, Woodbridge, VA 22193; (703) 670-2812.

> **Authors** — As a published author, you are an expert in your field. If you feel qualified and inclined, you might explore the possibilities of doing consulting work for some local, state, or federal government agencies. The above book should help you to orient yourself.

18:07   Selling to Mail Order Catalogs

While the major mail order catalogs drive a hard bargain — requiring as much as an 80% discount — they can move a lot of books. Not only that, but the exposure they give your books to all their customers will often result in spillover sales through bookstores. Where else could you find outlets who are willing to pay you so they can advertise your books to as many as 5,000,000 people?

Irena Chalmers Cookbooks have sold over 250,000 books through the Lillian Vernon catalog, which is mailed to over five million people. They have also sold many cookbooks through Jessica's Biscuit, a mail order cookbook catalog which is mailed to almost a million people. Indeed, they have found catalogs to be far more productive than book clubs.

There are some 6,000 companies in the U.S. that sell products through catalogs. In 1987, they mailed over 14 billion catalogs. In that same year, catalog sales were over $40 billion ($30 billion for consumer goods and $10 billion for business goods).

According to one Gallup Survey, 80% of the people who receive a catalog in the mail actually read some portion of the catalog, and 93% of the people who have bought something by mail or by phone within the past six months are avid catalog readers. In another survey, 33% of those surveyed said they would buy a book, record, or tape from a catalog.

To sell to catalogs, first research those catalogs which target the same audience as your book. If possible, get a sample copy of their catalog and review it to see if they offer any other books. Then send a finished copy of your book to those catalogs which you think would do the best job of presenting and selling your book. At the same time, enclose a Merchandise Data Sheet (see page 175 of *Mail Order Selling Made Easier*). This data sheet should provide all the details about your book, from its shipping weight and size to its potential markets.

Catalogs can be broken down into a number of different categories. Here are a few of the major categories:

* **General catalogs** — Sunset House, Lillian Vernon, Hanover House, Miles Kimball, Potpourri, Walter Drake, Harriet Carter, and others.

   The Harriet Carter catalog, for instance, featured 73 books in their most recent catalog — books on sports, cars, railroads, trivia, humor, word origins, crafts, and cooking. This catalog circulates to 30,000,000 people every year.

* **High-ticket catalogs** — Horchow, Neiman-Marcus, Joan Cook, Charles Keath, Bloomingdales, Adam York, Unicorn Gallery, and others.

* **Hi-tech catalogs** — Edmund's Scientific, Sharper Image, DAK, JSA, New Horizons, Video Playground, and others.

* **Games catalogs** — Game Room, Games, Fun House, Johnson Smith, Whole Mirth, FAO Schwarz, and others.

• **Children's catalogs**—Toys to Grow On, Childcraft, Giggletree, A Child's Collection, Children's Book and Music Center, Just for Kids, KidsRight, My Child's Destiny, Constructive Playthings, and others.

• **Cooking catalogs**—Jessica's Biscuits, Kitchen Arts and Letters, Wine and Food Library.

• **Business catalogs**—Quill, Small Business Success, Whole Work Catalog, Drawing Board Computer Supply, Lotus Computers, etc.

• **Catalogs for professionals**—Robert Anderson Publishing (healthcare catalog), Mix Bookshelf (music/broadcast), Firefighters Bookstore (firefighting), Jax Photo Books (photography), and others.

• **Remainder and general book catalogs**—Publishers Central Bureau, Edward R. Hamilton, Daedelus, Barnes & Noble.

• **Specialized catalogs**—Brookstone and Tools for Living (tools); Lee Ward, Dick Blick, and Boycan's (crafts); Dance Mart (dance); Genealogist's Bookshelf (genealogy); J.C. Whitney (auto); Traveller's Checklist (travel); Especially Maine (regional).

18:08 Resources for Selling to Catalog Houses

To help you sell to mail order catalog houses, here are a few magazines and directories which cover the catalog industry. Plus, I've listed several major catalog houses that feature books as well as other products.

Magazines

• **Catalog Age**, Six River Bend, P. O. Box 4949, Stamford, CT 06907-0949; (203) 358-9900. Hanson Publishing also publishes *Direct*.

• **Catalog Business**, 19 West 21st Street, New York, NY 10010-6805; (212) 741-2095. They also publish the biweekly tabloid, *DM News*.

Directories

• **Book Publishing Resource Guide**, Ad-Lib Publications, 51 N. Fifth Street, Fairfield, IA 52556-3226; (800) 669-0773; (515) 472-6617; Fax: (515) 472-3186. Among other listings, this directory features 420 mail order catalogs that carry books. Ad-Lib also publishes a special report titled, *How to Sell to Mail Order Catalogs*, which describes all the steps to selling a book or other product to mail order catalog houses. This report also lists 550 catalogs that feature books.

• **The Catalog of Catalogs**, Woodbine House, 10400 Connecticut Avenue #512, Kensington, MD 20895; (301) 949-3590. 8,000 listings.

• **The Directory of Mail Order Catalogs**, Grey House Publishing, Pocket Knife Square, Lakeville, CT 06069; (203) 435-0868; (800) 458-7664; Fax: (203) 435-0867. Lists 6,300 mail order catalogs but does not indicate which ones carry books.

- **Mail Order Product Guide**, Todd Publications, 18 N. Greenbush Road, West Nyack, NY 10994; (914) 358-6213. This directory lists companies which can supply products to catalogs. Your company should be listed in this directory.

- **National Directory of Catalogs**, Oxbridge Communications, 150 Fifth Avenue #636, New York, NY 10011-4311; (212) 741-0231; Fax: (212) 633-2938. Lists 4,350 mail order catalogs classified by subject. The newest and probably most useful directory of catalogs. $145.00.

Major Catalogs

To help you get started in making a list of key contacts, here are the addresses of four major mail order catalogs that carry books. For the addresses of other catalogs, see the directories on the previous page.

- **Hanover House Industries**, 1500 Harbor Boulevard, Weehawken, NJ 07087; 201-863-7300; Fax: (201) 319-3478. This company publishes the following four catalogs that carry gifts (and sometimes books): *Colonial Garden Kitchens* for crafts and cooking, *Hanover House Catalog* for low-priced gifts and gadgets, *Mature Wisdom* for people over 50, and *Old Village Shop* for low-priced gifts and gadgets.

- **Harriet Carter**, 425 Stump Road, Montgomeryville, PA 18936; (215) 361-5122. They feature many books in every catalog.

- **Publisher's Clearinghouse**, Jeannie Clarke, 382 Channel Drive, Port Washington, NY 11050; (516) 883-5432. Along with American Family Publishers, this company is one of the two major magazine subscription agencies (both offer $10,000,000 sweepstakes). Both are now offering books as well as magazines in their sweepstakes mailings.

  For instance, American Family Publishers have offered *Betty Crocker's Christmas Cookbook*, *Jane Fonda's New Workout & Weight-Loss Program*, *The Velveteen Rabbit Set*, four Little Treasury sets, and *Freebies for Cat Lovers*.

  In the beginning of 1989, Publisher's Clearinghouse began offering its first all-books catalog. Among the books they offered were *The Homeowner's Journal* by Vic Spadoccini and *Common Sense: The Complete Money Management Workbook* by Judy Lawrence. They also featured other practical books on cooking, crafts, consumer reference, self-improvement, personal finance, and children's books (both fiction and nonfiction). When they select a book, they buy from 2,000 to 10,000 copies at a time.

- **Publishers Central Bureau**, Barbara Rittenhouse, Frontlist Buyer, 201 E. 50th Street, New York, NY 10022; (212) 572-2624. While most of the books they feature are remainders, they also feature about 150 new quality paperbacks every catalog.

  Pathway has sold over 45,000 copies of *Do It*, a $2.25 paperback, through Publishers Central Bureau catalogs.

Authors — Be on the lookout for any catalogs which might be appropriate for your books. If you discover any, send them to your publisher so the special sales department can explore bulk sales to the catalog.

To receive catalogs in the subjects that interest you, just get your name on a couple of lists related to that subject. For instance, if you want to receive some of the photography related catalogs, subscribe to a photography magazine, or buy a camera or camera supplies by mail, or join an amateur photography club—anything to get your name on some lists.

18:09 Sales through Other Mail Order Dealers

Besides catalogs, there are a number of other ways to market your books through mail order book sellers. Here are a few of them:

- If you publish books on diet, health, exercise, crafts, or other subjects that would interest the readership of the large circulation Sunday magazines such as *Parade* and *USA Weekend*, contact National Syndications. This company buys remnant ad space in these magazines to advertise books which they buy from publishers at discounts of 65% to 70%. If they decide one of your books might appeal to their audience, they will test the ad. If it tests well, they will continue placing ads for the book. Depending on the title, they can move anywhere from 5,000 to 100,000 copies in a year. For more information, write to **National Syndications**, 230 Fifth Avenue #2010, New York, NY 10001; (212) 686-8680. They also publish the Publishers Choice book catalog.

  Among other books, National Syndications featured *How to Live with a Golfaholic* from Golfaholics Anonymous in *Parade* magazine.

- There are a good number of smaller enterprises which sell books by mail. Many of these mail order book dealers obtain their stock from one or two major sources (at discounts ranging from 50% to 70%) and then resell to their own customers. If your book appeals to the opportunity seeker, you should contact these major sources to see if they'd be interested in stocking your books. Since they require a discount of 60% to 80%, you shouldn't contact them unless you can afford to give such discounts.

  One major mail order book dealer source is **Premier Publishers**, P.O. Box 330309, Fort Worth, TX 76163-0309; (817) 293-7030. Premier can sell anywhere from a few hundred to a few thousand copies of your books each year. For instance, they sold about 300 copies of the precurser of *Mail Order Selling Made Easier* each year.

- If you'd rather sell directly to the mail order book dealers, you can advertise in *BookDealers World*, *Income Opportunities*, *Opportunity Magazine*, *Moneysworth*, or other magazines where people read the classifieds to find money-making opportunities. Wilshire Books and George Sterne's Profit Ideas are two publishers who have been using such mail order dealers for many years — and selling books as a result.

- When you sign up these independent dealers, you can offer them 50% to 70% terms depending on the quantity they order. These discounts are justified since all sales should be prepaid with no returns allowed (these are the standard terms).

  As an option, you can offer to dropship books for these dealers at a 50% discount plus a postage and handling fee. Under these arrangements, they only need to send you a check for the appropriate amount plus a label already made out to their customer. Then all you have to do is stuff the book into a shipping bag, attach the label and appropriate postage, and mail.

  Lowen Publishing has sold thousands of copies of *The Secretary's Friend* through dropship agreements with other independent publishers and marketers. They have also sold many copies through the Quill and Viking office supply catalogs.

18:10 Home Party Sales

How many of you have attended a Tupperware party? The Tupperware Company built up an incredible market almost solely on the basis of home party sales. Why not apply the same technique to advertise and distribute your books?

Lions Head Press has found that home party sales can be effective for selling religious books. They use individuals to demonstrate their entire line of books at in-home parties. Sales, thus far, have been encouraging.

18:11 Bartering for Books and Other Services

As long as I am exploring all possibilities, it is quite possible to use your books as exchange items for other services. I know of a number of poets who have bartered their poetry books for goods or services from family and friends.

When I published the third edition of my *Directory of Short-Run Book Printers*, I exchanged several hundred copies of the second edition of the *Directory* for books from other publishers. They, in turn, distributed the books to their customers or friends. In this way I made sure that the outdated books were distributed rather than trashed.

18:12 Sell Advertisements in Your Books

To increase the income from your books, you might consider selling advertisements for related products in the back pages of your books. Though some people would question whether such advertising would corrupt the editorial integrity of books, advertisements have not interfered with the quality of most magazines which carry advertising nor with the many directories (such as *Literary Market Place* and the *Thomas Register*) which also carry advertising.

Indeed, I see advertisements as being a service to readers, especially for users of directories. When we published the second and third editions of the *Directory of Short-Run Book Printers*, we accepted ads from book printers listed in the *Directory* as well as from typographers and binders who were not. Not only did the ads bring in extra money (enough, in fact, to pay for the entire editorial and production costs of the book), but the ads also allowed readers to catch a glimpse of how the printers viewed themselves—a glimpse I could not have provided in the actual listings. I believe that giving printers the opportunity to tell their story their way is an integral part of any really useful directory.

But why stop with advertising in directories? Why couldn't other books carry advertising as well? Recently, I saw an ad for a new quarterly fantasy magazine in a trade paperback fantasy novel. Such advertising might be the only feasible way for a quality magazine to reach the target audience for its editorial content. Why not give readers an opportunity to learn about related products or services?

Of course, you could also accept just about any advertising which targets the same market as your books. For example, romance novels could carry ads for soaps, beauty aids, and diet plans while westerns could carry ads for chewing tobacco or Marlboro cigarettes. Such ads may be getting too commercial, but they could help to hold the line on rising prices for mass-market paperbacks and for hardcovers as well. Perhaps there could be some selection criteria which would limit ads to certain clearly defined commercial products that you feel would be compatible with the book's content and style and which would actually be a service to the reader.

18:13 Remainder Sales: The Final Frontier

At some point in the life of a book, no matter how committed you are to keeping your books in print, you must consider whether or not to sell out any leftover stock to remainder dealers. Sometimes you will have to remainder a book simply because it is outdated or because the author wants to do another edition, but the major reason most books are remaindered is that the book is no longer selling enough copies to justify the costs of warehousing it.

Remaindering is actually just another way to keep a book alive rather than, as many publishers think, a way to bury a book. John Fielder of Westcliffe Publishers, which produces many fancy photo books, actually welcomes remaindering. It is, he says, a way to reach an entirely new market. When you cut the price of a book by half or more, you make your book affordable to a whole new group of book buyers. Indeed, a number of publishers are now actually publishing books for the remainder market. They don't really expect the books to sell that well in a bookstore at a high price, but they do expect them to sell quite well when they are marked down to the remaindered retail price.

True remainders are not damaged or returned copies which have been sitting on some bookseller's shelves for years; rather, true remainders are actual publishers' overstocks which have never been distributed. Most books are bought by remainder dealers at or below the publisher's actual productions costs (between 5% and 15% of the list price, or at a cost 1/4 to 1/3 that of the retail price the remainder will carry when sold in stores).

There are two basic ways to sell your books for remaindering:

1. You can offer a packaged deal to one or more remainder dealers. Send them copies of the titles you want to remainder, along with inventory information for each title. Once the dealers have had a chance to review the books, you can negotiate a price with them either over the phone or by mail. This is a quick and easy method to remainder a few titles.

2. You can offer a larger list of titles on a **bid-list** basis. Send the list to all remainder dealers who might be interested in bidding on the books. The list should include the following information about each book: title, name of author, other biographical details about the author that might encourage them to stock the book, the copyright date, original retail price, and remaining inventory. Offer review copies of any title they might be interested in reviewing more closely. In your cover letter, indicate a closing date for receiving bids, the terms of payment you expect, and information about how (and where) the books are stored. Under this method, the remainder dealer who offers the highest price for each book gets all the inventory for that book.

The major remainder dealers are Outlet Book Company (which, with $80 million in sales, does about half of all remainder business), Book Sales Inc. (with annual sales of $15 million), Book Thrift ($12 million in annual sales), and Sunflower Books ($10 million in annual sales). Their addresses are as follows. For the addresses of other remainder dealers, see Book Publishing Resource Guide:

• **Outlet Book Company**, Peter Schweitzer, Buyer, 225 Park Avenue South, New York, NY 10003; (212) 254-1600; Fax: (212) 529-2019.

• **Book Sales Inc.**, 110 Enterprise Avenue, Secaucus, NJ 07094; (201) 864-6341.

● **Bookthrift,** 45 West 36th Street, New York, NY 10018; (212) 947-0909.

● **Sunflower Books,** W. H. Smith Publishers, 112 Madison Avenue, New York, NY 10016; (212) 532-6600.

● The major chains (B. Dalton and Waldenbooks) also buy remainders.

Besides these book remainder dealers, you might also try marketing your leftover books to closeout dealers. Here are two major contacts in the closeout industry:

● **Promotion and Closeout Show,** Transworld Exhibits, 1850 Oak Street, Northfield, IL 60093. Over 3,000 buyers attend this show at the end of every April.

● **Libra Wholesale,** 1417 W. Brewster Street, St. Paul, MN 55105; (612) 645-2495; Fax: (612) 645-1050. Libra is one of many companies that specialize in buying close-outs, odd lots, and other merchandise for liquidation. They require a minimum of 10,000 items.

18:14 Books as Donations

If you would rather not sell your overstocked books at a loss or near loss, you can donate them to charity and take a deduction on your income taxes. Below are three services that will accept your excess inventory and channel these donations to worthy causes (schools, colleges, literacy groups, etc.) or sell them to fund scholarships and other grants. When you make such donations, you can deduct as much as twice your manufacturing costs in charitable tax deductions.

For more information, write to the following groups:

● **Charitable Book Program,** Robert Silver Associates, 307 East 37th Street, New York, NY 10016; (212) 686-5360.

● **Educational Assistance,** P. O. Box 3021, Glen Ellyn, IL 60138; (312) 690-0010.

● **National Association for the Exchange of Industrial Resources,** Cruz Ramos, Director of Donor Relations, 560 McClure Street, P. O. Box 8076, Galesburg, IL 61402; (309) 343-0704.

Authors — You, too, can qualify for tax deductions by donating your books to worthy causes. Check with your accountant to find out what deductions you can take.

Chapter 19

Book Spinoffs (For Publishers and Authors)

If you consider yourself a provider of information, entertainment, education, and/or enlightenment, then you don't have to limit your activities simply to publishing books. In most cases, you can take the same contents that are in your books and create new products—products that can help you to reach markets you could not reach in any other way. Any book—whether fiction or nonfiction, whether illustrated or text only, whether a bestseller or only an also-ran—can be adapted to other media.

Indeed, there are so many possibilities that the real question is not whether you can do it, but whether you want to do it. You must decide if adapting your books to other media is worth your time and effort—time and effort that will be taken away from your book publishing activities, time and effort that might be better spent promoting your current titles or creating new ones.

If you do decide to adapt your books, you have three basic options:

1. You can design, produce, and market the adaptations yourself.

2. You can license the rights to another company, as many book publishers and authors already do when they sell subsidiary rights.

3. You can work with another company. Such a joint project could be organized as a separate venture where each participating company provides a proportionate amount of money and personnel. Or it could be arranged so that one company is responsible for design and production while the other company is responsible for marketing and fulfillment. Or it could be some combination or permutation of these two possibilities.

In the rest of this chapter I will be describing many of the different ways you can adapt your books. I will not, however, be going into detail on how you should go about adapting and marketing your books under these different conditions (that would be a whole new book just by itself). For now just review the possibilities. If you decide that you'd like to pursue some of the different options, then begin by studying that field in greater detail. Subscribe to the trade magazines covering that field. Talk to retail shop owners. Attend exhibitions. Look before you leap.

19:01 Books into Books into Books

Once you've written and/or published a book, don't sit on your laurels. Rather, look for ways to change the format of your book so it will attract new audiences. Publishers already do this when they publish books in hardcover format, then trade paperback format, and then mass-market paperback format. At each change in format (and price), a new audience is reached. But you don't have to settle for three printed formats. A book can be adapted to a good number of other printed formats as well. Here are just a few of them:

- **New size** — Westcliff also publishes their big coffee-table books in a smaller size which they've trademarked by the title of Littlebooks. These Littlebooks sell for half what the bigger books cost and, thus, open up a new market for their titles.

- **Excerpts** — Most of the Littlebooks do not reproduce the entire text of the original but rather excerpt only a portion of the bigger book — aiming to reach a specific market. Hence, a photography book on Colorado might be broken up into separate editions for each area or city. Westcliff publishes separate titles for *Aspen*, *Vail*, and *Steamboat Springs*.

  Ten Speed Press excerpted *The New Quick Job-Hunting Map* from Richard Bolles's bestselling *What Color Is Your Parachute?*. This excerpt is regularly updated with new editions to supplement the original book. While the original book has sold over 3,000,000 copies, the smaller 64-page *Map* has sold more than 500,000 copies in all editions.

- **Anthologies and collections** — Why not publish an anthology using selected excerpts from some of your best books? Not only could such a collection sell quite a few copies on its own (if it were well edited), but it could also help to sell many of your other titles by providing readers with a sample of the other books. Such collections need not be limited to fiction titles (though I believe they would work best for fiction). Why not a selection from each of your regional travel guides? Or cookbooks?

- **Change titles** — While a rose by any other name would smell as sweet, title changes can help to increase sales of a book. For example, NAL changed the title of Maharishi Mahesh Yogi's *The Science of Being and Art of Living* to *Transcendental Meditation* right at the peak of interest in the TM program. As a result, they sold more books.

When St. Martins published Jack and Lois Johnstad's self-published book, *Attaining Financial Peace of Mind*, they changed the title to *The Power of Prosperous Thinking* (perhaps to draw a connection between that book and Norman Vincent Peale's *The Power of Positive Thinking*). Many paperback publishers will change the titles of books when they bring them out for the mass market.

• **Dress it up** — Irena Chalmers once described how a department store took one of her $5.95 cookbooks and dressed it up by tying a scarlet ribbon and some cinnamon sticks around it — and then charged ten dollars for the book! At Christmas time, such dressed-up books make perfect gifts.

• **Loose-leaf binders** — Loose-leaf publishing was originated by Richard Ettinger (one of the founders of Prentice-Hall) when one of his books became outdated by a change in the tax laws just as the book was coming off the press. To solve the problem, he tore off the covers of the books, removed the obsolete chapter, replaced it with the new information, and then published the new book in a loose-leaf binder. Loose-leaf publishing is especially useful for publications which need continual updating or for collections of forms and other illustrations which need to be duplicated with a copier.

• **Kits** — To supplement my new book, *Mail Order Selling Made Easier*, I designed two kits: the *Mail Order Worksheet Kit* (which includes full-size master copies of all the worksheets, forms, and and tables outlined in the book) and the *Mail Order Spreadsheet Kit* (which provides Lotus 1-2-3 compatible spreadsheet templates that allow users to explore how changes in prices, response rates, and costs could affect the profitability of their direct mail promotions).

• **Directories** — Susi Torre-Bueno of Rainbow Designs self-published her own needlework design books. Then, finding no national directory of such needlework books, she published such a directory, *The Index of Counted Thread*, to connect the thousands of craft shops with the 5,000 publishers in this field (most of them home-based businesswomen just like her).

When I first outlined the proposal for this book, I had intended to include listings of all the various book marketing channels in the appropriate chapters. But as I began to bring the information together, I realized that I couldn't possibly list all the resources without making this book too cumbersome to use (and too susceptible to becoming outdated very quickly). Hence, I decided to publish a separate directory. Since that time, the *Book Publishing Resource Guide* has taken on a life of its own.

• **Manuals and workbooks** — Many textbook publishers already provide workbooks and/or teacher's manuals to supplement their textbooks. Yet, why couldn't other publishers of nonfiction do the same? For example, a publisher of business books could well profit from providing the necessary forms to supplement a guide on direct marketing or personnel management or whatever.

To supplement its bestselling book on *Hang-Gliding*, Para Publishing published its *Hang Gliding Manual with Log*. Now in its seventh edition, the *Log* has sold over 75,000 copies while the original book has sold over 130,000 copies.

When I was writing the original edition of this book, I realized I could not begin to include all the forms, tables, and samples that a publisher should have access to. To supplement this book, then, I wrote and designed *Book Marketing Made Easier*, which includes everything from preparing a marketing strategy to planning budgets, forecasting sales, getting distribution, working with bookstores, and granting sub rights.

- **Purse books** — When Marilyn Ross self-published her book on genealogy, *Discover Your Roots*, she also contacted Dell about publishing excerpts from the book in their purse book series sold in supermarkets. While Dell rejected that proposal, they did contract to have her produce a new book on the same subject. Since her original book sold to bookstores, libraries, and schools, she was able to reach an entirely new audience through the purse books.

- **Large print books** — Over 400 large print titles are now produced each year. Among the leaders in this field are G. K. Hall and Doubleday (which operates a separate book club for large print editions, the Large Print Home Library). Large print editions allow you to market your books to readers with deteriorating eyesight, thus reaching an audience otherwise ignored by the traditional market. If your titles appeal to older people, you should consider issuing a separate large print edition (or selling the large print rights).

- **Diaries** — HarperCollins published *The Little House Diary*, which was based on the novels by Laura Ingalls Wilder.

- **Address books** — Bo-Tree Productions produces a number of address books including one on *Words of Women*.

- **Activity and coloring books** — Western Publishing produces many activity and coloring books based on licensed characters as well as some storybook characters.

- **Comics** — Various classics, from *Swiss Family Robinson* to *Huckleberry Finn*, have been published in comic format. Recently, a number of newer books have also been reproduced as comics or graphic novels.

- **Literary magazines** — Penguin Books introduced an English literary magazine, *Granta*, into this country in paperback format.

- **Limited editions** — William Morrow published a signed limited edition of John Irving's *A Prayer for Owen Meany*.

- **Boxed sets** — While most boxed sets feature fiction series such as *The Chronicles of Narnia* by C. S. Lewis, Ballentine has produced boxed sets of *The Pattern Library* and *The New York Times Gourmet*.

19:02 Audio/Video Adaptations

Though printed books should be around for some time to come, more and more people are choosing to get their information and entertainment through other media, especially audio and video formats. To meet their desire for a more lively format, publishers have begun to adapt books into a number of different audio and video formats including movies, TV programs, TV series, videotape format, read-aloud or dramatized audiotapes, records, and filmstrips.

• **Movies, TV programs, and TV series** — While few book publishers are currently producing movies or TV programming, several major publishers are connected to larger entertainment companies.

Simon & Schuster is a subsidiary of Gulf & Western Industries which also owns Paramount. Time-Life Books and Warner Books are part of the new Time Warner conglomerate which also owns the Warner movie studios and Home Box Office, among other media companies.

Most authors and publishers license movie/TV rights to experienced movie producers and production companies rather than attempt to produce such shows themselves.

With its production of the movie, *Animal House*, the *National Lampoon* magazine began its career as a movie producer as well as a magazine publisher. Why couldn't book publishers do the same?

• **Videotapes** — Many book publishers have begun to jump on the videotape bandwagon. As of 1985, there were over 40,000 videotape titles divided as follows: 13,000 general interest and educational; 10,000 health and science; 9,000 movies and entertainment; and 2,000 each of fine arts, children's programming, sports and recreation, and how-to titles. According to one study, by 1995 over 85% of all U.S. households will own a videotape player — and they will be spending $14 billion a year for videotapes.

Videotapes are already cheaper than books in some cases. For instance, Family Home Entertainment offers several $14.95 videotapes by T. Berry Brazelton which cost less that his books on the same subject (pediatrics).

Karl-Lorimar has sold over 1,000,000 copies of Jane Fonda's *Workout* video. Alfred Knopf has a bestselling series of videotapes featuring Julia Child.

Simon & Schuster publishes videos such as the *Silver Palate Good Times Live*, the L.L. Bean Guide series, *Jerry Baker's Lawn Care Tips*, and many more.

Wintergreen Press, a small Minnesota publisher, produced a video guide for parents, *Empty Arms: Reaching Out to You*, to accompany its books, *Empty Arms* and *Miscarriage: A Shattered Dream*.

Bookstores have been one of the effective places to market your sell-through videotapes. For instance, almost 25% of Waldenbooks's sales are now in the non-book area, including audio and video tapes.

Here, though, is another resource that should help you to market your videotapes (if you decide to produce your own). Telncom produces video preview programs highlighting little known or limited release videos. These programs are broadcast via national and local cable TV to 5.6 million homes. For more information, contact **Telncom**, 17819 S. Lysander Drive, Carson, CA 90746; (213) 979-9146.

To learn more about the video field, read the following two books:

Home Video: Producing for the Home Market – from Michael Weise, 3960 Laurel Canyon Boulevard #331, Studio City, CA 91614; (818) 905-6367.

Video Source Book – from National Video Clearinghouse, 100 Lafayette Drive, Syosset, NY 11791. This book provides data on the 40,000 plus video titles now on the market.

● **Audiotapes** – 85% of all households in the U.S. own at least one audiotape player; 60% have tape players in their cars. Sales of non-music audiotapes hit $100 million in 1985. One buyer at the Scribner's bookstores has said that the demand for books on cassettes is so large that each time they reorder, they order twice as many as the last time.

Recognizing this greater demand for books on tape, many book publishers (including Bantam and Simon & Schuster) have begun pushing their editors to obtain audio rights at the same time they buy book rights. Audiotapes have one great advantage over books: They can be listened to while driving. Tapes make a perfect companion during rush hour traffic.

As further signs of the importance of audio cassettes in the book trade, Bowker has published *On Cassette*, a bibliography of spoken word audio cassettes.

Newman sold over 100,000 copies of a 4-cassette package of Garrison Keillor's *News from Lake Wobegon* – more copies than many hardcover bestsellers.

● **Book/cassette packs** – Book and cassette packages are especially popular among producers of children's books and tapes because they allow children to read along with the tape.

HarperCollins published an entire series of "I Can Read" book and cassette packs. Other major producers of book/cassette packs for children include Price/Stern/Sloan, Kidstuff Books, and Yellow Moon Press.

Warner Audio Publishing offered travel tapes from Stephen Birnbaum covering the major European cities. Each tape came with a city map and a bonus travel tips cassette.

- **Records**—While records are rapidly being replaced by audiotapes, some companies are still producing records featuring the spoken word. The best known company in this field, of course, is Caedmon, which has been producing such records for many years, especially records of poetry, short stories, and plays for educational use. Nonetheless, because records do not have the portability of cassette tapes and because compact discs are beginning to replace records, records are not likely to play a large role in future book adaptations.

- **Compact discs**—A market for non-music compact discs has not yet developed.

- **Filmstrips**—Filmstrips are produced primarily for the school market. As more and more schools obtain videotape players, however, filmstrips will be used less and less.

19:03 Computer Related Adaptations

While some publishers have not done well with computer software or books, computer adaptations offer great possibilities. Electronic publishing sales are expected to rise to $21 billion by 1994. Here are just a few examples of how books can be adapted for computers:

- **Software for computers users**—Simon & Schuster published *The Fully Powered PC*, a combination of a book and software disc making an IBM-PC easier to use for nontechnical users.

- **Educational software**—Simon & Schuster's *Typing Tutor III* sold over 100,000 copies.

- **Business software and databases**—Many directories can profitably be transformed into computer databases on floppy disks. Because users demanded it, we produced a computer database version of *Book Publishing Resource Guide* called the *Book Marketing No-Frills Data Files*, which enables users to target only those sources which are interested in a particular subject (such as crafts, children's books, travel, science fiction, poetry, or any of 50 other subjects). We also offer the *PR FLASH No-Frills Data Files*, a $149.95 collection of disks listing over 11,000 key publicity contacts in magazines, newspapers, radio, TV, and syndicated columns.

- **Software for professionals**—The Center for Science in the Public Interest published *Nutrition Wizard* software for nutritional consultants. It is a combination electronic cookbook, nutritional reference, and diet analyst all rolled into one.

- **Home software**—CDA Electronic Publishing has published cookbooks, wine collector's books, and even the *Mr. Boston Bartender Guide* on discs. Simon and Schuster adapted *The Great International Paper Airplane Construction Kit* for the Macintosh computer.

Pinpoint Publishing published the *Micro Cookbook*, a software cookbook for IBM, Apple, and Commodore computers. At the request of Ortho Information Systems, they also produced *Computerized Gardening*, a software program for gardeners which Ortho now sells.

- **Novels on disc**—Addison-Wesley sold 50,000 copies of *The Hobbit*. Other interactive novels have been published by Bantam (*Sherlock Holmes in Another Bow*) and Simon & Schuster (*Star Trek, The Kobayshi Alternative*).

- **Electronic publishing**—Lee Foster published his travel book, *West Coast Travel*, on the CompuServe bulletin board. He is following that up with a disc version to be sold in bookstores.

- **CD-ROM**—The compact disc technology is opening an entirely new set of possibilities for publishers. Grolier has already published its *Academic American Encyclopedia* in CD-ROM format. Since the CD-Interactive standard allows for audio, video, text, and data interaction, CD-ROM products will eventually go beyond simple reference texts to fancier how-to and fiction texts for home use and entertainment.

Discovery Systems is one company that can prepare masters for your CD-ROM products and copies. As of August, 1988, they charged $1,500 for masters and $2.00 per each copy they make. For more information, contact **Discovery Systems**, 7001 Discovery Boulevard, Dublin, OH 43017; (614) 761-4287.

19:04 Toys and Games Adapted from Books

Books have been used for years as a means of both educating and entertaining children. Since the book that combines play value with content has a better chance of attracting and keeping a child's attention, book publishers have been creating pop-ups, board books, washable books, coloring books, and other activity books to bridge the gap between the ordinary book and toys in general.

Books can also be created as toys for adults, books such as the paper airplane construction kits and the new series from HarperCollins, which includes *Make Your Own Working Paper Clock* by James Rudolph and *Make Your Own Working Paper Steam Engine* by Kyle Wickware.

Books have also inspired new games and toys. Here are some examples of how other publishers have transformed their books into toys:

- **Toy/book packages**—Klutz Press has built its business by packaging a toy with a book describing how to use the toy. Klutz has done books on juggling (packaged with three small balls), kicking a hacky sack (with a hacky sack), throwing a boomerang (with a boomerang), and playing an harmonica (with an harmonica).

- **Toys**—WJ Fantasy has produced the Illustrators Collection of packaged toys which usually include paper toys, stickers, punch out figures, and other items centered around one theme such as *A Child's Chanukah Festival.* Each package is designed and illustrated by a prominent children's book artist.

  A few years ago I designed and wrote a book for Dover Publications on kinetic optical illusions. This book packaged together a number of cut-out patterns that would create illusions when the patterns were moved in a certain way. The book included an old-time movie carrousel, a Fechner-Benham disc, several flip books, four thaumatropes, the Ames window illusion, and a number of other wonderful illusions that kids could color, cut out, and assemble for themselves. Someday, as soon as I finish all my other projects, I hope to create another optical illusion kit featuring nonkinetic illusions.

- **Board games**—Milton Bradley manufactures a board game based on J. R. R. Tolkein's *The Hobbit.* Mayfair Games, distributed by Berkley Publishing Group, offers board games based on Anne McCaffrey's *Dragonriders of Pern* and Barbara Cartland's romance novels. And Victory Games has produced a game based on Dr. Ruth's nonfiction books called *Dr. Ruth's Game of Good Sex.*

- **Role-playing games**—Role-playing games have been produced based on the James Bond and Sherlock Holmes books as well as many science fiction and fantasy novels, including Iron Crown's Middle Earth games based on Tolkein's *Lord of the Rings.*

- **Jigsaw puzzles**—International Polygonics has manufactured puzzles based on *The Wind in the Willows, Treasure Island, Midsummer Night's Dream,* and *Peter Pan.* Similarly, American Publishing has produced jigsaw puzzles featuring characters from the Sesame Street TV show and Tolkein's *The Hobbit.*

- **Other puzzles**—Perigee Books distributed a puzzle, Mental Blocks (also known as Pandora's Blocks) created by artists Jacklyn Lambert and Jeffrey Samborski. The set of sixteen cubes could be manipulated into 96 different illustrations (and more than a million other combinations).

- **Model kits**—The Globe Playhouse, U.S. Capitol, and the House of Seven Gables are just a few of the buildings which can be created by the model kits from Kenilworth Publishing.

- **Card decks**—Western Publishing produces baseball trivia cards. Wingbow Press publishes a tarot deck to accompany *The Motherpeace Tarot Playbook* by Vicki Noble and Jonathan Tenney.

- **Dolls**—A Ramona Quimby doll based on the heroine of eight novels by Beverly Cleary has recently been offered by Morrow. Tide-Rider has produced a number of collectible dolls based on fictional characters (including Sherlock Holmes and Doc Watson).

As a November, 1987, *Publishers Weekly* article pointed out, "More than merely constituting additional products, these can be a highly effective means of increasing a character's visibility and generating greater book sales."

- **Doll/book sets** — HarperCollins offered a set featuring a copy of Maurice Sendak's *Where the Wild Things Are* and a doll based on a character from the book.

- **Paper dolls** — Dover Publications has published a good number of paper doll books over the years. Green Tiger Press published a *Spirit of the Flowers* paper doll box.

- **Plush** — Eden Toys produces stuffed animals and toys to coordinate with books featuring such characters as Babar, Paddington Bear, and Beatrix Potter's Peter Rabbit.

- **Plush/book sets** — Alfred Knopf packaged a stuffed Velveteen Rabbit to accompany the hardcover edition of Margery William's classic *The Velveteen Rabbit*. For $15.95 E. P. Dutton put together two Very First Books by Rosemary Wells with a plush version of Max, the rabbit featured in this series.

- **Other possibilities** — Balloons, buttons, pins, kites, windsocks, hobby kits, doll houses, action figures, and so on.

19:05 Posters and Calendars From Books

More publishers have probably adapted their books to posters and calendars than to any other format. Because publishers are already comfortable working with printed products and because they already have all the artwork ready to go, they can easily produce calendars and posters. Furthermore, calendars and posters are readily accepted into bookstores — the one market most publishers already serve through their distribution network.

To help stimulate your creative juices, here are just a few examples of how other publishers are adapting their books to various poster and calendar formats:

- **Posters** — Posters can be made from original paintings, storybook illustrations, book covers, commemorative posters, fine art reproductions, old engravings, movie posters, photographs, and even words.

  Art 101, for example, produced an entire series of Thousand Words posters featuring quotes by and about women, dance, Shakespeare, and other topics.

  Dover Publications regularly produces posters from public domain sources — including old advertising posters by Mucha and others.

  Fairfax Prints has produced fantasy art prints by Frank Frazetta, a number of which were originally painted for book covers.

Peaceable Kingdom Press offers posters from a good number of children's books, including *Goodnight Moon*, *The Runaway Bunny*, *The Story of Babar*, and *Where the Wild Things Are*. Over 1,000 bookstores carry their posters.

● **Art prints** — Art prints are reproductions of fine art in sizes ranging from postcards to posters. Many of the same companies that produce posters also produce art prints. For book publishers, one of the advantages of smaller art prints is that they can be shipped more easily than posters which must be shipped flat or in rolled cartons.

● **Maps** — Hammond, Rand McNally, and the American Map Company specialize in publishing maps, atlases, and globes. Only a few other publishers have done much with maps. Bradt Enterprises, for instance, has published maps to supplement its hiking guides. Warner Audio Publishing includes a free city map with each of its Stephen Birnbaum European Tour travel cassettes.

To be honest, I'm surprised that more travel guide publishers have not produced large-size maps to accompany their books. Such maps would seem to be a natural add-on sale. I know that I've always wished for a larger map when I've used travel guides.

● **Globes** — Rand McNally offers a world globe featuring Sesame Street characters. Sunstone Publications has produced a 3-D astrodome map of the night sky.

● **Wall calendars** — The most popular kind of calendar to produce is the wall calendar. There have been calendars featuring Tolkein characters, children's book illustrations, B. Kliban cats, travel book photos, and many, many others.

● **Desk calendars** — The Crossing Press published the *Women Writers Desk Calendar*. Price/Stern/Sloan adapted their bestselling book on Murphy's Laws to a desk calendar format.

● **Engagement calendars** — Galison Books produced the *Library of Congress Engagement Calendar* and the *National Gallery Book of Days*. Main Street Press produced the *Gay Engagement Calendar* and the *Mystery and Suspense Engagement Calendar*.

● **Page-a-day calendars** — Antioch and Workman both produce lines of page-a-day calendars. Andrews, McMeel & Parker published a *Sniglet-a-Day* calendar to supplement the bestselling *Sniglet* books.

19:06 Stationery and Other Paper Goods

Like posters and calendars, stationery and other paper goods are printed products which make it easy to adapt books to their formats. Hence, many book publishers have expanded their lines to include a variety of paper goods as well. Here are just a few examples:

- **Stationery**—C. R. Gibson offers stationery and accessories based on books by Beatrix Potter and Roger Tory Peterson.

  Quillmark offers a wide variety of stationery items based on books, including social stationery, invitations, address books, diaries, blank books, note cards, and thank you cards.

- **Note cards**—SRM Editions has published a line of note cards based on illustrations from Paul Goble's books, *The Girl Who Loved Wild Horses, Star Boy, Gift of the Sacred Dog,* and others.

  Fotofolio specializes in notecards taken from images produced by well-known photo-graphers and artists, from Edward Hópper to Jill Krementz.

- **Note pads**—Besides the *Sniglet-a-day* calendars, Andrews, McMeel & Parker also produced *Sniglet* note cards, greeting cards, magnetic memo pads, Post-it notes, and mugs.

  Quillmark produced notepads and note cubes featuring B. Kliban cats.

- **Note and memo boards**—Noteboards featuring Tolkein's *The Hobbit* and *Lord of the Rings* are available from Allen & Unwin.

  Cheers Workshop offers a wipe-off board illustrated with bear paws from Dennis Kyte's *The Last Elegant Bear.*

- **Postcards**—Dover Publications publishes a wide variety of postcard books featuring everything from photographs of New York to Mucha postcards to photos taken from Eadweard Muybridge's *Human Figures in Motion.*

  The *New York Review of Books* sells postcards featuring caricatures by David Levine of such literary notables as Marcel Proust and Virginia Woolf.

- **Greeting cards**—There are greeting cards for almost any occasion, from Valentines to Thanksgiving, from birthdays to graduations, from get well to farewell, from weddings to Mother's Day, and everything else in between.

  Abingdon Press published three full-color Christmas card booklets with poems and verses from the Bible.

  Redbird Productions has established a line of greeting cards based on illustrations from their self-published book, *Cream and Bread,* about growing up in a Scandinavian-Lutheran small town.

  Susan Polis Schutz began Blue Mountain Arts by publishing a book of her poetry illustrated by her husband, Steven Polis. She is now one of the bestselling poets of all time, and the greeting cards based on their works are among the major lines of independent greeting cards.

  Golden Turtle Press has published a line of greeting cards illustrated by Mollie Katzen, author/illustrator of the *Moosewood Cookbook.* Each card features a recipe inside.

- **Party invitations** — Dennis Kyte's *The Last Elegant Bear* is the basis for a line of party invitations produced by Cheers Workshop.

- **Gift wrap** — Harry N. Abrams offered *Giftwraps by Artists*, a series of wrapping-paper books created by noted artists, designers and craftspeople. Each book contained 16 sheets of wrapping paper plus an intro discussing the history and art of the patterns featured inside.

- **Gift tags** — Dover Publications, as part of its series of books featuring postcards, labels, stickers, and other stationery items, also publishes several books of gift tags.

- **Party goods** — Irena Chalmers Cookbooks licensed their logo to C. R. Gibson which imprinted the logo on a line of party goods, including paper plates, napkins, and gift tags. Chalmers then packaged some of these items with their cookbooks, thus giving them an opening into the gift and houseware departments of major department stores.

- **Labels, stickers, and decals** — Dover publishes a number of sticker and label books featuring images from the public domain such as Thomas Nast's Santa Claus and illustrations from *Alice in Wonderland*.

  Worcester Art Museum has a whole line of kitchen labels based on designs by such illustrators as George Cruikshank and Francois Millet.

  Broadman published a sticker book called *The Birth of Jesus* which includes 55 full-color reusable vinyl stickers.

- **Rubber stamps** — Inkadinkado manufacturers rubber stamps featuring illustrations by Edward Gorey. Kidstamps offers rubber stamps taken from children's book illustrations by Tomi DiPaola, Bill Peet, Sandra Boynton, and many others.

- **Bookmarks and bookplates** — Antioch Publishing built its business on its bookmarks featuring licensed and storybook characters.

- **Book bags and totes** — Ars Longa Productions produced a collection of silkscreened book bags featuring images from primitive as well as popular art.

  Afro-Bets offered sturdy canvas school bags imprinted with its Afro-Bets characters.

- **Miscellaneous paper items** — C. R. Gibson produces many paper goods featuring Beatrix Potter and Roger Tory Peterson (among others). These paper goods include photo albums, baby books, scrapbooks, diaries, notes, enclosures, gift wrap, and stationery.

  In its Little Gourmet series, Workman Publishing included such kits as the *Cookbook Lover's Kit* (with bookplates, helpers and recipe sheets), the *Kitchen Organizer* (a vinyl binder with stationery and note sheets), and the *Recipe Collector's Notebook*. Workman also offered *My First Travel Book* featuring a drawing pad, construction paper, and crayons.

19:07 Gifts and Accessories

While few publishers have ever manufactured gifts and accessories based on their books, some have licensed the rights to produce gifts to other companies. Here are some of the gift items that have been produced from books:

- **Mugs** — Andrews, McMeel & Parker currently markets *Sniglets* mugs through their Oz division. One of the mugs features the definition for "mugluk" — the stuff that collects in the bottom of coffee mugs that are not in use (i.e., peach pits, coins, old stamps, paper clips, etc.).
- **Figurines** — Royal Doulton produces china figurines, including a number of them based on characters from Beatrix Potter's books.
- **Jewelry** — Winnie the Pooh scrimshaw is available from Briarcliff Studios.
- **Music boxes** — Besides dishes, mugs, and figurines, Gorham also produces music boxes featuring Sesame Street and Paddington Bear.
- **Recipe boxes** — Cheers Workshop offers a recipe box decorated with illustrations from Dennis Kyte's *The Last Elegant Bear*. A Bear Paws cookie recipe is included inside the box.
- **Giftware** — Pelican Publishing offers Cajun Night giftware.
- **Miscellaneous items** — Butterfly Originals and Aviva Enterprises both offer many licensed products (Muppets, Garfield, Berenstain Bears, Snoopy), everything from sunglasses to banks, from pencil cases to erasers, from mirrors to small purses.

19:08 Clothing Related Items

T-shirts are the major clothing category that has been traditionally adapted from books. Dallas Alice offers screenprinted T-shirts featuring Babar, The Far Side, Bialosky and Friends, Beatrix Potter, and many other licensed characters as well as definitions from Workman's *Well-Defined Dictionary*. Art 101 offers Thousand Words T-shirts. Fairfax Prints markets Frank Frazetta T-shirt transfers.

But why should T-shirts be the only clothing adaptations? How about a "Fit for Life" exercise outfit? Or Stephen Birnbaum or Baedecker designer luggage? *Moosewood Kitchen* aprons? *The Cat in the Hat* hats? *Ball Four* baseball caps? *Paper Lion* football jerseys?

19:09 Food Related Items

With so many cookbooks published every year, why have there been so few cookbook related foods put on the market? The only one I am aware of is Cajun Magic Seasonings by Chef Paul Prudhomme. Are there any others? If not, why not? Certainly there should be some other gourmet foods that could tie into cookbooks. Or how about candies? Cookies? Breads? Other prepared food?

19:10 CMG Skin Care: An Example

Here's one final example of how a product can grow out of a line of books. Marjorie Ainsborough Decker, the Christian Mother Goose, wrote a number of books Christianizing basic fairy tales. Among her books are *Humpty Dumpty's Together Tales* about the togetherness of faith, *Nothing-Impossible-Possum Stories* about the positive power of faith, and *Grandpa Mole and Cousin Mole's Journeys* about the journey of faith.

Recently, in partnership with Ebenezer Toys, her press produced and marketed seven plush animals based on characters in her books. Finally, she also formulated three skin care products to ensure that "our precious children can have happy-soft skin." The three CMG Skin Care products included a body soap, a lotion, and an oil.

The moral of this story? Don't limit your vision. Almost anything can be related to your books if you take the time to make the connections that are most important to you (as either author or publisher). Take time to consider why you wrote or published a particular book. Then look to see if there are any other products, services, or ways of marketing that will help you to bring your message, idea, entertainment, or whatever to the attention of more people. Finally, decide whether you want to spend your time marketing this new product or service or you want to spend it writing and/or publishing a new book.

> **Authors** — If your book lends itself to some of these spinoffs, you might want to reserve merchandising rights for yourself — especially if you want to market the spinoffs yourself or license the rights to other companies. If so, make sure your contract retains these rights for you.

Chapter 20

Expansion Options for Publishers

As a publishing company grows, it begins to accumulate other resources besides its backlist of books and other knowledge besides its skill at editing and marketing books. Rather than let these other resources go to waste, you could make them an integral part of your publishing and marketing plans.

In Chapter 19, I have already described a number of different ways that book publishers can make use of their editing and marketing knowhow to create and distribute related products. In this chapter, I'd like to describe a few other ways that book publishers can expand on the basis of resources they accumulate as part of the publishing process.

20:01 Getting the Most from Your Mailing Lists

Time-Life Books's mailing lists are reportedly worth more than a million dollars in list rental income each year. That's about a dollar per name per year. What is your house list worth? Figure it out: At $50.00 per thousand, one name is worth five cents each time it is rented out. If you rent your house list twice a month (for a total of 24 times per year), your rental income would be $1.20 per name per year. Multiply that by the number of names on your house list, and you have a good estimate of what your house list could be worth.

You can, of course, rent your list for $60.00 or more per thousand. And you can rent it more than twice a month. A good list, in fact, can be rented three to four times a month with comparative ease, though most mail order experts would caution against renting your list out more often than that. Because you will want to mail your own offers to your in-house list, you don't want your list to get swamped with too much mail from other sources. Hence, about the maximum income you can expect to obtain from your house list is about $2.88 per name per year (at a cost of six cents per name, rented four times per month).

How do you go about renting your lists to other companies? There are two basic ways: 1) Handle it yourself, or 2) Let a list management company handle the maintenance and rental of your lists. Here are the ways a few major publishers have chosen to handle their house lists:

- Time-Life Books assigned its combined lists of over a million names to Woodruff-Stevens, a list management company which also handled lists for *Newsweek*, *McCall's*, Avon Fashions, Ideals Publishing Company, and Prentice-Hall.

- The Professional and Reference Division of McGraw-Hill appointed Mal Dunn Associates as the manager for its list of 391,000 names. Shepard's, a legal publishing subsidiary of McGraw-Hill, appointed CMG Information Services (a division of College Marketing Group) as its list manager.

- Dartnell rents out its own list of 120,000 active executive buyers. Its buyers have paid anywhere from $55.00 for a handbook to $635.00 for a training film. They update their list every day.

- Meredith Corporation has a separate division, Meredith List Marketing, which is responsible for maintaining and marketing their various house lists: 695,000 buyers of Frank Cawood health books, 15,000 active subscribers of *Prescription Drug News*, 220,000 buyers of the *Better Homes and Gardens Dieter's Cook Book*, and many other lists.

- Random House assigned its lists of book buyers to The Kleid Company, including over 22,000 buyers of Times Books (cookbooks, crossword puzzles, etc.), over 180,000 buyers of the *AMA Family Medical Guide*, and 24,000 buyers of the Audobon Society's *Encyclopedia of North American Birds*. The Kleid Company also handled the Simon & Schuster J.K. Lasser lists consisting of over half a million names.

- The Southwestern Company assigned its 315,000 1985 book buyers to Rubin Response Management Services. Southwestern's lists consisted primarily of women who had purchased high quality books (religion, reference, cooking and children's books), with an average order of $60.00.

- Better Health Publications gave Prescott List Management responsibility for managing its list of men who have bought a book on sexual nutrition. The list consists of 4,092 names of men over 50 years of age.

- Rodale offered its complete list of almost 8 million names through CompuName. Prices for their lists range from $55.00 per thousand for the total list to $60.00 per thousand for its subscriber lists to $75.00 per thousand for its multi-buyer lists.

- Enterprise Publishing has formed a separate division, Enterprise Lists, to handle list rentals and the production of a quarterly card deck. Its list consists of 215,000 book buyers and newsletter subscribers, all mail order generated buyers with an average purchase price of $44.00 (cash with order). They clean their list quarterly. They've rented their lists to *U.S. News and World Report*, Prentice-Hall, Xerox Corporation, *Boardroom Reports, Inc* magazine, and New England Business Services, among others.

- CareerTrack, a marketer of audio and video seminars, has its own sales teams that rents out its in-house list at the rate of 25 million names per year. At an average price of $80 per thousand, their annual income from list rentals would be $2 million.

- Ad-Lib Publications maintains and markets our own lists. Indeed, we sell both ways. We sell our list of book printers to book publishers via our *Directory of Book, Catalog, and Book Printers* and the computer mailmerge version of that *Directory*.

At the same time, we rent our list of buyers of the *Directory* to book printers. Since buyers of the *Directory* are clearly interested in buying book printing services, our list is the most targeted list in the industry for book printers to use. Currently, without any advertising at all, we rent our list about once a month. We feel that the rental of our list is a service to our customers since it puts them in touch with printers who are actively seeking short-run work from smaller publishers.

20:02 How to Market Your House Lists

If you turn over management of your lists to an outside list management service, they do all the marketing and promotion of the list, handle the updating of the list, and do all the fulfillment. You have only two responsibilities under such an arrangement: 1) to provide them with new and updated names on a regular basis (usually once a month), and 2) to approve the rental of your lists to any users (which means you have the responsibility to screen out any direct competitors or other companies who might make inappropriate offers to your lists).

Since many list management companies will not take on a list unless it has at least 25,000 names (or the potential to generate 25,000 names within a reasonable amount of time), you may have no choice but to handle your own lists. Even if your lists contain enough names, you may still prefer to keep your lists under your control. In such cases, here are some tips and suggestions on how to go about marketing your lists:

- Write letters directly to marketing managers at those companies which you feel would be most interested in using your lists. When describing your list, you should provide the following information if available:

1. The number of names on the list.

2. Whether the list consists of buyers or inquirers or both (with percentages).

3. To what kind of offer (or offers) did they respond.

4. What the average size of purchase was.

5. Dates of purchases (i.e., whether within the past three months, within the past year, within the last two years, or whatever).

6. Frequency of purchases (how many are multi-buyers, and can these names be rented separately).

7. Any information you have on the personal characteristics of the buyers (age, sex, occupation, median income).

Finally, let them know in what format the list is available (4-up cheshire, 2-up pressure sensitive, or whatever), in what ways the list can be sorted (by zip code, recency of purchase, multi-buyers, sex, income, or whatever), the cost per thousand, shipping charges, how payment is to be made, whether you guarantee accuracy of addresses (most lists guarantee a delivery rate of at least 95%), how often your list is cleaned, and the minimum number of names which may be ordered at one time.

To get a better idea of what information to provide and in what format, write for the media kits of several list owners and review how they describe their lists.

• Mail news releases describing your list to the major direct marketing and advertising magazines: *Direct Marketing, DM News, Direct, Target Marketing, Catalog Age, Catalog Business, Advertising Age*, and *Business Marketing*, among others.

• Advertise in these same magazines. Most of the major list owners and list brokers advertise regularly in these magazines. They wouldn't continue to advertise in these magazines if they were not getting a profitable response.

• Write for information on how to get listed in *Direct Mail List Rates & Data*. This directory, which describes over 55,000 different lists, is updated six times a year. Write to **Standard Rate & Data Service**, 3004 Glenview Road, Wilmette, IL 60091; (800) 323-4588. For a listing in the *Oxbridge Directory of Mailing Lists*, write to **Oxbridge Communications**, 150 Fifth Avenue #636, New York, NY 10011; (212) 741-0231.

• Inform major list brokers of the availability of your lists. **List brokers** are companies who act as intermediaries between list owners or managers and companies wanting to rent a list. While some brokers are also list managers, most are independent agents who make their money on the commission they receive from the list owner. The standard commission is 20% of the rental fee—a small price to pay for rentals you would not otherwise receive. Many of these list brokers are listed in the appendix of *Mail Order Selling Made Easier*.

• When you do send out your list for rental, be sure to seed your list with a few decoy names so you can track the usage of your list (to verify that the list renter only uses the list the one time, that the renter mails to the list within the time period stated in your contract, and to see that no unauthorized compiling of your lists occurs). These decoy names should be real people (friends, relatives, or associates) who can monitor their mail for any letters addressed to the code you have assigned them. Have them note the date they received the letter before they send it on to you.

If you'd rather not rely on friends or associates, there are companies which provide a similar service for a small annual fee plus a minimum charge per piece returned. Two such companies are:

U.S. Monitor Service, 86 Maple Avenue, New City, NY 10956-5092; (914) 634-1331.

National List Protection System, 16 Byron Place, Livingston, NJ 07039; (201) 992-6606.

20:03 Start Your Own Card Pack

As an adjunct to the rental of your mailing list and as an additional opportunity to promote your books, you could start your own card pack. Not only could you reserve as much as half the pack for your own titles, but you could also pay for the costs of the entire mailing by selling the remaining cards to noncompeting companies.

While you could start a card pack with as few as 10,000 names if the list is highly targeted, most such packs mail to at least 50,000 names. To publish a pack of 50 cards with a circulation of 50,000 would cost you between $20,000 and $30,000, depending on your in-house costs for marketing and administering the pack. Since each card you sell will bring in between $800.00 and $1000.00, you could pay for the entire pack by selling 25 to 30 cards.

To market your card pack, follow procedures similar to the steps listed above for marketing your mailing lists. Note, however, that your card pack should be listed in SRDS's *Card Pack Rates and Data* directory (which currently lists almost 600 card packs) rather than in its mailing list directory.

To learn more about starting up your own card pack, write to Solar Press for a copy of its booklet, *How to Publish a Direct Response Card Publication*. Solar Press is one of a number of card deck manufacturers:

• **Solar Press**, 11200 Frontenac Road, Naperville, IL 60566; (312) 983-1400; (800) 323-2751.

• **Preiss Printing Company**, 265 Bethpage-Spagnoli Road, Melville, NY 11747; (800) 645-9588; (516) 752-7100; (212) 895-4357.

- **Scoville Press,** 14505 - 27th Avenue N., Plymouth, MN 55441; (612) 553-1400.
- **Rose Printing Company,** 2503 Jackson Bluff, P. O. Box 5078, Tallahassee, FL 32314; (800) 227-3725; (904) 576-4151.
- **Collated Products Corporation,** 1300 Marros Road, Newark, DE 19711; (302) 731-4800.
- **Metropolitan Graphic Arts,** 930 Turrett Court, Mundelein, IL 60060; (800) 637-2659; (312) 674-8290.

Here's a list of a few book publishers with notes on how they handle the card packs they publish:

- John Wiley & Sons publishes three card decks which they market on their own: Engineers Action Cards (100,000 for $1,700), Financial Executive Action Cards (75,000 for $1,275), and Business/ Computer Action Cards (100,000 for $1,700).
- Enterprise Publishing offers the Enterprise Action Pack with a circulation of 100,000 for $1695 per card. Enterprise markets the pack on its own and also through Media Organization, a broker.
- Matthew Bender & Company markets its own card packs aimed at lawyers and accountants.
- Caddylak Systems markets its card pack of 100,000 book buyers through Direct Media List Management.
- Prentice-Hall offers four different card packs through Venture Communications. The four decks are: Prentice-Hall Business Management (100,000 circulation), Prentice-Hall Law (40,000), Prentice-Hall Tax (70,000), and Prentice-Hall Educators (100,000).
- McGraw-Hill offers its Business Leaders Direct Response Deck of 100,000 circulation through the management of Abelow Response. It also offers its Active Investor, Marketing Management, and Human Resources card packs through BRC Inc., another card pack management company.
- Rodale Books offers its Cookbook Buyers Pack through Leon Henry, a manager of lists and card packs.

20:04 Publish a Mail Order Catalog

If you are a smaller publisher with a limited number of titles of your own, you might consider organizing a catalog that includes related titles from other publishers. Keep the catalog focussed on a specific topic, such as health care, real estate, or child development. Start small, with perhaps only five or ten other titles, and expand as the demand requires. Besides using the catalog as a bounceback offer to your mail order customers, you might also offer it to targeted lists outside your own.

Here are a few examples of how other publishers are using catalogs to increase their income:

- Here at Ad-Lib, when we fulfill orders for our own books, we also enclose an 8-page brochure describing other books about printing, publishing, direct marketing, publicity, and advertising. We offer these books to help fill out our own line of books. Even though we only receive several thousand dollars a month in sales from this brochure, we still continue it because we feel it is a service to our customers.

- JLA Associates have put together a Small Business Success catalog which offers about thirty books and newsletters to help individuals start up and manage their own businesses. Currently, all orders received from the catalog are dropshipped direct from the original publisher. JLA stocks none of the books themselves.

- KTAV started the Jewish Gifts Catalogue, which includes not only books but also cookie cutters, games, crafts, toys, and gifts. Besides being sent to individual customers, the catalog is used by fundraising organizations within the Jewish community.

- Twenty First Century Publications advertises their catalog of new age and health-related titles in various national magazines. Along with their own titles, they also sell about 100 other titles from a number of different publishers. Since they also operate a bookstore, the books for the catalog do double duty as backup stock for the bookstore.

20:05 Other Mail Order Options for Directories

If you publish directories and other information resources, here are a few suggestions to help you to expand your services to those companies who are listed in your directories (or who advertise in your directories). These suggestions are taken from Russell Perkins's *Directory Publishing: A Practical Guide*.

- **Offer literature fulfillment services.** To make it easier for users of your directory to request information from different companies, you could offer to handle multiple requests for information. In such a case, you could fulfill all the requests yourself (by stocking appropriate literature from each participating company) or you could pass on the requests for information as they come in (just as many magazines now pass on requests for information via bingo cards inserted into the magazine). In either case, you would charge the companies for each request you fulfilled or passed on.

  The companies benefit by not having to add on extra staff to handle literature requests, and the users benefit by not having to write to many different sources.

- **Offer sample pack promotions.** Arrange to mail product samples from a number of different companies to all buyers of your directory. Under such an arrangement, each participating company would supply you with enough product samples (preferably small and unbreakable) to cover your user base. You would then mail out these samples with orders for the directory or as a separate mailing.

- **Include package inserts in all your outgoing mail.** While some companies might not want to advertise in your directory, they might be willing to pay you to stuff their promotional literature in with each outgoing order for your directory. They would provide you with sufficient inserts and pay you $40.00 or more per thousand inserts. If your directory has an annual circulation of 5,000 or more copies, a package insert broker could help you to locate interested companies. Here are the addresses of two well-known package insert brokers:

  Leon Henry Inc., 455 Central Avenue, Scarsdale, NY 10583; (914) 723-3176.

  Larry Tucker Inc., 607 Palisade Avenue, Englewood Cliffs, NJ 07632; (201) 569-8888.

- **Print discount coupons inside your directory.** For example, one publisher of an on-line database directory offers discount coupons for various database services. Not only are discount coupons an excellent way for advertisers to attract attention to their services, but they are also a bonus value for users of your directory (hence, they are an additional benefit that you can feature when advertising the directory). Here, again, you can use brokers to help you sell discount coupons. Russell Perkins recommends **Directory Discounts**, 2200 Union Center, Los Angeles, CA 90036.

20:06 Organize a Book Club

In 1986, book clubs sold over $698 million worth of books. Of the 200 or so book clubs now in existence, the majority are run as subsidiaries of book publishers, including the two biggest (Literary Guild and Book-of-the-Month Club). Here are a few examples:

- Macmillan recently sold its book club operation to NewBridge Communications which operates twelve different clubs for architects, astronomers, business executives, computer specialists, scientists, nurses, psychologists, owners of personal computers, and teachers.

- McGraw-Hill operates 7 different clubs, including ones for architects, personal computer owners, chemical engineers, civil engineers, electronics engineers, general engineers, and mechanical engineers.

- Time-Life Books owns Book-of-the-Month Club, BOMC Cooking and Crafts Book Club, Dolphin Book Club, Fortune Book Club, and Quality Paperback Book Club.

- The Mysterious Press joined with Book-of-the-Month Club to form the Mysterious Book Club.

- Doubleday/Bantam/Dell owns Literary Guild, Doubleday Book Club, Fireside Theater, International Collectors Library, Military Book Club, Science Fiction and Fantasy Book Club, Mystery Guild, and the Large Print Home Library.

- Watson-Guptil operates book clubs for artists, designers, and photographers.

- TAB Books operates the Aviators Guild, Computer Book Club, Electronics Book Club, and the How-to Book Club.

- Rodale offers the Prevention Book Club, Organic Gardening Book Club, Nature Book Society, and Practical Homeowner's Book Club.

- Other publishers offer clubs on dance (Princeton Book Company), ecology (Devin-Adair), history (Harcourt Brace Jovanovich), jewelers (Chilton), writing and art (Writers Digest Books), and religion (Word Books).

While book clubs would seem to be a natural extension of a book publishing program, there are many possible pitfalls to running a successful book club program. Indeed, Prentice-Hall recently sold their line of book clubs because they were not profitable enough.

20:07 Become a Distributor

Quite a few smaller book publishers have become distributors simply because they wanted to get better distribution for their own titles, especially outside the ordinary book trade channels. Since it usually doesn't cost any more to distribute fifty titles as does to distribute five titles, the publishers began to take on titles from other publishers as well. Similarly, some major publishers have agreed to distribute the books of smaller publishers to help cover their costs in setting up their own network of house sales representatives.

Should you become a distributor? That all depends on how much time you want to devote to working with other publishers to bring their books before the markets you are already approaching. To justify the expense and additional work load, you will probably need at least a 55% to 65% discount. Remember that you will not only have the costs of marketing the books, but you will have to pay warehousing, fulfillment, collection, and accounting costs as well.

To give you an idea of the variety of approaches publishers have taken in distributing books, here are a few examples:

- Gryphon House distributes children's books from over 80 publishers (16 of which are distributed under an exclusive arrangement). They use no sales reps, but rather distribute all books through mail order (via catalogs, book club programs, and book fairs). Gryphon sells to the library market, early childhood centers, and elementary schools.

• Samuel Weiser distributes books on metaphysics, astrology, the occult, health, and other subjects for over 200 different publishers. Most books are distributed on a nonexclusive basis to bookstores, other retail accounts, and individual book buyers.

• The Wilderness Press has added other publishers' titles that fit in with its line of trail guides and outdoor how-to books. All titles are distributed via such wholesalers as Bookpeople and also through a group of commissioned sales representatives. They sell more books through backpacking, skiing, and other sporting goods shops than they do through bookstores.

• In section 12:10 earlier in this book, we also listed the names of a number of major publishers who distribute books from smaller publishers to the book trade. In most cases, these major publishers use their own in-house reps to promote the titles of other publishers as well. Among these major publishers are Harper & Row, Random House, W. W. Norton, Farrar Straus Giroux, and Simon & Schuster.

• Voyageur Press recently began distributing books from other publishers. Ad-Lib Publications is one of Voyageur's first clients.

20:08 Operate Bookstores

In the early days of American publishing, publishers and bookstores were essentially one and the same. The bookstores published books which they then sold. Few other publishers even existed. Nowadays, few publishers own bookstores. Yet operating a bookstore would seem to be a natural outgrowth of some publishers' activities.

On the other side of the coin, in order to serve their local clientele and to fill gaps they see in the books now produced by publishers, a number of bookstores have begun publishing books. One bookstore in Tennessee published their own regional title which sold quite well. The Mysterious Book Shop started its own publishing arm. And Waldenbooks publishes a number of books under its own Longmeadow imprint.

Here are a few examples of bookstores operated by book publishers:

• Penguin operates seven company-owned stores in England and has recently franchised its first U.S. bookshop in Cambridge, Massachusetts. I would expect more Penguin franchised bookstores to come out of Penguin's promotion of its bookstore boutiques.

• Twenty First Century Publications operates a local bookstore here in Fairfield, Iowa. The bookstore grew out of their mail order catalog business. Since they were already stocking a wide variety of books for their catalog business, they decided to open a retail outlet as well.

- Llewellyn Publications has operated a bookstore in downtown Saint Paul, Minnesota for a good number of years. Llewellyn also publishes a mail order catalog featuring books on astrology and the occult, including titles from other publishers.

- Besides publishing their own books and a regional arts newspaper called *Uncle Jam*, Fragments West also operates The Cobblestone Gallery, a book and card shop. In this case I'm not sure which came first, the publisher or the bookstore.

- Dover Publications operates a bookstore at their publishing headquarters in New York. Because they publish so many titles themselves, the bookstore only features their own books.

- In the basement of its New York headquarters building, McGraw-Hill operates one of the best technical/professional bookstores in the country.

- Bantam Doubleday Dell recently sold the Doubleday Book Shop chain to B. Dalton.

- Globe Pequot Press operates the Globe Corner Bookstore, a travel specialty bookstore in Boston.

20:09 Publish a Newsletter or Magazine

Many book publishers also publish magazines (or newsletters, or newspapers), and many magazine publishers also publish books. Here are just a few of them: Time-Life Books, Atlantic Monthly Press, McGraw-Hill, Chilton Books, Rodale Press, Fragments West, Prentice-Hall, Reader's Digest Books, Field Publications, R. R. Bowker, Modern Handicraft, Motorbooks International, Dustbooks, Our Sunday Visitor, Parents Magazine Press, Warren Gorham & Lamont, Watson-Guptill, Williams & Wilkins, H. W. Wilson, Enterprise Publishing, Verbatim Books, Consumer Guide Books, Matthew Bender, and Writers Digest Books.

One of the advantages of publishing newsletters and magazines is that they can provide you with material for new books. Not only can you create books by collecting articles together under a general theme, but you can also develop books out of major articles in your magazine. Magazines also put you into contact with some of the best writers in the subjects you specialize in publishing. Hence, you have a means to draw upon the best talent for your books.

Magazines and newsletters also give you a strong promotional base for marketing any new books you publish. Certainly Writers Digest Books makes good use of its connection with the magazine. McGraw-Hill also makes good use of the magazines it publishes, including *BYTE* and *Popular Computing*, to promote its new computer books. At the very least, you can use any unsold ad space to advertise your books.

● Howard J. Ruff sent $2.00 discount coupons to the readers of his newsletter, *Financial Success Report*, to promote one of his new books. The coupons, though, were only good if the readers bought the book at one of the major chain stores such as B. Dalton or Waldenbooks. As a result of this promotion, his book soon rose to the top of the chain's bestseller lists. Once on these lists, it didn't take long for the book to also appear on other major bestseller lists including the *New York Times* list.

● Free Spirit Publishing started a newsletter for gifted teenagers, their parents and teachers that supplements their *Gifted Kids Survival Guides* and other books.

● The *Book Marketing Update* and *Book Promotion Hotline* newsletters grew out of a need to keep our book marketing series (*1001 Ways to Market Your Books*, *Book Publishing Resource Guide*, and *Book Marketing Made Easier*) up-to-date. Since then, they have grown into a full-fledged independent entity—and profit center.

20:10 Miscellaneous Businesses

Here's a list of a few other businesses that publishers have gone into at one time or another. You might find that some of them will fit well into your own expansion plans.

● **Advertising agencies**—Some publishers have formed advertising agencies to take advantage of the standard 15% agency discount for placing advertisements in magazines.

On the other hand, Ad-Lib Publications grew out of Ad-Lib Consultants, which was a consulting service specializing in the design, development, and promotion of toys and gifts. While the consulting part of our business is now only a small part of our operation, it still functions as our advertising agency (as well as serving a few other smaller companies).

● **Export representatives**—Feffer and Simons, one of the major export representatives for books, was a subsidiary of Doubleday before Baker & Taylor bought it. Both HarperCollins and John Wiley & Sons have international subsidiaries which function as foreign agents for a number of other publishers.

● **List management services**—Meredith Corporation has a division, Meredith List Marketing which not only handles the management and marketing of its own list but also manages a variety of independently owned lists. Business Mailers Inc., a major supplier of lists of medical professionals, is a subsidiary of Macmillan.

● **Telemarketing services**—Grolier Telemarketing, a subsidiary of Grolier, offers inbound and outbound telemarketing services to other companies.

- **Printing**—Acropolis Books also operates Colortone Press, a high quality four-color printing company. Williams & Wilkins is a division of Waverly Press, another book printer. Offset Paperback Book Manufacturers and Delta Lithograph are divisions of the same company that owns Bantam Doubleday Dell.

  Eerdmans Publishing, Westview Press, Naturegraph Publishers, and Rand McNally are other publishers who also print books. If you own a printing press and are not using it fully for the production of your own books, it makes sense to use the unfilled time to produce books for other publishers.

- **Real estate agencies**—Meredith Corporation, publishers of *Better Homes and Gardens*, has franchised BH&G real estate agencies all over the country.

- **Radio shows**—Tyndale House Publishers produces *First Edition*, an author interview show.

- **Licensing**—Rather than licensing a specific book title, Rand McNally licensed the company name for a series of travel videos from Lightning Video. Because it was giving its name to the series, it had full approval rights on all videos that were sold under its name and received royalties on all copies sold.

- **Brand name products**—You don't have to license your company name to take advantage of its brand name; you can develop and market your own brand name products. Of course, before you can do that, you have to build up and promote your company name as a brand name. That takes time, money, and commitment.

- **Speakers bureau**—Matthew Bender and Company, a legal publisher, has formed a speakers bureau for its authors. They book their authors for media appearances as well as seminars and other meetings. Why not form your own speakers bureau as well?

As you read the next chapter, you might come up with some other ideas for new products and services that your company can develop. For example, how about giving seminars (or setting up a conference or trade show)? Or how about offering consulting services? Or how about establishing an institute (such as the Writers Digest Writing School)?

Even though the next chapter is directed primarily at authors, book publishers should also find it interesting. Read on. But before you do, the following section presents one more consideration for expansion-minded publishers.

20:11 To Buy or To Sell—That Is the Question

Perhaps one of the quickest ways to expand is to buy up other publishing companies (or other companies outside the publishing field). Thus,

Bantam bought Doubleday; Maxwell bought Macmillan; Random House bought Knopf, Crown, and others; Viking Penquin bought New American Library; Putnam bought Family Line, Inc.; Simon & Schuster bought Prentice Hall; and so on.

But you don't have to be one of the major companies to participate in this merger mania. Many mid-size publishers have also expanded through buying other companies.

- Addison-Wesley recently bought Aris Books, a publisher of fancy cookbooks.

- Globe Pequot Press, through editorial acquisitions and through buying various regional publishing houses such as East Woods Press, is planning to become the largest publisher of regional titles in the country.

Of course, the flip side of this question is to decide when and if you will sell out to another publisher. Why would you ever want to sell out? Here are several reasons why publishers have sold out to other publishers:

1) **Personal reasons**—With smaller companies owned and managed by one or two principals, sometimes personal reasons cause them to sell their company. Perhaps because of a major illness. Or because they have other things they want to do with their lives. Or because of family demands.

2) **Financial reasons**—Some smaller companies go bankrupt for one reason or another, or they get overloaded with debt. The only way to survive is to sell out to another publisher. If the smaller publisher is a corporation, there is also the possibility of a hostile takeover.

3) **Growth reasons**—Many smaller publishers continually live on a shoestring, from one month to the next, never quite able to expand as they would like to. By selling to a larger company that has the money and other resources to finance expansion, a smaller publisher can finally realize its full potential for growth.

4) **Temptation beyond reason**—Sometimes another publisher comes along with a truckload of cash that simply can't be ignored. So the smaller publisher succumbs to temptation and sells the company.

Selling out, then, does not need to be a disaster. Indeed, it may all be part of your company's (or your own) growth cycle.

Chapter 21

Authors: How to Capitalize on Your Books

My advice is not to create something totally different from what you are now selling until you have pursued every means of marketing your existing information. The best strategy is to repackage your bestselling, proven products and market them to a brand new audience. . . .

Don't be shy about selling your repackaged information for a higher price. People want your information but may not have the time or desire to read a book. They will gladly pay more to get the same information presented in a convenient form. That's why you see the exact same information sold as a $10 book, a $25 cassette series, a $40 non-credit course, a $75 videotape, a $100 newsletter, a $150 per hour consultation, a $250 seminar, etc.

— Mark Nolan, *Information Marketing Newsletter*

No other publication establishes the credentials of an author the way the publication of a book does. Until you've written a book and had it published, you will always be an incomplete writer in the eyes of many people. Why is this? I don't know. Perhaps it's because books are more substantial, more impressive. Maybe it's because the book stands or falls on your work alone. Whatever the reason, you should be ready to capitalize on the increase recognition that publication of a book gives your work.

This chapter lists some of the ways that you can use your new-found recognition to expand the audience for your creative endeavors — and make more money in the process. While some of these opportunities will come your way unasked, don't wait for them to happen. Instead, envision what you really want, and then create it on your own.

21:01 Sell Your Writing Skills

Once you have demonstrated that you can write a book that merits
publishing, you will find that many new opportunities begin to open up for
you in the writing field. Here are just a few of them:

- You'll finally be able to convince a literary agent to take on your work.
  Few agents will represent authors who only produce short pieces
  simply because there's not enough money in selling articles and short
  stories. The agents have to be able to justify the time and money they
  spend on representing their clients. Representing one book is more
  cost-effective for them than trying to sell dozens of articles to generate
  the same amount of income.

- Magazine editors will take you more seriously since you have
  demonstrated that you can produce major works. Also, by getting your
  book published, you've passed a screening test far more rigorous than
  any magazine writer. Your book is one out of 35,000 new titles, while a
  magazine article is only one out of half a million or more features.

- With the publication of your book, you become an instant expert.
  Again, I'm not sure why this is the case, but it is a fact of life. People
  will seek you out for advice. Editors will pay more attention to your
  article proposals, especially those having to do with your area of expertise (as indicated by your book). You might even find yourself
  teaching Ph.D. candidates even though you have nothing more than a
  B.A. or high school diploma.

- You'll also find more doors open to you in the business world and
  other areas where your knowledge and/or writing skills (again, as
  evidenced by your book) are needed. Indeed, you could well be offered job opportunities that are more in line with what you really want
  to do with your life.

- A published book will increase your chances of obtaining grants to
  continue developing your skills as a poet or fiction writer. Foundations
  and other organizations are more willing to support authors who have
  demonstrated that they can produce a significant amount of work.

21:02 One Book Two Ways

Once you have established your reputation as an expert on one subject, why not write another book on the same subject. Not only is it easier
to write another book on the same subject, but you will also be able to use
many of the same contacts to promote, market, and distribute your new
book. Just as a publisher benefits from specializing in specific areas, so
can a writer.

Here are a few examples of how other writers have drawn upon their previous books to create new books:

• Sheldon Gerstenfeld, a veterinarian, wrote one book on *Taking Care of Your Cat*. Then, using much of the same information and advice, he wrote another book on *Taking Care of Your Dog*. Both books used the same cover design, format, and style (thus saving the publisher time and money in designing and producing the books). Later, Gerstenfeld wrote still another book, *The Bird Care Book*, which incorporated much of the same information and made use of the same book design.

• Archie Satterfield and Eddie Bauer put together three related books for Addison-Wesley, all using the same format and design. The first book, *The Eddie Bauer Guide to Cross-Country Skiing*, was followed by two other books aimed at a more general audience, *The Eddie Bauer Guide to Family Camping* and *The Eddie Bauer Guide to Backpacking*.

• When Durk Pearson and Sandy Shaw wrote their book on *Life Extension*, they filled it with many complicated and technical articles, which made the book difficult for the average reader to follow. Nonetheless, the book sold over a million copies. To make the information in the book more accessible to the average person, they wrote a second book, *The Life Extension Companion*, which used less technical language to make the same points as the first book. Recently, they've written a third book, *The Life Extension Weight Loss Program*, to reach an even greater audience.

• This book you're now reading could easily be adapted to address two new markets. If I ever get the time and incentive to follow up on the idea, I'd like to write a second book aimed at small businesses, to be titled *1001 Ways to Sell Almost Anything*, and a third book aimed at consultants and other professionals, to be titled *1001 Ways to Sell Yourself (and Your Services)*. Though each book would be organized in the same way and draw upon much of the same information, the detailed resources and examples would be different. While any business or professional could gain many insights and ideas from reading this book, they'd gain even more from reading a book aimed directly at them.

• It's possible to write one book aimed, for instance, at doctors and another one aimed at patients. Both books could contain much of the same information; only the angle of approach would be different. For instance, in my *Directory of Book Printers* I included several sections giving publishers pointers on how to select a book printer and work with that printer to produce a high quality yet inexpensive book. Recently I've taken that same information and adapted it to a report aimed at printers who want to develop more short-run business. The report, *How to Sell Your Short-Run Production Services to Book Publishers*, shows book printers how to adapt their advertising and actual capabilities to serve the short-run needs of book publishers.

- Peter McWilliams essentially wrote the same book three different times. First he wrote *The Word Processing Book*, then *The Personal Computer Book*, and then *The Personal Computer in Business Book*. While each book contained much of the same information, each was aimed at a different market. Each, in turn, became a national best-seller. He even followed up the word processing book with another book, *Questions and Answers on Word Processing*, based on questions readers had asked him to answer. Later, he published a special edition of the word processing book for the IBM computer, *Word Processing on the IBM*.

21:03 Self-Publishing Successes

For those of you who are thinking of self-publishing your own book, here are a few examples of other writers who have done so successfully— and then sold their book to a major publisher in order to gain even wider distribution.

- Norman Dacey self-published *How to Avoid Probate* and sold 10,000 copies on his own before the book was picked up by Crown, who then went on to sell over a million copies of the book.

- After having triple bypass surgery at the age of 32, Joseph Piscatella was forced to change his eating habits. As a result, he and his wife developed 400 recipes for foods low in salt, sugar, and fat. In the spring of 1983, he self-published 5,000 copies of *Don't Eat Your Heart Out*. Within a month the entire edition had sold out. Later that fall Workman Publishing published the book, printing 30,000 copies in their first edition. Since that time, they've sold well over 170,000 copies of the book at the rate of about 6,000 copies per month.

- Mildred Newman and Bernard Berkowitz self-published *How to Be Your Own Best Friend*. The book sold so well in their local area (the West Coast) that Random House paid them a $60,000 advance for the rights to publish the book nationally.

- When Jim Everroad lost his job as a high school athletic coach, he decided to become a sportswriter. The first job he tackled was to write an article describing the exercises he had developed to tighten his pot belly. After selling the article to a newspaper, he expanded it into a full book (6,000 words plus several dozen photographs) and printed a first edition of 3,000 copies. That edition sold so quickly that he ordered another edition of 50,000 copies, which he sold primarily in his own home region of Indiana. Later the book was discovered by Price/Stern/Sloan who published a national edition of the book, which became a bestseller. The book has since sold over 2,000,000 copies.

- Spencer Johnson and Kenneth Blanchard originally self-published *The One Minute Manager* because they wanted to sell their book at a $15.00 cover price (a price few major publishers would have dared set for such a slim book). After they had sold more than 20,000 copies of the book in a very short time, seventeen publishers bid for the rights to republish the book. Since then, the book has sold millions of copies and been on the bestseller lists for both hardcovers and trade paperbacks.

- After twenty years in show business, Mike Martineau self-published his own novel, *The Strokers*, about the rise to stardom of a British rock musician. He started out by distributing the novel only to bookstores in the Virgin Islands where he lived. Tourists there bought out the first and second printings of the novel (one store sold over 7,000 copies alone). Hallmark Press, a Miami publisher, then took over the publication of the book. Meanwhile, Martineau sold movie rights to Joseph E. Levine Presents for a $25,000 option against a final pickup price of $250,000. He also received $35,000 for writing the screenplay for the movie.

- When he began having problems keeping up with orders for his self-published book, *How to Keep Your Volkswagen Alive: A Manual of Step-by-Step Procedures for the Compleat Idiot*, John Muir asked his friend Ken Luboff to take over. John Muir Publications has now sold over 2 million copies of the book.

- Wess Roberts paid for and promoted four printings of his book, *Leadership Secrets of Attila the Hun*. After getting a strong endorsement for the book from H. Ross Perot, Roberts decided to approach New York publishers once again. As a result, Warner Books featured the book as their hardcover lead title for March, 1989, and the book went on to become a bestseller. Foreign rights sales were made to publishers in England, Holland, Spain, Germany, Norway, Sweden, Mexico, and Brazil, among others. Total advances ran into six figures. Plus Literary Guild bought book club rights, Nightingale-Conant bought audio rights, and *Success* magazine bought first serial rights.

- Here are just a few other books that were originally self-published and went on to become bestsellers:
  Feed Me, I'm Yours by Vicki Lansky
     (now published by Bantam)
  The Handbook of Higher Consciousness by Ken Keyes, Jr.
  Looking Out for #1 by Robert Ringer
  Mary Ellen's Best of Helpful Hints by Mary Ellen Pinkham
     (now published by Warner)
  What Color is Your Parachute by Richard Nelson Bolles
     (now published by Ten Speed Press)
  You Can Heal Your Life by Louise Hay

21:04 How to Make Money on Remainders

Unless your book becomes a steady backlist seller, your book will sooner or later be dropped by your publisher. You then have the choice to let the book die at a remainder house or to buy up the remainder copies yourself and try to promote them on your own. If you do decide to promote them on your own, you will become, in effect, your own publisher. You can then use many of the tips and suggestions in this book to market your book.

Exposition Press, a vanity press, has a division which specializes in distributing remaindered books for authors who buy up the stock from their publishers. They pay 50% royalty for all books sold by them. For more information, contact **Imprint Publishers**, 1701 Blount Road, Section C, Pompano Beach, FL 33069; (305) 979-3277.

21:05 Syndicating Your Expertise

Having a book published establishes your credentials both as a writer and as an expert. You can use both these credentials to syndicate your knowledge via radio stations and newspapers or to obtain a position as a commentator on a radio or TV show.

Here are a few examples of what other authors have done:

- **Syndicated newspaper columns** — Mary Ellen Pinkham, author of a number of books on helpful hints, writes a syndicated column that is carried by over 125 newspapers with a combined circulation of well over ten million readers.

  Peter McWilliams, author/publisher of a number of computer books, wrote a weekly column on personal computers for the Universal Press Syndicate. The column was carried by over 75 newspapers with a circulation of ten million, making him one of the most widely read computer journalists in the country.

  Tom Peters, co-author of *In Search of Excellence*, wrote a weekly syndicated newspaper column on business management for the Tribune Company.

- **Television features** — Besides the weekly newspaper column, Tom Peters also appeared weekly on the cable TV show, *Business Times*.

  After publishing her books on helpful hints, Mary Ellen Pinkham joined *Good Morning America* for two years as a commentator on helpful hints for the home.

- **Syndicated television show** — Howard Ruff, author of *How to Prosper During the Coming Bad Years*, had a nationally syndicated TV show, *Ruff Times*.

- **Syndicated radio series** — Beverly Nye, self-publisher of *A Family Raised on Sunshine*, syndicated her own series of shows on homemaking tips to radio stations across the country. Not only did the radio stations pay her royalties for airing the show, but she was able to use the show to plug her own books.

- **Magazine columnist** — Herschell Gordon Lewis, author of *Direct Mail Copy That Sells* and *More Than You Ever Wanted to Know about Mail Order Advertising*, writes a regular column for *Direct Marketing* magazine. At the end of each column, the magazine prints a short biography which plugs his books and his copywriting services.

  I write a regular book review column for *Small Press* magazine. Not only do I get paid for writing the column, but I also get regular exposure to one of the prime audiences for my books on marketing and publishing.

  Lear's magazine ran a monthly feature based on *Bradshaw On: The Family* by John Bradshaw. Bradshaw also prepared a series based on this book for the Public Broadcasting System.

- **Newsletter columnist** — For two years I wrote a regular column about book marketing for the COSMEP newsletter. Although I received no compensation for this column, I did receive a short plug for my books.

21:06 Publish Your Own Newsletter

Once you've established your expertise, you might consider publishing a newsletter, especially if your expertise is in a rapidly changing field. Newsletters can command high prices and, because they are shorter than books, can be easier to produce. The major drawback to newsletters is that they do require a long-haul commitment to meeting deadlines (whether monthly, bimonthly, or quarterly). Because of the high startup costs of getting subscribers, it's not worth publishing a newsletter if you don't intend to continue publishing it for at least two years.

For more information on publishing newsletters, write to the following two resources: **The Newsletter Associaton**, 1401 Wilson Boulevard #403, Arlington, VA 22209; (703) 527-2333 (publishers of the *Hotline* newsletter); and **Newsletter Clearinghouse**, 44 West Market Street, Rhinebeck, NY 12572; (914) 876-2081 (publishers of the *Newsletter on Newsletters*).

- Howard Ruff's *Financial Success Report* at one time had 115,000 subscribers paying $109.00 per year (that works out to over $12 million per year in subscription income).

- Pam Young and Peggy Jones, authors of *Sidetracked Home Executives*, publish a bimonthly newsletter, *S.H.E.s On Track*, which helps to promote their other books, cassette tapes, and Home Executive Kit.

● For several years Robert Ringer, author/publisher of *Winning Through Intimidation*, *Looking Out for #1*, and *Restoring the American Dream*, published a newsletter, *The Tortoise Report*, which was essentially an expression of his personal philosophy. Several hundred thousand subscribers paid $59.00 per year for the monthly newsletter.

21:07 Speak Out Your Knowledge

As the author of a book, you will often be asked to speak before groups. At some point you will have to decide if you will charge for your speaking services or continue to offer them gratis. To be honest, the lecture circuit could provide you with more income than your writing. For instance, Mary Cunningham, author of *Powerplay*, commands $10,000 per speaking engagement. Angela Davis, Betty Friedan, Jane Fonda, and Joan Mondale all get $5,000 per talk.

To learn more about earning money as a speaker, read Jeffrey Lant's book, *Money Talks* or Herman Holtz's *Speaking for Profit*. If you decide to get serious about a career as a speaker, explore the following resources:

● **National Speakers Association**, 3877 N. 7th Street #350, Phoenix, AZ 85014; (602) 265-1001. The association for professional speakers.

● **International Platform Association**, P. O. Box 250, Winnetka, IL 60093-9990; (312) 446-4321. Since 1831, the professional association of the lecture circuit.

● **Toastmasters International**, P. O. Box 9052, Mission Viejo, CA 92690; (714) 858-8255. Contact them to get the address for a local group where you can build your speaking skills before a supportive group.

● *Sharing Ideas Among Professional Speakers*, 18825 Hicrest Road, P. O. Box 1120, Glendora, CA 91740; (800) 438-1242; (818) 335-8069. Dottie Walters, editor and publisher of this newsletter, also operates Walters International Speakers' Bureau.

Here are a number of ways to earn money as a speaker:

● **Engage a lecture agent to represent you.** Like other agents, they work on a commission (usually anywhere from 15% to 30%). For a list of such agents, see the appendix of Jeffrey Lant's *Unabashed Self-Promoter's Guide* or Richard Weiner's *Professional's Guide to Public Relations Services*.

● **Register with speakers bureaus** who work on a nonexclusive basis. Speakers bureaus assist organizations looking for speakers to address their meetings and conventions. When they book a speaking engagement for you, the speakers bureau will charge a percentage of your speaking fee (generally somewhere between 20% and 30%).

- **The possibilities for speaking are almost endless.** Not only can you speak at local club meetings, but you can also speak for sales meetings, seminars, conventions, association meetings, company training programs, on cruise ships, and anywhere else that people go to find useful information. Almost every company and association has need of speakers at least once a year (for their annual conference or meeting) and many require speakers more often than that (for monthly sales meetings, training programs, and other educational seminars).

- **Organize your own seminars.** Once you've had some experience as a speaker, you might consider setting up seminars, such as the "Implementing In Search of Excellence" seminars (informally known as skunkcamps) put on by Tom Peters. The skunkcamps are only one of five services offered by the Tom Peters Group; the other four are consulting, research, publishing, and audio/video products.

  Gordon Burgett conducts hundreds of seminars every year. All of his seminars and books cover the same subjects: freelance writing, travel writing, making money as a speaker, and giving seminars. His speaking seminar is now available as an audiotape course. For more information, write to **Communications Unlimited**, P.O. Box 6405, Santa Maria, CA 93456; (805) 937-8711.

- **Offer workshops.** For instance, the author/publisher of *Christmas in the Air* offers a Christmas workshop every fall.

- **Organize your own conventions.** That's what Howard Ruff did. In the late 1970's he organized a number of Ruff Times National Conventions featuring well-known political and business figures giving advice on how to survive in the coming hard times. The cost for the full three-day convention in 1979 was $95.00. Many conventions, of course, charge much more than that.

21:08 Making Money as a Teacher

While speaking before large groups might pay better, teaching classes can often be more fulfilling. Teaching is an especially good way to gain experience talking before groups, and it is possible to arrange the classes you teach so you are well compensated for your time. Here are a number of possibilities:

- **Teach continuing education classes** for adults. Most high schools and colleges offer evening and weekend courses for adults who are not able to attend classes during the day. These continuing education courses are usually noncredit courses, so even if you don't have a teaching certificate, you may still teach these classes. Indeed, as an author, you are probably more experienced and qualified than many of the other people teaching such courses.

Since most schools charge students a fee (anywhere from $20 to $50) for a three to ten hour course, the teacher usually gets paid a portion of the course fees collected (anywhere from 30% to 60%). Hence, if 30 students were to take one of your courses, you could well make $500 or more for a five hour course. Plus, you can assign your book as the textbook for the course and gross another $300 or more. Since you will undoubtedly be teaching a course related to your book, it is certainly reasonable to draw upon your book as the course text.

Another benefit of teaching continuing education classes is that your course (and book) will be publicized before as many as a million potential customers. For instance, when a large university system offers your course in its continuing education program, it might send out catalogs announcing its courses to an entire metropolitan community.

Many of the seminars that Gordon Burgett teaches every year are offered through colleges and continuing education programs.

Joyce Carlisle, author/publisher of *The Avocado Lovers' Cookbook*, has taught a course on Cookbook Publishing and Marketing through the Open University. The fee for the one-day course was $55.00.

• **You could also teach correspondence courses** like the ones offered by the Writer's Digest School.

• If you write cooking, craft, or how-to books, you could arrange to **teach classes at local stores,** community centers, or shopping centers.

Jack Mandel, author of the *Arts, Fine Crafts, and Collectibles Directory*, regularly teaches business workshops at Bloomingdale's and Macy's department stores. Not only do they pay him to put on the workshop, but they also pay for the books used in the workshop.

• **You could even open your own school.** For example, if you write cookbooks, why not open a cooking school. Not only could the school bring in additional money, but it could also give you a place to test new recipes or cooking techniques.

One thing I've learned in all the years I've taught classes and spoken before groups is that the teacher always learns more than the student. This, perhaps, is the strongest argument that can be made for teaching at least a few classes a year. You will always come away from such classes with renewed enthusiasm for your subject, renewed interest and, if my experience is any indication, a mind bursting with ideas for new books. So, get out there and enjoy.

21:09 Making Money as a Consultant

If you are not comfortable speaking before large groups, you can still put your expertise to work as a consultant. No matter what your subject area, somewhere at sometime someone is going to need your expertise — and be willing to pay well for your services.

To learn more about setting yourself up as a consultant, read Jeffrey Lant's book, *The Consultant's Kit*, Herman Holtz's *How to Succeed as an Independent Consultant*, or Kate Kelly's *How to Set Your Fees and Get Them*. All three books are superb.

You might also want to subscribe to *Consulting Opportunities Journal*, P. O. Box 430, Clear Spring, MD 21722; (301) 791-9332.

Here are a few ways other writers and publishers are putting their expertise to work as consultants:

- **Become a consultant** — Sheilah Kaufman, author of eleven cookbooks including *Sheilah's Fearless Fussless Cooking*, does consulting for gourmet food, gift, and houseware companies. She also travels around the country teaching cooking classes.

  Besides producing about 50 seminars every year on construction estimating and project management, the R. S. Means Company also publishes software and offers consulting services (where they send experts to work with construction companies on site).

- **Offer consulting services via the mail** — Herschell Gordon Lewis, author of a number of books on direct marketing, has his own business called Communicomp, which offers direct mail copywriting for a wide variety of companies and organizations including the UN Children's Fund, Grolier Enterprises, Heritage House, and American Bankers Insurance Company. All his business is conducted through the mail and by phone.

- **Offer consulting services via the phone** — The Beckley Group offered their Million Dollar Advisory Service via a toll-free phone number to all subscribers of their Beckley Report newsletter. Any subscriber could call at any time to get advice from one of their trained real estate advisors.

  As the author of a number of books on book marketing as well as the editor and publisher of the *Book Marketing Update* and *Book Promotion Hotline* newsletters, I also offer consulting advice via the phone to anyone having questions about book publishing and marketing. For this service, I charge $100.00 per hour (or, in effect, $1.67 for each minute it takes to answer your questions).

- **Franchise your consulting services** — Carole Jackson, author of the multi-million copy bestseller, *Color Me Beautiful*, has franchised Color Me Beautiful consultants all over the country. When Acropolis Books came out with a new book, *Always in Style with Color Me Beautiful* by Doris Pooser, their 30-city publicity campaign was fully supported by Color Me Beautiful consultants in each of those cities.

- **Establish an institute** — John Naisbitt, author of the bestselling book *Megatrends*, has organized an institute to study trends. The institute offers consulting services, a newsletter, and seminars, plus a number of annual reports.

One of Tom Peter's five businesses, as noted above, is a research institute. The institute provides research data and other information to support the other businesses in his group.

- **Establish a center**—Jed Diamond, author of *Inside Out: Becoming My Own Man*, and Carlin Diamond, author of *Love It, Don't Label It*, have organized the Center for Prospering Relationships to promote the principles and practices they believe in. Both books were published by their own press, Fifth Wave Press.

  Lee and Marlene Canter, who started off by self-publishing their first book *Assertive Discipline: A Take Charge Approach for Today's Educator*, have since trained over 400,000 educators in their Assertive Discipline program.

- **Form an association**—Chase Revel formed the American Entrepreneur's Association to promote his line of business start-up manuals. Through the association's *Entrepreneur* magazine and other services, it actually provides much support for business newcomers.

21:10 Become a Legal Expert Witness

A number of authors have found a lucrative sideline income from appearing as expert witnesses for various legal questions. As a legal expert, you may be called upon to investigate cases, testify at trials, give depositions, counsel attorneys, or provide other advice either by mail or over the phone. The standard fee for such work is around $100 or more an hour. If you have to go out of town to do on-site investigations or testify at a trial, the standard fee is anywhere from $500 to a $1000 per day, plus expenses.

How do you become an expert witness? First, of course, you need to be an expert. While writing a book on a particular subject will authenticate your expertise, you should also have a lot of experience in that subject because you will have to stand up to cross examinations in court. Being an expert witness can be hard work since you must do your homework for each case, so if you are not enthusiastic about studying or learning more about your subject, you should not get into this field.

If you do decide to become a legal expert, visit your local law library (at the county courthouse or local law school) and check out the directories of legal experts. Review these directories to see if your area or areas of expertise are listed. If so, write to those directories and request an application to be listed. Here are three such directories:

- **Expert Witness Directory**, National Forensic Center, 17 Temple Terrace, Lawrenceville, NJ 08648; (609) 883-0550.

- **National Medical Advisory Service**, 7910 Woodmont #700, Bethesda, MD 20814; (301) 913-0002.

- **Technical Advisory Service for Attorneys**, 1166 Dekalb Pike, Bluebell, PA 19422; (215) 275-8272.

Dan Poynter, author of *The Parachuting Manual* and *Parachuting, The Skydiver's Handbook*, is one author who also does expert witness work. Besides being the author of eight books on the subject, Dan also spent seven years as a skydiving instructor and is still an active member of several parachuting associations.

Dick Murdock, a former railroad engineer and author of a number of books about the old days of railroading in northern California, also does legal expert work for railroads. As a side benefit to his legal expert work, Dick recently sold 1,000 copies of one of his railroading books to a law firm which specializes in railroad cases (and for whom Dick has often done consulting).

21:11 A Few Unusual Spinoffs

Jim Everroad, author of the two million copy bestseller, *How to Flatten Your Stomach*, endorsed and marketed the Belly Burner, an exercise device. Commercials for this product appeared on TV all over the country. A copy of his book was enclosed as a bonus with every order for the Belly Burner.

Chef Paul Prudhomme, author of *Louisiana Kitchen*, published a catalog featuring cast-iron skillets and other cookware necessary for preparing Cajun foods, plus his own brand of herbs and seasonings, Cajun Magic Seasonings, and several Cajun delicacies known as Tasso Ham and Andouille sausage (both of which are prepared in his manufacturing plant in Melville, Louisiana). He distributed these catalogs through his three Louisiana Kitchen restaurants in New Orleans, New York, and San Francisco, as well as to people who had written in asking for more information. He advertised the catalog in *The New Yorker* and *Cook's Magazine* as well as on the Owen Spann syndicated radio show.

Drawing on her reputation as a romance novelist, Barbara Cartland has gone on to endorse lines of bedsheets, greeting cards, perfume, and vitamins. She also recorded an album of love songs.

21:12 Fringe Benefits

One of the fringe benefits of being a writer is that you are often sent free products to review. I know of a number of cookbook writers, for instance, who have received dozens of blenders or microwaves to test while they were preparing cookbooks featuring those machines.

When writing his book on word processing, Dan Poynter received a free Xerox word processor to review. Similarly, when Peter McWilliams was producing all his books on computers and word processing, he would receive a new machine to review almost every month. He had machines sitting in his hallways, kitchen, even his bathroom.

While preparing my books on publishing, I've received a good number of complimentary review copies of books on publishing and marketing (all of which I've reviewed in *Book Publishing Resource Guide*).

When you are preparing a new book, don't overlook the possibility of receiving complimentary review copies of materials that you require in your research. It never hurts to ask for such review copies. Remember, if you feature anything in your book, you will be giving it publicity that no amount of advertising could possibly buy.

These fringe benefits may not amount to much, but they do help you to cut down your up-front costs in producing a book. So don't be shy about making an honest request for review material needed for your book.

21:13 Do It Once, and Sell It Forever

When John Shuttleworth started *The Mother Earth News* magazine, his guiding principle was this: Do it once, and sell it forever. And that's just what he did. Not only did he write and edit the bimonthly magazine, but he also wrote a syndicated newspaper column three times a week, hosted a spot radio program five times a week, wrote several books, conducted dozens of seminars, and ran a mail order business.

How did he do all this? By doing something once and then selling it over and over again. He'd write a magazine article and then whittle it down to three or four key paragraphs for the newspaper column. He'd then take the newspaper column, make a few minor changes in it, and use it as the script for his radio spots. One of the books he wrote was essentially a collection of his newspaper columns. And all the material was used as background for his seminars.

There's no reason you can't do the same with your books. Just follow John's golden rule: **Do it once, and sell it forever.**

Chapter 22

What to Do Next

This book, as I noted in the introduction, was designed to be a potpourri of ideas, examples, tips, and suggestions to encourage you to explore new ways to market your books. I hope the book has achieved this purpose for you. To be honest, I'd be surprised if you didn't come away from this book with at least a dozen new promotional possibilities for your books.

As a caution, however, I'd like to repeat what I said in the introduction. Don't get so excited about all the possibilities for marketing your books that you try to do everything at once. It won't work. Instead, focus your attention on those markets and promotional methods that offer the best possible return for your time and money. Remember the old 80/20 rule. Put your attention on your prime markets first because those markets are the ones that are going to produce the vast majority of your sales and profits.

22:01 The Ad-Lib Book Marketing Library

As you undoubtedly noticed, I've referred a good number of times to three other books that I have written: *Book Marketing Made Easier, Book Publishing Resource Guide*, and *Mail Order Selling Made Easier*. This book plus those three books were designed to be used as a unit. Each complements and supplements the others.

Book Marketing Made Easier provides all the forms and records any publisher would need to prepare and carry out an effective marketing program to the book trade (bookstores, libraries, and schools). Every step is covered—from preparing a marketing strategy, forecasting sales, and planning budgets to researching the media, sending out press releases, and obtaining reviews; everything from getting distribution and working with bookstores to exhibiting books and granting subsidiary rights. This book, in short, takes a lot of the fuss and bother out of organizing an effective marketing program, thus allowing you more time to do the actual marketing.

On the other hand, *Book Publishing Resource Guide* lists more than 8,000 key contacts for the major book marketing channels: wholesalers ... distributors ... sales representatives ... chain stores ... book clubs ... catalogs that feature books ... card packs ... mailing lists ... book fairs and conventions ... foreign rights representatives ... remainder dealers ... marketing co-ops ... publicity services ... and a number of other marketing services. Plus it includes a select list of book reviewers (almost 3,000 newspaper editors and reviewers from 400 top newspapers as well as 700 magazine editors and reviewers). Each listing includes names, addresses, phone numbers, topics of interest, and other applicable information. This directory will help you to tailor your promotional campaigns to fit each new book you publish.

Mail Order Selling Made Easier is loaded with practical, easy-to-use instructions to help anyone—whether a mail order neophyte or a direct mail veteran—develop and carry out successful direct marketing programs. Learn how to select the best products. Learn how to calculate the costs of your direct mail promotions and determine your break-even point. Learn how to design effective direct mail promotions. Learn how to find and test the most appropriate lists for your promotions. Learn how to handle refunds and shipping delays. If you have any questions about the nitty-gritty of mail order, you will find the answer here.

All four books (including this one) were designed to work together as a unit. I do hope you will read all four of them. If you'd like copies of the other three books, ask your bookstore to order them. Or, if the books are not available locally, you may order them from **Ad-Lib Publications, 51 N. Fifth Street, P. O. Box 1102, Fairfield, IA 52556-1102; (800) 669-0773; (515) 472-6617; Fax: (515) 472-3186.**

22:02 Book Marketing and PR Flash No-Frills Data Files

In the process of publishing several directories and two newsletters, Ad-Lib has developed a database of 18,000 marketing and media contacts for promoting books. We have divided these contacts into two data files: the *Book Marketing No-Frills Data Files* and the *PR Flash No-Frills Data Files*. Both sets of data files are available for IBM-PC, Macintosh, or compatible computers in a variety of file formats including tab-delimited ASCII, comma-delimited ASCII, dBase, and SYLK. When ordering, specify the file format compatible with your database program.

Book Marketing No-Frills Data Files

The Book Marketing No-Frills Data Files include 7,500 key book marketing contacts divided into four sections:

- **1,325 book wholesalers**, including 210 distributors, 150 publishers who also distribute books, 475 wholesalers, 380 paperback jobbers, and 160 sales representatives.
- **1,450 book markets**, including 330 bookstore chains, 180 book clubs, 305 mail order catalogs, 160 top independent general booksellers, 70 remainder dealers, and 100 rights buyers.
- **1,590 book services** (card packs, mailing lists, book fairs and conventions, bibliographies, directories, exhibit services, publishing associations, publicity services, and much more).
- **3,110 specialty booksellers.**

PR Flash—National Publicity No-Frills Data Files

The *PR Flash No-Frills Data Files* consists of the following five sections featuring more than 11,000 national media contacts:

- **3,690 newspaper** editors and book reviewers.
- **3,210 magazine** editors, book reviewers, and serial rights buyers.
- **2,460 radio** shows, stations, and networks, including those that do phone interviews.
- **970 television** shows, stations, and networks, including 250 national TV contacts.
- **755 syndicates**, syndicated columnists, news services, and free-lance writers.

Each set of No-Frills Data Files sells for $149.95. Buy both sets and save—only $249.95 for all 18,500+ key contacts. That's only 1.35¢ per name. For less than it would cost you to rent a portion of this database list just once, you can own the entire database and use it as often as you like. No other database or directory offers so much for so little cost.

22:03 Other Books and Reports

Besides the four books in the Ad-Lib Book Marketing Series, Ad-Lib also publishes two other books and four reports that might be of interest to book publishers and authors.

Specialty Booksellers Directory

The *Specialty Booksellers Directory*, published in July, 1987, lists the names, addresses, buyers, and topics of interests for over 2,100 specialty booksellers. These stores specialize in one or more of the following subjects: children's books, computers, business, crafts, cookbooks, house and garden, aviation, gay/lesbian, social issues, travel, science, animals and pets, psychology, new age, history, art, poetry, education—50 topics in all!

By January 1991, the *Specialty Booksellers Directory* will be replaced by a series of special reports customized by subject interest. Whatever your area of specialization, Ad-Lib will create a report that lists the booksellers who specialize in that subject. The reports will list store names, buyers, addresses, and phone numbers plus provide labels for listings—all for only $8.00 per hundred names.

Directory of Book Printers

The *Directory of Book Printers*, published at the end of each year, lists almost 500 book printers in the United States, Canada, and abroad. It doesn't matter where you live. With this directory, you can locate a quality book printer who specializes in the quantities, sizes, and bindings you want to use—at a price you can afford. I've had many book publishers call me after using this directory to tell me how much money they saved on their printing bills. I know one publisher who saved $8,000, another who saved over $5,000. Even more important, though, for most publishers are the hassles and delays that they avoided by being able to match their printing job to the printer's capabilities.

Special Marketing Reports

Ad-Lib Publications also publishes five special marketing and publicity reports ($30.00 each):

- **How to Sell to Mail Order Catalogs** — Describes all the steps you need to follow to sell a book or other product to mail order catalog houses. Also lists 550 catalogs tht carry books, tapes, and other items.

- **How to Sell to Premium/Incentive Users** — Besides showing how to approach premium/incentive users directly, this report describes how to use reps and promotion houses to sell your book or other product as a premium. Also lists 252 premium sales reps and 139 incentive promotion houses. 51 pages.

- **Mail Order Worksheet Kit** — This kit includes full-size master copies of all worksheets and records outlined in *Mail Order Selling Made Easier*. 50 pages.

- **Radio Phone Interview Shows: How to Do an Interview Tour from Home** — This report lists 890 radio shows that feature phone interviews with authors and other experts. It also describes all you have to do to set up the interviews. Finally, it also includes 22 pages of addresses formated to copy onto labels with any photocopy machine.

- **The Top 250 National TV News, Talk, and Magazine Shows** — This report features the top 200 national television shows that feature interviews, news, or reviews. Over 100 pages of details on who to contact and how to book a guest appearance on a national TV talk show.

22:04 Book Marketing Newsletters

Book Marketing Update is a 32-page bimonthly newsletter for anyone wanting to sell more books. It is chock-full of information, resources, tips, and tidbits to help you market your books more effectively. Here's what our readers have to say: "As each issue comes, I think, *There's no way you can top this* — and your next one does." ... "The management of our two companies have found your newsletter to be the finest newsletter about our business that we have ever seen." ... "It's super! Packed with helpful tips. Well-written and interesting to read." $48.00 per year.

Book Promotion Hotline is a weekly newsletter that features 75 to 100 up-to-date key book marketing contacts each issue, including book clubs, catalogs, editors, radio/TV shows, special sales opportunities, wholesalers, and more. All names, addresses, and phone numbers are verified by phone each week, so you know the information is absolutely reliable. Even if you only follow up on 3 or 4 contacts each week, you should gain more sales and media attention as a result of this newsletter than you would ever get from a display ad costing five times as much. $150.00 per year (includes a subscription to *Book Marketing Update*).

22:05 Other Services

Since I like to practice what I preach, I have been slowly expanding the services that I offer to other publishers and writers. For a number of years now, I've been doing consulting in the design, development, and promotion of toys and books in my local area. Now my consulting services are available to anyone within reach of a phone.

I now offer a toll-free telephone advisory service for anyone with questions regarding the marketing of their books. Call **(800) 699-0773**. The charges for this service are $100.00 per hour, billed by the minute to your credit card (either MasterCard, VISA, or American Express). Use as many minutes as you need to have your questions answered.

Finally, I am available to speak to groups of publishers and writers. In the past few years I've spoken to dozens of groups around the country. If you know of a group that would like me to speak on publishing, marketing, or publicizing books, have them give me a call at **(800) 669-0773**.

Well, we've come to the end of this book. I hope you enjoyed it and found it useful. Please send me your success stories. I love to hear how other publishers market their books — and, in most cases, I share this information with the readers of my newsletter. Meanwhile, enjoy yourself. And sell those books!

John Kremer

Bibliography

The following books are the major resources used in writing this book. For a complete bibliography of books, magazines, and other publishing resources, see *Book Publishing Resource Guide*. To order most of the following books, call toll-free **(800) 669-0773**.

Ballou, Melinda-Carol, Marie Kiefer, and John Kremer, *Specialty Booksellers Directory* (Fairfield, IA: Ad-Lib Publications, 1987)

Bodian, Nat, *Book Marketing Handbook, Volumes One and Two* (New York: R. R. Bowker, 1980)

Bodian, Nat, *Publishers Direct Mail Handbook* (Phoenix: Oryx, 1985)

Carter, Robert, editor, *Trade Book Marketing* (New York: Bowker, 1983)

Corwin, Stanley J., *How to Become a Bestselling Author* (Cincinnati: Writer's Digest Books, 1984)

Glenn, Peggy, *Publicity for Books and Authors* (Huntington Beach, CA: Aames-Allen, 1984)

Huenefeld, John, *The Huenefeld Guide to Book Publishing, Fourth Edition* (Lexington, MA: Mills-Sanderson, 1990)

Kremer, John, *Book Marketing Made Easier* (Fairfield: Ad-Lib, 1986)

Kremer, John, *Book Publishing Resource Guide* (Fairfield: Ad-Lib, 1987)

Kremer, John, *Book Marketing No-Frills Data Files* (Fairfield: Ad-Lib, 1990)

Kremer, John, *Directory of Book Printers* (Fairfield: Ad-Lib, 1991)

Kremer, John, *Mail Order Selling Made Easier* (Fairfield: Ad-Lib, 1991)

Kremer, John, *PR FLASH: The National Publicity No-Frills Data Files* (Fairfield: Ad-Lib, 1990)

Lant, Jeffrey, *How to Make a Whole Lot More Than $1,000,000 Writing, Publishing, and Selling How-To Information* (Cambridge, MA: JLA Associates, 1989)

Lant, Jeffrey, *The Unabashed Self-Promoter's Guide* (Cambridge: JLA Associates, 1983)

McHugh, Jack, *McHugh Publishing Reports* (Framingham, MA: McHugh, 198-), various reports (4 pages to 72 pages)

Parkhurst, William, *How to Get Publicity* (New York: Times Books, 1985)

Poynter, Dan, *Book Fairs* (Santa Barbara, CA: Para Publishing, 1986)

Poynter, Dan, *The Self-Publishing Manual* (Santa Barbara: Para, 1989)

Richards, Pamela Spence, *Marketing Books and Journals to Western Europe* (Phoenix: Oryx Press, 1985)

Ross, Marilyn and Tom, *Book Promotion and Marketing* (Buena Vista, CO: Communication Creativity, 1988)

Ross, Marilyn and Tom, *The Complete Guide to Self-Publishing* (Cincinnati: Writer's Digest Books, 1980)

Ross, Marilyn and Tom, *How to Publish City & Regional Books* (Buena Vista: Communication Creativity, 1987)

Index

Y

About the Author

John F. Kremer is the president and publisher of Ad-Lib Publications, in Fairfield, Iowa.

He is the author of a number of books on publishing and marketing, including *Book Marketing Made Easier, Book Publishing Resource Guide, Mail Order Selling Made Easier, Directory of Book Printers,* and *Specialty Booksellers Directory.*

He is also the developer of the *PR FLASH No-Frills Data Files, Book Marketing No-Frills Data Files,* and *Mail Order Spreadsheet Kit.*

Illustration by Max Vague

In addition, he is the author of four special reports: *How to Sell to Mail Order Catalogs*; *How to Sell to Premium/Incentive Users*; *Radio Phone Interview Shows: How to Do an Interview Tour from Home*; and *The Top 250 National TV News, Talk, and Magazine Shows.*

Finally, he is also the author of *Tinseltowns, U.S.A.*, a trivia quiz book.

John is a member the Mid-America Publishers Association, Publishers Marketing Association, COSMEP, Minnesota Independent Publishers Association, Marin Small Publishers Association, and American Booksellers Association.

Besides editing and publishing the *Book Marketing Update* and *Book Promotion Hotline* newsletters, John also writes the Books for the Trade column for *Small Press* magazine.

John is single, 41 years old, never been married, but highly eligible. Besides being a superb slow-pitch softball pitcher, he also plays walleyball, basketball, and radios. He rides a three-speed bicycle to work.